Applied Decision Analysis and Economic Behaviour

ADVANCED STUDIES IN THEORETICAL AND APPLIED ECONOMETRICS
VOLUME 3

THE SPECIAL SCOPE OF THE SERIES

The fortress of econometrics has often been laid siege to from one or a few sides only. According to their inspiration or inclination, authors have laid stress on model specification, parameter estimation, testing and prediction or more generally the use of models (prediction in particular being a rare bird in econometric literature). Special topics, such as errors in the variables, missing observations, multi-dimensional data, time-series analysis, dynamic specification, spatial autocorrelation, were dealt with as and when the need arose.

No econometric exercises will ever be complete. Nevertheless, in setting up such an exercise as part of an operational economic investigation, one may reasonably be expected to try and encompass in it as many aspects of econometric modelling as may present themselves. This series is devoted to the publication of work which, as far as possible, addresses all aspects of a ''complete econometric modelling'' approach; for instance, spatial econometrics or policy optimisation studies which account explicitly for the specification, estimation or analysis of components of those models in the widest sense, including any complementary components from the environment in which the economic model must operate.

The very objective of the series may limit its extensions; but as André Gide put it (Les faux monnayeurs), ''il est bon de suivre sa pente, pourvu que ce soit en montant''.

All correspondence should be addressed to A.J. Hughes Hallet or to J.H.P. Paelinck at the Erasmus University, PO Box 1738, 3000 DR Rotterdam, The Netherlands.

Applied Decision Analysis and Economic Behaviour

edited by

A.J. Hughes Hallett

1984 **MARTINUS NIJHOFF PUBLISHERS**
a member of the KLUWER ACADEMIC PUBLISHERS GROUP
DORDRECHT / BOSTON / LANCASTER

Distributors

for the United States and Canada: Kluwer Academic Publishers, 190 Old Derby Street, Hingham, MA 02043, USA
for the UK and Ireland: Kluwer Academic Publishers, MTP Press Limited, Falcon House, Queen Square, Lancaster LA1 1RN, England
for all other countries: Kluwer Academic Publishers Group, Distribution Center, P.O. Box 322, 3300 AH Dordrecht, The Netherlands

Library of Congress Cataloging in Publication Data

Applied decision analysis and economic behavior.

(Advanced studies in theoretical and applied econometrics ; 3)
1. Economic policy--Mathematical models--Addresses, essays, lectures. 2. Decision-making--Mathematical models--Addresses, essays, lectures. 3. Uncertainty--Mathematical models--Addresses, essays, lectures. 4. Rational expectations (Economic theory)--Addresses, essays, lectures. I. Hallett, Andrew Hughes. II. Series.
HD75.5.A65 1984 338.9'00724 84-6148
ISBN 90-247-2968-8

ISBN 90-247-2968-8 (this volume)
ISBN 90-247-2622-0 (series)

PRINTED IN THE NETHERLANDS

CONTENTS

INTRODUCTION

The optimisation of economic systems over time, and in an uncertain environment, is central to the study of economic behaviour. The behaviour of rational decision makers, whether they are market agents, firms, or governments and their agencies, is governed by decisions designed to secure the best outcomes subject to the perceived information and economic responses (inlcuding those of other agents). Economic behaviour has therefore to be analysed in terms of the outcomes of a multiperiod stochastic optimisation process containing four main components: the economic responses (the dynamic constraints, represented by an economic model); the objective function (the goals and their priorities); the conditioning information (expected exogenous events and the expected future state of the economy); and risk management (how uncertainties are accommodated).

The papers presented in this book all analyse some aspect of economic behaviour related to the objectives, information, or risk components of the decision process. While the construction of economic models obviously also has a vital role to play, that component has received much greater (or almost exclusive) attention elsewhere. These papers examine optimising behaviour in a wide range of economic problems, both theoretical and applied. They reflect a variety of concerns: economic responses under rational expectations; the Lucas critique and optimal fiscal or monetary policies; market management; partly endogenous goals; evaluating government reactions; locational decisions; uncertainty and information structures; and forecasting with endogenous reactions.

The book has been partitioned accordingly into sections dealing with Expectations, Uncertainty, Policy Models, Market Management, and Decentralisation. In the first section Turnovsky and Stemp provide a theoretical examination of the macroeconomic stabilisation problem under rational expectations and show that optimal policy rules turn out to be time consistent if the adjustment costs are relatively large. Karp and Havenner present a more general discussion of the determination of optimal macroeconomic policies in the light of the Lucas critique, and reach similar conclusions. Then Holly and Corker undertake an empirical study of optimal monetary policies under rational expectations, using a large scale econometric model of the U.K. economy.

In the section on uncertainty, Shmueli and Tapiero consider how to make predictions in a market containing several interdependent products and rational agents. Sandblom and Eiselt's paper returns to the macroeconomic arena and looks into the consequences of attempting to steer an economy with policies determined either under parameter uncertainty or conflicting parameters from different models. These are empirical exercises. The paper by Deleau, Le Van and Malgrange then introduces the idea of efficient interventions in the face of significant uncertainties, arguing that target variances should be traded off against one another along an 'uncertainty frontier' in the same way that their achievements are in a (deterministic) Pareto allocation of policy efforts.

The third section focusses on endogenising decisions as part of the modelling process. Desai, Keil and Wadhwani model policy reactions when there is switching between different regimes because governments change. Their study is set in the classic situation of an incomes policy in a political cycle. An allied problem is the generation of multiperiod predictions for an economy where policies are endogenised through a feedback rule. Friedmann's contribution is to study a prediction mechanism which accounts for the mutual interactions between predictions and policies. In a more conventional contribution, Baum uses optimisation techniques as a yardstick with which to judge historical policy performance.

The management of commodity markets is the subject of the fourth section. Here Dixon and Chen examine the effects of different price support levels on the stability of incomes in a rational agricultural market. In particular they contrast the case where the support level is allowed to respond to market developments to the case where that level is fixed in advance. Ghosh, Gilbert and Hughes Hallett investigate the scope and costs of price stabilisation in an international commodity market, and then examine the information structure of successful intervention rules. Their conclusion is that it is the contents of the information set (specifically the anticipations variables) rather than the type of decision rule which is important.

The final section deals with decentralised planning. The contribution of Neese and Pindyck considers economic performance when decision making is decentralised between fiscal and monetary authorities. Using an econometric model of the U.S. economy, the effects of different private behaviour patterns (ranging from ignoring or passively reacting to other agents, to actively persuing optimal equilibrium strategies) are compared empirically to cooperative decision making. Moving to the level of industry planning, Petkovski examines the stability and control of a multi-sector hierarchical system where decisions are taken with varying frequencies depending on the level of the decision unit in the hierarchy. Finally, Hanjoul and Thisse remind us that the optimisation of conflicting targets is just as necessary over space as it is over time intervals. They review the optimal location of firms within an industry, when firms are now the decision makers.

In practice much of this work is likely to involve large complex models with extensive dynamics and many interacting sectors. In the epilogue, Kendrick puts forward some rules for presenting and encoding such models. These rules are part of the recent attempts to design 'modelling languages' which will make complicated models more accessible and intelligable to the general user.

The special feature common to these papers is that they try to internalise some of the components of the decision process in order to make the modelling of economic behaviour more systematic. This is done at least as much to get information on the decision structure as it is to select actual policies. Since one learns by doing, these papers emphasise that there is a serious issue of experimental design in order that the right questions should be asked. Experiments are vitally important since they are the nearest we may come to testing alternative specifications of the components of the decision model because (a) there is no possibility of manipulating an economic system under repeatedly identical experimental conditions (indeed there is no possibility of 'live' experiments), (b) there is an inherent randomness in human behaviour not found in physical systems, (c) there are observation and measurement problems which can never be fully overcome.

Obviously there is no reason to expect nature (or indeed governments) to perform the crucial controlled experiments which will enable us to distinguish between alternative specifications of these components. In that case 'laboratory' experiments, not 'live' ones, must be conducted. The whole decision model should be subject to severe testing during its construction *and* the derivation of policy recommendations, with the aim of correcting specifications which would later appear to have led to mistaken policy proposals. The case against explicit optimisation in empirical work usually focusses on the difficulty of formulating and accomodating the risks, the priorities, and the information system adequately. Yet if, as is now generally accepted, it is necessary to use an explicit model (and probably an econometric one, whether simple or sophisticated) to ensure the accountability and mutual consistency of projections, then by the same token a decision model explicit in all four components is crucial for exactly the same reasons.

Warwick, February 1984 — A.J. Hughes Hallett

PART I

EXPECTATIONS

CHAPTER 1

OPTIMAL STABILISATION POLICIES UNDER PERFECT FORESIGHT

Peter J. Stemp *Australian National University and the University of Illinois*
Stephen J. Turnovsky *University of Illinois, USA*

1. INTRODUCTION

The problem of choosing between inflation and unemployment rates continues to be a fundamental one in most modern economies. The question of the optimal choice of trade-off between them has been investigated by a number of authors. The earliest studies, conducted in the mid 1960's were purely static; see, for example, Lipsey (1965) and Brechling (1968). Subsequently, the analysis was extended to a dynamic context on the assumption that inflationary expectations, known to be a critical aspect of the trade-off, follow some gradual evolutionary process such as an adaptive scheme; see, for example, Phelps (1967, 1972) and Turnovsky (1981). These authors derive an optimal path in which the inflation rate adjusts gradually towards some steady-state equilibrium, while the unemployment rate converges slowly towards its natural rate. The transitional dynamic adjustment path depends upon the parameters characterising the economy and the preferences of the policy maker, including in particular, the rate of time discount.

Contemporary macroeconomic theory is dominated by the rational expectations hypothesis. In this chapter, we analyse the inflation-unemployment trade-off under the assumption that expectations satisfy perfect foresight, which is the deterministic analogue to rational expectations. We show that while the economy can jump instantaneously to a zero rate of inflation, there is a trade-off between an initial once-and-for-all jump in the price level and the subsequent gradual adjustment of unemployment to its natural rate.

An important, and widely discussed, aspect of optimal policy determination under rational expectations, concerns the question of the time consistency of the optimal policy; see, for example, Kydland and Prescott (1977) and Turnovsky and

Hughes Hallett, A.J. (ed.) Applied Decision Analysis and Economic Behaviour
©1984, Martinus Nijhoff Publishers. Dordrecht/Boston/Lancaster
ISBN 90-247-2968-8. Printed in The Netherlands

Brock (1980). In our analysis we show that for the objective function we consider the solution is indeed time consistent for a wide range of parameter values, although for a relatively modest modification of the cost function, the optimal solution is rendered always time inconsistent.

2. A DYNAMIC MACROECONOMIC MODEL

The analysis of this chapter will be based on the following macroeconomic model which is derived under the assumption that labour supply is greater than labour demand; i.e., $N^S > N^D$.

$$Y = D(Y^D, r-\pi, A) + \quad G \tag{1.1a}$$

with partial derivatives $0 < D_1 < 1,\ D_2 < 0,\ D_3 > 0$

$$Y^D = Y - T + rb - \pi A \tag{1.1b}$$

$$A = m + b \tag{1.1c}$$

$$m = L(Y, r, A) \tag{1.1d}$$

with partial derivatives $L_1 > 0,\ L_2 < 0,\ 0 < L_3 < 1$

$$N^D = N^D(v) \qquad N^{D'} < 0 \tag{1.1e}$$

$$N^S = N^S(v) \qquad N^{S'} > 0 \tag{1.1f}$$

$$Y = f(N^D) = Y(v) \qquad Y' < 0 \tag{1.1g}$$

$$U = (N^S - N^D)/N^S = U(v) \qquad U' > 0 \tag{1.1h}$$

$$w = \alpha(\bar{U} - U) + \pi \tag{1.1i}$$

$$\pi = p, \quad \text{except at points where P jumps} \tag{1.1j}$$

In addition,

$$\dot{v} = v(w - p) \tag{1.2a}$$

and $$\dot{m} = \theta(G - T + rb) - pm \tag{1.2b}$$

and $$\dot{b} = (1 - \theta)\ (G - T + rb) - pb \tag{1.2c}$$

The variables in this model are given in table 1.1.

Table 1.1. The definitions of the variables

Y	=	real output
Y^D	=	real private disposable income
D	=	real private expenditure
G	=	real government expenditure
r	=	nominal interest rate
π	=	expected rate of inflation
$r-\pi$	=	real interest rate
P	=	price level
p	=	$\dot{P}/P$ = actual rate of inflation
M	=	nominal money supply
m	=	M/P = real money supply
B	=	nominal supply of bonds
b	=	B/P = real supply of bonds
A	=	real private wealth
W	=	nominal wage rate
v	=	W/P = real wage rate
w	=	$\dot{W}/W$ = rate of nominal wage inflation
N^D	=	demand for labour
N^S	=	supply of labour
f	=	production function
U	=	rate of unemployment
$\bar{U}$	=	natural rate of unemployment

Equation (1.1a) is the product market equilibrium condition, in which real private demand increases with real private disposable income and real private wealth and decreases with the real rate of interest. Equation (1.1b) defines real private disposable income to be real factor plus returns on government bonds, less expected capital losses on financial wealth (the expected inflation tax on real private wealth) and exogenous real taxes. Real private wealth is defined in equation (1.1c). Equilibrium in the money market is described by equation (1.1d) where the demand for real money balances depends upon the real level of income, the nominal rate of interest and real private wealth.

The supply of, and demand for, labour are given by equations (1.1e) and (1.1f).

Both are monotonic functions of the real wage (with the indicated signs). Equations (1.1g) and (1.1h) likewise describe the production function and the rate of unemployment as being the difference between the supply of and demand for labour as a percentage of the labour supply. The production function is written on the assumption that $N^D < N^S$.

Equation (1.1i) is a simple Phillips curve with the rate of wage inflation increasing with excess demand in the labour market and with the expected rate of inflation. It is a standard version of the 'expectations hypothesis' with the unitary coefficient on expectations reflecting the 'accelerationist' view. Equation (1.1j) states that inflationary expectations satisfy perfect myopic foresight; i.e., the instantaneous expected rate of inflation equals the instantaneous actual rate of inflation. This equation is assumed to hold everywhere, except at points where there are jumps in the price level, in which p becomes infinite.

The dynamics of the system are described in equations (1.2a)–(1.2c). The first of these equations defines the evolution of real wages, while equations (1.2b) and (1.2c) describe government financial policy and the evolution in the stocks of financial assets it generates. Specifically, these equations assert that the government deficit consists of government expenditure plus the interest payments on government debt less tax revenues and that a fraction θ of this deficit is financed by money creation, with the balance $(1-\theta)$ being financed by issuing bonds.[1] The specific forms of these two equations is obtained by transforming the original government budget constraint, which involves the adjustment of the nominal stocks of money and bonds, to the corresponding adjustments in the real quantities of these variables.

The equations sets (1.1) and (1.2) describe the economy faced by the policy maker. We assume that the policy maker regards a state of zero inflation (stable price level) and a fixed rate of unemployment, δ say, as globally optimal. Given these long-run targets we assume that the policy maker's objective is to choose government expenditure policy (G) and monetary policy (θ), after allowing for the optimal initial jump in the price level so as to minimise the following loss function

$$L \equiv c|U(0) - U_o| + \tfrac{1}{2} \int_0^\infty e^{-\gamma t} [ap^2 + (U-\delta)^2]dt \qquad (1.3)$$

where U_o is the previously inherited rate of unemployment, and U(0) is the endogenously determined initial unemployment rate following the jump in the price level (see below).

Note that in general the natural rate of unemployment $\bar{U} \neq \delta$. This reflects the fact that the rate of unemployment which the economy tends to approach, i.e. $\bar{U}$, may not coincide with the level that the policy maker finds socially optimal. The parameter a $(0 < a < \infty)$ reflects the relative importance attached to inflation and unemployment in the intertemporal objective. As a increases, the policy maker is concerned increasingly with inflation; as a decreases the objective is weighted more heavily toward unemployment. The parameter $(0 < \gamma < \infty)$, which measures the rate of time preference, reflects the degree of myopia of the policy maker; the larger γ the more myopic he is. It will be demonstrated later that by an appropriate choice of an initial jump in the price level P, the initial rate of unemployment U(0) can be chosen. This instantaneous initial jump in unemployment from its inherited rate is assumed to impose adjustment costs on the economy and these are reflected in the cost parameter c. Note that these initial costs are assumed to be proportional to the absolute magnitude of the jump. This form of cost function turns out to be time consistent for a wide range of parameter values. By contrast, if these initial costs are represented by the more familiar quadratic cost function, time inconsistency always obtains.

In order to solve the policy optimisation problem it is first convenient to use equations (1.1) to express the short-run rate of inflation and the short-run interest rate in terms of the endogenous variables A, m, and b, and the policy variables G and T. These solutions are given by[2]

$$p = p(U, m, b, G, T) \tag{1.4a}$$

with the partial derivatives $p_U < 0, p_m < 0, p_b \gtreqless 0, p_G < 0, p_T > 0$;

and $$r = r(U, m, b) \tag{1.4b}$$

with the partial derivatives $r_U < 0, r_m < 0, r_b > 0$.

Note that (1.4a) implies that an increase in government expenditure is deflationary, while an increase in exogenous tax receipts is inflationary. The reason for these seemingly perverse effects is seen from (1.1a) and (1.1d). In order for product market equilibrium to be maintained, an increase in G must be matched by a reduction in private demand, which with output and wealth fixed instantaneously, is met by an increase in the real interest rate. But since the nominal interest rate is independent of G, this increase takes the form of a reduction in the inflation rate. And likewise for a change in T. However, it should be stressed that these effects are only partial; they do not allow for the jumps in the price level induced by such policy changes, which in turn will impact on the rate of inflation. Given that U = U(W/P), m = M/P, and b = B/P and that the nominal wage rate W, and the nominal asset supplies M and B are all constrained to move continuously, the complete effect of an increase in G on the instantaneous rate of inflation is given by the expression

$$\frac{dp}{dG} = -\left[p_U\, U' \frac{W}{P^2} + p_m \frac{M}{P^2} + p_b \frac{B}{P^2}\right] \frac{\partial P}{\partial G} + p_G$$

where U′ denotes the partial derivatives of U with respect to P. In addition to the partial effect which is negative, as noted, there are the induced effects operating through the jump in the price level and this has several induced positive effects. First, by lowering the real wage this reduces unemployment, thereby stimulating inflation. Secondly it reduces the real stock of money and bonds and a sufficient condtion for the combined net effect of this to be inflationary is that the wealth elasticity of the demand for money be less than unity. In short, the induced effects of an increase in G are all inflationary and indeed on balance are likely to dominate the perverse partial deflationary effect.

Differentiating (1.1h) with respect to t and combining with (1.1i) and (1.2a), we obtain

$$\dot{U} = \beta(\bar{U} - U) + \epsilon(\pi - p) \tag{1.5}$$

where for convenience we let $\beta \equiv U'v\alpha$, $\epsilon \equiv U'v$.

The question arises as to when the jumps in the price level will take place. Intuitively it seems reasonable that this will occur at the points where the policy variables are likely to undergo discrete changes, which is at the beginning of the period of optimisation.[3] Invoking this assumption it follows that π=p, thereafter.

The objective facing the policy maker can now be summarised by the following optimisation problem:

$$\min_{\theta, G} c|U(0) - U_o| + \tfrac{1}{2}\int_0^\infty e^{-\gamma t}[ap^2 + (U - \delta)^2]\,dt \tag{1.6}$$

subject to[4]

$$p = p(U, m, b, G, T) \tag{1.7a}$$

$$r = r(U, m, b) \tag{1.7b}$$

$$\dot{m} = \theta\,[G - T + rb] - pm \tag{1.7c}$$

$$\dot{b} = (1 - \theta)[G - T + rb] - pb \tag{1.7d}$$

$$\dot{U} = \beta(\bar{U} - U) \tag{1.7e}$$

where $W(0) = W_o$, $M(0) = M_o$, and $B(0) = B_o$ are all predetermined and P(0) is endogenous. The initial quantities m(0), b(0), and U(0) are endogenous and satisfy the constraints

$$m(0) = M_o/P(0) \tag{1.8a}$$

$$b(0) = B_o/P(0) \tag{1.8b}$$

$$U(0) = U(W_o/P(0)) \tag{1.8c}$$

Since the function describing the loss associated with the initial jump in the price level, i.e., $c\,|U(0) - U_o|$, is nondifferentiable at $U(0) = U_o$, the optimisation problem specified by equations (1.7a)–(1.7f) and (1.8a)–(1.8c) can most easily be solved by decomposing it into the following two problems:

Problem 1:

Find $L_1 = \text{Min } c(U(0) - U_o) + \tfrac{1}{2}\int_0^\infty e^{-\gamma t}[ap^2 + (U-\delta)^2]\,dt$ (1.9a)

subject to $U(0) \geqslant U_o$ (1.9b)
and equations (1.7a)–(1.7e) and (1.8a)–(1.8c)

Problem 2:

Find $L_2 = \text{Min } c(U_o - U(0)) + \tfrac{1}{2}\int_0^\infty e^{-\gamma t}[ap^2 + (U-\delta)^2]\,dt$ (1.10a)

subject to $U_o \geqslant U(0)$ (1.10b)
and equations (1.7a)–(1.7e) and (1.8a)–(1.8c)

The solution to the original problem associated with the loss function given by (1.6) is then a solution for which $U(0) \geqslant U_o$ if $L_1 \leqslant L_2$, or a solution for which $U_o \geqslant U(0)$ if $L_2 \leqslant L_1$.

3. DETERMINATION OF THE OPTIMAL SOLUTION

To solve the optimisation problems specified by both problems 1 and 2 we first write down the Hamiltonian function as follows

$$\begin{aligned} H \equiv {} & \tfrac{1}{2} e^{-\gamma t}[ap^2 + (U-\delta)^2] \\ & + \mu e^{-\gamma t}[\dot{m} - \theta(G - T + rb) + pm] \\ & + \lambda e^{-\gamma t}[\dot{b} - (1-\theta)(G - T + rb) + pb] \\ & + \eta e^{-\gamma t}[\dot{U} - \beta(\bar{U} - U)] \end{aligned} \tag{1.11}$$

where $\mu e^{-\gamma t}$, $\lambda e^{-\gamma t}$, and $\eta e^{-\gamma t}$ are the discounted Lagrange multipliers associated with the dynamic equations (1.7c)–(1.7e) respectively. The Euler equations with respect to m, b, U, G, and θ are respectively given by[5]

$$\dot{\mu} = app_m + \mu[-\theta r_m b + p_m m + p + \gamma] + \lambda[-(1-\theta)r_m b + p_m b] \tag{1.12a}$$

$$\dot{\lambda} = app_b + \mu[-\theta(r_b b + r) + p_b m] + \lambda[-(1-\theta)(r_b b + r) + p_b b + p + \gamma] \tag{1.12b}$$

$$\dot{\eta} = U - \delta + app_U + \mu[-\theta r_U b + p_U m] + \lambda[-(1-\theta)r_U b + p_U b] + (\beta+\gamma)\eta \tag{1.12c}$$

$$app_G + \mu[-\theta + p_G m] + \lambda[-(1-\theta) + p_G b] = 0 \tag{1.12d}$$

$$\mu = \lambda \tag{1.12e}$$

In addition the dynamics of m, b, and U are given by equations (1.7c)–(1.7e). Equations (1.12a)–(1.12d) can be solved to give the evolution of the variables μ, λ, η, π, m, b, and U along the policy maker's optimal path.

In addition, the optimal solution must satisfy the following transversality conditions as $t \to \infty$,

$$\lim_{t\to\infty} m\mu e^{-\gamma t} = 0 \tag{1.13a}$$

$$\lim_{t\to\infty} b\lambda e^{-\gamma t} = 0 \tag{1.13b}$$

$$\lim_{t\to\infty} U\eta e^{-\gamma t} = 0 \tag{1.13c}$$

Furthermore, the fact that m(0), b(0) and U(0) are endogenously determined in accordance with (1.8a)–(1.8c) imposes the constraints

$$b(0) = \phi_1 m(0), \qquad \text{where } \phi_1 \equiv B_0/M_0 \tag{1.14a}$$

$$U(0) = U[\phi_2 m(0)], \qquad \text{where } \phi_2 \equiv W_0/M_0 \tag{1.14b}$$

Accordingly, the following transversality conditions must also be satisfied at the initial time 0 (see, for example, Kamien and Schwartz (1971)):

For Problem 1,

If $U(0) > U_o$, then

$$\mu(0) + \phi_1\lambda(0) + U'\phi_2[\eta(0) - c] = 0 \tag{1.15a}$$

but if $U(0) = U_o$, then

$$\mu(0) + \phi_1\lambda(0) + U'\phi_2[\eta(0) - c] \leqslant 0 \tag{1.15b}$$

For Problem 2,

If $U_o > U(0)$, then

$$\mu(0) + \phi_1\lambda(0) + U'\phi_2[\eta(0) + c] = 0 \tag{1.16a}$$

but if $U_o = U(0)$, then

$$\mu(0) + \phi_1\lambda(0) + U'\phi_2[\eta(0) + c] \geqslant 0 \tag{1.16b}$$

The solution given by the system of equations (1.12)–(1.16) can be simplified considerably. First, (1.12d) and (1.12e) imply

$$p = \frac{\mu[1 - p_G A]}{ap_G} \tag{1.17a}$$

Also, combining equations (1.12a), (1.12b) and (1.12e) implies a second relationship between p and μ

$$p = \frac{\mu[r_m b - r_b b - r + (p_b - p_m)A]}{a(p_m - p_b)} \tag{1.17b}$$

In general, equations (1.17a) and (1.17b) cannot both be satisfied simultaneously unless

$$p = \mu = 0 \qquad \text{for all t} \tag{1.17c}$$

Moreover, combining (1.17c) with (1.12e) implies

$$\lambda = 0 \qquad \text{for all t} \tag{1.17d}$$

Hence, using (1.17a)–(1.17d), the optimal path reduces to

$$\eta = (\beta + \gamma)\eta + U - \delta \tag{1.18a}$$

$$\dot{U} = \beta(\bar{U} - U) \tag{1.18b}$$

$$p = 0 \tag{1.18c}$$

$$\dot{m} = \theta [G - T + rb] \tag{1.18d}$$

$$\dot{b} = (1 - \theta)[G - T + rb] \tag{1.18e}$$

$$\lim_{t \to \infty} U\eta e^{-\gamma t} = 0 \tag{1.18f}$$

Equations (1.18a)–(1.18f), together with the transversality conditions (1.15a,b) and (1.16a,b), determine the optimal path for unemployment and inflation. Using (1.17c) and (1.17d), the latter simplify to the following:

For Problem 1:

$$\text{If } U(0) > U_o \text{ then } \eta(0) = c \tag{1.19a}$$

$$U(0) = U_o \text{ then } \eta(0) \leqslant c \tag{1.19b}$$

For Problem 2:

$$\text{If } U_o > U(0) \text{ then } \eta(0) = -c \tag{1.20a}$$

$$U_o = U(0) \text{ then } \eta(0) \geqslant -c \tag{1.20b}$$

Equations (1.18a), (1.18b), (1.18f), and the transversality conditions given by equations (1.19) and (1.20) can then be used to solve for the optimal path for U as follows. Integrating (1.18b), yields

$$U(t) = \bar{U} + (U(0) - \bar{U})e^{-\beta t} \tag{1.21a}$$

where U(0) is the initial value of U(t), following the jump, which is to be determined. Substituting (1.21a) into (1.18a) and integrating again, we find that

$$\eta(t) = -\frac{(\bar{U} - \delta)}{\beta + \gamma} + \frac{[\bar{U} - U(0)]}{2\beta + \gamma} e^{-\beta t} + De^{(\beta + \gamma)t} \tag{1.21b}$$

where D is an arbitrary constant. In order for the transversality condition (1.18f) to be satisfied we require D = 0. Then substituting equations (1.19) and (1.20) into (1.21b), and comparing the loss functions for Problems 1 and 2, we can show that the optimal solution to the general problem is given by

$$U(0) = \bar{U} + \frac{(2\beta + \gamma)}{\beta + \gamma} [\delta - \bar{U}] - (2\beta + \gamma)c, \quad \text{if } U_o < U(0) \tag{1.22a}$$

or, if $U_o = U(0)$,

$$\bar{U} + \frac{2\beta+\gamma}{\beta+\gamma}(\delta - \bar{U}) - (2\beta+\gamma)c \leqslant U(0) \leqslant \bar{U} + \frac{(2\beta+\gamma)}{\beta+\gamma}[\delta - \bar{U}] + (2\beta+\gamma)c \qquad (1.22b)$$

or $$U(0) = \bar{U} + \frac{(2\beta+\gamma)}{\beta+\gamma}(\delta - \bar{U}) + (2\beta+\gamma)c, \quad \text{if } U_0 > U(0) \qquad (1.22c)$$

From (1.22b) it will be observed that if the inherited unemployment rate, U_0, lies in a specific closed interval, bounded by

$$\bar{U} + \frac{(2\beta+\gamma)}{\beta+\gamma}(\delta - \bar{U}) - (2\beta+\gamma)c \leqslant U_0 \leqslant \bar{U} + \frac{(2\beta+\gamma)}{\beta+\gamma}(\delta - \bar{U}) + (2\beta+\gamma)c \qquad (1.23)$$

then it will be optimal for no initial jump in the unemployment rate to occur. However, if U_0 lies outside this interval, then the unemployment rate will jump instantaneously to the nearest boundary of this closed interval. The boundaries of the closed interval depend upon: the natural rate of unemployment, $\bar{U}$; the target rate of unemployment, δ; the cost associated with the initial jump in the unemployment rate, c; the coefficient of unemployment in the Phillips curve, β; the rate of time preference of the policy maker, γ. Several special cases are worth noting.

(i) If the cost associated with the initial jump increases without limit, $c \to \infty$, then it will never be optimal to have an initial jump in unemployment and $U(0) = U_0$.

(ii) If the cost associated with the initial jump vanishes, $c \to 0$, then the initial unemployment rate will always jump to a level given by

$$U(0) = \bar{U} + \frac{2\beta+\gamma}{\beta+\gamma}(\delta - \bar{U})$$

(iii) If the policy maker is perfectly myopic, $\gamma \to \infty$, then it will never be optimal to have an initial jump in unemployment provided $c > 0$.

(iv) If the desired target rate of unemployment equals the natural rate, i.e. $\delta = \bar{U}$, then the boundaries of the closed interval in (1.23), $\bar{U} \pm (2\beta + \gamma)c$, are symmetric about the natural rate $\bar{U}$.

Note that these jumps in the unemployment rate, when they occur, are mirrored by jumps in the price level. Indeed, it is the initial jump in the price level which, given the instantaneous stickiness of the nominal wage, permits the initial jump in the unemployment rate to occur. Differentiating (1.8c), the relationship between the two jump variables is given by

$$\frac{dP}{P_0} = \frac{U_0 - U(0)}{U' \cdot (W_0/P_0)}$$

Once the initial value of U(0) has been obtained the implied optimal path for U is derived by substituting for U(0) into the solution given by equation (1.21a). To characterise the path of unemployment more precisely, we shall assume throughout the rest of this chapter that

$$U_0 > \bar{U} \geqslant \delta \tag{1.24}$$

That is, we assume that the inherited unemployment rate exceeds the natural rate, which in turn is at least as great as the socially desirable target. Using this assumption, figures 1.1a and 1.1b illustrate the time paths of the unemployment rate and price level in the three cases corresponding to: (i) a 'small' initial downward jump in the unemployment rate, such that $U_0 > U(0) > \bar{U} \geqslant \delta$; (ii) a 'large' initial downward jump in unemployment, such that $U_0 > \bar{U} > U(0) \geqslant \delta$; and (iii) no initial jump in the unemployment rate, such that $U(0) = U_0$.

Starting from inherited values of U_0 and p_0, the optimal policy calls for inflation to be reduced instantaneously to zero and for unemployment to jump to U(0), after which it evolves towards its natural rate $\bar{U}$. In the case where the parameters c, β, γ are such as to render only a small jump as being optimal, the unemployment rate approaches its natural rate from above. In the case where a large initial jump is optimal, the unemployment rate falls initially below the natural rate and subsequently approaches it from below. In the final case of no initial jump, the optimal unemployment rate simply evolves continuously (from above) towards its natural rate. The two figures also illustrate the trade-off between the initial once-and-for-all jump in the price level and the subsequent intertemporal adjustment in the unemployment rate. The lower the rate of unemployment desired along the optimal path, the larger is the required initial increase in the price level.

Although the optimal solution has been derived formally, a more heuristic approach to the problem is also possible. It can be seen that the optimal objectives can be decomposed into several components, each of which is associated with a different policy instrument. Thus the first objective is to minimise the loss associated with inflation; that is, to minimise

$$\int_0^\infty p^2 e^{-\gamma t}\, dt \tag{1.25}$$

Note that (1.4a) stated p = p(U, m, b, G, T). Therefore, given values of U, m, b, and T, it is possible to ensure that p = 0 for all t, by appropriately adjusting government expenditure G.

The second objective is to choose the money-bond mix (θ) so that the discounted present values of m and b converge to zero. Such an objective has not been postulated

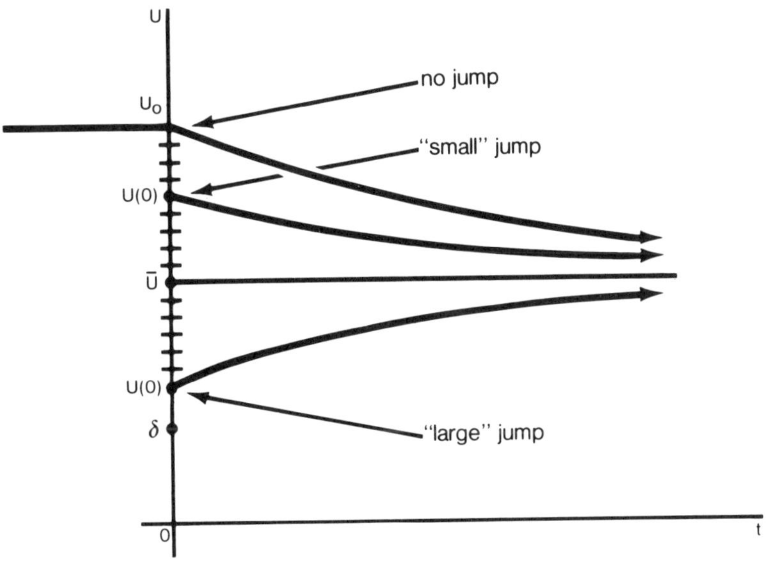

Figure 1.1a. Time path for unemployment

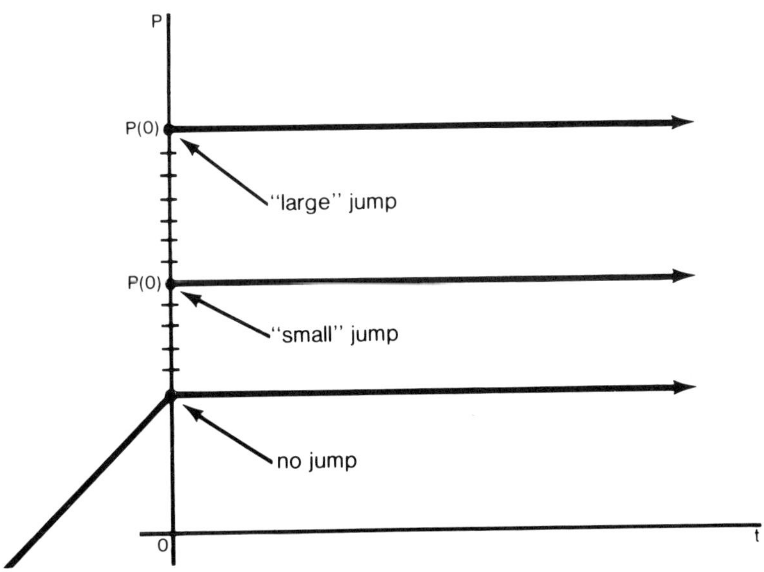

Figure 1.1b. Time path for price level

as being a formal requirement of the model but can be justified by considering the model here as having been derived from an underlying optimisation for the consumer. Such conditions would then appear as transversality conditions for the consumer's optimisation problem.

The third objective is to minimise the loss function associated with the time path for unemployment; i.e., to minimise

$$c|U(0) - U_0| + \tfrac{1}{2}\int_0^{\infty} e^{-\gamma t}[U - \delta]^2\, dt \tag{1.26}$$

Since U is independent of fiscal and monetary policy, a global minimum can be achieved by choosing an optimal value for the initial condition U(0). Recalling (1.21a), the formal solution of this problem gives precisely the same results as those given by equations (1.22a)–(1.22c).[6]

4. TIME CONSISTENCY OF THE OPTIMAL SOLUTION

Given the possibility of jumps through the price level, the question of the time consistency of the solution to the optimal policy problem specified by equations (1.6), (1.7a)–(1.7e) naturally arises. More precisely, is the optimal path chosen at time $t = 0$ consistent with the optimal path that would be chosen at some time in the future, say at $t = 1$? Clearly it is desirable that this be the case.

Figure 1.2a gives an example which is time consistent. This time consistency will occur provided $\bar{U}$ lies within the closed interval

$$\bar{U} + \frac{(2\beta + \gamma)}{\beta + \gamma}(\delta - \bar{U}) - (2\beta + \gamma)c \leqslant \bar{U} \leqslant \bar{U} + \frac{(2\beta + \gamma)}{\beta + \gamma}(\delta - \bar{U}) + (2\beta + \gamma)c \tag{1.27}$$

In this example, an initial jump will take the unemployment rate to the boundary of this closed interval. Thereafter, the dynamic path given by equation (1.21a) will drive U monotonically towards $\bar{U}$, which by (1.27) lies within the closed interval. Since the dynamic path never leaves the closed interval after the initial jump, and since it is not optimal to jump within the closed interval, this solution is time consistent.

Figure 1.2b illustrates what will happen if the inequalities in (1.27) do not hold. In this case the solution is time inconsistent. As before, the initial jump takes unemployment to the boundary of the closed interval. However, if (1.27) does not hold, $\bar{U}$ lies outside the closed interval. Accordingly the dynamic path given by (1.21a), which following the initial jump directs U monotonically to $\bar{U}$, takes U out of the

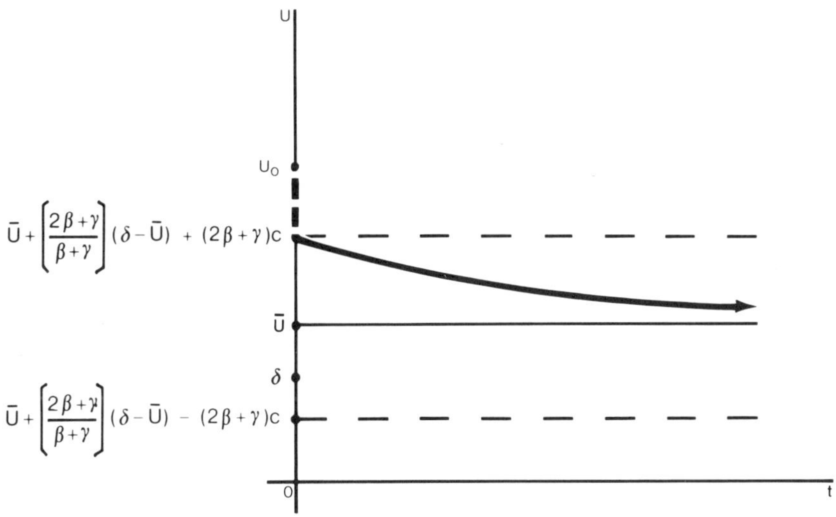

Figure 1.2a. Example of time consistent solution

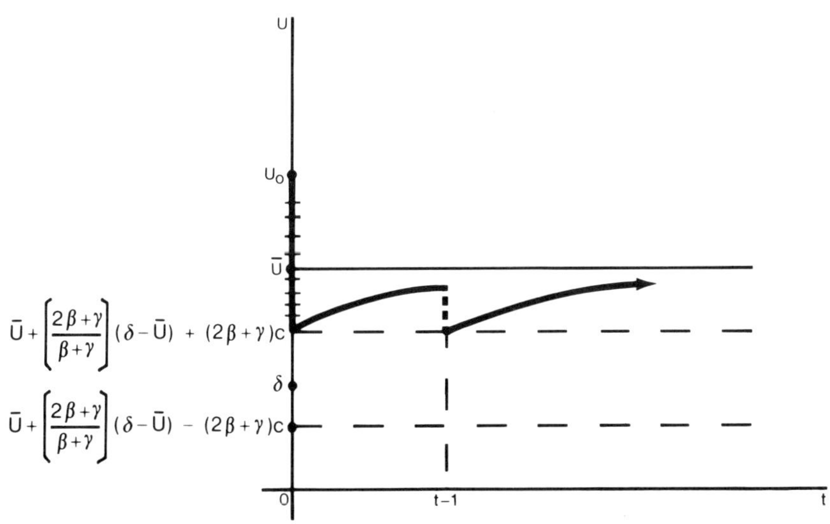

Figure 1.2b. Example of time inconsistent solution

closed interval. Figure 1.2b shows what happens if the decision maker recomputes the optimal policy at t = 1. Clearly a jump back to the boundary of the closed interval is optimal and hence the solution is time inconsistent.

Note that if the desired target rate of unemployment equals the natural rate ($\delta = \bar{U}$) then the inequalities (1.27) are always satisfied and the time path of unemployment is time consistent. Also, if we consider the examples given in figures 1.1a and 1.1b, then the case of a small jump is represented by figure 1.2a and is thus time consistent; while that of a large jump is illustrated in figure 1.2b and is clearly time inconsistent. In general, given values of the natural rate of unemployment, $\bar{U}$, and the parameters β, γ, and c, it is always possible for the policy maker to choose his desired target rate of unemployment δ so as to ensure that the time path for the optimal unemployment rate is time consistent.

It is important to be aware that this property of the time consistency of the optimal path is sensitive to the specification of the loss function attached to the initial jumps. If, for example, this is replaced by the seemingly natural quadratic function, so that the objective function (1.3) becomes

$$L = \tfrac{1}{2} c[U(0) - U_o]^2 + \tfrac{1}{2} \int_0^\infty e^{-\gamma t}[ap^2 + (U - \delta)^2]\,dt \qquad (1.28)$$

then it is shown in the Appendix that the optimal value for U(0) is given by

$$U(0) = \frac{cU_o + \dfrac{\bar{U}}{2\beta + \gamma} + \dfrac{\delta - \bar{U}}{\beta + \gamma}}{c + \dfrac{1}{2\beta + \gamma}}$$

so that

$$U(0) - \bar{U} = k_1\left[(U_o - \bar{U}) + \frac{\delta - \bar{U}}{c(\beta + \gamma)}\right] \qquad (1.29)$$

where

$$k_1 = \frac{c(2\beta + \gamma)}{1 + c(2\beta + \gamma)}$$

However, if following an initial jump from U_o to U(0), the policy maker immediately recomputes his optimal policy now using U(0) as a given value, the corresponding optimal desired initial condition U(0+) say, now becomes

$$U(0+) - \bar{U} = k_1\left[U(0) - \bar{U} + \frac{\delta - \bar{U}}{c(\beta + \gamma)} \right] \tag{1.30}$$

$$= k_1^2\left[(U_o - \bar{U}) + k_1(k_1 + 1)\frac{\delta - \bar{U}}{c(\beta+\gamma)}\right]$$

Since $U(0+) - \bar{U} \neq U(0) - \bar{U}$, the recomputed path is not continuous following the initial jump. Hence the problem with a loss function specified by (1.28) does not have a time consistent solution.

5. CONCLUDING REMARKS

This chapter has analysed the optimal intertemporal inflation and unemployment in a dynamic macro-model in which inflationary expectations satisfy perfect foresight. We have shown that the inflation rate can be driven to zero, although there is a trade-off between an initial once-and-for-all jump in the price level, and an associated jump in the unemployment rate (if such jumps are indeed optimal), and the subsequent evolution of unemployment towards its natural rate.

Whether or not there is an initial jump in the price level has been shown to depend upon certain given aspects of the economy, such as the natural rate of unemployment, the slope of the unemployment-wage inflation Phillips curve, and the cost imposed on the economy by the initial jump in unemployment. In addition, it depends upon certain parameters that can be chosen by the policy maker, such as the socially desired target rate of unemployment and his rate of time preference. These factors, together with the precise specification of the loss function, affect the time consistency or otherwise of the optimal policy.

The basic properties of the optimal policy under perfect foresight derived in this chapter differ dramatically from the optimal policy obtained for models in which expectations evolve sluggishly, such as when they are generated adaptively. An important consequence of this is that preconceptions about the mechanisms by which expectations are formed can radically alter the policy maker's optimal strategy in controlling inflation and unemployment.

APPENDIX

In this Appendix we briefly discuss the case of initial quadratic costs, so that the objective of the policy maker is the minimise

$$L = \tfrac{1}{2}\, c[U(0) - U_o]^2 + \tfrac{1}{2} \int_0^\infty e^{-\gamma t}[ap^2 + (U - \delta)^2]\, dt \tag{A.1}$$

subject to equations (1.7a)–(1.7e) and (1.8a)–(1.8c) of the text.

The optimal path again reduces to equations (1.18a)–(1.18f), together with a transversality condition. The following transversality condition must now be satisfied at the initial time t = 0:

$$\mu(0) + \phi_1\lambda(0) + U'\phi_2[\eta(0) - c[U(0) - U_o]] = 0 \tag{A.2}$$

Using (1.17c) and (1.17d) this reduces to

$$\eta(0) = c[U(0) - U_o] \tag{A.3}$$

The optimal solution for $\eta(t)$ must again satisfy (1.21b), where once again we require D = 0. Then substituting (A.3) into (1.21b) we derive

$$U(0) = \frac{cU_o + \dfrac{\bar{U}}{2\beta + \gamma} + \dfrac{\delta - \bar{U}}{\beta + \gamma}}{c + \dfrac{1}{2\beta + \gamma}} \tag{A.4}$$

The implied optimal time path for U is obtained by substituting for U(0) from (A.3) into the solution (1.21a). At the same time, the rate of inflation is set to zero in accordance with equation (1.18c).

NOTES

1. Equations (1.2b) and (1.2c) are derived from

$$\frac{\dot{M}}{P} = \theta[G - T + rb]$$

$$\frac{\dot{B}}{P} = (1 - \theta)[G - T + rb]$$

2. In deriving the restrictions on the partial derivatives in (1.4a) and (1.4b), we have assumed that

$$D_1 m + D_2 < 0$$

$$D_1 b + D_2 < 0$$

3. This result can be proved formally. Using a modification of the proof of Vind's Theorem (see Arrow and Kurz (1970, p. 51)) it is possible to show that since the Hamiltonian is convex in U, an optimal solution will not have a jump except possibly at the initial time point.
4. Throughout the rest of this chapter we shall assume that p and r can be described by affine functions.
5. The equation $\partial H/\partial\theta = 0$ reduces to $(\mu - \lambda)\ [G - T + rb] = 0$. Since monetary policy would be ineffective if $G - T + rb = 0$, we have assumed that G and T have been chosen so that $G - T + rb \neq 0$ for all finite values of time, t. In this case (1.12e) reduces to $\mu = \lambda$, as given.
6. This result can be derived formally as follows. Suppose the objective is to minimise

$$L = c\,|U(0) - U_o| + \tfrac{1}{2}\int_0^\infty e^{-\gamma t}(U - \delta)^2 dt$$

Substituting for U(t) from (1.21a) gives

$$L = c\,|U(0) - U_o| + \tfrac{1}{2}\left[\frac{(\bar{U} - \delta)^2}{\gamma} + \frac{2[U(0) - \bar{U}]\,[\bar{U} - \delta]}{\beta + \gamma} + \frac{[U(0) - \bar{U}]^2}{2\beta + \gamma}\right]$$

$$= c\,|U(0) - U_o| + \phi(U(0)).$$

We can now divide the general problem into two sub-problems as follows:

Problem 1: minimise $L_1 = c(U(0) - U_o) + \phi(U(0))$, subject to $U(0) \geqslant U_o$; and

Problem 2: minimise $L_2 = c(U_o - U(0)) + \phi(U(0))$ subject to $U_o \geqslant U(0)$.

Differentiating the appropriate expressions for L_1 and L_2 with respect to U(0) then yields expressions equivalent to (1.22a)–(1.22c).

REFERENCES

Arrow, K.J. and M. Kurz (1970), *Public Investment, the Rate of Return, and Optimal Fiscal Policy,* John Hopkins Press, Baltimore and London.

Brechling, R. (1968), 'The trade-off between inflation and unemployment', *Journal of Political Economy,* 76, pp. 712-737.

Kamien, M.I. and N.L. Schwartz (1971), 'Sufficient conditions in optimal control theory', *Journal of Economic Theory,* 3, pp. 207-214.

Kydland, F. and E. Prescott (1977), 'Rules rather than discretion: The inconsistency of optimal plans', *Journal of Political Economy,* 85, pp. 473-491.

Lipsey, R.G. (1965), 'Structural and deficient demand unemployment reconsidered', in: A.M. Ross (ed.), *Employment and the Labour Market,* University of California Press, Berkeley, California.

Phelps, E.S. (1967), 'Phillips curves, expectations of inflation and optimum utilisation over time', *Economica,* 24, pp. 254-281.

Phelps, E.S. (1972), *Inflation Policy and Unemployment Theory,* Norton, New York.

Turnovsky, S.J. (1981), 'The optimal intertemporal choice of inflation and unemployment', *Journal of Economic Dynamics and Control,* 3, pp. 357-384.

Turnovsky, S.J. and W.A. Brock (1980), 'Time consistency and optimal government policies in perfect foresight equilibrium', *Journal of Public Economics,* 13, pp. 183-212.

CHAPTER 2

TOWARD THE RESURRECTION OF OPTIMAL MACROECONOMIC POLICIES

L. Karp *Texas A and M University, USA*
A. Havenner *University of California, Davis, USA*

1. INTRODUCTION

The recognition of rational expectations has lead some to conclude that control theory is not an appropriate technique for determining policy. This conclusion is incorrect. The presence of rational expectations on the part of the public merely requires that policy makers solve a more sophisticated control problem, as we demonstrate below. Section 2 reviews the problem of the 'inconsistency' of optimal policies in a world of rational expectations. The problem forms the basis for the rational expectations criticism of control theory. Section 3 casts the policy making process as a dynamic Stackelberg game. After examining the mathematics of the anomaly, which hinges on the inapplicability of the Principle of Optimality, several types of control solutions which do not exhibit the anomaly are discussed. Section 4 summarises the results.

2. POLICY CONSISTENCY

Rational expectations require that economic agents recognise that tomorrow's world is affected by the decisions of policy makers. Agents form expectations of policy makers' decisions, and these expectations influence their own choices. Thus, the decisions of future policy makers affect the economic environment not only directly, but also through their influence on the present actions of the public.

The application of control theory to policy problems requires the estimation of a dynamic model. The reduced form of this model is used as a system of state equa-

Hughes Hallett, A.J. (ed.) Applied Decision Analysis and Economic Behaviour

ISBN 90-247-2968-8. Printed in The Netherlands

tions in the control problem; the objective functional measures the (discounted) payoff or cost in the current and future periods. It is customary to assume that the reactions of agents are captured in the reduced form of the model. This implies that agents' current decisions depend on the controllers' (policy maker's) current and previous policies. It is at this point that the application of control theory runs afoul of rational expectations, which postulates that the agents' reactions also depend on future policies.

If the policy maker behaves as described in the previous paragraph, his policies will be 'consistent', but not optimal. They are consistent in the sense that the policy maker takes the current state (and the agents' reactions) as given, and optimises over the future. If the policy maker behaves in this way at each point in time, rational agents will become aware of this, and adjust their choices. The requirement that the policy maker behave consistently constrains his choice of policies. It may be optimal for today's policy maker to compel his successor to follow a certain rule in order to induce the public to behave in a certain way –we show in the next section that the leader's payoffs monotonically decrease in the number of revisions– but if that rule is not the optimal policy for the state at which the successor finds himself it is disallowed. It is this requirement of consistency, combined with rational expectations, that causes Kydland and Prescott to trumpet the demise of optimal control in macroeconomic policy (1977, p. 487):

> 'The implication of this analysis is that . . . active stabilisation may very well be dangerous and it is best that it not be attempted. Reliance on policies such as a constant growth in the money supply and constant tax rates constitute a safer course of action.'

These are strong conclusions –indeed, overly strong, as will be seen below– and they deserve careful consideration.

3. POLICY AS A DYNAMIC GAME

It simplifies the exposition to assume that there are only two players, policy makers and the public, and that decisions occur in continuous time. Player i, i = ℓ (leader), f (follower), wants to choose u_i to maximise

$$J_i(u_\ell, u_f) = \int_0^T L_i(x, u_\ell, u_f, t)dt \tag{2.1}$$

where u_i is player i's control vector, x is the state, the argument t allows exogenous changes, and T (possibly infinite) is the end of the game. The evolution of the state is governed by

$$\frac{dx}{dt} = \dot{x} = f(x, u_\ell, u_f, t) \qquad x(0) = x_o \tag{2.2}$$

Before examining the relation between this differential game and the control problem, it is useful to review static Stackelberg games and their solutions. Player i chooses u_i, a vector rather than a function, to maximise $J_i(u_\ell, u_f)$, $i = \ell, f$. Assuming an interior solution, the follower's first order condition gives $\partial J_f(u_\ell, u_f)/\partial u_f = 0$. This implicitly defines the follower's reaction function. The leader then maximises $J_\ell(u_\ell, u_f)$ over both u_ℓ and u_f, taking the reaction function as a constraint. The static Stackelberg game is equivalent to a constrained optimisation problem. The relation between Stackelberg differential games and control problems is analogous.

3.1 Failure of the Principle of Optimality

The following solution to the Stackelberg differential game was proposed by Simaan and Cruz (1973a, b). Assuming an interior solution, the follower's Hamiltonian and first order conditions (suppressing the arguments x, u_ℓ, u_f, t) are given by

$$H_f = L_f(.) + y f(.) \tag{2.3}$$

$$\partial H_f / \partial u_f = 0 \tag{2.4}$$

$$-\partial H_f / \partial x = \dot{y} \tag{2.5}$$

Equation (2.2) and appropriate transversality conditions, which depend on whether T and x(T) are given, constitute the remaining first order conditions. The follower's costate variable, y, gives the marginal value to the follower of an increase in the state. As in the static game, the first order conditions implicitly determine the follower's reaction function. Here they depend on the entire trajectory of the leader's controls, rather than the controls at a single point. The leader treats (2.4) as an ordinary constraint; he treats the follower's costate variable, y, as a state, the equation of motion of which is given by (2.5). The leader is faced with the control problem of choosing $u_\ell(t)$ and $u_f(t)$ to maximise (2.1), subject to (2.2), (2.4), (2.5) and the follower's transversality conditions.

The only way in which this differs from a standard control problem is that the initial value of the 'state' y is not given. The value of the follower's costate at T is given by the transversality conditions, so its value at t=0 is determined up to a constant by the entire trajectory of controls. The leader implicitly determines y(0) through his choice of controls. The leader's Hamiltonian is given by

$$H_\ell = L_\ell(.) + \eta_1 f(.) - \eta_2 \, \partial H_f / \partial x + \Theta \, \partial H_f / \partial u_f \ , \tag{2.6}$$

where η_1 and η_2 are the leader's costate variables associated with the states x and y, respectively, and Θ is the constraint multiplier for (2.4). Since y(0) is free, $\eta_2(0)=0$.

Suppose that the follower does not have rational expectations, and that the leader is allowed to revise his policy at some point τ in the interval (0, T). The leader first announces a policy $u_\ell(t)$ for all t in the interval (0, T). This policy, and the follower's response, determines the value y(t) over that interval. The costate variable η_2 evolves according to the equation

$$\dot{\eta}_2 = -\,\partial H_\ell(.)/\partial y \quad . \tag{2.7}$$

Since $\dot{\eta}_2 \neq$ o in general, this implies that $\eta_2(\tau) \neq 0$. That is, at τ the leader could increase his payoff by an increase or reduction in the follower's costate, $y(\tau)$. However, $y(\tau)$ is fully determined by the transversality conditions at T and the leader's control trajectory over (τ, T). This implies that if the leader were allowed to revise at τ he would want to change the trajectory over (τ, T) which he had announced at t = 0. The Principle of Optimality does not hold. The 'failure' of the Principle of Optimality is due to the nature of the control problem resulting from the Stackelberg game. The Principle states that if the controller takes as given the state resulting from an optimal control path over (0, τ), and re-solves his probelm at τ, then the optimal control path over (τ, T) will be the same as that determined at t = 0. In this problem, however, the controller (the leader) is not given y(0), and if he is permitted to revise at τ, or at any other point, he is not given y at that point; rather, it is determined by his future actions.[1] Therefore, the Principle of Optimality is inapplicable in this problem, i.e., consistent policy makers will always renege, and deviate from their announced strategies.

In the situation described above, the policy makers lead in a differential Stackelberg game; they are permitted to revise their policies during the game, but the follower is not sufficiently astute to anticipate this revision. This appears to describe the world that policy makers believed they inhabited until the mid-1970's. The rational expectations critique pointed out that if the public anticipated revision, a different result would obtain. Suppose that the policy maker will revise at some time τ, and that both he and the public are aware of this. At $t = \tau$ the policy maker must take the state of the economy $x(\tau)$ as given, but as argued above, he considers $y(\tau)$ as free. He determines his optimal policy over (τ, T) and this determines $y(\tau)$. Since the optimal policy over (τ, T) depends on the state x at $t = \tau$, write $y(\tau) = y(x(\tau))$ where the function $y(x(\tau))$ is determined by the leader's maximisation problem over (τ, T). Now consider the interval (0, τ). The follower is faced with an ordinary control problem, since he treats u_ℓ as exogenous over the entire interval of play. Over the interval $(0, \tau)$ the knowledge, of both the leader and the follower, that the leader will revise at τ induces the additional constraint

$$y(\tau) = y(x(\tau)) , \tag{2.8}$$

i.e., the follower is not fooled and the problem must be solved with the follower's costate variable a function of the actual state at the time of revision, $x(\tau)$.

3.2 Binding contracts

Designate $J(x(\tau))$ as the optimal value of the game to the leader over (τ, T) given $x(\tau)$ and given that he revises at τ. The leader's problem, with revision and rational expectations, is

$$\max_{u_\ell, u_f} \int_o^\tau L_\ell(.)dt + J(x(\tau)) \tag{2.9}$$

s.t. (2.2), (2.4), (2.5) and (2.8)

The trajectory that satisfies this problem clearly is feasible for the original (open loop) problem with no revision. The addition of the constraint (2.8) lowers the total payoff to the leader. To demonstrate this last assertion it is necessary only to show that the solution to (2.9) does not in general [2] solve the original problem. Suppose that it did. Then the trajectories for $x(t)$ and $u_i(t)$ must be the same for the original problem (open loop, without revision) and the problem given by (2.9). Since the controls are determined implicitly as functions of $x(t)$ and $y(t)$, this implies that $y(t)$ must be the same for both problems. But in the problem (2.9), $y(\tau)$ is chosen to maximise $J(x(\tau))$. However, as stated above, for the original problem $\eta_2(\tau) \neq 0$ in general, so $y(\tau)$ is not the value of y at τ that maximises the original problem over (τ, T). This contradiction implies that the open loop controls, which are optimal [since they are not constrained by (2.8), and thus include the constrained case as a subcase], are not identical to the controls that result from solving (2.9). In summary, the solution that results when the leader is able [3] to revise at a particular point during the interval of play, and both the leader and the follower are aware of this, gives the leader a lower payoff than when he uses open loop controls (announces an optimal trajectory and does not deviate from it).

If the leader is allowed to revise twice, and the follower is aware of this, the same argument can be used to show that the leader's payoff is lower than when he revises only once. Repeating the argument n times verifies that in a world of rational expectations, the leader's payoff is nonincreasing (strictly decreasing, except when

$\eta_2 \equiv 0$) in the number of revisions he is permitted. As the number of revisions, n, gets large, the intervals between revisions become small. As n goes to infinity, the leader is constantly revising: he always takes the current state as given and is behaving consistently.

The conclusion is that consistent behaviour is suboptimal, and contrary to what might be expected, for the leader 'more consistency' is worse than 'less consistency'. Thus, there is an incentive, in the form of higher payoffs, for the leader to commit to binding contracts on his performance if any can be devised. In many cases, such as flood plain improvements or Federal Reserve assistance to prevent bank failure, such commitments may be relatively easy to implement, perhaps requiring only a highly visible announced policy. If a binding macroeconomic stabilisation policy were possible, the leader would willingly agree to commit himself and succeeding leaders to the policy that is best for him, which is the original (standard) open loop solution with no revision. The optimal policies need not be stationary –indeed, they will not be except at a stationary equilibrium– but rather will allow for exogenous changes in the economy, as evidenced by the time dependence of f(.) and L_i(.).

3.3 Threats

The possibility of constraining future policy makers not only makes the open loop policy credible, but also implies the existence of other types of policies which may give the leader a still higher payoff. Suppose that the leader has a set of targets for the follower's controls. If he is able to penalise the follower for deviations from these targets, he may persuade the follower to approximate them, thus increasing his (the leader's) payoff. As a limiting case, the leader may have sufficient power to persuade the follower to exactly track any set of targets. In that case the leader effectively chooses the follower's controls, and solves a team problem rather than a game. The question is, how is the leader to penalise the follower for deviations from targets that the leader sets? One possibility is for the leader to choose a particular state dependent control rule. Recall that the open loop controls considered above were written as functions of time alone, and that the follower took the leader's control values as given rather than the control rule considered now.

For simplicity, suppose that the leader's only interest is in keeping the state in some set A_1 and his own control in some set A_2. In this case his target for the follower's control consists of some set A_3 [4] such that when $x \in A_1$, $u_\ell \in A_2$ and $u_f \in A_3$, the solution to equation (2.2) lies in A_1. The leader may announce any closed loop rule which maps A_1 into A_2, and maps the complement of A_1 into the set or element most damaging to the follower. That is, the leader uses his feedback rule as a threat to persuade the follower to cooperate. For this strategy to be successful, the threat must be sufficiently damaging to the follower if carried out, and the follower must believe that there is a high probability that it would be carried out. Damage depends on the specifics of the problem, and nothing can be said about its satisfaction in general. Credibility relies on the possibility of compelling future policy makers to follow the announced closed loop strategy. If the strategy is successful, then x remains in A_1, and the problem of time inconsistency does not arise. Since the consistency of the solution is contingent upon the state being in A_1, we may regard this as a form of state-dependent consistency. For $x \in A_1$ the Principle of Optimality holds.

To make the discussion concrete, let A_1 be a tolerable range for the rate of inflation, A_2 a range for the growth of the money stock, and A_3 a range for the rate of private borrowing or wage demands. When the public's controls correspond to levels that maintain an acceptable inflation rate and growth in the money stock, all is well. The severity of monetary policy when the inflation rate exceeds tolerable limits disciplines the public by assuring them that inflation will be in the targeted range, thus making, for example, wildly speculative schemes uneconomic.

As this example indicates, there is a danger of mistaking a very perverse policy for an optimal closed loop policy. One possible 'threat' for the monetary agencies is to hold to fixed money growth in all situations; i.e., the closed loop policy maps the entire domain of x into A_2. If the departure from the tolerable range, A_1, is not due to the public's behaviour, but to events beyond their control, such as the world economic situation, then the discipline is not only wasted on the public, but is counterproductive since, for $x \notin A_1$, the closed loop control need not be the best available. It was chosen to keep the state in A_1, not to return it to that set should it ever depart from it. If it is not in the leader's own interest to impose the penalty whenever $x \notin A_1$, whether because of exogenous shocks or follower recalcitrance, then the Principle of Optimality fails again. In this case a binding contract can restore credibility to the threat, but notice the difference from section 3.1 above. If the penalty is tripped by events not under the follower's control, the leader may not choose to enter the contract, knowing that a threat contracted to force the follower into an infeasible region may make both parties worse off.

3.4 Feasibility with threats

The idea of using a state dependent strategy as a disguised threat and thereby forcing the follower to accept a certain solution has been exploited by Papavassilopoulos and Cruz (1980) –P&C– and Basar and Selbuz (1979) –B&S– to solve the linear-quadratic game (a linear equation of motion and a quadratic objective function). Since the linear-quadratic structure is frequently used in economics, the solution is of practical interest. The method consists of two steps. First, the leader solves his problem as a team problem, that is, he optimises over both his own controls and those of the follower. He then chooses a representation of his (the leader's) control (see below), which he presents to the follower as his control rule. This representation qualifies as a closed loop control law if, when the follower takes it as given, he solves his problem by choosing the controls that satisfy the leader's team problem.

To illustrate the method, we review an example given by P&C. Let the state, x(t) and the controls $u_f(t)$ and $u_\ell(t)$ be scalars, and the state equation be given by $x = x + u_f + u_\ell$. The leader solves a control problem using both controls; this gives linear feedback rules of the form $u_f = f(t)x(t)$ and $u_\ell = g(t)x(t)$. Define a new state, $y(t) = \int_0^t x(\tau)d\tau$ which gives the history of the state. The leader announces his controls $u_\ell = h(t)x(t) + k(t)y(t)$. This is what is meant by a representation of the leader's control. Then the follower is faced by a system given by $\dot{x} = (1 + h(t))x + k(t)y + u_f$ and $\dot{y} = x$. The follower solves his control problem subject to these two equations and likewise obtains a control rule of the form $u_f = p(t)x(t) + q(t)y(t)$. The leader's problem (an inverse control problem) is to find functions h(t) and k(t) so that $f(t)x(t) = p(t)x(t) + q(t)y(t)$ and $h(t)x(t) + k(t)y(t) = g(t)x(t)$.

B&S discuss the problem in discrete time and allow the leader to choose a rule of the form $u_\ell = G_1x(t) + G_2x(t-1)$. The matrices G_1 and G_2 are found by solving a system of equations recursively. B&S give a sufficient condition for a solution to exist.[5] This condition cannot be simply expressed in terms of the parameters of the problem, but requires calculation. They state that numerical experimentation indicates that if the condition is not satisfied when the leader has one-step-memory, it is usually possible to satisfy it by allowing the leader the history of the state in the more distant past. This is not surprising, because each piece of information enlarges the class of control rules available to the leader. (The situation is analogous to including more explanatory variables in a regression).

By solving the team problem first, the leader ensures the feasibility of the solution he is attempting to force onto the follower (unlike the raw threat case above). Since the leader receives the payoff to his team solution, he would have no desire to revise his control rule at a later date and the Principle of Optimality holds. Thus, the follower knows the leader will perform as promised even without binding contracts.

4. SUMMARY AND CONCLUSIONS

It is well known that the solution to a game is in general very sensitive to the assumptions made, and the game between policy makers and the public is no exception. Stating that the public has rational expectations implies that a game is being played, but does not determine the rules of the game, i.e., the players' sets of admissible control rules. It is our feeling that the Kydland-Prescott time consistency argument, which they use in their 1977 paper to call for fixed money growth rates (quoted in section 2 above) and in a later article to endorse a balanced budget constitutional ammendment (Kydland and Prescott (1980), p. 80), has had an effect on the profession entirely out of keeping with its (lack of) robustness to assumptions. While their logic is correct in the narrow context of their model, there are more plausible views of the world which yield contrary results and it is certainly premature to abandon control solutions because of rational expectations. Indeed, in this chapter we present three widely-applicable cases in which control solutions are appropriate in the presence of rational expectations.

First, by demonstrating that the leader's payoff is a decreasing function of the number of revisions permitted, we show that there is an incentive for the leader to enter contracts that bind him to the standard open loop optimal control solution, circumventing the time-inconsistency problem. Binding contracts need not be legal documents, only arrangements in which the cost of reneging exceeds the gains so that in many cases an announced policy will suffice. For example, imagine the costs to the Federal Reserve of accommodating large-scale Treasury borrowing after repeatedly denying that it would do so.

Second, it may be possible in some cases for the leader to cow the follower with damaging and believable threats. In this case the Principle of Optimality may or may not fail depending on the parameters of the individual problem, but it need not fail necessarily. In some cases the leader can improve his position by entering a binding contract to make the threat believable; if the prescribed follower policy is feasible, the game has been reduced to a control problem.

Finally, since there are really no constraints on the sophistication of the policies available to the leader, we can imagine the leader solving the team problem and then an inverse optimal control problem, at least in the linear-quadratic case. Then, even with rational expectations, the follower will wish to perform exactly as planned; as indeed will the leader. Again, there is no time-inconsistency problem. The formal requirement for this solution is access to the history of the state, a requirement that is not at all binding in the case of macroeconomic policy. With this far more realistic set of assumptions, the time-inconsistency problem does not occur.

NOTES

1) The feedback functions themselves change at τ, not just their values. The anticipated $x(\tau)$ is the actual $x(\tau)$, but if the leader is permitted to revise his policy the newly determined costate variable y differs from the anticipated, invalidating the Principle of Optimality. This effect of the leader's anticipated future actions on the follower's is termed noncausality by Hughes Hallett (1983), who evaluates the suboptimality implied by ignoring it.
2) The exception is when $\eta_2 \equiv 0$.
3) By 'able' we really mean 'will'. The leader at τ is concerned with the payoff over (τ, T) and ignores the effect of his decision on the follower over $(0, \tau)$.
4) A_3 may depend on x and u_ℓ.
5) A technical aspect of B&S's approach is that they assume that the follower is unable to act in the last period. As the number of periods becomes large, this restriction becomes unimportant. Incidentally, although the objective functions are quadratic and both the equation of motion and feedback rules are linear, the solution does not satisfy the certainty equivalence principle.

REFERENCES

Basar, T. and Selbuz, H. (1979), 'Closed loop Stackelberg strategies with applications in the optimal control of multilevel systems', *IEEE Transactions on Automatic Control,* AC-24, pp. 166-179.

Hughes Hallett, A.J. (1983), 'Optimal strategies for dynamic games and the incentive to cooperate', *International Journal of Systems Science,* 14, pp. 179-200.

Kydland, F.E. and E.C. Prescott (1977), 'Rules rather than discretion: the inconsistency of optimal plans', *Journal of Political Economy,* 85, pp. 473-491.

Kydland, F.E. and E.C. Prescott (1980), 'Dynamic optimal taxation, rational expectations and optimal control', *Journal of Economic Dynamics and Control,* 2, pp. 79-91.

Papavassilopoulos, G.P. and J.B. Cruz, Jr. (1980), 'Sufficient conditions for Stackelberg and Nash strategies with memory', *Journal of Optimisation Theory and Applications,* 31, pp. 253-260.

Simaan, M. and J.B. Cruz, Jr. (1973a), 'On the Stackelberg strategy in nonzero-sum games', *Journal of Optimisation Theory and Applications,* 11, pp. 533-555.

Simaan, M. and J.B. Cruz, Jr. (1973b), 'Additional aspects of the Stackelberg strategy in nonzero-sum games', *Journal of Optimisation Theory and Applications,* 11, pp. 613-626.

CHAPTER 3

OPTIMAL FEEDBACK AND FEEDFORWARD STABILISATION OF EXCHANGE RATES, MONEY, PRICES AND OUTPUT UNDER RATIONAL EXPECTATIONS

S. Holly and R. Corker
London Business School, U.K.

1. INTRODUCTION

This paper examines the role of an optimal stabilisation policy for output, prices and the exchange rate in an open economy. The market in foreign exchange is assumed to be efficient and forward-looking in the sense of the rational expectations hypothesis, but the domestic goods and labour markets are assumed to respond sluggishly. As was originally stressed by Dornbusch (1976), if in these circumstances a government attempts to reduce the rate of inflation by monetary contraction then the real exchange rate appreciates causing a loss of international competitiveness. Only as the domestic price level adjusts slowly towards its lower equilibrium will the real exchange rate move back towards its previous level.

As a related theme we consider the structure of the optimal policy and decompose it into a feedback policy –which with any costs of adjustment gives a distributed lagged response to unanticipated disturbances in the economy– and a forward-looking (or feedforward) policy which gives a distributed lead response to disturbances which are anticipated to occur in future periods. This establishes a duality with the types of responses to anticipated and unanticipated shocks in rational expectations models. As an example of this, Wilson (1979) extended Dornbusch's analysis of exchange rate dynamics to show that if a change in monetary policy is anticipated by the foreign exchange market, the exchange rate will shift prior to the period in which the change occurs.

In this paper we permit both the monetary authority and the foreign exchange market to respond to both anticipated and unanticipated shocks. Thus, if it is widely anticipated that oil prices will shift in the near future both the monetary authority and the foreign exchange market can respond immediately. The forward-looking characteristics of an optimal stabilisation policy are a neglected area of control theory

Hughes Hallett, A.J. (ed.) Applied Decision Analysis and Economic Behaviour

ISBN 90-247-2968-8. Printed in The Netherlands

mainly because of a tendency to ignore anticipated shocks to exogenous variables, or else to rule them out by extracting the signal part of exogenous processes to control and then treating the remaining noise as strictly unanticipated. This of course is to fail to distinguish between closed loop and pure feedback control (Tse (1974), Hughes Hallet and Rees (1983)).

The structure of feedback and feedforward are established for the case of a linear model with additive disturbances and preferences represented by a quadratic objective function. Later we examine how this might look empirically by using a large nonlinear model of the UK economy[1]. The structure of the model has had to be modified slightly to allow us to ensure that the spot exchange rate is determined by arbitrage. This is done in such a way that the current differential between domestic and foreign interest rates (after allowing for risk and transactions costs in a heuristic way) is matched by rationally expected changes in the exchange rate.

The nonlinearity of the model poses some computational problems for the study of responses to anticipated and unanticipated disturbances since we cannot derive explicit analytical optimal decision rules. Instead we use a method proposed by Holly and Zarrop (1983) to determine optimal open loop policies under rational expectations. Repeating the calculation after the addition of a shock effectively allows us to uncover the (approximate) feedback and feedforward components by numerical differentiation. The response surface of the optimal policy provides useful insights into the role of economic policy under rational expectations in the foreign exchange market, and suggests that shocks striking the economy via fluctuations in the real exchange rate can be ameliorated.

2. FEEDBACK AND FEEDFORWARD

In this section be briefly examine the structure of an optimal decision rule for economic policy, ignoring, for the present, the role of expectations. Since the results are well known in the literature (Chow (1975)) we confine ourselves to a statement of the problem.

Suppose a linear model with additive stochastic errors can be written

$$y_t = Ay_{t-1} + Bx_t + Ce_t + \epsilon_t \tag{3.1}$$

where y_t is a vector of m endogenous variables, x_t a vector of n policy instruments, e_t a vector of q exogenous variables and ϵ_t a vector of random disturbances with zero mean and known covariance. The objective function is quadratic in expected deviations of targets and instruments from desired values

$$E(J) = \tfrac{1}{2} E \sum_{t=1}^{T} \left\{ \delta y_t' Q_t \delta y_t + \delta x_t' N_t \delta x_t \right\} \tag{3.2}$$

where

$$\delta y_t = y_t - y_t^d ; \quad \delta x_t = x_t - x_t^d$$

and the superscript indicates desired values. The symmetric weighting or penalty matrices Q_t and N_t are assumed to be positive semi-definite and positive definite respectively. The optimal decision rule is the time varying function

$$x_t = L_t y_{t-1} + h_t \tag{3.3}$$

where

$$L_t = - [N_t + B'P_tB]^{-1} B'P_tA \tag{3.4}$$

$$h_t = - [N_t + B'P_tB]^{-1} \left\{ B'P_tC\bar{e}_{t,t} - N_t x_t^d - B'(Q_t y_t^d + k_t) \right\} \tag{3.5}$$

where

$$P_t = Q_t + (A + BL_t)' P_{t+1} (A + BL_t) + L_t' N_t L_t \tag{3.6}$$

$$k_t = (A + BL_t)' \left\{ P_{t+1} (Bh_t + C\bar{e}_{t,t}) - Q_t y_t^d - k_{t+1} \right\} - L_t' N_t x_t^d \tag{3.7}$$

The boundary conditions for these two difference equations are given by

$$P_{T+1} = Q_T ; \quad k_{T+1} = 0 \tag{3.8}$$

and $\bar{e}_{i,j} = E_i e_j$ indicates an expectation formed at time period i with respect to time period j. L_t is commonly referred to as the feedback gain, while h_t is the tracking gain. The feedback gain is a time varying function of the structure of preferences and the system constraints represented by A and B. It is designed to attenuate unanticipated innovations in ϵ_{t-1} which it is assumed are observable without error (i.e. no filter is required) through obervations on y_{t-1}. The variation in y_{t-1} will be wholly attributable to ϵ_t only if $E_{t-1} e_{t-1} = e_{t-1}$. That is if exogenous variables in the current period are observable. This may not always be the case. A small open economy to which the rest of the world is exogenous is unlikely to observe the current state of world trade without error; though precise measurements of interest and exchange rates in the current period would be available. This means that some of the revision to policy occurring at time t may be due to new information about e_{t-1} though of course the feedback response of x_t does not differentiate between the source of any disturbance.

Note that the policy revision is with reference to an open loop policy, i.e. the policy determined at time period t–1 conditional on information available at t–1 and to be implemented at time period t in the absence of any disturbances.

In addition to the feedback response to y_{t-1} there can also be a current period shift in economic policy because of alterations in expectations about future exogenous variables. These changes in expectations affect current economic policy through h_t, the second term on the right hand side of (3.3). This term is normally referred to as the tracking gain in the control literature. But because of the important role it plays in generating a current period economic policy response to *anticipated* disturbances to exogenous variables we shall refer to it as the *feedforward* term [2]. The lead response to an anticipated impulse in exogenous variables at some future period τ, can be written down analytically (Baum (1980)) from equations (3.3) to (3.7). Given the close loop decision rule (3.3) and the forward difference equations (3.6) and (3.7) we have

$$\frac{\partial x_t}{\partial e_\tau} = F_t B \left[G_{t+1} \cdot G_{t+2} \cdot \ldots \cdot G_\tau \right] \left\{ I + BF_\tau S_\tau \right\} C \tag{3.9}$$

where

$$F_t = N_t + S_t B^{-1}$$

$$S_t = Q_t + P_{t+1}$$

$$G_t = (A + BL_t)' S_t$$

This means that if policymakers revise their expectations about what values exogenous variables will take in the future there will be an immediate policy adjustment, with the strength of response dependent on intertemporal preferences, model structure and the distance between the current period, t, and the period, τ, in which the change occurs.

It can be seen then, from equations (3.3) to (3.7), that the optimal closed loop policy is comprised of both a backward-looking distributed lag feedback response to unanticipated disturbances and a forward-looking distributed feedforward response to anticipated disturbances.

3. RATIONAL EXPECTATIONS IN THE FOREIGN EXCHANGE MARKET

The exchange rate in the version of the LBS model currently used for forecasting and policy analysis is based on the monetary theory of the balance of payments (Ball, Burns, Warburton (1977)). The UK, as a small open economy, is assumed to be a price taker. The UK demand for money is assumed to be a simple function of income and interest rates:

$$m_t - p_t = y_t - \phi r_t \tag{3.10}$$

where lower case letters denote logs; m_t is the UK demand for money, p_t a price index, and y_t income. The world demand for money has equivalent arguments in world variables:

$$m_t^W - p_t^W = y_t^W - \theta rw_t \tag{3.11}$$

The theory of purchasing power parity, when applied to traded goods, implies that in the long run the real exchange rate is independent of nominal magnitudes:

$$p_t + s_t - p_t^W = k_t \tag{3.12}$$

where k_t is the real exchange rate. Onto this long run formulation is grafted a dynamic adjustment process –attributable to adjustment costs, information lags and uncertainties, determinants of the real exchange rate such as North Sea oil, as well as some short run asset substitution effects proxied by domestic and world interest rates and the borrowing requirement of the government (Beenstock, Budd and Warburton (1981)). This formulation of the exchange rate is backward-looking and does not permit the exchange rate to respond to 'news' or to anticipated disturbances. It can also imply that there are unexploited arbitrage opportunities. To overcome this difficulty we modified the structure of the LBS model so that the spot exchange rate is determined by an efficient markets condition but not necessarily that there is perfect capital mobility. Net holdings of foreign exchange are a function of the expected change in the exchange rate and the uncovered interest rate differential:

$$K_t = \lambda\left\{{}_t s^e_{t+1} - s_t + r_t - rw_t\right\} + k_o \tag{3.13}$$

where K_t is the net position, and k_o a constant, s_t the spot exchange rate, r_t the domestic interest rate and rw_t the overseas interest rate. Finally, ${}_t s^e_{t+1}$ is the expectation of the exchange rate at time t+1 conditional on information available at t. Speculative capital flows are then simply the first difference of K_t. On the assumption of a freely floating exchange rate and no direct foreign reserves intervention by the government, the spot exchange rate must adjust to clear the market in foreign exchange. The flow on the capital account is then just the negative of the flow on the current account. Thus

$$K_t = K_{t-1} - BAL_t \tag{3.14}$$

by successive substitution we then reach an exchange rate equation

$$s_t = {}_t s^e_{t+1} + r_t - rw_t + \frac{1}{\lambda}\left\{BAL_t + CBAL_{t-1}\right\} \tag{3.15}$$

where BAL_t is the balance of payments on current account, and $CBAL_t$ the cumulative BAL_t. Under perfect capital mobility lambda is infinity, so equation (3.15) reduces to the infinitely elastic arbitrage relationship widely used in the analytical literature (e.g. Buiter and Miller (1981)).

Forward substitution in (3.15) shows that the spot exchange rate is dependent on current and future expected interest rates and the current and future expected state of the balance of payments:

$$s_t = \sum_{i=o}^{\infty}\left\{r_{t+i} - rw_{t+i} + \frac{1}{\lambda}(BAL_{t+i} + CBAL_{t+i-1})\right\} \tag{3.16}$$

Although these are endogenous variables we could in principle substitute them out and express the spot exchange rate as a function of future expected exogenous variables, among which would be numbered the policy instruments. In equation (3.16), the exchange rate is entirely a forward-looking 'jump' variable which responds only to current unanticipated and future anticipated shocks.

It should be clear that there is a duality between the forward-looking, anticipatory behaviour of the foreign exchange market and the forward-looking anticipatory behaviour of an optimising economic policy maker. In this framework economic policy is formulated as the solution to an intertemporal problem determined jointly with the rational intertemporal optimising behaviour of the private sector.

4. OPTIMAL POLICY IN RATIONAL EXPECTATIONS MODELS

There are a number of technical difficulties associated with establishing the optimal policy when expectations are forward-looking. The dynamic programming solution provided by equations (3.3) to (3.7) is not appropriate (Chow (1980)) when, in the linear case, the constraints are of the form

$$y_t = Ay_{t-1} + Bx_t + Ce_t + D_t y_{t+1} + \epsilon_t \tag{3.17}$$

where ${}_t y^e_{t+1}$ is the rational expectation of y_{t+1} formed on the basis of information available at t, and terminal conditions on the expectations process preclude speculative bubbles. However, it is possible to use open loop with feedback techniques such as the penalty function method of Holly and Zarrop (1983) to determine the current period optimal policy. There still remains a problem even with non-recursive methods because of the time inconsistency issue originally raised by Kydland and Prescott (1977). One way around the difficulty is to assume that the open loop with feedback solution is a Nash equilibrium solution under which neither the private sector nor the government has an informational advantage. For this condition to hold we require that equation (3.17) reflects the first order optimality conditions (plus transversality conditions) of a forward-looking optimising private sector (Holly (1983)). Time inconssistency does not arise in these circumstances (Brandsma and Hughes Hallett (1984)).

Technically the objective function is minimised while ensuring that expectations are consistent, i.e. for the case of the exchange rate we require ${}_t s^e_{t+1} = s_{t+1}$. This is achieved by the augmented objective function

$$J' = J + \sum_{t=1}^{T} ({}_t s^e_{t+1} - s_{t+1})^2 \tag{3.18}$$

The unconstrained minimum of the second term on the RHS of (3.18) is then the consistent expectations solution after we have imposed a terminal condition. This is assumed to take the form

$${}_t s^e_{T+1} = (1 + q) s_T \tag{3.19}$$

where q is the rate of change of the exchange rate between period T−1 and period T. A variety of methods have been proposed for the numerical solution of rational expectations models (Fair (1979), Anderson (1979), Lipton et al. (1983), Buiter (1981), Driffill (1982)) but with the exception of the method of Driffill, none of them is able to determine an optimal policy. By minimising the augmented objective function we can determine the optimal response of the policy maker to both anticipated and unanticipated disturbances while also allowing for the fact that expectations will alter endogenously in response to the policy. But for this to be reasonable we must assume that the government announces its objective function and how it will respond to different types of disturbance. It is clear that the exchange rate will respond quite differently, depending upon what policy regime the government is perceived or assumed to be operating.

It is important to stress that the 'optimal' policy is simply that policy which minimises (3.2). If the structure of preferences alters or the government switches from pursuing one target to another the optimal responses will alter. Providing information to the private sector about possible switches in regime is a very important element in any economic policy. If the private sector continued to believe that the government was pursuing a money supply target when in fact a policy shift had occurred to an exchange rate target, the response of the economy to disturbances could be quite different from what they would be if the adoption of the exchange rate target was widely known and understood.

5. EMPIRICAL RESULTS

Macroeconomies are subject to a continuous sequence of both unanticipated (innovations in equation residuals) and anticipated shocks. In these circumstances economic policy entails a continuous process of systematic revision as new information becomes available. The actual frequency with which policy adjustments are made will vary depending on the quality and reliability of information, uncertainty about its accuracy, and the freedom with which policy instruments can be varied given institutional and political constraints. These inside and outside policy lags are equally as relevant to whatever kind of economic policy is being pursued, whether it is a standard countercyclical policy, or a money supply policy, or whatever. Information uncertainty and the time policy makers take to respond will usually mean that governments will not react to every fluctuation in economic activity. In this paper we confine ourselves to considering optimal responses to just two reasonably large disturbances.

(a) First, oil prices were reduced permanently by twenty percent, allowing the change to be unanticipated and also anticipated four periods before it occurs.
(b) Second, we imposed an unanticipated wages shock of five percent for one year.

For these disturbances we examined the optimal economic policy responses under a variety of different policy regimes.

(a) a naive money supply target
(b) a naive exchange rate target
(c) an inflation and output target

The policy instruments we employ vary between policy regimes. When the relationship between fiscal and monetary policy is captured by the budget constraint of the government, severe limitations are placed upon the number of independent policy instruments available to the policy maker. We have assumed that interest rates are freely determined in the money market so that the primary instruments are fiscal in the form of government's current expenditure, the basic tax rate and value added tax.[3] We also chose to place restrictions on the frequency with which both the basic tax rate and VAT could be altered to ensure that they were only allowed to change at the time of the budget in the second quarter of each calendar year. This was achieved by including the first difference of both the basic tax rate and VAT as 'targets' in the objective function and heavily penalising changes in all quarters other than the second quarter of each year.

5.1 The multiplier effects of a fiscal expansion

Before we examine the closed loop optimal response of the policy maker to anticipated disturbances we report the open loop responses of the model. These dynamic multipliers are calculated both for the forward-looking and the backward-looking exchange rate, even though for all the subsequent results we report only the forward-looking exchange rate equation is used. An initial comparison of this kind helps to show how much difference anticipation can make to the dynamic responses of a model, a point originally given prominence by Lucas (1976).

In Chart 3.1 we show the response of the model to a step increase in government expenditure of £300m at 1975 prices. For the anticipated step increase –something which only has meaning for the forward-looking exchange rate case– it is assumed that the step increase begins in period 5. Because of a technical restriction on the number of time periods, the charts show the line for the anticipated step disturbance stopping four periods short of the other two lines. This has some bearing on the nature of some of the results on which we shall comment later.

The output multiplier shows the conventional pattern of rising and then falling. For the anticipated case, output rises even before the expected fiscal expansion, but after an initial expansion which is actually greater than for the other two cases, the crowding-out effect is more marked. The reason for this can be found in the chart for inflation (the rate of change of consumer prices). Prices rise in anticipation of the fiscal expansion and reduce consumption. The main reason for this can be found in the behaviour of the nominal exchange rate which falls immediately by more than two percent. For the unanticipated case, with a forward-looking exchange rate, the downward jump in the exchange rate is much more marked, falling approximately five percent immediately.

In contrast, the response when the exchange rate is backward-looking is quite different. At first the exchange rate appreciates. The reason for this is that the money supply only grows with a lag after a fiscal expansion, so that the initial increase in output shifts the demand for money function upwards and causes the exchange rate to appreciate. The response of unemployment to a fiscal expansion is broadly similar for all three cases though the initial fall in unemployment is greater for the unanticipated case.

Chart 3.1. Multiplier effects of a fiscal expansion

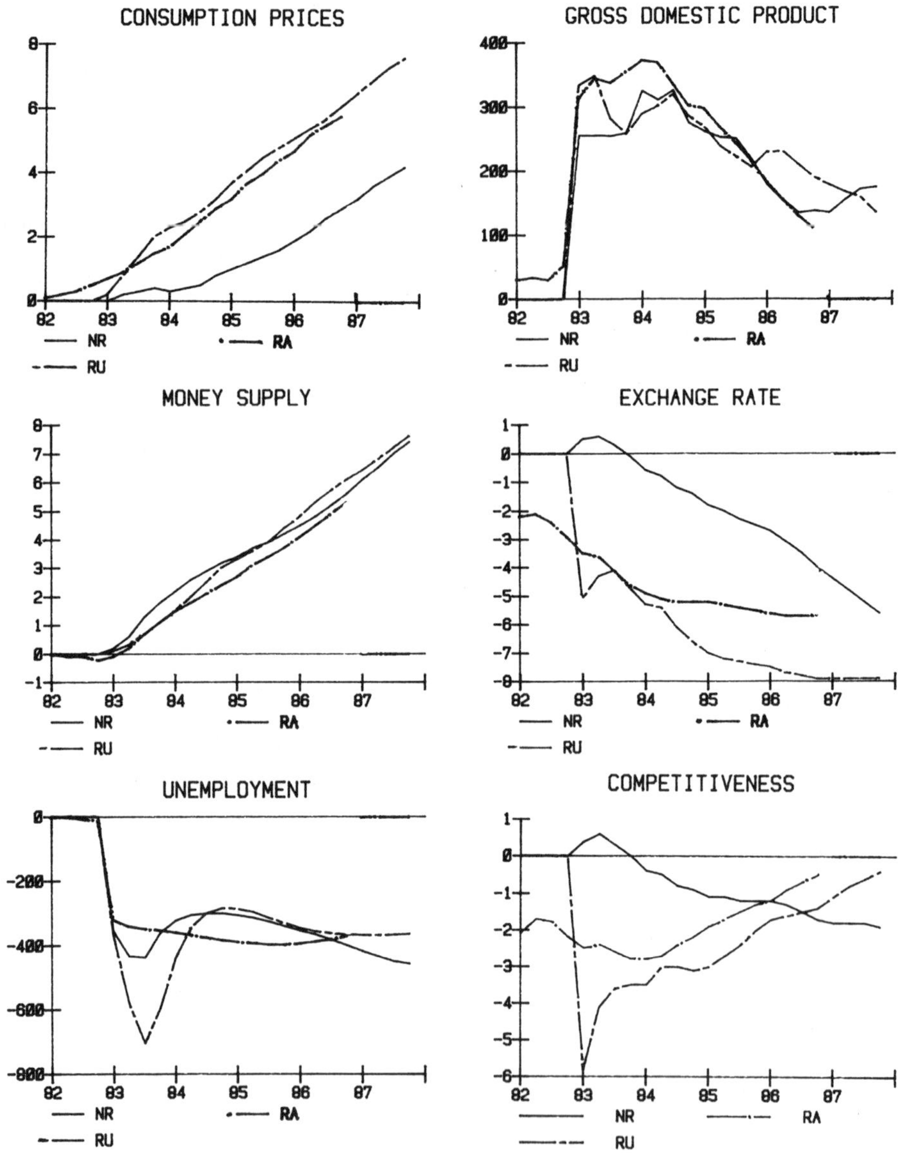

NR : non-rational
RA : rational and anticipated
RU : rational and unanticipated

The final variable is competitiveness, or the real exchange rate, measured in this case by relative domestic and world wholesale prices in a common currency. In most of the literature on the response of the exchange rate to monetary policy (Dornbusch (1976), Buiter and Miller (1981)) the effect of a monetary contraction is considered. For our case of an implicit fiscal/monetary expansion with a forward-looking exchange rate and with sluggishly responding domestic prices, there is an immediate fall in the real exchange rate. But with a gradual rise is domestic prices there is a rise in the real exchange rate, and by the end of the period the real exchange rate is almost back to its previous value. The overall difference in the behaviour of prices, the money supply, the exchange rate, and competitiveness, under anticipated and unanticipated shifts in fiscal policy is due to the different integral effects. The integral fiscal effect is twenty five percent less for the anticipated expansion relative to that for the unanticipated expansion. Nevertheless, both cases indicate that the model is tending towards a steady state effect, with no change in the real exchange rate or real money balances, and with crowding out of expenditure. There is an anomaly, however, in the behaviour of unemployment. The reason for this is that in the LBS model, increases in government expenditure have almost a one-to-one effect on public sector employment which is not fully offset by the crowding out of private sector employment. So while output as a whole may be crowded out by a fiscal expansion, there is a positive employment effect.

5.2 An oil price shock

We have stressed in section 2 how an optimal economic policy can be designed to attenuate both anticipated and unanticipated disturbances; and how when combined with the forward-looking behaviour of the private sector –confined in this paper to the foreign exchange market– this produces both lead and lagged optimal responses. Under the closed loop policy we assume that the foreign exchange market is aware of the government's intentions and believes them, so that the anticipated effects of the policy are fully internalised in the exchange rate.

In this section we consider the effects of a permanent twenty percent fall in the price of oil. First we report the effects when it is assumed that the government does not respond in any way to the disturbance.

Because of North Sea oil changes in oil prices have a markedly different effect on the U.K. economy relative to the effect on the majority of industrialised countries. A shift in oil prices has a direct impact on the revenues available to the government from taxation on North Sea oil production. Because the U.K. is a net exporter of oil, a rise in oil prices improves the current balance of payments while it tends to cause the balance of payments of net importers to worsen. There is also a supply side effect through changes in input prices relative to primary factor prices and through changes in the real exchange rate altering the shares of traded and non-traded goods sectors in total output. However, these supply side aspects are not, at present, well modelled in the LBS model since it is strongly orientated, as are most of the main macro-economic models, to the demand side through the income and expenditure accounts.

Because fiscal and monetary policy are linked through the budget constraint of the government, changes in revenue from North Sea oil are reflected in changes in the borrowing requirement and therefore –in the absence of offsetting fiscal adjustments– in changes in the money supply. This major feature of the U.K. economy is reflected in the results shown in Chart 3.2. Since the foreign exchange market is assumed not to expect that the government will attempt to offset the consequences for its revenue of lower oil prices, the exchange rate depreciates immediately in response to an unanticipated twenty percent fall. Initially, because of lower input prices, domestic prices fall. But this is overtaken quite quickly by the exchange rate depreciation causing other prices to rise. Output benefits from lower oil prices, partly because of the improvement in competitiveness –though this is rapidly eroded by rises in domestic prices– and partly because lower world oil prices stimulate world economic activity and this increases U.K. exports. [4]

Lower oil prices also lower world prices so that in combination with higher U.K. domestic prices, competitiveness after two years actually goes against the U.K. Theoretically one would anticipate that a fall in oil prices would be reflected in an overall improvement in U.K. competitiveness –a fall in the real exchange rate– and this would imply adjustments on the supply side and changes in the shares of the traded and non-traded goods sector in total output. The observed increase in the real exchange rate at the end of the period is partly due to the fall in world prices as well as to the possibility that the real side of the economy has not yet fully responded to the swings in competitiveness.

When the change in oil prices is expected, the exchange rate falls in anticipation; though, again, because the integral effect is smaller the fall in the exchange rate is not as great. Domestic prices actually rise because of the lower exchange rate before the oil price shock, and then fall again with the lower oil prices, only to rise subsequently as the effect of a depreciating exchange rate works through. This form of anticipatory behaviour is the most significant feature of rational expectations models and has the most serious implications for any dynamic analysis of both economic policy –which must take account of anticipation– and the responses of econometric models.

So far we have assumed that the government responds passively to the down-

Chart 3.2. Oil price shock effects (anticipated/unanticipated) under a neutral policy

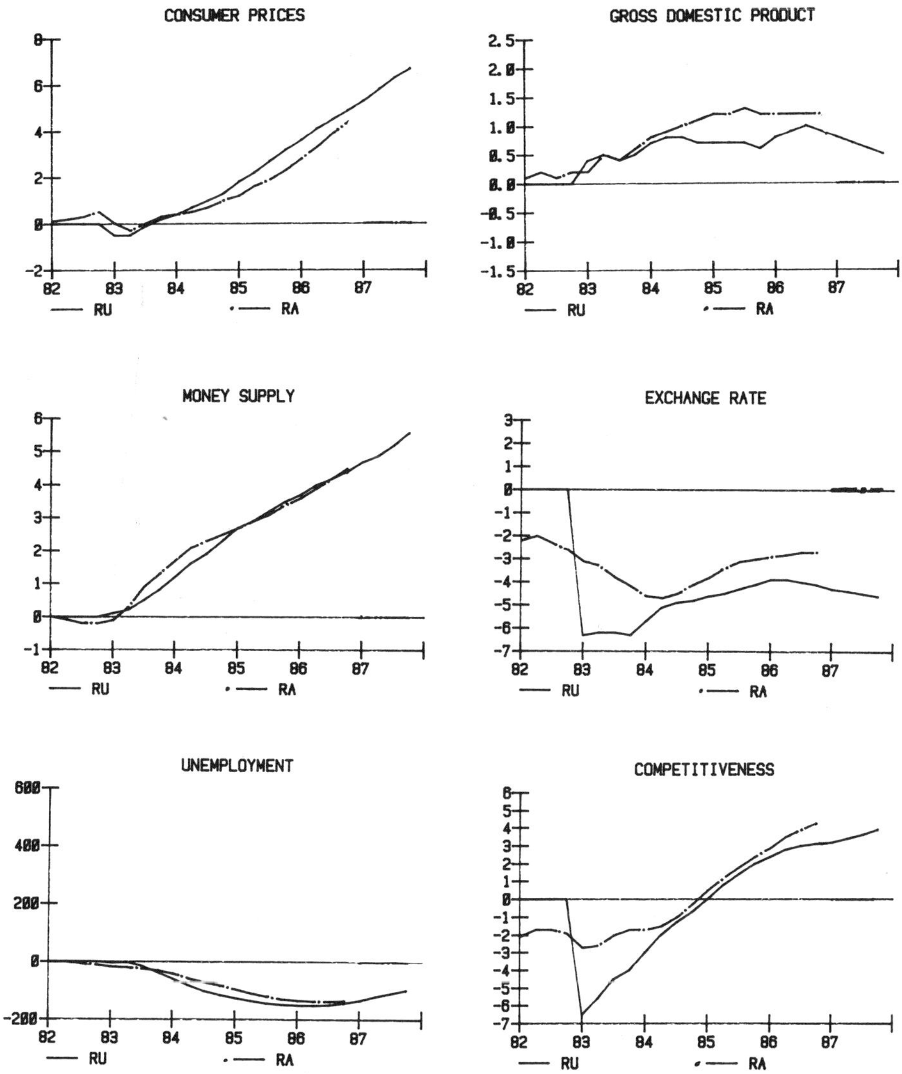

RA : rational and anticipated
RU : rational and unanticipated

ward shift in oil prices. But this need not be so. The output and employment effects of lower oil prices are beneficial, but prices end up much higher. It is possible to envisage a very wide range of policy responses in these circumstances depending upon both the objectives a government sets itself, the policy instruments it has at its disposal, and the priorities it attaches to different forms of economic performance.

Monetary targets

In the last decade a number of governments have adopted the money supply as an intermediate target. Under our first policy regime we assume that all the government attempts to do is to try to eliminate the unfavourable effects of the oil price fall on its revenue and the money supply by adjusting current expenditure and direct taxes. Given that we are studying the response surface of an optimal policy we have simply set the desired value for the stock of money equal to the path obtained in the absence of the oil shock. We are therefore deliberately abstracting from any consideration of what the underlying economic strategy is in terms of the levels of economic variables. The underlying strategy may well describe some transient path for the economy towards a preferred state. We are therefore examining responses about this path. The weights used are shown in column 1 of table 3.1. For this exercise only current government expenditures and the basic tax rate have been used as instruments. The results for both an anticipated and unanticipated shock are as shown in Chart 3.3. In comparison with a passive policy, shown in Chart 3.2, the behaviour of the economy is markedly different. For the unanticipated case the exchange rate does fall in the first eighteen months but then it appreciates. Competitiveness does improve for about a year but is then reversed, so the real exchange rate ends up higher in the end. Part of the reason for this is that domestic prices fall, relatively, until almost the end of the period. One consequence, however, is that the beneficial output effects are reversed; output actually falls in the first year but grows subsequently, though not as fast as under the passive policy. Unemployment is much worse in the initial years but eventually falls back to the level it would have been in the absence of the oil shock. The reason for the initial contraction in output and employment can be seen from the diagrams for government expenditure and tax rates. Government expenditure is cut by more than five percent in the first year but then brought back almost to its base level by year five. Tax rates, on the other hand, are increased by approximately 3 pence in the pound by the last year so that overall the shortfall in revenue is financed by raising personal taxes.

The results for the anticipated shock case are broadly similar. Though the exchange rate does appreciate initially, government expenditure is cut in anticipation of the fall in oil prices and this depresses output prior to the oil price fall. Somewhat

Chart 3.3 Oil price shock effects (anticipated/unanticipated) with a monetary target

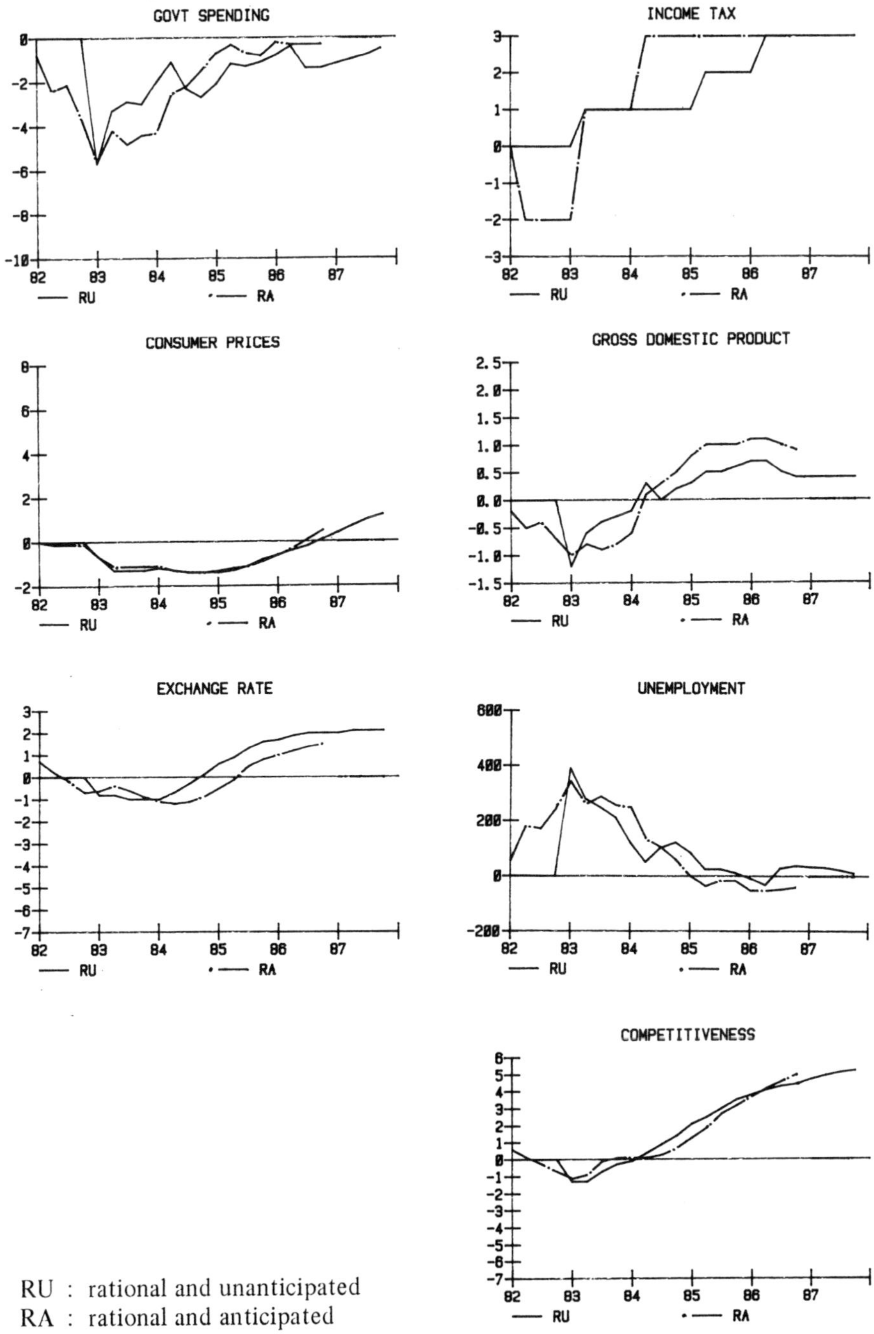

RU : rational and unanticipated
RA : rational and anticipated

anomalously, tax rates are cut in anticipation of the oil price change and then raised. The reason for this probably lies in the drawn out effects of government expenditure. Cuts in personal tax are used in the first year to offset the first year effects of the cut in government expenditure on the money supply. These feedforward policy responses are a clear demonstration of how, parallel with the forward-looking behaviour of the foreign exchange market, the government's optimal response involves forward-looking anticipatory adjustments to economic policy.

An exchange rate target

The behaviour of a floating exchange rate is an important, though not the only, mechanism by which the effects of monetary and fiscal policies are transmitted to the domestic economy. The relationship between monetary and fiscal policy and the exchange rate is not a hard and fast one since domestic and foreign disturbances can alter the exchange rate. Given that we have assumed that domestic prices are sticky, this means that fluctuations in the real exchange rate will directly affect domestic output and employment and prices. Artis and Currie (1981) have, therefore, suggested that exchange rate targets could provide as good a policy regime for stabilising prices as a monetary target.

We therefore switched policy regimes, from neutralising the effects on the money supply of an oil price fall to neutralising the effects on the nominal exchange rate. Artis and Currie (1981) have argued that a monetary supply target is superior to an exchange rate target if the disturbance is to the foreign price level. While an oil price shock is initially reflected in a change in foreign prices, the effect, other things being equal, cannot be permanent since it is a relative price change. Moreover, even in the short run it cannot be interpreted as a pure foreign price level shock, along the lines of Artis and Currie, because of the consequences of oil prices for revenue in the U.K. Despite these qualifications, in Chart 3.4 we show the result when government current expenditure and taxes[5] are now used to neutralise the effects on the nominal exchange rate of an oil price shock.

Taking the unanticipated case first, the stabilisation of the nominal exchange rate is achieved by initially cutting the money supply over the first two years and then allowing it to grow as an almost mirror image of the behaviour of the nominal exchange rate in Chart 3.3. However, fiscal adjustments are necessary to engineer changes in the money supply, so the demand for money, output and the exchange rate are also affected. To offset this government expenditure is cut dramatically, while income tax is also cut. Although these results may not be especially plausible, and suggest a respecification of the objective function, they do show up the differential impact of government spending and private spending (as affected by changes

Chart 3.4. Oil price shock effects (anticipated/unanticipated) with an exchange rate target

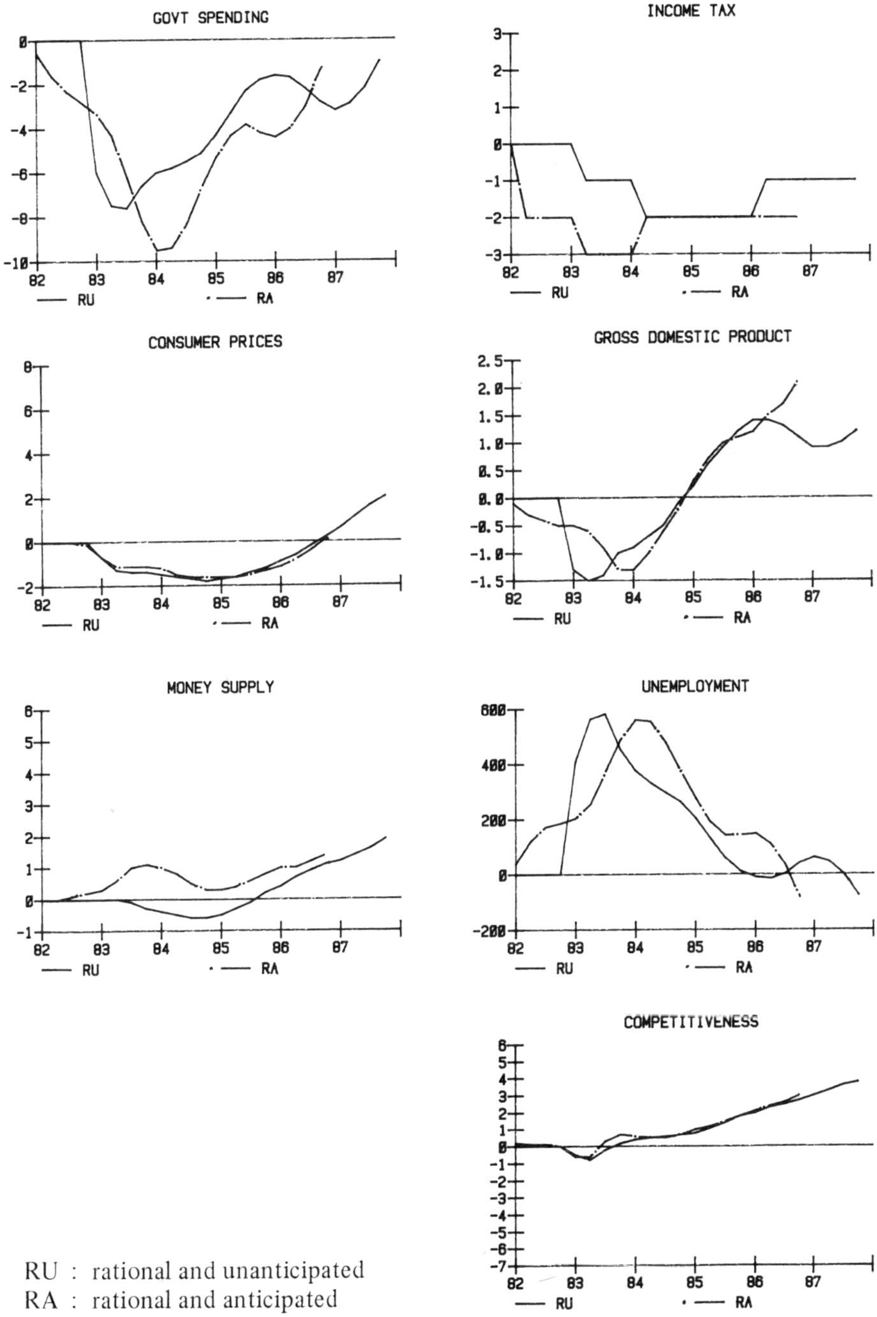

RU : rational and unanticipated
RA : rational and anticipated

in taxes) on the balance of payments and on the demand for money. The fall in output in the first two years is due to a cut in public sector output, offset partly by cuts in income tax. In comparison with the case of a monetary target the variability of consumer prices is greater, though not by very much. So if one's sole interest were with price stability, for this particular shock monetary targets are superior to exchange rate targets. The initial deflationary impact on output is also greater. Under both targets the real exchange rate follows a broadly similar pattern, but with an appreciation of the real exchange rate in the last year which is greater under the monetary target.

With the exception of the money supply, the results for the anticipated case are very similar to the unanticipated case. Government expenditure and taxes are cut in anticipation, so that output falls before the oil price falls. The money supply, in contrast to the unanticipated case, rises immediately. The reason for this is that because the exchange rate attempts to appreciate in anticipation, the money supply has to be expanded immediately to offset it.

5.3 A wages shock

In this section we consider the effects of an unanticipated shock to manufacturing wages in the form of an autonomous rise of five percent over the period of a year. Because of 'knock on' effects, this shock is also transmitted to the rest of the private sector, though not necessarily to the full extent.

The results of a neutral policy are shown in Chart 3.5. Higher nominal wages produce a boost to private consumption; but this is more than offset by the effect on exports of a rapid deterioration in competitiveness, by a fall in investment because of lower profits, as well as by a fall in the real money stock causing interest rates to rise and an edging up of the exchange rate. The rise in public sector wages[6] raises the public sector borrowing requirement which is also raised because of lower tax revenues from lower output. This eventually feeds through to the money supply. Prices rise in response to the cost push, but the rise is moderated at first by a higher exchange rate and lower domestic demand. The exchange rate eventually reverses itself as interest rates moderate, and begins to fall. Output also begins to recover and the rate of change of prices then falls.

A monetary target

Under a monetary target regime the rise in the money supply is prevented by the rises in income tax shown in Chart 3.6, and by cuts in government expenditure in the first ten quarters. Thereafter, however, government expenditure starts to rise

Chart 3.5. Unanticipated wages shock under a neutral policy

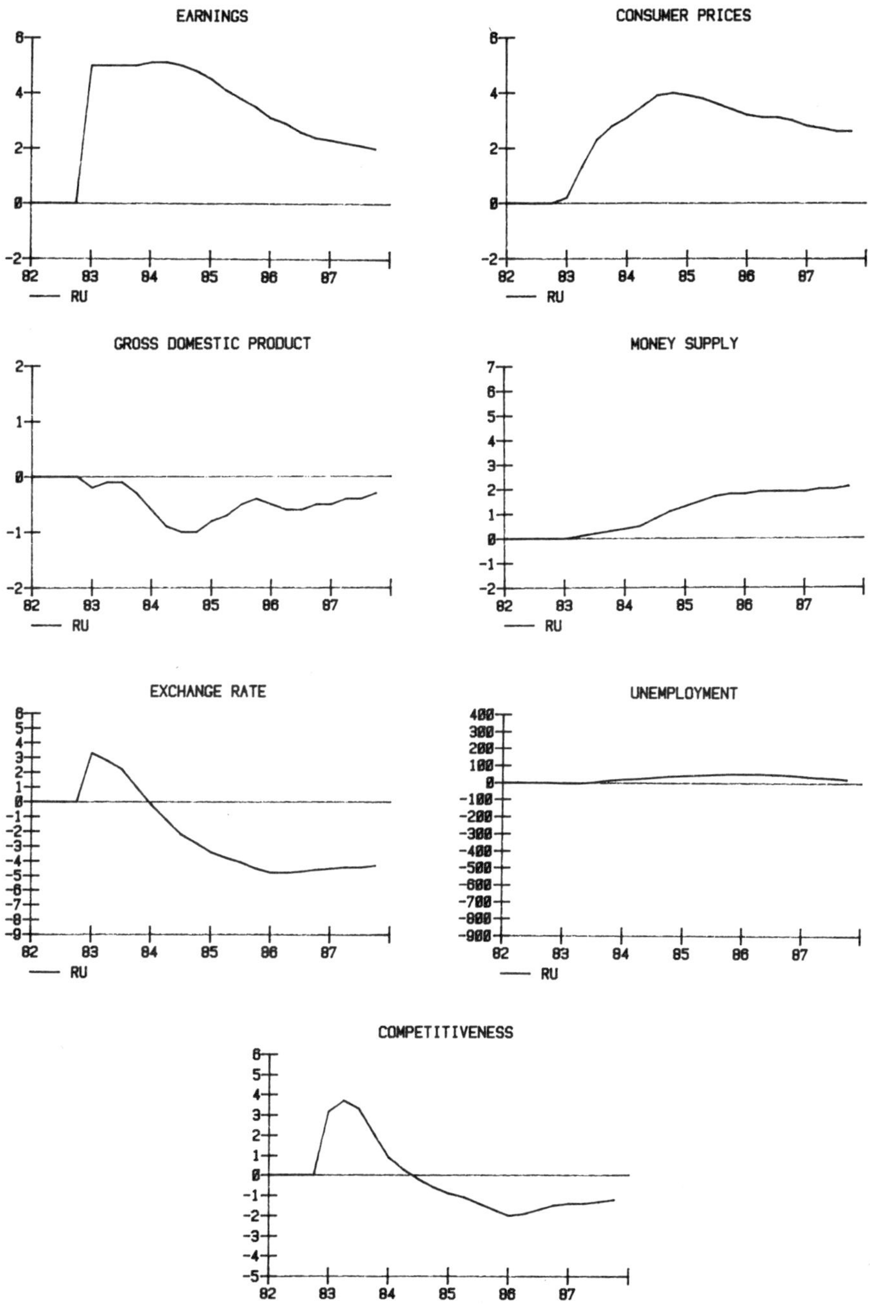

Chart 3.6 The effects of an unanticipated wages shock under monetary and exchange rate targets

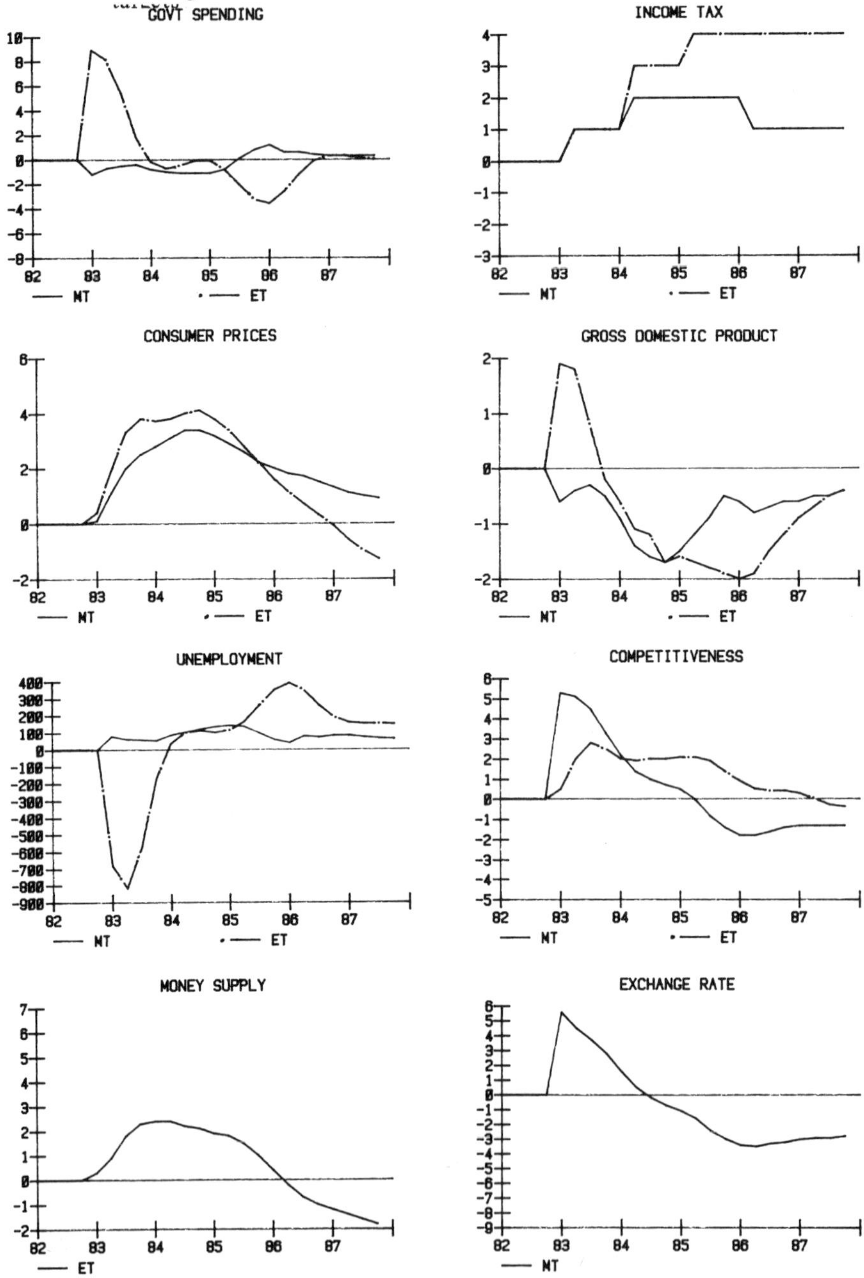

MT : monetary target
ET : exchange rate target

again. In contrast to the neutral policy case, the initial appreciation of the nominal exchange rate is much more marked, while the long run depreciation is less. The deflationary impact of the wages shock is intensified by the non-accomodating fiscal and monetary policy; in fact GDP at its maximum is 1.65 percent less than in the absence of the shock. The rise in consumer prices over the first two years however is hardly moderated by the non-accomodating policy; prices peak at 3.4 percent higher compared with 4 percent. But in the long run the price level returns to its former level, compared with a long run level of 2.5 percent higher in the absence of a monetary policy.

An exchange rate target

Under a nominal exchange rate target, monetary and fiscal policy is accomodating in order to prevent the exchange rate adjusting. This is mainly achieved, initially, by moderating the fall in real money balances through an expansion of the money supply. This is achieved, as shown in Chart 3.6, by large increases in public expenditure in the first year. But, with the need to prevent subsequent falls in the exchange rate, government expenditure is cut in the second and third years and brought back to its original level by the end of the fifth year. Tax rates, in contrast, are steadily increased. Prices initially rise by marginally more than under a neutral policy, but by the end price rises are actually lower. Output is initially held up by the increase in government expenditure, but it eventually falls by more than either when a monetary target is pursued or when policy is neutral. However, total output lost is actually about the same under either a monetary or exchange rate target regime.

In terms of price variability there is not much to choose between a naive monetary policy and a naive exchange rate policy. If anything, prices are slightly less variable under a monetary policy. The wages shock we have been examining can be interpreted, in the terms of Artis and Currie (1981), as a shift in the aggregate supply function. They concluded that in a fairly open economy, exchange rate targets would be superior to money supply targers for price stabilisation. But, even though the effects of price shocks on aggregate demand in the LBS model are very strong, Artis and Currie's conclusion does not seem to be borne out by our results because of the implicit real balance effects on consumption and the relative price effects on exports. Similarly our results do not support the study of Artis and Karakitsos (1982) which used a version of the LBS model without a forward-looking exchange rate equation and concluded, albeit for a much more general loss function, that a monetary target was inferior to a combination of a monetary and an exchange rate target. The empirical results suggest that the robustness of Artis and Currie's analytical conclusions may be sensitive to the specification of the model and indicate that further analytical work is needed.

A countercyclical monetary and fiscal policy

Because of its effects on competitiveness and profits, the effect of the wages shock is enough to simultaneously raise prices and bring about a fall in output and employment. In these circumstances the fiscal and monetary authorities could choose to prevent the fall in output. The results of this simple countercyclical policy are shown in Chart 3.7. The objective function is shown in column 5 of table 3.1.

Under this policy most of the reflationary impact is achieved by cuts in income tax. Government spending is expanded but not by much and in some periods is actually cut. Initially higher interest rates –due to lower real money and unchanged income– hold the exchange rate up. But as interest rates fall the exchange rate depreciates, ending up almost 7.5 percent lower. The money supply and domestic prices are also much higher so that the short run cost-push boost is reflected in a permanent rise in the price level.

Inflation and output targets

In this final exercise we expanded the policy options to include both prices and output. Since an aggregate supply shock has the effect of simultaneously raising prices and lowering output, we face a problem in using government expenditure and income taxes as instruments. We therefore substituted VAT for income tax in our objective function. The penalties used are shown as column 6 in table 3.1. The results of the optimisation are shown in Chart 3.8.

In comparison with the simple output stabilisation task discussed above, a better degree of control can be exercised over both output and prices. These particular results suggest very large cuts in value added tax from 3.5 percentage points in the first year to a maximum of 8 percentage points in the third year. This has two consequences. It helps to moderate the rise in consumer prices and to stimulate consumption. Higher demand helps to offset the effect of lower profits on investment. The higher growth path for money forces the exchange rate down immediately despite higher interest rates so that competitiveness does not deteriorate as badly. The result of all this is that output actually rises. Given that the stabilisation policy seeks changes in neither prices nor output, the expansion in output is offset by cuts in government expenditure which then lower total employment.

The reasonableness of these results is open to question. Even though the wages shock is only temporary, the government appears to be getting drawn into a cycle of cuts in VAT and expenditure. The exchange rate still falls, the money supply is higher, and, even though consumer prices can be influenced, the other wholesale

Chart 3.7. The effects of an unanticipated wages shock under an output stabilisation target

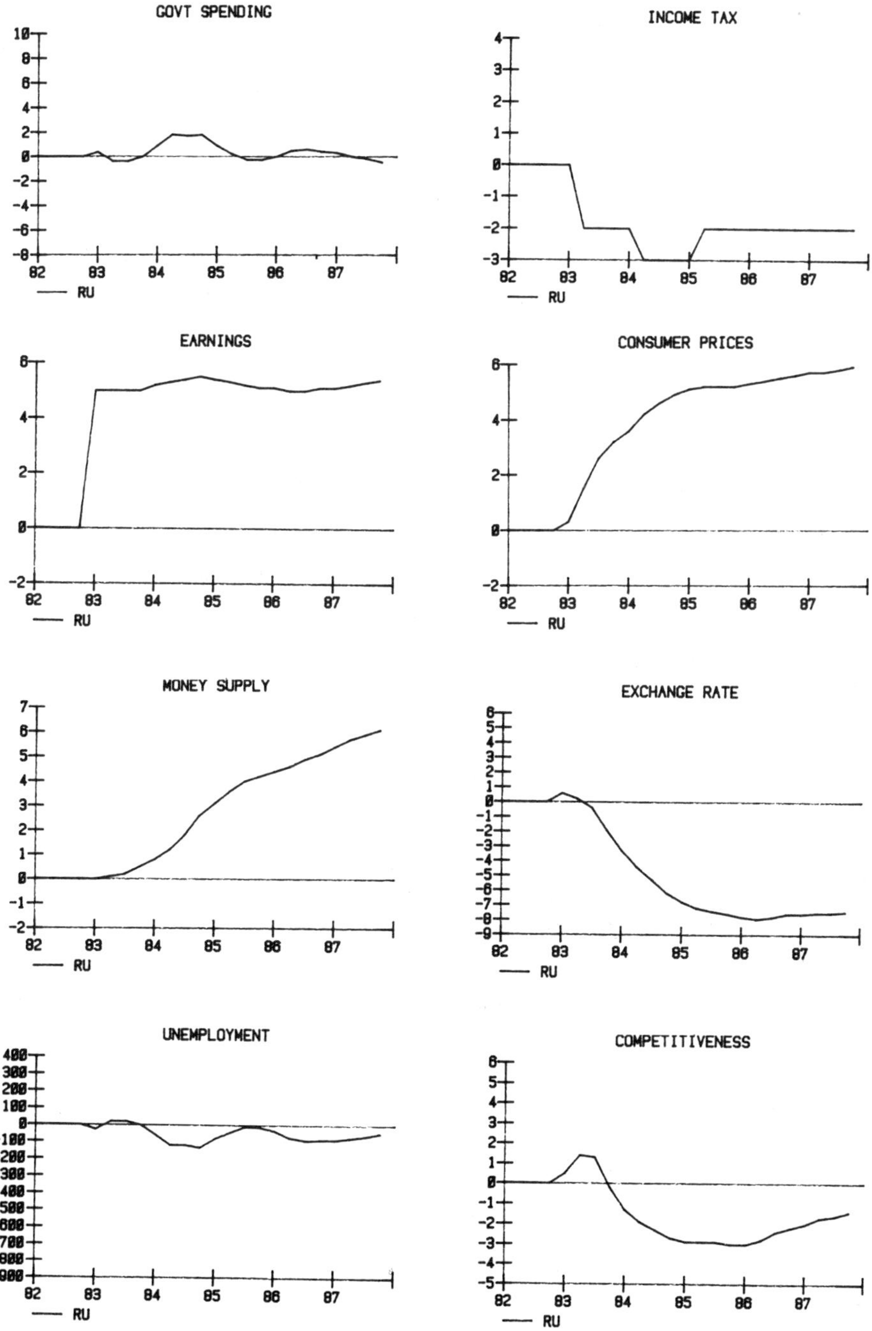

Chart 3.8. Unanticipated wages shock under inflation and output targets

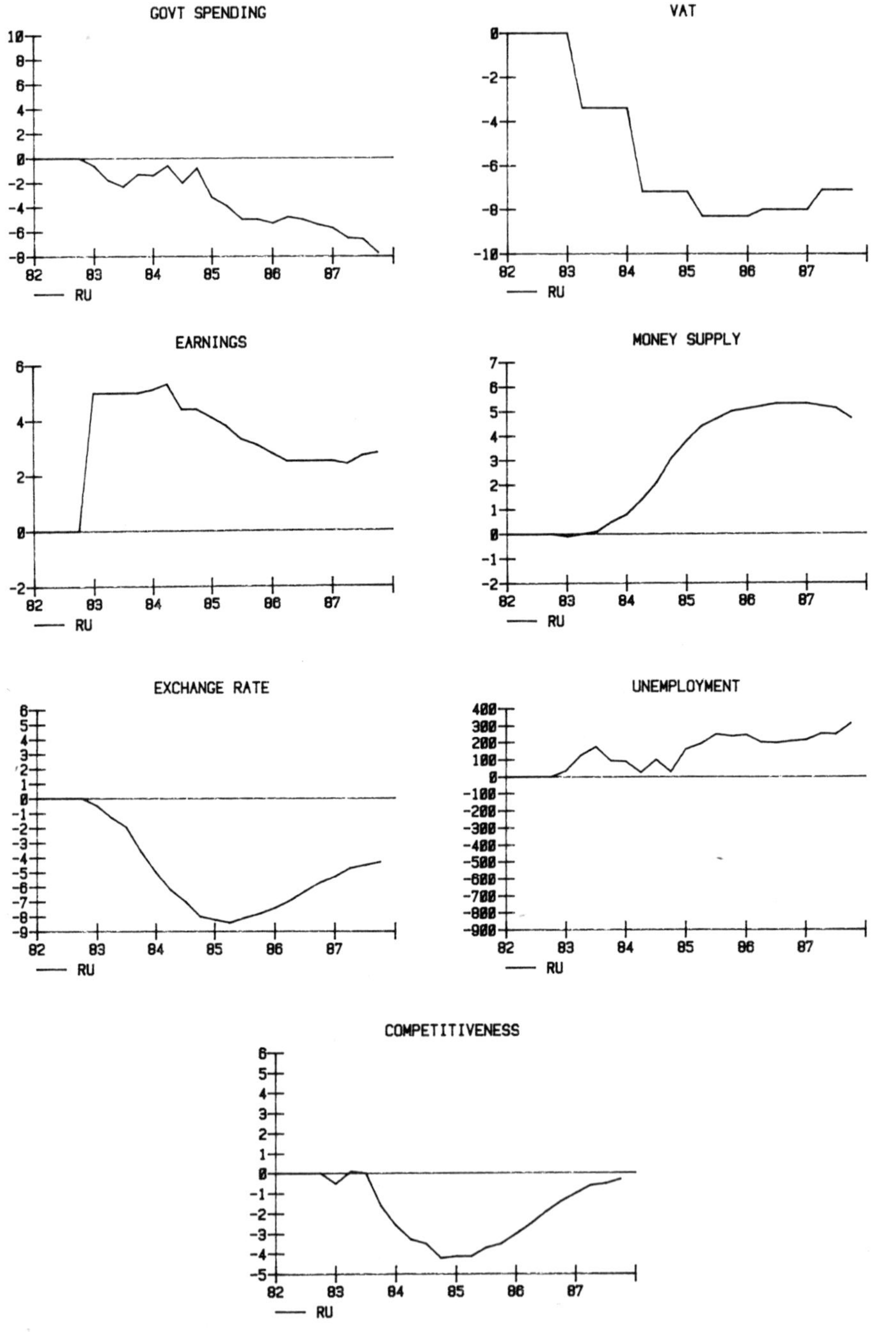

and input prices which are not affected by VAT still rise.

6. SUMMARY AND CONCLUSIONS

The empirical results we have reported have been for illustrative purposes, but they demonstrate how it is feasible to design feedback and feedforward policy when the foreign exchange market is forward-looking. Optimal responses to both anticipated and unanticipated disturbances have been examined. The results are obviously of a partial nature since we have considered a relatively small set of targets and instruments and subjected the model to a very narrow range of shocks. While this makes the interpretation easier, a real world policy involves a more or less continuous process of adjustment to a multiplicity of disturbances, the precise sources of which are difficult to identify separately. In this stochastic environment, clear cut distinctions between different intermediate targets such as the money supply and the exchange rate become hard to maintain.

Table 3.1. Penalties used in objective function

	(1)**	(2)**	(3)	(4)	(5)	(6)
Targets						
P						5×10^{3}
Y					10^{-5}	10^{-1}
M	10^{-5}		10^{-5}			
S		1.5×10^{2}		10^{3}		
ΔTRY*	10^{2}	10^{2}	10^{2}	1	1	
ΔVAT*						1
Instruments						
G	10^{-6}	10^{-6}	10^{-6}	10^{-6}	10^{-6}	10^{-6}
TRY	1	1	1	1	1	
VAT						3×10^{-3}

* Penalties in second quarter, otherwise 10^{9}

** Penalties for both anticipated and unanticipated shocks

P : consumer prices

Y : gross domestic product

M : sterling M3

S : effective exchange rate

G : government current expenditure

TRY: basic tax rate

VAT: value added tax

NOTES

1) The London Business School Econometric Model, see LBS (1982).
2) This obviously conflicts with its usage in the control engineering literature. But it is a rarely used term in practice and is ripe for arrogation by economists.
3) We could have increased the flexibility of policy by permitting the monetary authority to intervene directly in the foreign exchange market by buying and selling currencies. This would have entailed including a term in changes in foreign currency reserves within the bracket governed by $1/\lambda$ in equation (3.15).
4) There is a small model of the world which is run in tandem with the LBS model (see Beenstock and Dicks (1983)).
5) The objective function penalties are shown in column 2 of table 3.1.
6) We assume that a neutral policy means that cash limits on public expenditure are not used.

REFERENCES

Anderson, P.A. (1979), 'Rational expectations forecasts from nonrational models', *Journal of Monetary Economics,* 5, pp. 67-80.

Artis, M.J. and D.A. Currie (1981), 'Monetary targets and the exchange rate: a case for conditioning targets' in W.A. Eltis and P.J.N. Sinclair (1981).

Artis, M.J. and E. Karakitsos (1982), 'Monetary and exchange rate targets in an optimal control setting', *PROPE Discussion Paper* No. 30, Imperial College, University of London.

Ball, R.J., T. Burns and P.J. Warburton (1979), 'The London Business School model of the U.K. economy: an exercise in international monetarism', in P. Ormerod (ed), *Economic Modelling,* Heinemann, London.

Baum, C.F. (1980), 'On the sensitivity of optimal control solutions', *Journal of Economic Dynamics and Control,* 2, pp. 205-208.

Beenstock, M., A. Budd and P.J. Warburton (1981), 'Monetary policy, expectations and real exchange rate dynamics', in Eltis and Sinclair (1981).

Beenstock, M. and G. Dicks (1983), 'An aggregate monetary model of the worl economy', European Economic Review, *20, pp. 261-286.*

Brandsma, A.S. and A.J Hughes Hallett (1984), 'Noncausalities and time inconsistency in dynamic noncooperative games: the problem revisited', *Economics Letters,* 14, pp. 123-130.

Buiter, W.H. (1981), 'Saddlepoint problems in rational expectations models', University of Bristol (mimeographed).

Buiter, W.H. and M.H. Miller (1981), 'Monetary policy and international competitiveness: the problems of adjustment', in Eltis and Sinclair (1981).

Chow, G. (1975), *Analysis and Control of Dynamic Economic Systems,* John Wiley, New York.

Chow, G. (1980), 'Economic policy evaluation and optimisation under rational expectations', *Journal of Dynamic Economics and Control,* 2, pp. 1-13.

Dornbusch, R. (1976), 'Exchange rate dynamics', *Journal of Political Economy,* 84, pp. 1161-1176.

Driffill, E.J. (1982), 'Optimal money and exchange rate policies', *Greek Economic Review,* Dec. 1982, 1*.

Eltis, W.A. and P.J.N. Sinclair (eds.) (1981), *The Money Supply and the Exchange Rate,* Clarendon Press, Oxford.

Fair, R.C. (1979), 'An analysis of a macroeconomic model with rational expectations in the bond and stock markets', *American Economic Review*, 69, pp. 539-552.

Holly, S. (1983), 'Dynamic inconsistency and dynamic games in intertemporal optimisation models: a resolution of the Kydland and Prescot conundrum', *CEF Discussion Paper No. 108*, London Business School.

Holly, S. and M.B. Zarrop (1983), 'On optimality and time inconsistency when expectations are rational', *European Economic Review*, 20, pp. 23-40.

Hughes Hallett, A.J. and H.J.B. Rees (1983), *Quantitative Economic Policies and Interactive Planning*, Cambridge University Press, Cambridge and New York.

Kydland, F. and E. Prescott (1977), 'Rules rather than discretion: the inconsistency of optimal plans', *Journal of Political Economy*, 83, pp. 473-490.

Lipton, D., J. Poterba, J. Sachs and L. Summers (1982), 'Multiple shooting in rational expectations models', *Econometrica*, 50, pp. 1329-1333.

LBS (1982), 'London Business School Econometric Model: a technical manual', London Business School (mimeographed).

Lucas, R.E. (1976), 'Econometric policy evaluation: a critique', in K. Brunner and A. Meltzer, *The Phillips Curve and Labour Markets*, North Holland, Amsterdam.

Tse, E. (1974), 'Adaptive dual control methods', *Annals of Economic and Social Measurement*, 3, pp. 65-84.

Wilson, C.A. (1979), 'Anticipated shocks and exchange rate dynamics', *Journal of Political Economy*, 87, pp. 639-647.

PART II

UNCERTAINTY

CHAPTER 4

ADAPTIVE ECONOMETRIC FORECASTING BY AN APPROXIMATE FILTERING-SMOOTHING ALGORITHM: THE CASE OF THE ISRAELI MEAT SECTOR

A. Shmueli and Charles S. Tapiero
The Hebrew University, Jerusalem, Israel

1. INTRODUCTION

Applications of control related techniques to econometric models in planning and forecasting are not new. These have evolved ever since economists have realised the potential application of the Kalman filter to economic estimation problems (see Athans (1974), Athans and Kendrick (1974), Day and Groves (1975), Lainiotis (1971), Mehra (1974), Sarris (1973), Turnovsky (1976) and Upadhyay (1976)). Subsequent experience with the Kalman filter in econometrics has been disappointing however, having to bridge a communication gap between engineers and economists as well as resolve the (almost) lack of information in economics for specifying precisely a model's parameters. As a result, filtering has not been found to be an adequate substitute to standard econometric estimation procedures. The combination of filtering techniques, together with the gamut of econometric instruments has, however, been shown of potential interest in econometrics and in planning (see Feldstein (1971), MacRae (1975), Mehra (1972) and Ruddel (1975)). This is particularly true if we recognise the non-stationary character of parameter estimates in economic models which point to fast changing economies and structural change (e.g., see the October 1973 special issue of Annals of Economic and Social Measurement as well as Cooley, Rosenberg and Wall (1977), Pagan (1978) and others). We can relate such observations more closely with the recent developments in adaptive filtering (such as Mehra (1972)) and dual control (e.g., Feldbaum (1965), BarShalom and Tse (1976), Kang and Kendrick (1975, 1976), Pekelman and Rausser (1978) and Tse (1974)). In these cases, filtering techniques (linear or non-linear, approximate or not) are used for on-line system identification (or parameter estimation in the language of

Hughes Hallett, A.J. (ed.) Applied Decision Analysis and Economic Behaviour
©1984, Martinus Nijhoff Publishers. Dordrecht/Boston/Lancaster
ISBN 90-247-2968-8. Printed in The Netherlands

economists) of time-varying parameters.

In the sections that follow we shall use the filtering and econometric approach jointly in a problem of adaptive econometric forecasting of the Israeli meat sector. Our econometric model of this sector was described in Shmueli and Tapiero (1982) and its optimisation for stabilising the meat markets in Israel has been conducted by Shmueli and Tapiero (1980). Here, we begin by re-formulating the standard econometric estimation and forecasting problems as filtering problems (section 2). We then compare the performance of an (reduced form) econometric and an adaptive forecasting scheme for the Israeli meat sector data (section 4), and show that the adaptive forecast algorithm which we present in section 3 yields more accurate forecasts. Evidently further research, particularly in the estimation of variable parameter econometric models and further empirical experience in the application of filtering approaches to econometric problems, is required. The combination of econometric and filtering techniques used here may also be found a useful means for resolving, even if only by approximation, the extremely complex problems of estimation and forecasting in time-varying parameter models.

2. STATE SPACE REPRESENTATION AND PARAMETERS ESTIMATION IN A SIMULTANEOUS EQUATION ECONOMETRIC MODEL

The reduced form of econometric models is usually employed for forecasting and policy analysis. For most purposes the reduced form can be expressed as a first order vector difference equation (or a first order vector differential equation in continuous time). To do so, consider the structural form of an econometric model with lagged dependent variables:

$$B_0 y_t + B_1 y_{t-1} + \ldots + B_m y_{t-m} \qquad (4.1)$$

$$+ \; D_0 X_t + \ldots + D_n X_{t-n} + u_t = 0$$

where

y_t = a vector a M state (endogenous) variables

x_t = a vector of P input (exogenous) variables

u_t = a vector of disturbances, normally distributed and serially uncorrelated

$B_i, D_j; i=0,1,\ldots m, \; j=0,1,\ldots n;$ parameter matrices

If we define new matrices A_i, C_i such that $A_i = B_0^{-1} B_i$, $C_i = -B_0^{-1} D_i$ and $v_t = -B_0^{-1} u_t$, then y_t can be written as a lagged vector equation of the following form:

$$y_t = A_1 y_{t-1} + \ldots + A_m y_{t-m} + C_0 X_t + \ldots + C_n X_{t-n} + v_t . \tag{4.2}$$

The state-space representation (4.2) can be defined as a first order difference equation system:

$$\bar{y}_t = A\bar{y}_{t-1} + CX_t + \bar{v}_t , \tag{4.3}$$

where (primes denote transpose)

$$\bar{y}_t' \triangleq [y_t', y_{t-1}' \ldots, y_{t-m+1}'; x_t', x_{t-1}', \ldots, x_{t-n+1}']$$

$$\bar{y}_{t-1}' \triangleq [y_{t-1}', \ldots \; y_{t-m}'; x_{t-1}', \ldots x_{t-n}']$$

$$\bar{v}_t' \triangleq [v_t', 0, \ldots, 0, \ldots, 0]$$

and x_t is as defined earlier. The matrices A and C are defined as follows:

$$A \triangleq \begin{bmatrix} A_1, A_2, \ldots, A_{m-1}, A_m, C_1, C_2, \ldots, C_{n-1}, C_n \\ I \quad 0 \quad \ldots \quad 0 \qquad 0 \quad 0 \quad 0 \quad \ldots \quad 0 \qquad 0 \\ 0 \\ \qquad \ddots \\ \qquad\qquad 0 \\ \qquad\qquad I \\ 0 \qquad \ldots \quad 0 \qquad 0 \quad 0 \qquad \ldots \qquad 0 \\ \qquad\qquad\qquad I \\ \qquad\qquad\qquad 0 \\ \qquad\qquad\qquad\qquad \ddots \\ 0 \quad 0 \quad \ldots \quad 0 \qquad 0 \quad 0 \qquad \ldots \quad I \qquad 0 \end{bmatrix} \qquad C \triangleq \begin{bmatrix} C_0 \\ 0 \\ \vdots \\ 0 \\ I \\ 0 \\ \vdots \\ 0 \end{bmatrix}$$

An extension of (4.3) to include time-varying parameters is straightforward and given by

$$\bar{y}_t = A_t \bar{y}_{t-1} + C_t X_t + \bar{v}_t \tag{4.4}$$

where A_t and C_t are as defined above, but with the non-stationary (time-varying) parameters A_{it} and C_{jt} for i = 1, . . . m and j = 1, . . . n. For notation convenience, we rewrite equation (4.2) as

$$y_t = \Pi \bar{x}_t + v_t \tag{4.5}$$

where y_t and v_t are as defined before, and

$$\Pi \overset{\Delta}{=} [A_1 \ldots A_m, C_0, \ldots, C_n] \tag{4.6}$$

Finally the newly defined predetermined variables vector $\bar{x}_t$ consists of

$$\bar{x}'_t \overset{\Delta}{=} [y'_{t-1}, \ldots y'_{t-m}, x'_t, \ldots x'_{t-n}] \tag{4.7}$$

In terms of classical econometric notation, we can proceed from equation (4.1) and write it as

$$\Gamma y_t + B\bar{x}_t + u_t = 0 \tag{4.8}$$

where $\Gamma = B_0$, $B = [B_1 \ldots B_m, D_0, \ldots D_n]$ and $\bar{x}_t$ is as defined in (4.7). As a result, Γ is an MxM matrix, B is an MxN matrix where N = mM + p(n+1), and $\bar{x}_t$ is an Nx1 vector. Further we also assume that:

(a) $u_t \sim N(0, U)$ and is serially uncorrelated, or U is a diagonal matrix.
(b) ψ is the covariance matrix of the structural-form consisting of MxM blocks each containing $(M+N)^2$ elements. That is ψ is an M(M+N) x M(M+N) covariance matrix of the M(M+N) vector of the structural parameters arranged by equations (i.e., by rows of $[\Gamma, B]$).

The implications of these assumptions will be clarified later on. The reduced form of the econometric model (4.8) is then simply rewritten as shown in (4.5), where $\Pi = -\Gamma^{-1}B$. As a consequence of assumption (a), v_t is serially uncorrelated with variance-covariance diagonal matrix V:

$$v_t \sim N(0, V); \quad V = \Gamma^{-1}U(\Gamma^{-1})' . \tag{4.9}$$

Finally, we define a state vector θ_t of dimension MxN, composed of the reduced form parameters arranged by equation:

$$\theta'_t = [\Pi_{11}, \ldots \Pi_{1N}; \Pi_{M1} \ldots \Pi_{MN}] \tag{4.10}$$

where $\mathrm{cov}(\theta_t, \theta'_t)$ is denoted by an MNxMN matrix Ω_t. Also, we can define an MxMN matrix F_t of predetermined variables

$$F_t = \begin{bmatrix} \bar{x}'_t & & & 0 \\ & \cdot & & \\ & & \cdot & \\ 0 & & & \bar{x}'_t \end{bmatrix} \tag{4.11}$$

so that the reduced form model (4.5) becomes

$$y_t = F_t \theta_t + v_t \,. \tag{4.12}$$

In other words, by letting θ_t be the parameters and F_t contain predetermined and known variables, we have rewritten the reduced form as an equation we shall call the observation equation. In such an equation, θ_t is unknown but generated by some (Markovian) process while V is also specified in terms of U and Γ. Since the data patterns change over time, as they become available, this means that F_t is also a non-stationary matrix. Finally, y_t, although unknown at time t, is ex post determined and reflected in the vectors $\bar{x}_t$. Evidently, at a given instant of time, a non-linear relationship between the θ', Γ and B exists such that one can be found from the other. As time passes by, and new observations on y_t become available, then the estimates of θ and its components are updated.

When parameters θ_t are non-stationary, reflecting changes in the economic system, we may postulate some continuous evolution process for such parameters. This procedure is fundamentally different from that of econometricians who conventionally assume that parameters are constants throughout the estimation and planning horizon. Although several authors have suggested tests to verify the stationarity of parameters (e.g., Brown et al. (1975)), the non-stationary character of parameters in econometric models has not been dealt with. Here we assume that there is an underlying Markovian process describing the evolution of the reduced-form parameters over time:

$$\theta_t = G_{t-1}\theta_{t-1} + L_{t-1}\epsilon_{t-1} \tag{4.13}$$

where θ_t is defined in (4.10), $\epsilon_t \sim N(0, W_t)$ and G_t and L_t are known matrices. Typical cases would be to let θ_t be purely random parameters

$$\theta_t = \theta_{t-1} + \epsilon_{t-1}$$

or letting parameters grow with known or estimated trend etc.

The model (4.12) – (4.13) which we rewrite below

$$\begin{cases} \theta_t = G_{t-1}\theta_{t-1} + L_{t-1}\epsilon_{t-1} \\ y_t = F_t\theta_t + v_t \end{cases} \tag{4.14}$$

is a simultaneous equations version of the Dynamic Linear Model (DLM) of Harrison and Stevens (1976). In our case, if we let Γ (or B_0 in (4.1)) be a diagonal (identity) matrix, and if U is also diagonal and the solution of (4.14) is reduced to a single equation estimation problem (since the parameters are independent), which we resolve M times.

The system (4.14), with some reservations to be dealt with in the next section, now has a standard formulation. Thus, using classical results from Kalman and Bucy (1961), Athans (1974), Athans and Kendrick (1974), Chow (1975) and others, we write the conditional estimates of θ_t as the solution of the recurrence equations (Tapiero (1977)):

$$\begin{cases} \hat{\theta}_{t|t} = E\left\{\theta_t | y_0, y_1 \ldots . y_t\right\} \\ \Omega_{t|t} = \text{cov}\left\{\theta_t | y_0, y_1 \ldots y_t\right\} \end{cases} \tag{14.15}$$

Assuming the following prior statistics

$$\begin{cases} E(\theta_0) = \theta_{0|0} \\ \text{cov}(\theta_0, \theta_0') = \Omega_{0|0}, \end{cases} \tag{4.16}$$

with V and the sequences y_t, F_t, W_t, L_t, G_t known, then the conditional estimates are recursively given by:

$$\hat{\theta}_{t|t} = \hat{\theta}_{t|t-1} - H_t(F_t\hat{\theta}_{t|t-1} - y_t) \tag{4.17}$$

$$\hat{\theta}_{t|t-1} = G_{t-1}\hat{\theta}_{t|t-1} \tag{4.18}$$

$$H_t = \Omega_{t|t-1}\, F_t'[F_t\Omega_{t|t-1}\, F_t' + V]^{-1} \tag{4.19}$$

$$\Omega_{t|t-1} = G_{t-1}\Omega_{t-1|t-1}\, G_{t-1}' + L_{t-1}W_tL_{t-1}' \tag{4.20}$$

$$\Omega_{t|t} = \Omega_{t|t-1} - H_tF_t\Omega_{t|t-1} \tag{4.21}$$

Note that in the special case where $G_t = I$ only the updating stage matters for estimating the means. If, in addition, $L_t = 0$ (i.e. all parameters are constants), then the same will hold for the estimation of the covariances. However, several of the assumptions regarding our knowledge of the system structure (4.14) and its parameters (such as W, L, G, etc) will be violated in practice. It is then possible to alter the equations of (4.17) – (4.21), and apply adaptive filtering techniques which in principle are filtering equations expanded to include those elements of the parameter estimates which are unspecified in (4.14). This can lead to very complex computational problems and to problems in non-linear filtering (see Mehra (1972, 1974), Tapiero (1977)). In the next section we shall consider an algorithm for such a problem.

Finally, although the reduced form parameters are *non-linear* functions of the econometric structural parameters, the system in (4.14) is *linear* in the equivalent state vector θ_t and thus fulfills the fundamental assumptions required for application of the Kalman filtering algorithm. Also, equation (4.13) provides a departure from standard econometric procedures, by letting the econometric reduced form parameters be non-stationary and subject themselves to modelling. To do so, some prior knowledge (empirical or otherwise) is required.

3. THE ADAPTIVE ALGORITHM

In practice, the assumptions made regarding the system parameters in (4.14) cannot be maintained. Particularly the problem specifying initial (prior) estimates for $\theta_{0|0}$ and $\Omega_{0|0}$ are acute. A possible definition of such parameters might be made on a priori grounds arising from experimental design, nature's laws (as is common in physical-engineering applications), previous results, etc. In econometrics, the methods above are not appropriate and we are forced to turn to other approaches. Suppose (as is customary in econometric applications) that at time t a sample of observations on y_t and $\bar{x}_t$ are given for $t = -1, -2, \ldots -T$. Forecasts for $t = 1, 2, \ldots \tau$ are required. Using standard principles, econometric theory yields consistent and asymptotically unbiased estimators for $\theta_{0|0}$ and $\Omega_{0|0}$ (e.g., by maximum likelihood, two stage and three stage least squares, etc.). Assume (for computational feasibility) time invariant parameters in the econometric model and known variances for the error vector. Then, for the simultaneous equations model, econometric estimation provides estimates for $\hat{\Gamma}$, $\hat{B}$, $\hat{U}$, $\hat{\psi}$ (see equation (4.8) together with assumptions (a) and (b)). From (4.5) and (4.9) we can obtain consistent and asymptotically unbiased estimates of Π and hence for $\theta_{0|0}$ (by using (4.12) and V). Denote these estimates by $\hat{\theta}$ and $\hat{V}$ respectively. To obtain an estimate of $\text{cov}(\theta_{0|0}, \theta_{0|0}) = \Omega_{0|0}$ we apply Theorem 1 of Goldberger et al. (1961):

$$\Omega = K\psi K' \quad \text{and} \quad \hat{\Omega} = \hat{K}\hat{\psi}\hat{K}' \tag{4.22}$$

where ψ is defined by assumption (b) in the previous section, and K is an $M \times M(M+N)$ matrix,

$$K = \Gamma^{-1} \otimes [\Pi, I] \tag{4.22}$$

with $\otimes$ denoting a direct product. Π is given in equation (4.10) and $[\Pi, I]$ is of dimension $N \times (M+N)$. If we set $E(\theta_0) = \theta_{0|0} = \hat{\theta}$, $cov(\theta_0, \theta_0) = \Omega_{0|0} = \hat{\Omega}$, $V = \hat{V}$,, then $\hat{\theta}$, $\hat{\Omega}$ and $\hat{V}$ provide prior estimates for the system model defined in (4.14) in the previous section. Nonetheless, the econometric estimation indicated above can not be confused with the estimation of (4.14), since the latter involves a change of concept in the estimation procedure. While the classical estimation procedure in econometrics assumes parameters to be unknown constants, with asymptotically normal and consistent point estimators, the system (filtering) estimates assume that parameters are, in fact, *random variables* and point estimates serve only as centrality measures of the parameters' distributions at the initial time. Further, in our case, the prior estimates $\theta_{0|0}$, $\Omega_{0|0}$ are not constants, but random realisations with some probability distribution. Redictions at $t = 0$ (based on the sample information on $(0, -T)$ are given by extrapolations of $y_k (0 < k \leqslant \tau)$ and are of course a function of $\theta_{k|0}$, which is a function of $\theta_{0|0}$ and the covariance $\Omega_{0|0}$ only (together with other known or assumed parameters in our model).

However, when data on the endogenous and exogenous variables y_t and x_t respectively becomes available, some parameter estimate updating is required. For our parameters $\theta_t (t > 0)$ the filtering estimates can be appropriate. For updating θ_0 (or any subsequent parameters $\theta_1, \theta_2, \ldots \theta_\tau$) using the observed data or added empirical evidence, we can use a smoothing procedure (e.g. Tapiero (1977, p. 419) to obtain estimates $\theta_{t|\tau}$ where $\tau \geqslant t$. This results in the ex post forecasting approach which is often used in econometrics to test the precision and forecasting ability of econometric models. But this procedure for updating $\hat{\theta}_{0|0}$ is used here to incorporate the information contained in the additional observations into the model. As such, it also includes the information we have specified in the parameters' evolution (4.13). Such updating cannot, of course, be obtained by repeating on-line the econometric model estimates, since we will inevitably assume again that the parameters are time-invariant for the remaining horizon. As a result, although a truly 'initial guess' of initial conditions $\theta_{0|0}$ and $\Omega_{0|0}$ can be obtained by standard econometric techniques, these 'guesses' can be improved subsequently by 'smoothing' them on the basis of the new evidence accumulated, the presumed non-stationarity of the parameters of the parameters to be estimated, and the recursive filtering (smoothing) equations. The procedure thus followed is represented graphically below:

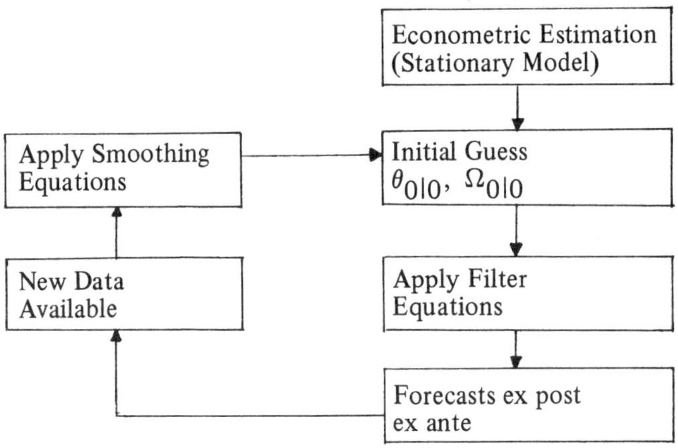

Figure 4.1. The estimation-filtering Algorithm

When data on the period $(1, \tau)$ for which forecasts are required is not available, we use the ex ante forecasts based on the information in $(0, -T)$. While in the ex post case F_t is known at each t (since it contains measurements of y_t and x_t only), in the ex ante forecasts F_t is not known. Two difficulties then arise. The first difficulty consists in finding an appropriate method for generating future values of the independent variables. The second, conditional on the first, is to establish the implications of such 'future' F_t's for the estimation problem (4.14) and the subsequent forecasts we derive from it. When only exogenous variables are included in $\bar{x}_t$, namely $\bar{x}_t = [x_t, x_{t-1} \ldots, x_{t-T}]$, and these future variables are generated probabilistically as shown later on, then at time $t = 0$,

$$\hat{y}_k = \hat{F}_k \hat{\theta}_{k|0} \qquad \text{with}$$

$$F_k = E(F_k = \bar{x}_k \otimes I) \qquad 0 \leqslant k \leqslant \tau$$

are best forecast of the dependent variables y_k, where E(.) is the expectation operator. However this will involve more uncertainty in our forecasts due to the uncertainty about F_k (Feldstein (1971)).

When the lagged endogenous variables y_t are included in $\bar{x}_t$ as well, the estimation problem in (4.14) becomes more non-linear. This occurs in the definition of F_k which has elements that are themselves functions of past θ_t, $t < k$. Further, since each θ_t is itself a function of its previous states $\theta_{t-1}, \theta_{t-2}, \ldots$, the observation equation (4.12) will also be non-linear in the equivalent state vector θ. To see this non-linearity clearly, suppose that $\hat{\theta}_{0|0}$ in (4.14) is found be using the information in (–T, 0) and with F_1 initially known (since lagged values of y_1, namely $y_0, y_{-1}, y_{-2}, \ldots$ are assumed given). The first period k = 1 prediction is then given by

$$\hat{y}_1 = F_1 \hat{\theta}_{1|0} \cdot \tag{4.24}$$

For k = 2, we have

$$y_2 = F_2 \theta_2 + v_2 \cdot \tag{4.25}$$

But F_2 includes values in y_1 which are not known but estimated as $\hat{y}_1$ by (4.24). As a result, $F_2(y_1)$ is some unknown function of y_1. Since also at k=2 $\theta_2 = G_1\theta_1 + L_1\epsilon_1$ the quantities $F_2(y_1)$ and θ_2 are non-linear functions of θ_1; thus

$$y_2 = \bar{F}_2(F_1, \theta_1, \theta_2) + \bar{\bar{F}}_2(\theta_1, \theta_2, v_1, v_2) \tag{4.26}$$

with $\bar{F}_2$ and $\bar{\bar{F}}_2$ representing nonlinear functions of F_2 in the states θ_1, θ_2. If F_1 is known, as we have assumed, and since θ_t, u_t and ϵ_t are mutually uncorrelated, a mean prediction of y_2 would be

$$E(y_2 | y^0) = F_1 \cdot E(\bar{F}'_2(\theta_1, \theta_2) | y^0) \tag{4.27}$$

where

$$\bar{F}_2(F_1, \theta_1, \theta_2) = F_1 \bar{F}'_2(\theta_1, \theta_2) \, . \tag{4.28}$$

Hence for k = 2, the solution is still quite simple since $\bar{\bar{F}}'_2$ is of degree two only. For example, supposing that $G_t = L_t = I$ and $\bar{x}'_t = y'_{t-1}$ (i.e. there are no exogenous variables) we have

$$\hat{y}_1 = (y_0 \otimes I)\hat{\theta}_{0|0} \tag{4.29}$$

Then

$$y_2 = F_2\theta_2 + v_2 = y_1\theta_2 + v_2 \tag{4.30}$$

which, since v_t, θ_t and ϵ_t are uncorrelated, implies

$$y_2 = (y_0 \otimes I)(\hat{\theta}_{0|0}\, \hat{\theta}'_{0|0} + \Omega_{0|0}) \, . \tag{4.31}$$

For higher period predictions (k > 2) we obtain much more complicated terms. It is because of such difficulties that an approximate filtering (rather than an exact one) approach is required. Typically, we could find some linearisation scheme (such as through a Taylor series approximation) which could render the nonlinearities in F tractable. Here, we shall propose an approach based on the definition of auxiliary equations in the forecasting scheme which will reduce our problem to be on an essentially linear structure.

The auxiliary equations used interactively by estimating one set of parameters (the F_t's) off-line, while the remaining parameters θ_t are estimated on-line. In this sense, the approximate filtering algorithm is a 'ping pong' procedure which generates the parameter estimates F'_{t-1} and θ_t's recursively and interactively. The auxiliary equations essentially allow us to treat the ex ante forecasting scheme (with F_t's unknown) as an ex post one, with 'observations' F_t leading to ex ante forecasts generated by an off-line auxiliary equation. The algorithm is represented in the flow diagram, figure 4.2 below.

Suppose that F_t contains only exogenous variables, thus $\bar{x}'_t = [x'_{t-1}, \ldots x'_{t-n}]$, $F_t = x_t \otimes I$, and let the off-line forecasts of x_k, $k > 0$ be generated by an auto-regressive process

$$\bar{x}_t = \mu \bar{x}_{t-1} + \eta_{t-1}; \qquad x_0 \text{ given} \tag{4.32}$$

where η_{t-1} is a zero mean normal disturbance with variance-covariance matrix Λ. The matrix μ has a structure similar to that of A in (4.3) and is estimated by standard econometric procedures using the available sample information (0, –T). For each $k > 1$,

$$\hat{\bar{x}}_k = \hat{\mu} \bar{x}_{k-1}; \qquad \bar{x}_0 = \text{given} \tag{4.33}$$

where $\hat{\mu}$ is an estimator of μ. Then $\hat{y}_k = (\bar{x}_k \otimes I)\hat{\theta}_{k|0}$ are consistent forecasts of y_k which use stochastic predictors for $\bar{x}_k$ and thus have greater variance then in the ex post forecasts. The stochastic nature of $\bar{x}_k$ is, in addition, a function of the covariance matrix of μ. That variance-covariance matrix is estimated as $\Sigma(\ddot{\mu})$ from (4.33). The forecasts provided by (4.33) are fed into $\hat{F}_t$ for use in (4.14). As a result, the first difficulty pointed out earlier in the solution of our filtering problem is resolved, albeit at the cost of an increased variance due to the auxiliary auto-regressive process (4.32).

Where lagged endogenous variables are included in our definition of $\bar{x}_t$, (4.32) generates observations on y_t. In our formulation, this 'instrument' for forecasting F_t (for the estimation of θ_t) presumes that actual observations are conditioned by the past history of the process and that η_t and u_t are uncorrelated. This procedure

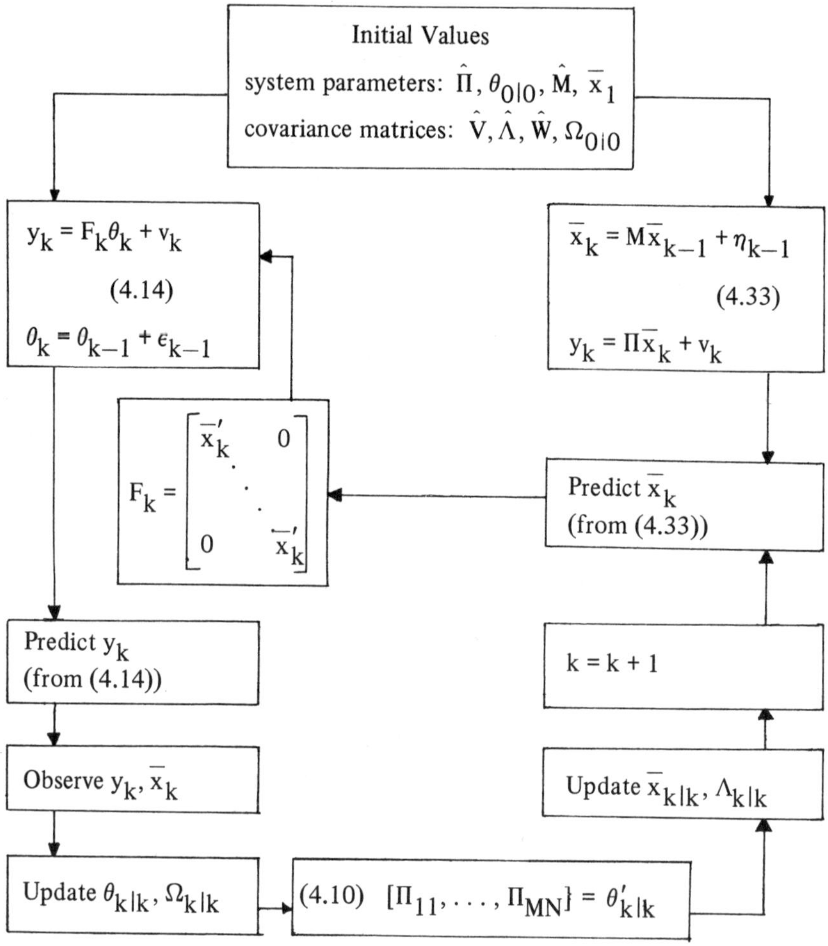

Figure 4.2. The 'ping pong' adaptive forecasting scheme

of postulating an auto-regressive process for observations generation is only an approximation, which maintains the linearity of our estimating precedures at the cost of the uncertainty implicit in the model we have postulated. In this sense, the filtering algorithm is only an approximation to the true filtering problem defined earlier.

An adaptive algorithm which would up-date estimates as additional observations are obtained and revise the conditional forecasts can now be formulated as consisting of two models:

The off-line model

$$\begin{cases} \bar{x}_k = \mu \bar{x}_{k-1} + \eta_{k-1} & \text{Model} \\ y_k = \Pi \bar{x}_k + v_k & \text{Observation} \\ \text{and } \hat{V}, \hat{\Lambda} \text{ and } x_0 \text{ given} & \end{cases}$$

The on-line model

$$\begin{cases} \theta_k = G_{k-1}\,\theta_{k-1} + L_{k-1}\,\epsilon_{k-1} & \text{Model} \\ y_k = F_k\,\theta_k + v_k & \text{Observation} \\ \text{and } \hat{V}, \hat{W}, \hat{\theta}_{0|0} \text{ and } \Omega_{0|0} \text{ given} & \end{cases}$$

At time k, y_k and $\bar{x}_k$ are observed. The observations are used in (4.14) to revise the estimates $\theta_{k|k}$, $\Omega_{k|k}$. The revision of $\theta_{k|k}$ automatically updates the estimates of Π which are used to update the filtered estimates $\bar{x}_k$. Using the revised estimate $\bar{x}_k$, future values of $\bar{x}_j$, $k<j<\tau+k$, are derived. They are components of the F_j's which serve to forecast a revised series of y_j for $k<j<\tau+k$.
Note that at time k the observed $\bar{x}_k$ is used as initial value, and for the filtering part of the process which yields the estimates $\hat{\theta}_{k|k}$, $\Omega_{k|k}$.

4. AN EMPIRICAL APPLICATION: ADAPTIVE FORECASTING OF THE MEAT SECTOR

The econometric model we consider is the meat sector model developed by Shmueli and Tapiero (1980, 1982) for the period 1968–74 using monthly time series. The model has empirical estimates of the most important relations linking consumption, imports, production, inventories, and prices. Broadly speaking the model consists of four types of meat: (1) fresh beef, (2) frozen beef, (3) fresh uncleaned broilers, and (4) cleaned broilers, both fresh and frozen. Frozen beef is imported, stored and marketed by the government. Fresh beef and broilers are locally produced and marketed in an essentially free market, while frozen broilers are stored and marketed by the government. Figure 4.3 aims to capture the relationships between the sector's various segments and the process by which means it reaches the consumer. Other aspects (both institutional and statistical) of the meat sector are treated in detail in the

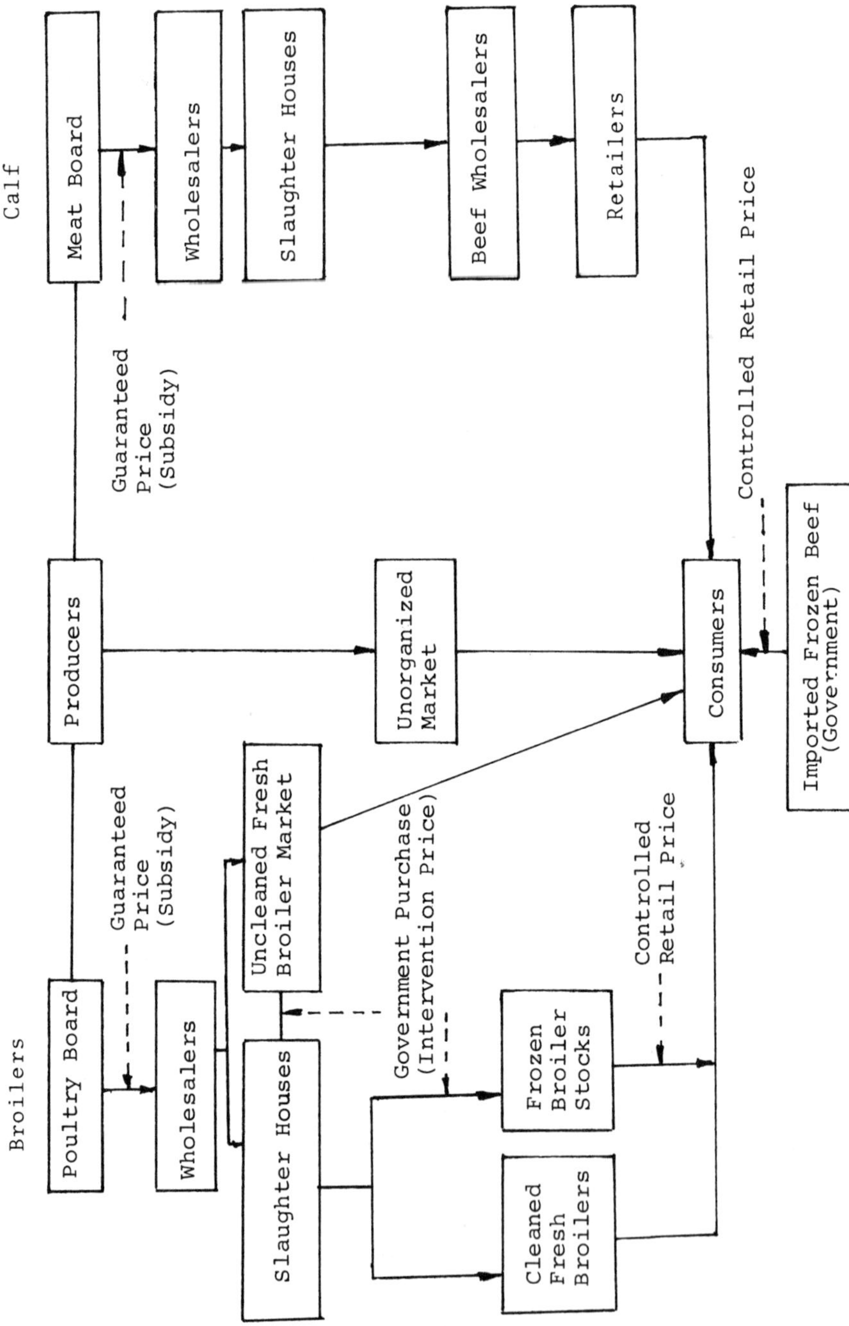

Figure 4.3. Main flows in the meat sector

references given above.

The model contains 10 stochastic equations and 12 identities which constitute the structural form. In addition to the 22 endogenous variables, there are 6 instrumental (control) variables which are treated as exogenous and 9 exogenous (uncontrolled) variables. The long lags in the model imply a complex dynamic structure. To estimate the model we have used a three-stage least squares estimation approach with restrictions,[1] using monthly time series data (January 1968 – June 1974) on the organised markets.[2] For computational convenience we have estimated a linear model (attempts to estimate a non-linear model did not produce better estimates). The v_t were tested for serial correlation, and this hypothesis was rejected (using the Durbin-Watson test) at a 5% level.

The forecasting was performed for 23 months (July 1973 – May 1975). The first 12 forecasts are therefore within the sample period. First we used the standard reduced-form forecasting approach and then we used the adaptive forecasting algorithm for a simulataneous model with time-invariant parameters. The initial values for $\theta_{0|0}$ were the derived reduced-form parameters; $\Omega_{0|0}$ and $\hat{V}$ were derived by (4.22) and (4.9) respectively. $\hat{V}$ and $\hat{\psi}$ being obtained from the three-stage least squares (3SLS) estimation phase.

The resulting time paths for four endogenous variables, the per capita consumption of each type of meat, are shown in figures 4.4 to 4.7. Each figure outlines three time paths: the actual path; a forecast based on the 3SLS (reduced-form) estimates; and a forecast based on the adaptive forecasting algorithm. June 1974 is the end of the sample period.

The main feature of the diagram is that the adaptive forecasts show a filtered and smoothed path compared with the 3SLS forecasts. Thus they did not capture the extreme points of the actual path but, considering the whole forecasting period, they provide the better forecasts, as can be seen from the ususal RMSE criterion (table 4.1).[3] The improvement is between 17 and 55 percent, with the greatest improvement corresponding to the worst 3SLS forecast.

Table 4.1. Per capita meat consumption: comparison of three-stage least squares and adaptive forecasting, using the RMSE criterion

Variable	RMSE 3SLS	RMSE Adaptive	Percent improvement by adaptive algorithm
Fresh beef	0.039	0.028	28
Frozen beef	0.163	0.126	23
Uncleaned broilers	0.315	0.142	55
Cleaned broilers	0.249	0.208	17

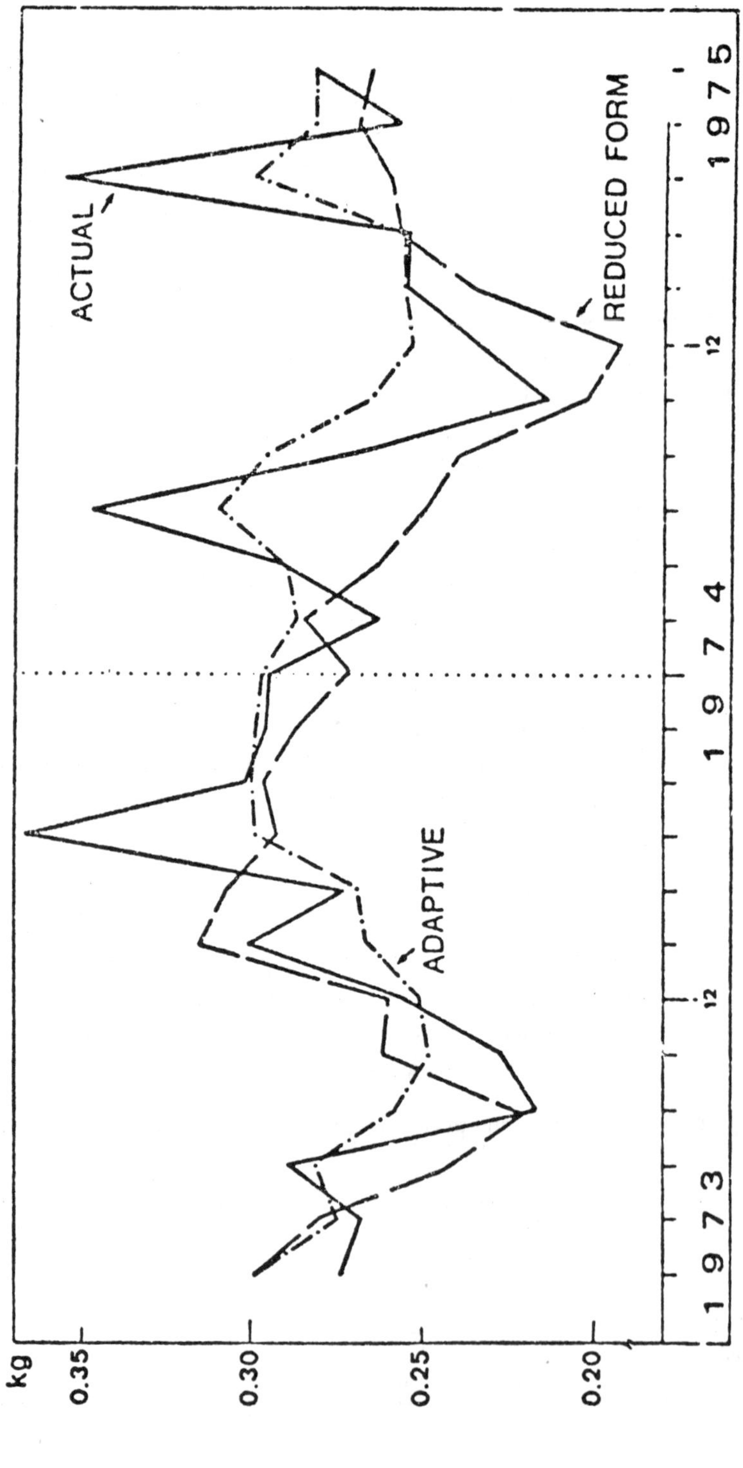

Figure 4.4. Per capita consumption of fresh beef

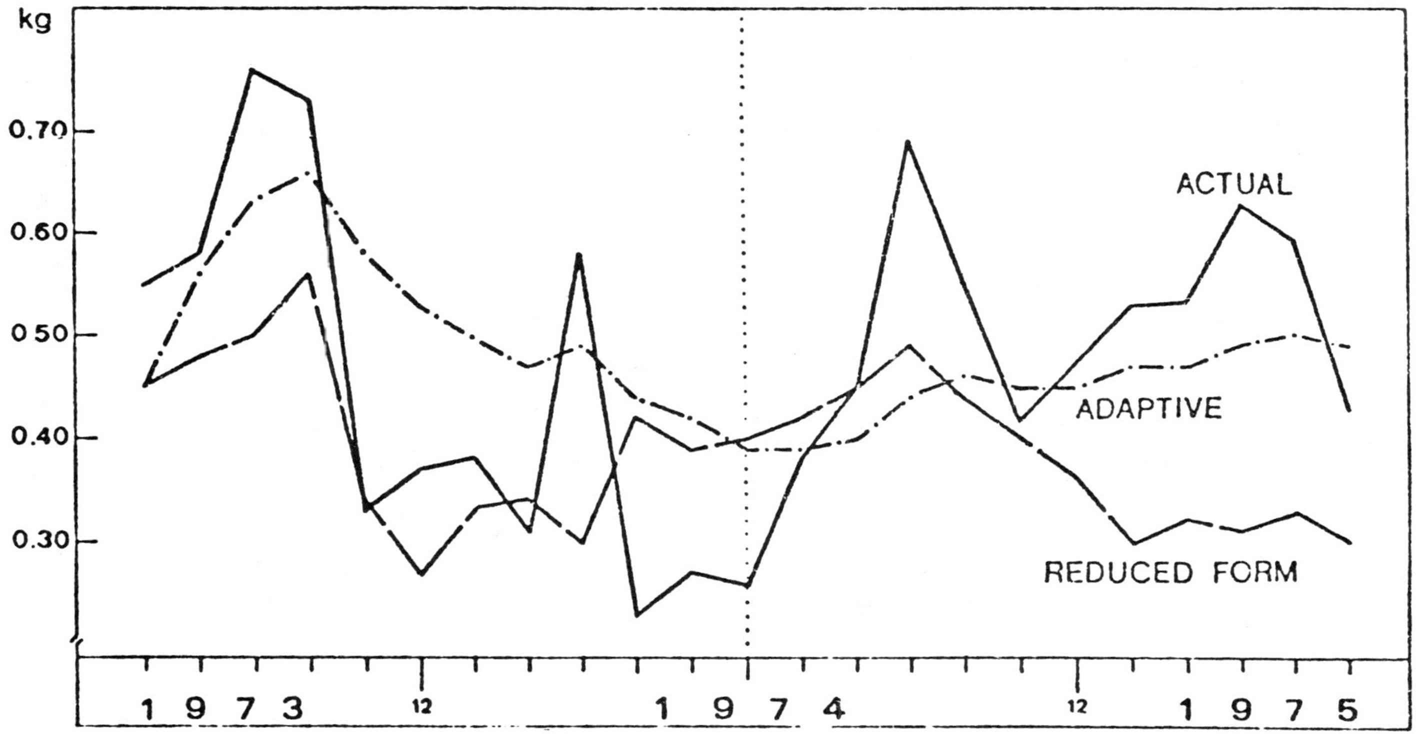

Figure 4.5. Per capita consumption of frozen beef

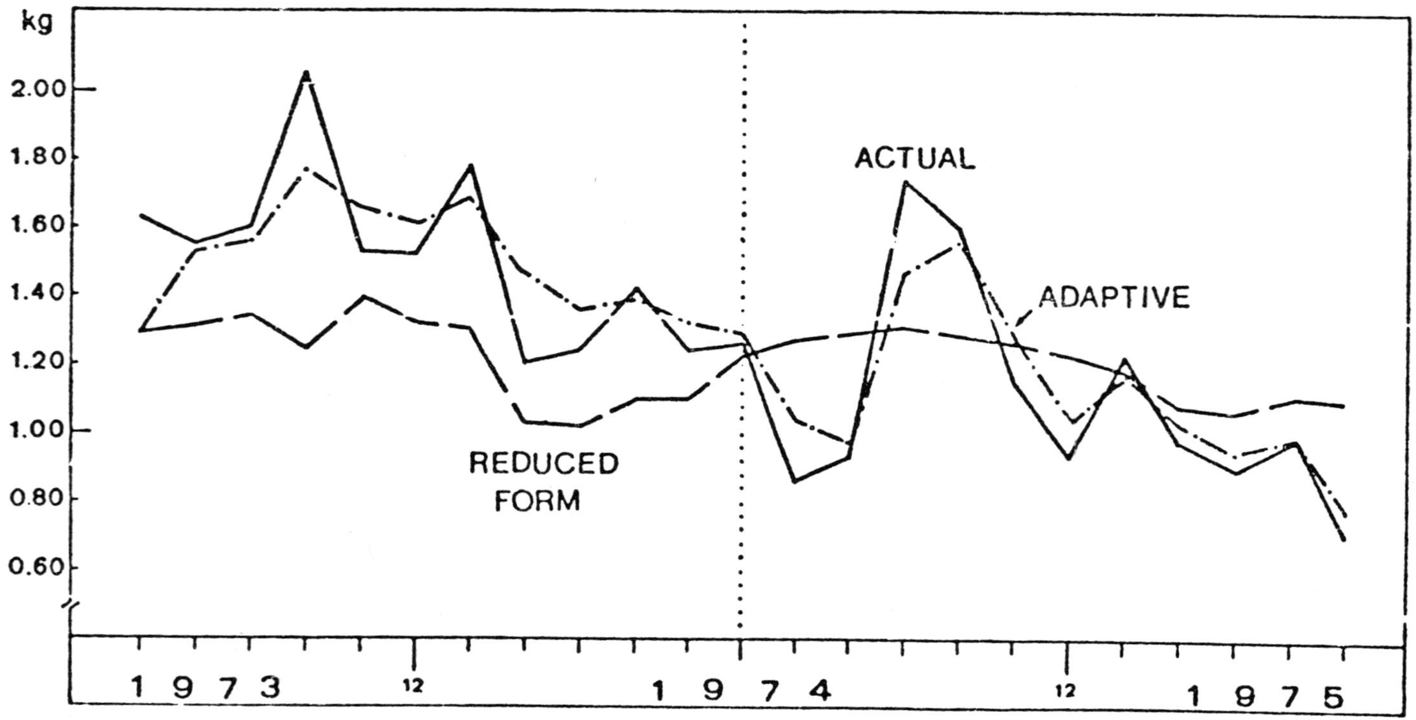

Figure 4.6. Per capita consumption of uncleaned broilers (fresh)

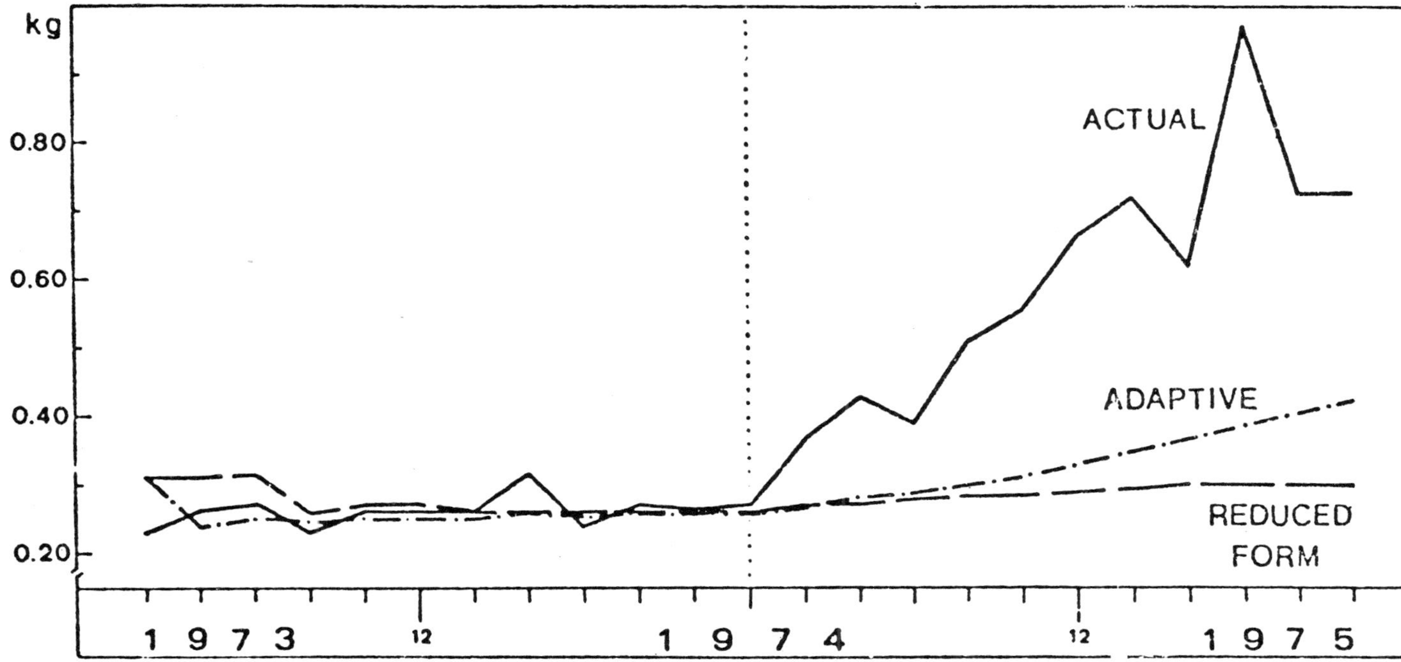

Figure 4.7. Per capita consumption of cleaned broilers (fresh and frozen)

5. CONCLUSIONS

We have shown the applicability of the Kalman filter algorithm and forecasting in econometrics. The results show that, even with the standard Kalman algorithm with constant parameters, one can improve estimates and forecasts.

The updating process which characterises the algorithm enables the model to deal with structural changes and with dynamics which classical econometric estimation fails to deal with.

The deviation from the classical least-squares approach by the use of filtering-smoothing algorithms enables us, for example, to estimate time-varying parameters. Cases of multi-process bi-furcating models, structural changes, and non-stationarity can also be handled by techniques which are based on the same kind of filtering-updating algorithms.

There are however some problems in applying these engineering-oriented techniques to econometrics. Most of them cause the problem to become non-linear due to parameter uncertainty. Optimal solution to the problem would require a non-linear optimisation technique which estimates the parameters and the state vector simultaneously. Here, we have proposed an approximated solution to the problem which is based on a decomposition into two auxiliary models. The empirical application considered in this chapter, the Israeli Meat Sector econometric model, has shown the benefits and improved precision of the adaptive forecasting scheme at least for this model.

NOTES

1. Resulting from the utility maximisation used to derive the demand functions.
2. That is, sales through the marketing boards and the major cooperatives such as Tnuva. Coverage is confined to the organised markets because (a) the only reliable data refer to them; and (b) government policy is operative only in the organised markets. This limited coverage may bias the results.
3. Note that the criterion to be minimised is the mean square error for both estimation techniques. The difference is, however, that the least-squares forecaster is the conditional mean given all the available observations, while the Kalman filtering forecaster is conditional on the updated mean and the covariance of the parameters.

REFERENCES

Ando, A. and C. Palash (1976), 'Some stabilisation problems of 1971-75 with an application of optimal control algorithms', *American Economic Review,* 66.

Annals of Economic and Social Measurement. Special Issue on Time-Varying Parameters, II (October 1973).

Athans, M. (1974), 'The importance of Kalman filtering methods for economic systems', *Annals of Economic and Social Measurement,* 3, pp. 49-63.

Athans, M. and D. Kendrick (1974), 'Control theory and economics: A survey, forecasts and speculations', *IEEE Transactions on Automatic Control,* AC-19, pp. 518-524.

Bar Shalom, Y. and E. Tse (1976), 'Caution, probing and the value of information in the control of uncertain systems', *Annals of Economic and Social Measurement,* 5, pp. 323-338.

Brown, R.L., J. Durbin and J.M. Evans (1975), 'Technique for testing the constancy of regression relationships over time', *Journal of the Royal Statistical Society,* Series B, pp. 149-192.

Chow, G.C. (1974), 'Identification and estimation in econometric systems: A survey', *IEEE Transactions on Automatic Control,* AC-19, pp. 855-862.

Chow, G.C. (1975), *Analysis and Control of Dynamic Systems,* John Wiley and Sons, New York.

Chow, G.C. (1976), 'The control of non-linear econometric systems with unknown parameters', *Econometrica,* 44, pp. 685-695.

Cooley, T., B. Rosenberg and K.D. Wall (1977), 'A note on optimal smoothing for time-varying coefficient problems', *Annals of Economic and Social Measurement,* 4, pp. 453-456.

Day, R.H. and T. Groves (eds.) (1975), *Adaptive Economic Models,* Academic Press, New York.

Feldbaum, A.A. (1965), *Optimal Control Systems,* Academic Press, New York.

Feldstein, M.S. (1971), 'The error of forecasting econometric models when the forecast preperiod exogenous variables are stochastic', *Econometrica,* 39, pp. 55-60.

Friedman, B.M. (1975), *Methods in Optimisation for Economic Stabilisation Policy,* North Holland, Amsterdam.

Goldberger, A.F., A.L. Nagar and H.S. Odeh (1961), 'The covariance matrices of reduced-form coefficients and of forecasts for a structural econometric model', *Econometrica,* 29, pp. 556-573.

Harrison, P.J. and C.F. Stevens (1976), Bayesian forecasting', *Journal of the Royal Statistical Society,* 38, Series B, No. 3, pp. 205-247.

Kalman, R.E. (1960), 'A new approach to linear filtering and prediction problems', *Transactions ASME Journal of Basic Engineering,* 82, pp. 34-45.

Kalman, R.E. and R.S. Bucy (1961), 'New results in linear filtering and prediction theory', *Transactions ASME Journal of Basic Engineering,* 83, pp. 95-107.

Kang, B.H. and D. Kendrick (1975), 'An economist's guide to adaptive control of linear systems with random parameters', Project on Control in Economics, Report No. 75-4, University of Texas, Austin, TX.

Kendrick, D. and B.H. Kang (1975), 'An economist's guide to wide-sense dual control', Project on Control in Economics, Report No. 75-1, University of Texas, Austin, TX.

Lainiotis, D.G. (1971), 'Optimal adaptive estimation: Structure and parameter adaptation', *IEEE Transactions on Automatic Control,* AC-16, pp. 160-170.

MacRae, E.C. (1975), 'An adaptive learning role for multi-period decision problems', *Econometrica,* 43, pp. 893-906.

Mehra, R.A. (1972), 'Approaches to adaptive filtering', *IEEE Transactions on Automatic Control,* AC-17, pp. 693-698.

Mehra, R.A. (1974), 'Identification in control and econometrics: Similarities and differences', *Annals of Economic and Social Measurement,* 3, pp. 21-47.

Pagan, A. (1978), 'A unified approach to estimation and inference for stochastically varying regression coefficients', Core Discussion Paper No. 7814, University of Louvain, Belgium.

Pekelman, D. and G.C. Rausser (1978), 'Adaptive control: Survey of methods and application',

Special Issue on Applied Optimal Control, in: A. Bensoussan, P. Kleindorfer and C.S. Tapiero (eds.), *Management Science,* 24.

Ruddel, W.C. (1975), 'Recursive estimation algorithms for economic research', *Annals of Economic and Social Measurement,* 4, pp. 397-406.

Sarris, A. (1973), 'A Bayesian approach to estimation of time-varying regression coefficients', *Annals of Economic and Social Measurement,* 2, pp. 501-523.

Shmueli, A. and C.S. Tapiero (1982), 'The Israeli meat sector: An econometric model', *European Journal of Agricultural Economics,* 9, pp. 65-86.

Shmueli, A. and C.S. Tapiero (1980), 'Optimal stochastic control and stabilisation of the Israeli meat sector', in: A. Bensoussan, P. Kleindorfer and C.S. Tapiero (eds.), *Applied Stochastic Control in Econometrics and Management Science,* North Holland, Amsterdam.

Tapiero, C.S. (1977), *Managerial Planning: An Optimum and a Stochastic Control Approach,* (2 vols), Gordon Breach Science Publ., New York.

Tse, E. (1974), 'Adaptive dual control methods', *Annals of Economic and Social Measurement,* 3, pp, 65-84.

Turnovsky, S.J. (1976), 'Optimal stabilisation policies for stochastic linear systems: The case of correlated muliplicative and additive disturbances', *Review of Economic Studies,* 43, pp. 191-194.

Upadhyay, T. (1976), 'Applications of adaptive control to economic stabilisation policy', *International Journal of Systems Science,* 7, pp. 641-650.

CHAPTER 5

CONTROLLING AN ECONOMETRIC MODEL USING DIFFERENT COEFFICIENT SETS

C.-L. Sandblom and H.A. Eiselt
Concordia University, Montreal, Canada

1. INTRODUCTION

In optimisation experiments with macroeconometric models, there are many sources of uncertainty and error that should be taken into consideration. An issue which has received much attention during the last decade is how random disturbances in the model equations will affect optimal policies. Another issue and one which seems to have been overlooked is the effects of coefficient estimates of different refinement on the determination of optimal policies.

In this chapter we use the CLEAR model, which is a 35-equation linear econometric model of Canada, and optimise it in four different versions. To ensure a realistic setting for the control experiments, a suitable piecewise quadratic objective function involving the unemployment and inflation rates is minimised, and the control variables are restricted to move between reasonably tight lower and upper bounds.

The four model versions represent coefficient estimates of the one- and two-stage least-squares type, with different corrections for serial correlation. An optimal control trajectory from one model version is then used to simulate the other three versions; this procedure is repeated for each of the model versions. To put the results in proper perspective, a historical simulation of each model version is also performed and included in the analysis. We then study the resulting payoff matrix of welfare function values with regard to dominance or any other notable feature. This exercise will give the model builder valuable knowledge about the robustness of his model; it will also be useful if estimating an even more refined model version is contemplated.

An outline of the paper is as follows. In the next section we will briefly describe

Hughes Hallett, A.J. (ed.) Applied Decision Analysis and Economic Behaviour

ISBN 90-247-2968-8. Printed in The Netherlands

the CLEAR model and the setup of the control experiments. It should be noted that we use bounds on the controls and no costs in the objective function for employing the controls. In section 3 we discuss the approach of simultaneously using different models or model versions for control experiment purposes; we also present the numerical results obtained and an analysis of these. Section 4 concludes the chapter by summarising the findings and by offering some remarks about the usefulness of the approach.

2. OPTIMISING THE CLEAR MODEL

The CLEAR (Canadian Linear Econometric Applied Research) model was constructed for the purpose of performing a variety of economic policy experiments, mainly optimal control. The Bank of Canada RDX2 model (Bank of Canada, 1976) and its data base were used in the building of CLEAR. The RDX2 model has more than 300 equations (CLEAR has only 35); yet both models are quarterly, highly interdependent (CLEAR even more than RDX2) and possess a similar very elaborate polynomial lag structure. By being linear and more aggregated, CLEAR should have more specification error than RDX2; this is however compensated for by more advanced estimation techniques than are practical for large scale models. Also, corrections for serial correlation will to some extent counter-balance the oversimplification committed by adhering to linearity; this is borne out by CLEAR's quite impressive tracking ability. Finally, as the optimisation will be performed only over a fairly short period (3 years, i.e. 12 quarters), the linearity restriction is not unreasonable. For a complete account of the model as well as its simulation, forecasting and shock response performance, see Banasik (1978) and Banasik and Sandblom (1981).

The estimation period of CLEAR is from the first quarter of 1961 to the last quarter of 1973, i.e. there are 52 data points in the estimation. Four versions of the model are considered, all resulting from least-squares multiple regression estimation, with the Hildreth-Lu correction for serial correlation. The first two versions, STAGE1 and STAGE1R are both the result of one-stage least squares estimation. Although both these have coefficients that are adjusted for serial correlation error, only in STAGE1R are the lagged errors used in the simulation of endogenous variable estimates. The other two versions of the model, STAGE2A and STAGE2R, result from corresponding two-stage least-squares estimation. STAGE2, the proper analogue of STAGE1, had to be replaced by STAGE2A in which the autocorrelation coefficient was constrained not to exceed 0.9 (this happened in four cases in STAGE2 which led to awkward coefficient estimates). Crudely speaking we can rank the model versions in ascending order of sophistication as STAGE1, STAGE1R, STAGE2A, STAGE2R. For a full description of the estimation procedures, see Banasik and Sandblom (1981).

As an objective for the optimal control experiments in this chapter we will measure the welfare cost by the following auxiliary objective function W, which is to be minimised:

$$W = \sum_t \left\{ (\text{unemployment}_t - 2)^2 + (\text{inflation}_t - 3)^2 \right\}$$

where the unemployment and annual inflation rates are expressed in percent, and the summation is done over the twelve-quarter period, starting with the first quarter of 1970 (1970.1) to 1972.4. Unemployment rates of 2% or less are discarted from the objective function, as are inflation rates of 3% or less; the objective function is therefore piece-wise quadratic with so-called 'dead zones'. The 2% and 3% targets were selected based on the actual historical values for the planning period. See Sandblom and Banasik (1981) where the general form of the objective function is also discussed. The experiments are conducted by performing fiscal economic policy only; the control variable is government non-wage expenditure, GONW, which in all experiments was constrained to move between about \$1046 million and \$1992 million. This corresponds to twice the actual historical bandwidth of this period, which was about \$1282 million to \$1755 million. For the simulation and optimisation experiments, we used the GRG-type CONOPT code (see Drud, 1978 and Drud and Meeraus, 1980), as implemented on the Concordia University CDC Cyber computer. Experiments with CLEAR using the above type of objective function are reported on in Sandblom and Banasik (1981, 1984); for a discussion of the bounded control approach and a justification of the bandwidth selected, see Sandblom, Banasik and Parlar (1981).

3. THE EXPERIMENTS

Thus having four different versions of the same model at our disposal, we may ask which of these would be the best for optimal control purposes. It would appear that this question could only be answered if we know which of the models 'best' represents the economy being considered; this view is maintained by Christ (1975) who compared several models of the U.S. economy. We will now show that some light might be shed on this issue by extending the following idea due to Chow (1977); see also Chow (1981, Ch. 11) and Rüstem (1982).

For each of the four model versions, we compute an optimal trajectory of the control variable over the planning period 1970 first quarter (1970.1) to 1972.4. Each of these four trajectories is then in turn used to *simulate* each of the four model versions, and the resulting welfare cost value is recorded. The results of these simulations are shown in table 5.1 below, where for comparison we also display the welfare cost values resulting from historical simulation. For example, if GCNW values that are obtained from optimising STAGE2A are used to simulate STAGE1R, a W-value of 108.14 will result.

Table 5.1 Welfare cost values for different model versions and optimal control trajectories

Simulating model version	Optimal control trajectory from model version				
	STAGE1	STAGE1R	STAGE2A	STAGE2R	Historical
STAGE1	68.41	85.43	133.75	82.52	562.16
STAGE1R	86.87	84.27	108.14	86.52	409.42
STAGE2A	189.29	185.00	178.79	181.30	198.74
STAGE2R	162.49	160.47	159.01	158.12	186.87

The payoff matrix in table 5.1 has several interesting features. First of all we note that each element in position (i, i), i.e. along the main diagonal, is the smallest in its respective row. This is of course necessary for logical consistency, since such elements correspond to minimising the welfare cost for the respective model version. Secondly we notice that the STAGE2R row element-wise is smaller than the STAGE2A row. In other words, the STAGE2R model dominates the STAGE2A version, yielding better results (lower welfare costs) no matter which optimal trajectory is chosen; this is true even if the historical trajectory of the control variable GCNW is included in the comparison. Similarly we conclude that both the STAGE1 and the STAGE1R models dominate the STAGE2R version; this time, we have to exclude the historical GCNW simulation from the comparison. No conclusion can be drawn from comparing STAGE1 with STAGE1R.

From the above observations it appears that the STAGE1 and STAGE1R model versions are preferable from a controllability point of view, but it certainly does not mean that they should be selected in preference to any of the other two model versions for practical policy making. This is because we do not know if the one-stage versions better reflect the underlying economy being modelled. In fact, the rightmost (historical simulation) column seems to indicate a poorer performance of the one-stage models when used for simulation. That the two-stage versions actually perform significantly better as regards tracking ability is shown in Banasik and Sandblom (1981), where it is also seen that STAGE2R is the obvious best choice if a good tracking ability is what we are looking for. On the other hand, if realistic shock response properties are more important, then the same paper shows that STAGE2A should be selsected.

Let us now scan the payoff matrix of table 5.1 with respect to any possible column dominance. That is, we are now interested to see if any particular optimal policy rather than any particular model is better than the others. It is a priori clear that no clear-cut dominance can be found, since we already know that the elements along the main diagonal constitute row-minima. The exception is of course the historical column, which, not unexpectedly, is dominated by all the other columns. If we believe that the one-stage models should be taken as seriously as the two-stage versions, it appears that STAGE2R has an edge over STAGE2A, performing significantly better for the one-stage version. However, if we judge the two-stage optimal policies based only on their performance for the two-stage models (i.e. disregarding the one-stage models as unimportant), then we cannot say much about which of the two-stage policies should be selected. The advantage of STAGE2A for its own optimal policy (178.79 versus 181.30) is perhaps slightly lighter than that of STAGE2R for its own optimal policy (158.12 versus 159.01), but this slight edge in favour of STAGE2A has to be seen against the big edge of STAGE2R for the one-stage models.

The above analysis leads us to conclude that none of the models is clearly superior to the others for the purpose of finding a robust optimal policy. However, if we assign more importance to the more sophisticated model versions (in view of their better tracking properties), we might come out in favour of using the STAGE2R optimal policy.

For a further analysis, let us plot the optimal GCNW control trajectory computed for the different model versions. This is done in figure 5.1 below, where for reasons of comparison the historical values are shown as well.

We note in figure 5.1 that the optimal GCNW values have a tendency to stay at the upper or lower bounds, occasionally jumping from one to another in a so-called 'bang-bang' fashion. In Sandblom, Banasik and Parlar (1981) it is shown that this bang-bang property becomes more pronounced the narrower the bounds are. (For example, with a bandwidth corresponding to the historical range, the bounds were hit each time whereas for a bandwidth of five times the historical range, the bounds were hit only eight out of twelve times).

From figure 5.1 we can see that all four model versions agree for the first four quarters but that they then diverge; there is a common downward trend at the end of the second year and at the beginning of the third. Otherwise the versions tend to behave in different ways with no clearly discernible pattern; particularly towards the end of the three-year planning period. As only the first few quarters of any optimal plan will ever be carried out (after that it will always be reoptimised in the light of whatever new information has become available; c.f. the sliding window con-

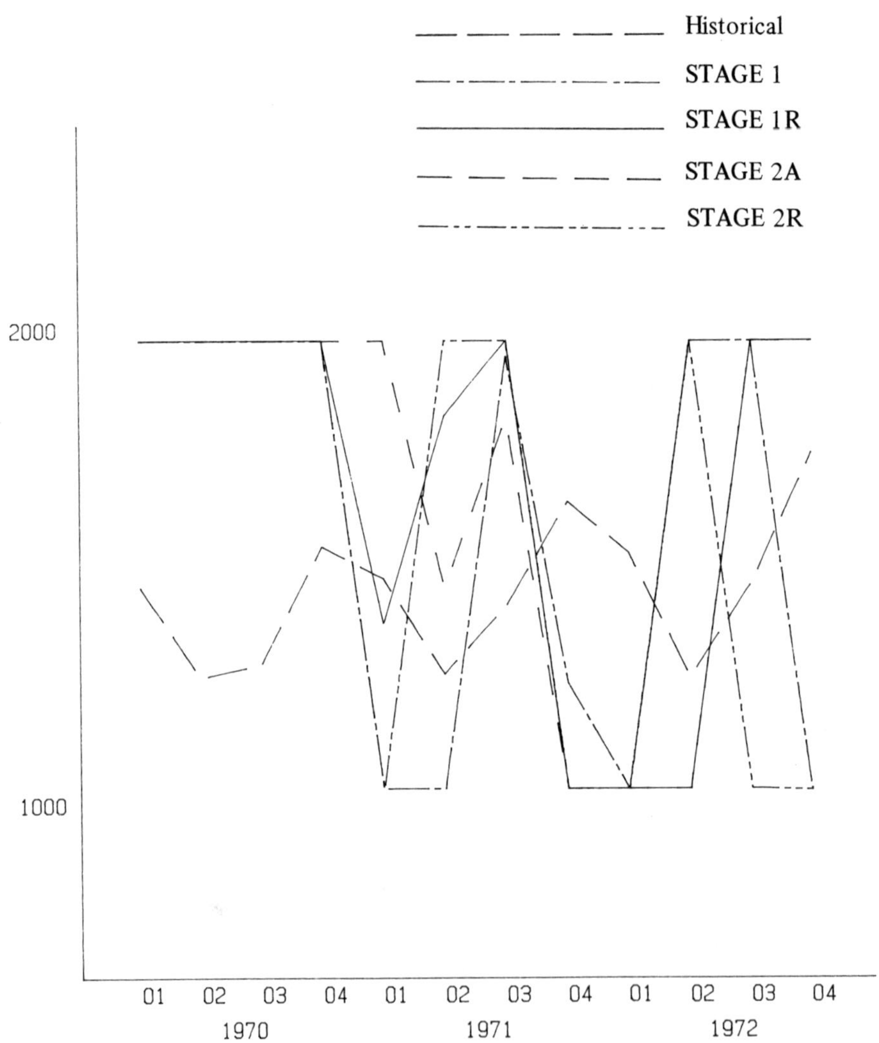

Figure 5.1. Historical values of GCNW (government non-wage expenditure) compared with optimal values for different model versions. Millions of 1961 dollars.

cept discussed in Sandblom and Banasik, 1984), thé inconclusive behaviour at the end of the twelve-quarter period is of no great concern. Far more important is the unanimous agreement between all four models' versions about the behaviour of the optimal policy during the first year, which is to say at the upper bound.

Yet another possibility to study the effects of the various model policies is to plot and analyse the deflated gross national expenditure (UGNE) time paths generated by the four model versions. This is done in figures 5.2 and 5.3 below; in figure 5.2 we show the UGNE paths for STAGE2R with the different optimal GCNW trajec-

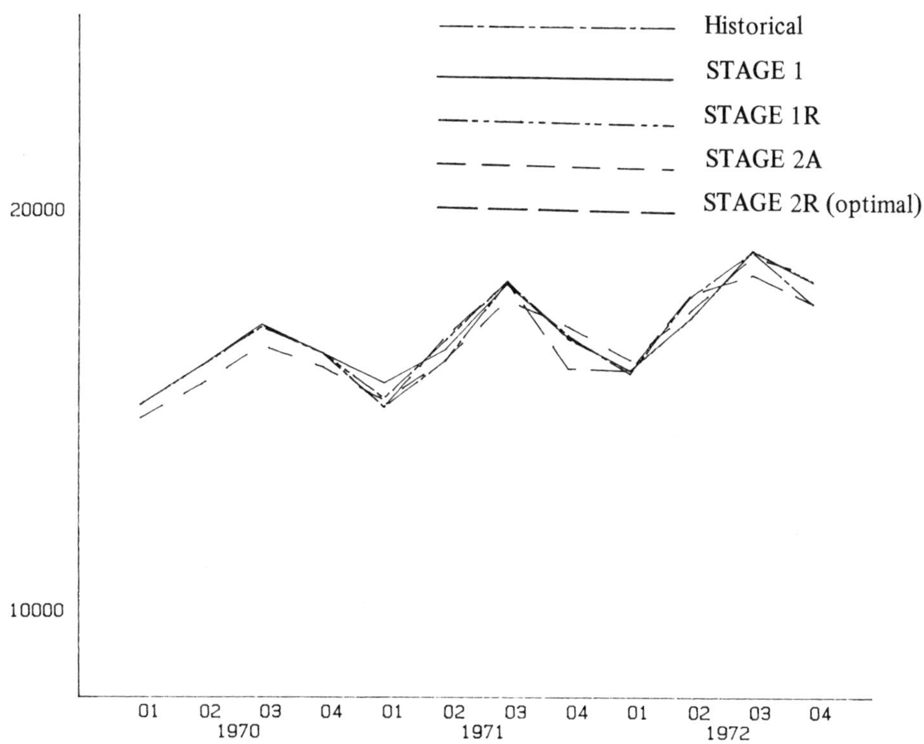

Figure 5.2. Values of UGNE (deflated gross national expenditure) for historical STAGE2R simulation compared to values obtained by using optimal GCNW-values from different model versions. Million of 1961 dollars.

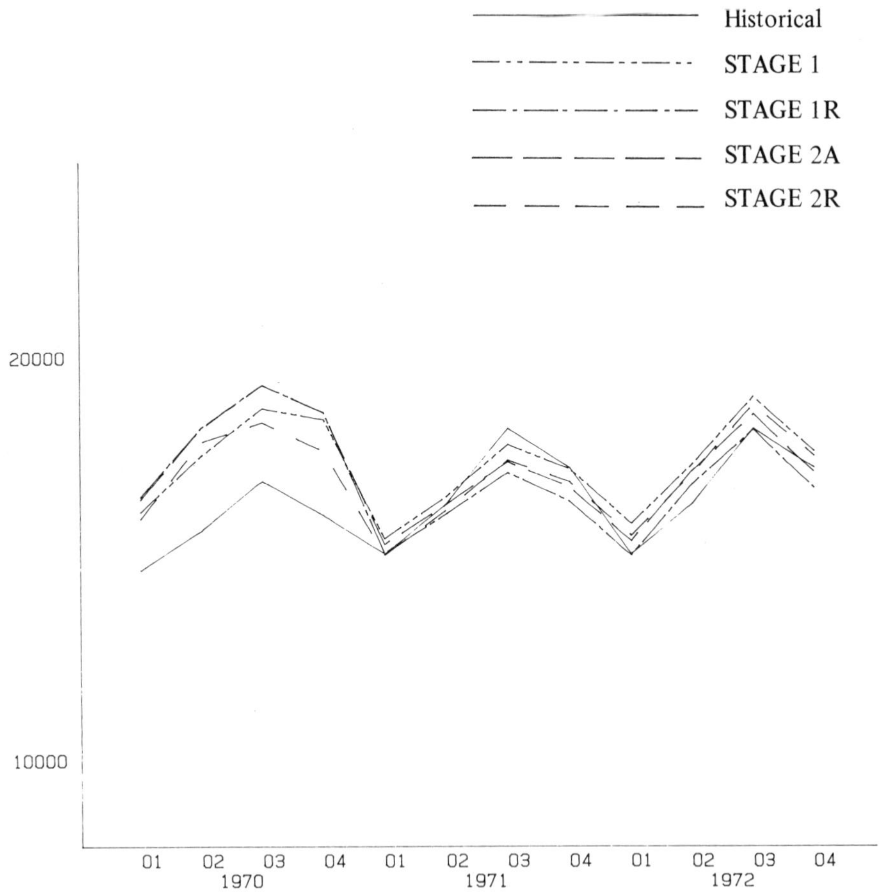

Figure 5.3. Historical values of UGNE (deflated gross national expenditure) compared to values obtained by simulation of different model versions using optimal GCNW-values obtained from STAGE2R. Millions of 1961 dollars.

tories generated from the other model versions. In figure 5.3 we have plotted the UGNE paths generated by simulating each of the four model versions with the optimal STAGE2R GCNW trajectory in the input data. For reasons of comparison, the UGNE values corresponding to historical simulation are shown as well. Crudely speaking, we can say that the concern in figure 5.2 is on how the model STAGE2R performs; in figure 5.3 our concern is the optimal policy resulting from model STAGE2R.

In figure 5.2 we note that the UGNE values obtained by simulation using optimal GCNW values coincide during the first four quarters. This is due to the fact that GCNW coincides for all model versions for the first four quarters (as we saw in figure 5.1). During these four quarters, the historical simulation values of UGNE are consistently below those obtained by optimising GCNW. This is a natural effect of the fact that in the control solutions, the GCNW during the first four quarters are at the upper bound and therefore higher than the corresponding historical values. The same tendency for UGNE also applies to the rest of the planning period, except for the end of the third and the beginning of the fourth quarter, and the very last quarter. The UGNE values resulting from simulation using optimal GCNW values also have a tendency to fluctuate less; this is an effect of the countercyclical feature of the optimal controls.

By examining figure 5.3 we find that the simulated values of UGNE are in general above the actual historical values, at least during the early part of the planning period; this is not surprising as GNCW is then at its upper bound. We also note that the fact that the GNCW values used in figure 5.3 are especially attuned to STAGE2R (being optimal for this version) results in a tendency of UGNE for this model version to fluctuate less than the others.

The analysis can now be carried further by investigating the behaviour of other variables, particularly those in the objective function. This would however be outside the scope of this chapter, which is to demonstrate the idea and the usefulness of the approach described above.

4. SUMMARY AND CONCLUSIONS

In this chapter we have shown how different versions of the same model can be compared against each other for the purpose of optimal economic policy making. The results were summarised in a payoff table of welfare cost values for the different experiments. The payoff table was then analysed and some interesting features regarding the various models and policies were found. The analysis was then carried further by investigating the behaviour of the key variable UGNE for the various experiments. On balance it could be seen that the STAGE2R version is probably in this case the best version of our type of experiment.

Although our discussion is based on very limited experiments with only one model, one control variable and for one given planning period, the usefulness of the approach should be obvious. It is also clear that instead of having a particular model in different versions, corresponding to coefficient sets of varying refinement, one could also choose to experiment with different models, all having coefficient sets of similar refinement. This analysis can then be integrated (in Step 10) into the elaborate twelve-step procedure for using econometric models in macroeconomic policy formulation, that was suggested by Chow (1979 and 1981, Ch. 12).

NOTES

This work was supported, in part, by the Social Sciences and Humanities Research Council of Canada under grant number 410-79-0350-R1 which is gratefully acknowledged. We are also indebted to Arne Drud for his CONOPT code, and to Kathie Brown for assistance with the diagrams.

REFERENCES

Banasik, J.L. (1978), 'A condensed and linearised version of the RDX2 model of the Canadian economy'' MBA thesis, Concordia University, Montreal.

Banasik, J.L. (1978), 'A condensed and linearised version of the RDX2 model of the Canadian economy', MBA thesis, Concordia University, Montreal.
Montreal (mimeo).

Bank of Canada (1976), 'The equations of RDX2 revised and estimated to 4Q72', *Bank of Canada Technical Reports,* No. 5.

Chow, G.C. (1977), 'Usefulness of imperfect models for the formulation of stabilisation policies', *Annals of Economic and Social Measurement,* 6, pp. 175-187.

Chow, G.C. (1979), 'Effective use of econometric models in macroeconomic policy formulation' in S. Holly, B. Rüstem, and M.B. Zarrop (eds.), *Optimal Control for Econometric Models,* MacMillan, London, pp. 31-39.

Chow, G.C. (1981), *Econometric Analysis by Control Methods,* John Wiley and Sons, New York.

Christ, C.F. (1975), 'Judging the performance of econometric models of the U.S. economy', *International Economic Review,* 16, pp. 54-74.

Drud, A. (1978), 'An optimisation code for nonlinear econometric models based on sparse matrix techniques and reduced gradients', *Annals of Economic and Social Measurement,* 6, pp. 563-580.

Drud, A. and A. Meeraus (1980), 'CONOPT – A system for large scale dynamic nonlinear optimisation – User's manual', Version 0.105, Development Research Center, World Bank, Washington, D.C.

Rüstem, B. (1982), 'Optimal policies with rival models: compromise solutions, game and minmax strategies', Report EE.Con. 82.41, Imperial College of Science and Technology, University of London (mimeo).

Sandblom, C.L. and J.L. Banasik (1981), 'Optimal and suboptimal controls of a Canadian model', in J.M.L. Janssen, L.F. Pau and A. Straszak (eds.), *Dynamic Modelling and Control of*

National Economies, Pergamon Press, Oxford, pp. 71-78.
Sandblom, C.L., J.L. Banasik and M. Parlar (1981), 'Economic policy with bounded controls', Department of Quantitative Methods, Concordia University, Montreal (mimeo).
Sandblom, C.L. and J.L. Banasik (1984), 'Optimising economic policy with sliding windows', *Applied Economics*, 16, pp. 45-56.

CHAPTER 6

THE UNCERTAINTY FRONTIER AS A GLOBAL APPROACH TO THE EFFICIENT STABILISATION OF ECONOMIC SYSTEMS: EXPERIMENTS WITH THE MICRO-DMS MODEL

M. Deleau *Ministry of Economics and Finance, Paris, France*
C. Le Van *CNRS, CEPREMAP, Paris, France*
P. Malgrange *CNRS, CEPREMAP, Paris, France*

1. INTRODUCTION

The application of optimisation methods to macroeconometric models is now current practice. In recent years, stress has been put on the potentialities of such methods for purposes of analysis (see Chow (1975)). In a previous article, we proposed some analytical results about the global 'stabilisation' properties of a given economic model (Deleau and Malgrange (1979)). Our approach applies to a linear (or linearised) system with implicit) quadratic objective functions. It uses the concept of 'uncertainty frontier', which characterises 'efficient' stabilisations and gives a synthetic expression of the tradeoffs between objectives (e.g. how much do you 'destabilise' prices in the process of stabilising unemployment.

This article offers a short summary of available analytical results (Part 2). They are then applied to a macroeconometric model, MICRO-DMS (Brillet (1982)), which is a small scale version of the annual DMS model of the French economy (Fouquet et al. (1978)).

2. MATHEMATICAL FORMULATION AND RESULTS

2.1 Linear-quadratic systems in final form

2.1.1 The concept of uncertainty frontier

We consider the following linear model, in final form:

Hughes Hallett, A.J. (ed.) Applied Decision Analysis and Economic Behaviour

ISBN 90-247-2968-8. Printed in The Netherlands

$$x = Md + s \tag{6.1}$$

with $-x(n \times 1)$ = objectives
$-d(p \times 1)$ = instruments
$-s(n \times 1)$ = uncontrolled variables.

Model (6.1) can be thought of as a linear stationary approximation of a non-linear model in the neighbourhood of a given trajectory; and x, d, s can be interpreted in terms of deviations from that trajectory. In the following, we consider the problem of stabilising system (6.1) around this trajectory, i.e. of getting x 'as close as possible' to the null vector. We assume $p < n$, and that s is a random vector, with zero mean and variance-covariance matrix S with typical elements (s_{ij}).

A policy is a function which associates a value for the instruments d with every value taken by the uncontrolled variables s, namely $d = T(s)$. We assume that the only constraints bearing on the choice of T are *informational constraints* (see Marschak and Radner (1972) for a general exposition, and Deleau and Malgrange (1972) for applications). The two polar cases are of course the perfect information case (s is known when action d is taken) and the null information case (the only feasible policies are constant-action policies).

In the following, we consider the set of quadratic objective functions of the form $x'Cx$, C being any definite positive and diagonal matrix (this last condition is not essential. Furthermore we will consider only policies T with zero mean since any optimal T has this property.

If a particular policy T with zero mean is chosen, x is a random vector with variance-covariance matrix Σ as follows:

$$\Sigma(T) = E(MT(s) + s)(MT(s) + s)' \tag{6.2}$$

where E denotes the expectation operator.

Running T across the set of feasible policies generates an associated set of attainable variance-covariance matrices for the objectives. Since we restrict ourselves to diagonal quadratic objective functions, only the variances of the objectives have to be taken into account. 'Efficient stabilisations' (i.e. optimal for such diagonal quadratic objective functions) correspond to the (lower) frontier of the set of attainable variances. For any 'point' on this frontier, it is not possible to reduce the variance of one objective without increasing that of another. This frontier will be called the *uncertainty frontier* associated with system (6.1) for the informational constraints under consideration. The characteristics of an uncertainty frontier thus reflect:

- the model properties (matrix M);
- the stochastic characteristics of the uncontrolled variables;
- the informational constraints bearing on the choice of d.

To illustrate this last remark, the uncertainty frontier corresponding to the null information case reduces to a 'point'; namely the vector of the variances of s, which are also the 'ex ante' variances of the objectives.

The following proposition gives an idea of the 'shape' of an uncertainty frontier for a model of type (6.1). Such a frontier is denoted $\mathcal{R}$.

Proposition 1: Any uncertainty frontier is a manifold of R^n, with dimension at most equal to $n-1$, convex with respect to the origin.

It can be observed that duality results exist between the (efficient) variance vectors of $\mathcal{R}$ and the system of weights put on the objectives (see Deleau and Malgrange (1979)).

2.1.2 The perfect information case

Under perfect information, the optimal policy associated with a diagonal definite positive matrix C is known to be linear and equal to:

$$T = -(M'CM)^{-1} M'C . \tag{6.3}$$

We assume the model not to be degenerate; M is of rank p. Then, there exists a $(n-p)n$ matrix, R, with rank $n-p$, such that $RM = 0$. The following proposition then holds (see Deleau and Malgrange (1979)).

Proposition 2: The variance-covariance matrix, S, of vector s being assumed of full-rank, the uncertainty frontier of system (6.1) with perfect information corresponds to the diagonals of all positive, semi-definite matrices Σ of rank $n-p$ such that

$$R \Sigma R' = RSR' \tag{6.4}$$

This proposition reflects the essential nature of efficient stabilisation of system (6.1) under perfect information: such stabilisation yields variance-covariance matrices 'as weakly definite-positive as possible' (i.e. of rank $n-p$), which implies efficient vectors in terms of the variances of the objectives, given that not all combinations of objectives can be stabilised (indicated by the structure of R).

This proposition can be made more precise for the particular and frequently considered case where there is one instrument less than objectives. Then R is a line vector $(r_1, \ldots, r_n)$ and efficient Σ matrices are all of rank 1.

Proposition 3: (Deleau and Malgrange (1979)): If $p = n-1$, the uncertainty frontier $\mathcal{R}$ under perfect information can be represented by:

$$\sum_{i=1}^{n} |r_i| \sqrt{\sigma_{ii}} = \sqrt{\sum_{i,j} r_i r_j s_{ij}} \tag{6.5}$$

These results can also be extended to the case of quadratic objective functions where C is not necessarily diagonal, and to other information structures (see Deleau and Malgrange (1979)).

2.2 Linear quadratic systems in state-variable form

We now consider a linear dynamic model in state-variable form:

$$x(t) = Ax(t-1) + Bd(t) + \epsilon(t) \tag{6.6}$$

where $\epsilon(t)$ is a stationary white noise, with variance-covariance matrix S. It is generally assumed for such systems that, when action d(t) is taken, $x(t-1)$ at least is known but not necessarily $\epsilon(t)$. For quadratic objective functions, the optimal policies are linear and of the following type:

$$d(t) = T(t)[Ax(t-1) + \hat{e}(t)] \tag{6.7}$$

where $\hat{e}(t)$ is the expected value of $\epsilon(t)$ conditional upon information at time t. T(t) is a p x n matrix which is not stationary for finite-horizon problems.

The case of an infinite horizon can of course yield stationary optimal policies. Provided A is stabilisable (i.e. there exists a p x n matrix G such that A + BG is stable) and if a non-zero weight[1] is put on every component of x in $x'Cx$, Proposition 4 below gives a straightforward extension of Proposition 2.

As before, B is assumed of maximal rank and U is a $(n-p) \times n$ matrix with rank $(n-p)$ such that $UB = 0$. Then

Proposition 4: If A is stabilisable, the stationary uncertainty frontier of system (6.6), when $\epsilon(t)$ is known at t, is generated by all semi-definite positive matrices Σ with rank $n-p$ such that:

$$U \Sigma U' = UA \Sigma A'U' + USU' . \tag{6.8}$$

When $\epsilon(t)$ is not known at t ($x(t-1)$ being still known), the same formula applies with

$$\Sigma = \tilde{\Sigma} + S \tag{6.9}$$

with $\tilde{\Sigma}$ semi-definite positive of rank $n-p$.
This proposition is a slight modification of Deleau and Malgrange (1979).

The specification of results (6.8) or (6.9) for $p = n-1$ and in terms of standard errors no longer gives (in general) hyperplanes but hyperbolic surfaces formed from differences or sums of squares. An illustration is given in section 2.3 below.

Finally, we recall the formulae giving the optimal stationary policy for a stabilisable model A and a positive definite matrix C:

$$T = -(B'HB)^{-1} B'H \tag{6.10}$$

with H defined by

$$H = C + A' [H - HB(B'HB)^{-1} B'H] A \tag{6.11}$$

Equation (6.11) can be solved using an iterative procedure. These results will be used in section 3.5.

2.3 An illustration

We consider the following very simple model:

$$x_1(t) = ax_1(t-1) + d(t) + \epsilon_1(t)$$

$$x_2(t) = bx_2(t-1) + d(t) + \epsilon_2(t)$$

with $\epsilon_1(t)$, $\epsilon_2(t)$ independent and of variance 1. In addition, a and b are assumed positive. In the static case (terms in $x(t-1)$ not taken into account), the uncertainty frontier under perfect information is given by:

$$\sqrt{\sigma_{11}} + \sqrt{\sigma_{22}} = \sqrt{2}$$

(see Proposition 3).

If only $\epsilon_1(t)$ is known, a straightforward extension gives the following equation

$$\sqrt{\sigma_{11}} + \sqrt{\sigma_{22} - 1} = 1$$

These two frontiers are drawn in figures 6.1 and 6.2.

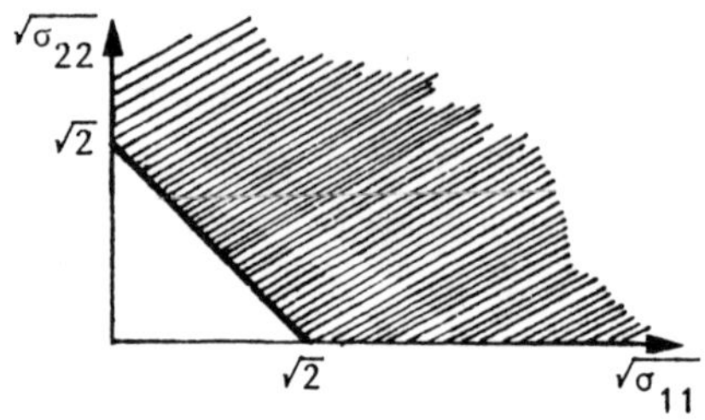

Figure 6.1

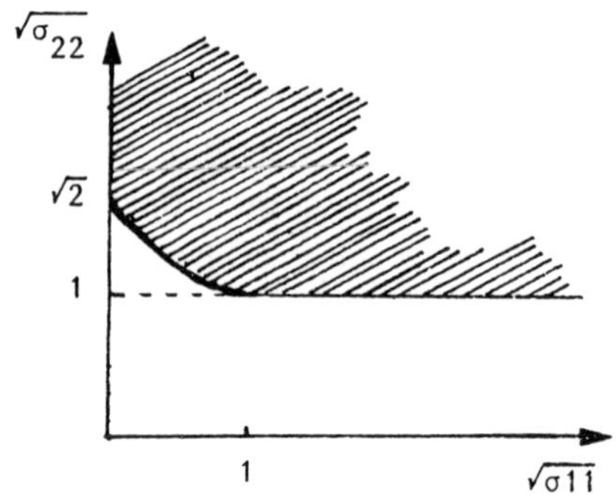

Figure 6.2

Figures 6.3 to 6.8 give the uncertainty frontier for optimal stationary dynamic stabilisations (equation (6.8)). Figures 6.4 and 6.6 correspond to cases where trying strongly to stabilise one objective may actually destabilise the other (infinite variance). In such cases, so long as a non-zero weight is put on this last objective, a boundary exists for the reduction of the variance of the first. For dynamic macromodels it may happen that the uncertainty frontier has, as in figure 6.6, ***a narrow 'angle'*** which implies a very limited field for efficient stationary stabilisation (see an example in Deleau and Malgrange (1979)). This will generally occur when divergent dynamics (for example, wage-price dynamics) are present in the model.

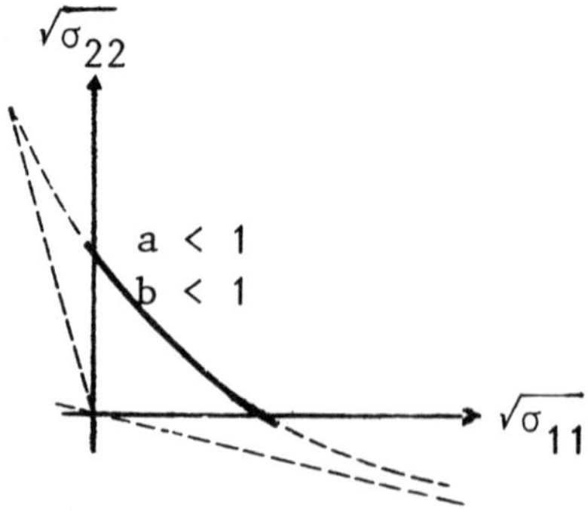

Figure 6.3

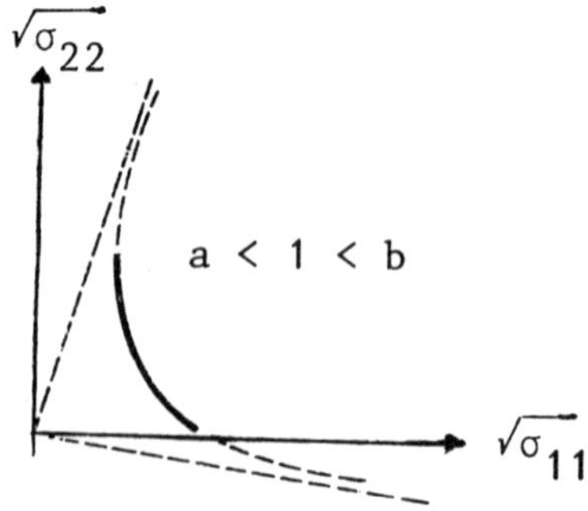

Figure 6.4

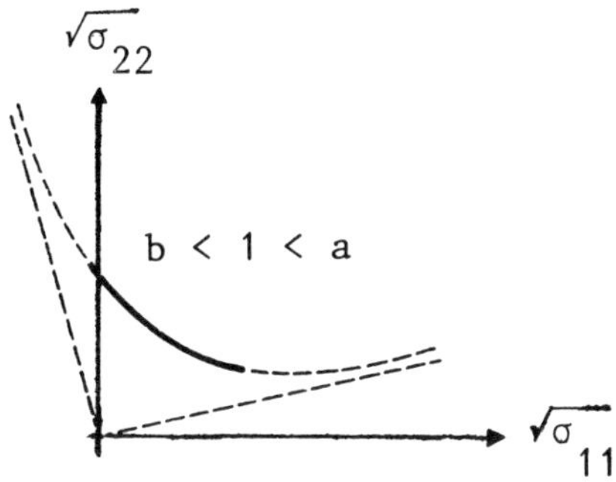

Figure 6.5

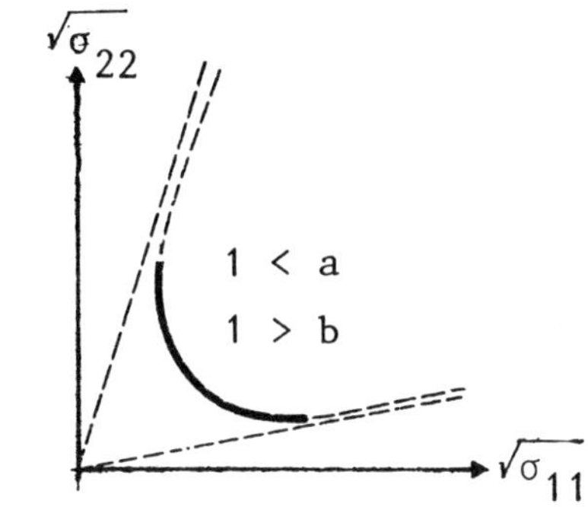

Figure 6.6

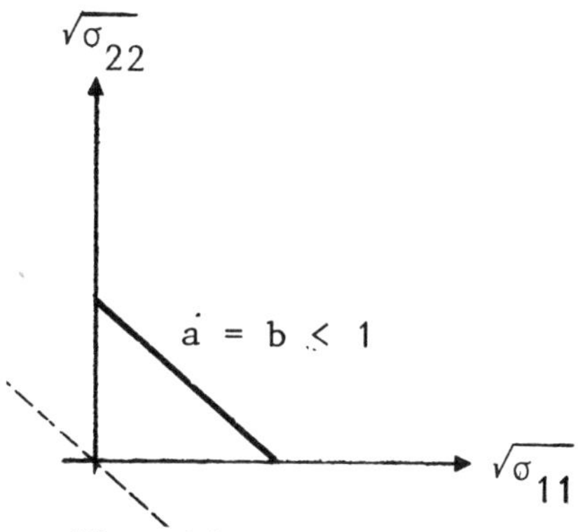

Figure 6.7

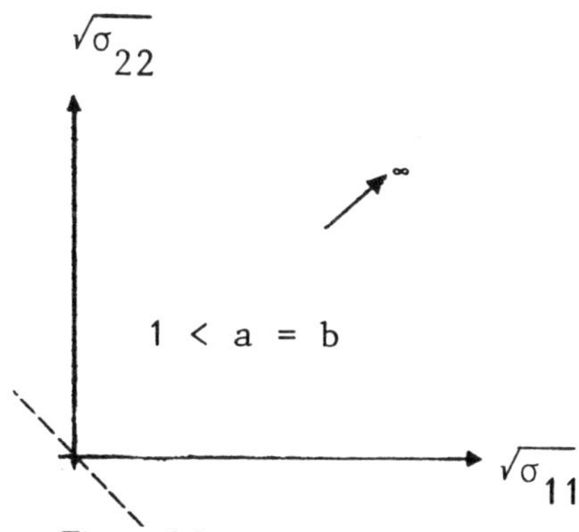

Figure 6.8

3. AN APPLICATION TO MICRO-DMS

3.1 The model

MICRO-DMS is a very small-scale version (Brillet (1982)) of the annual model DMS used by INSEE, in particular for five-year planning projections for the French economy (see Fouquet et al. (1978)). The DMS model has 2500 equations, but MICRO-DMS has only 17 which are set out in table 6.1. In that table, equation (1) defines desired non-agricultural employment as a linear function of production (complementary factors), and equation (2) defines actual non-agricultural employment. Total employment is given by equation (3). Job demand is given by equation (4); hence the definition of unemployment rate is given by equation (6).

Next, equation (5) is a measure of the capacity utilisation rate; equation (7) is a Phillips equation without money illusion (WA being the *real* wage rate). Equation

Table 6.1. MICRO-DMS: The equations

(1) $ND = (Q - \overline{QZ}) / \overline{PRODT}$

(2) $\text{Log}\dfrac{NA}{NA_{-1}} = \underset{(3.9)}{0.326}\ \text{Log}\dfrac{ND}{NA_{-1}} + \underset{(4.0)}{0.00882} + \epsilon_2 \qquad \sigma_{\epsilon_2} = 0.547 \times 10^{-4}$

(3) $N = NA + \overline{NZ}$

(4) $\dfrac{PD}{1.0131^t} = \underset{(-14)}{-0.55}\dfrac{(N - \overline{N})}{1.0131^t} + \underset{(31.5)}{797} + \epsilon_4 \qquad \sigma_{\epsilon_4} = 6660$

(5) $TU = 1.37\, Q/K$

(6) $UN = PD/(PD+N)$

(7) $\text{Log}\dfrac{WA}{WA_{-1}} = \underset{(-3.3)}{-0.994}UN + \underset{(8.4)}{0.0803} + \epsilon_7 \qquad \sigma_{\epsilon_7} = 0.204 \times 10^{-3}$

(8) $TP = [(Q - \overline{QZ})(1 - \overline{TAX}) - WA \times NA] / K$

(9) $C/(WA \times N + \overline{RDX}) = \underset{(193)}{0.877} + \epsilon_9 \qquad \sigma_{\epsilon_9} = 0.348 \times 10^{-3}$

(10) $I/K = \underset{(10.2)}{0.658}(I/K)_{-1} + \underset{(3.7)}{0.149}TP + \underset{(4.6)}{0.056}(Q/Q_{-1} \qquad \sigma_{\epsilon_{10}} = 0.181 \times 10^{-5}$

$\quad \overline{TU}/TU) + \underset{(2.5)}{0.145} + \epsilon_{10}$

(11) $DI = C + I + \overline{DA}$

(12) $\text{Log}(M/DI) = \underset{(-5)}{-0.265}\ \text{Log}(1 - TU) + \underset{(40)}{1.744}\overline{OUV} \underset{(-35)}{-3.7} + \epsilon_{12} \qquad \sigma_{\epsilon_{12}} = 0.632 \times 10^{-3}$

(13) $\text{Log}(P/P_{-1}) = \underset{(6.1)}{0.562}\ \text{Log}\left[\dfrac{P.WA.N}{Q} / \left(\dfrac{P.WA.N}{Q}\right)_{-1}\right] \qquad \sigma_{\epsilon_{13}} = 0.103 \times 10^{-3}$

$\quad \underset{(-3.5)}{-1.143}(TP - \overline{TP})_{-1} + \underset{(1.5)}{0.239}(TU - \overline{TU})$

$\quad + \underset{(3.9)}{0.022} + \epsilon_{13}$

(14) $\text{Log}(X/\overline{DM}) = -\underset{(-3.3)}{1.355}\ TU + \underset{(4)}{0.717}\ \text{Log}(\overline{PE}/P)$ $\qquad \sigma_{\epsilon_{14}} = 0.854\text{x}10^{-3}$

$+\underset{(6.8)}{0.387}\ \overline{OUV} + \underset{(36)}{12.6} + \epsilon_{14}$

(15) $Q = DI + X - M$

(16) $SE = (P\ X)/(\overline{PE}\ M)$

(17) $K = 0.963\ K_{-1} + I_{-1}$

List of symbols for table 6.1.

Endogenous variables

C	Real household consumption
DI	Total real domestic demand
I	Real productive investment
K	Real productive capital
M	Real imports
N	Total employment
NA	Employment except agriculture
ND	Optimal employment except agriculture
P	Domestic price index
PD	Level of unemployment
Q	Total real valued added
SE	Foreign trade imbalance
TP	Profit rate
TU	Capacity utilisation rate
UN	Unemployment rate
WA	Real wage rate
X	Real exports

Exogenous variables

$\overline{DA}$	Real autonomous expenditures
$\overline{DM}$	Foreign demand
$\overline{N}$	Labour force trend
$\overline{NZ}$	Employment in agriculture
$\overline{OUV}$	Indicator of the degree of openness
$\overline{PE}$	Foreign price index
PRODT	Productivity trend
$\overline{QZ}$	Real value added in agriculture
$\overline{RDX}$	Real autonomous disposable income
$\overline{TAX}$	Value added tax
$\overline{TP}$	Trend of profit rate
$\overline{TU}$	Trend of capacity utilisation rate

(8) then provides a definition of the profit rate, and equation (9) is a standard consumption function.

As in the original model, investment is determined by a combination of accelerator and profitability mechanisms (equation (10)). Equations (12) and (14) are standard imports and exports equations.

The price equation, (13), describes a dynamic adjustment of prices to costs, with an influence of capacity utilisation and profits. Equation (16) is a measure of foreign trade imbalance (exports over imports in value terms). Finally, equation (17) defines capital accumulation.

The short run output multiplier of public expenditure is rather low, 0.71, due to the effects of increases in imports and to the weakness of consumption effects. The latter weak multiplier is associated with the rather inert wages and employment variables in this model. In fact the output multiplier can be decomposed as follows:

Variable	Q	C	I	DA	X–M	P%
Multiplier	0.71	0.11	0.16	1.00	–0.56	0.023

Eight variables appear with a lag: NA, N, WA, Q, K, I, P and TP. In fact, as shown below, the actual dynamic order of the system is five.

3.2 The long run system

The relations given in table 6.1 are specified so as to allow for the existence of a 'long run solution' (for more details about this concept, and the associated methodology, see Deleau, Malgrange and Muet (1981 or 1982)). Such a solution is characterised by constant growth rates (not necessarily identical for all the variables of the system) and an identity between the expected, or desired, values and the actual values.

In the present case, there exist three basic different growth rates, which are defined exogenously:

- g for Q, C, I, $\overline{DA}$, X, M and K (given by the assumption about the growth of $\overline{DA}$),
- n for NA, ND, N, PD (given by the assumption about the growth of $\overline{N}_0$),
- ρ for P and $\overline{PE}$ (given by the assumption about the growth of $\overline{PE}$).

The growth rate of real wage is then equal to $\frac{1+g}{1+n} - 1$.

These growth rates are taken to be equal to 0.0515 for g, 0.0131 for n, 0.0631 for ρ. These figures represent the average growth rates of the relevant variables on the sample period 1960–1978.

Finally, the initial levels associated with a long run solution should satisfy the relations of the 'long run system' given in table 6.2. It can be seen that the causalities implied by this long run system are very different from those associated with the short run one:

- the capacity utilisation and profit rates are simultaneously determined, indepedently of the rest of the system,
- the unemployment rate is also predetermined.

Table 6.2. MICRO-DMS: The long run system

(E10) $(1-0.658)(g+\delta) = 0.149TP^* + 0.056(1+g-\overline{TU}/TU^*) + 0.0145$

(E13) $(1-0.562)\rho = -1.143(TP^*-\overline{TP}) + 0.239(TU^*-\overline{TU}) + 0.022$

(E7) $(1+g)/(1+n) - 1 = -0.994UN^* + 0.0803$

(E6) $PD^* = N^*\, UN^*/(1-UN^*)$

(E4) $N^* = \overline{N}_0^* - (PD^*-797)/0.55$

(E3) $NA^* = N^* - \overline{NZ}^*$

(E2) $ND^* = NA^*$

(E1) $Q^* = \overline{QZ}^* + ND^*.\overline{PRODT}$

(E5) $K^* = 1.37\, Q^*/TU^*$

(E17) $I^* = (g+\delta)K^*$

(E8) $WA^* = [(Q^*-\overline{QZ}^*)(1-\overline{TAX}) - K^*\, TP^*]/NA^*$

(E9) $C^* = 0.877\,(WA^*.N^* + \overline{RDX}^*)$

(E11) $DI^* = C^* + I^* + \overline{DA}^*$

(E12) $\text{Log}\, M^* = \text{Log}\, DI^* - 0.265\, \text{Log}\,(1-TU^*) + 1.744\,\overline{OUV}^* - 3.7$

(E15) $X^* = Q^* + M^* - DI^*$

(E14) $P^* = \overline{PE}^*[(\overline{DM}^*/X^*)\exp(12.6 + 0.387\overline{OUV}^* - 1.355TU^*)]^{1/0.717}$

(E16) $SE^* = (P^*.X^*)/(\overline{PE}^*.M^*)$

The first property follows from the formulation of investment and price equations, the second from the Phillips equation. This last feature is a very common one in macroeconomic models; whereas they are 'demand models' in the short run, the associated long run system is of a supply type with some kind of 'natural unemployment rate' (see Courbis (1980), Deleau, Malgrange and Muet (1981, 1982), Le Van (1983), Malgrange (1982)).

3.3 A linear stationary representation

The existence of a long run solution for the model is used to obtain a particular linear approximation.

First the following transformation of variables is made:

$$x_t = \text{Log}\,\frac{X_t}{(1+x)^t}$$

with X_t = original variable.
x = associated long run growth rate.

The long run solution of the original model then appears as a stationary solution of the transformed system, which is linearised around this stationary solution. The result is given in table 6.3.

We turn now to the use of this last model within the stabilisation framework of Part 2. Three objective variables are defined, namely unemployment (pd), prices (p), foreign trade (se). Three decision variables are also selected: public expenditures ($\overline{da}$), tax rate ($\overline{TAX}$), exchange rate (through $\overline{pe}$). In fact, it will be seen that $\overline{da}$ and $\overline{TAX}$ have almost collinear effects. Hence, either ($\overline{da}$, $\overline{pe}$) or ($\overline{TAX}$, $\overline{pe}$) are used.

Finally, the uncontrolled uncertain variables are identified with the residuals of the behavioural equations (see table 6.3), plus the difference between actual foreign demand ($\overline{dm}$) and its trend. They are assumed to be independent, zero mean, random variables, with variances estimated through OLS techniques. This specification of uncertainty is of course crude and incomplete (see Fair (1980)) but it constitutes a useful first approximation.

Given this choice of variables, the system can be put into a standard state variable form. This is done below.

Table 6.3. MICRO-DMS: A linearised stationary approximation

(L1) $nd = 1.092\ q$

(L2) $na = 0.326\ nd + 0.674\ na_{-1} + \epsilon_2$

(L3) $n = 0.676\ na$

(L4) $pd = -12.31\ n + 0.0010\ \epsilon_4$

(L5) $TU = 0.856\ (q-k)$

(L6) $UN = 0.0408(pd-n)$

(L7) $wa = -0.994\ UN + wa_{-1} + \epsilon_7$

(L8) $TP = 0.31\ q - 0.202(wa+na) - 0.081\ k - 0.29\ \overline{TAX}$

(L9) $c = 0.533\ (wa+na) + 1.14\ \epsilon_9$

(L10) $i = 1.68\ TP + 0.665\ q + 0.728\ TU + k + 0.658\ (i_{-1}-k_{-1}) - 0.665\ q_{-1} + \epsilon_{10}$

(L11) $di = 0.77\ c + 0.138\ i + 0.092\ \overline{da}$

(L12) $m = di + 1.84\ TU + \epsilon_{12}$

(L13) $p = 1.28(n+wa-q) + 0.546\ TU + p_{-1} - 1.28(n_{-1}+wa_{-1}-q_{-1})$
$- 2.61\ TP_{-1} + \epsilon_{13}$

(L14) $x = -1.36\ TU - 0.717\ p + 0.717\ \overline{pe} + \epsilon_{14} + \overline{dm}$

(L15) $se = p + x - m - \overline{pe}$

(L16) $q = 0.785\ c + 0.141\ i + 0.171\ x - 0.192\ m + 0.094\ \overline{da}$

(L17) $k = 0.916\ k_{-1} + 0.084\ i_{-1}$

3.4 Short run uncertainty frontiers

We first consider the short run reduced form which is given by:

$$\begin{bmatrix} pd \\ p \\ se \end{bmatrix} = \begin{bmatrix} 0.145 & -\ 0.198 & -\ 0.318 \\ 0.017 & -\ 0.023 & -\ 0.037 \\ 0.225 & -\ 0.307 & -\ 0.627 \end{bmatrix} \begin{bmatrix} \overline{TAX} \\ \overline{da} \\ \overline{pe} \end{bmatrix} + \begin{bmatrix} \eta_1 \\ \eta_2 \\ \eta_3 \end{bmatrix} \qquad (6.12)$$

The effects of any instrument have the same sign on each target, with a strong collinearity for $\overline{TAX}$ and $\overline{da}$. Prices are very rigid in the short run, as is usual in macroeconometric models.

The η_i variables are of course linear combinations of the original uncontrolled variables ϵ_i and $\overline{dm}^2$, with the following variance-covariance matrix:

$$S = \begin{bmatrix} 0.0212 & 0.00008 & -0.0065 \\ 0.00008 & 0.00112 & -0.00058 \\ -0.0065 & -0.00058 & 0.0136 \end{bmatrix}$$

This matrix reflects the short run rigidity of prices, as well as the secondary importance of cross-effects.

The linearity of the model allows for a decomposition of the ex ante variances of the objectives (the diagonal of S), with respect to the various original residuals. This is done in table 6.4.

Table 6.4. Decomposition of ex ante variables

	ϵ_2/na	ϵ_4/pd	ϵ_7/wa	ϵ_9/c	ϵ_{10}/i	ϵ_{12}/m	ϵ_{13}/p	ϵ_{14}/x	$\overline{dm}$/x
η_1	<u>0.194</u>	<u>0.382</u>	0.001	0.058	0.001	0.011	0.003	0.011	<u>0.342</u>
η_2	0.082	0.018	<u>0.280</u>	0.015	ϵ	0.002	<u>0.515</u>	0.002	0.086
η_3	0.001	ϵ	0.002	<u>0.219</u>	0.004	0.001	0.015	0.001	<u>0.738</u>

A rather clear decomposition appears:

- the (ex ante) uncertainty on employment is mainly due to the uncertainty in the 'job market' equations (58%) and in foreign demand (34%).

- the uncertainty in prices is largely caused by the uncertainty in prices and wages (80%).
- the uncertainty about the foreign balance rests heavily on the uncertainty about foreign demand (74%) and also about consumption (22%).

Since $\overline{TAX}$ and $\overline{da}$ are collinear, we restrict ourselves to the pair $(\overline{da}, \overline{pe})$. The application of Proposition 3 gives the following relation between standard errors of objectives:

$$e_p + 0.113\, e_{pd} + 0.0007\, e_{se} = 0.037 \tag{6.13}$$

where e_i denotes the standard error of objective i.

It can be seen that neglecting either p or pd raises their variances moderately, when the other two objectives are perfectly stabilised. In contrast, a perfect stabilisation of prices and employment very strongly destabilises the foreign balance: its standard error rises to 5300% against 12% ex ante! This is due to the near perfect collinearity of instruments $\overline{da}$ and $\overline{pe}$ with respect to the objectives p and pd.

The relative insensitivity of prices in the short run, as reflected by equation (6.12), justifies paying particular attention to the stabilisation of se and pd only, using either $\overline{pe}$ or $\overline{da}$ to do so. The uncertainty frontiers corresponding to perfect information are given in figure 6.9.

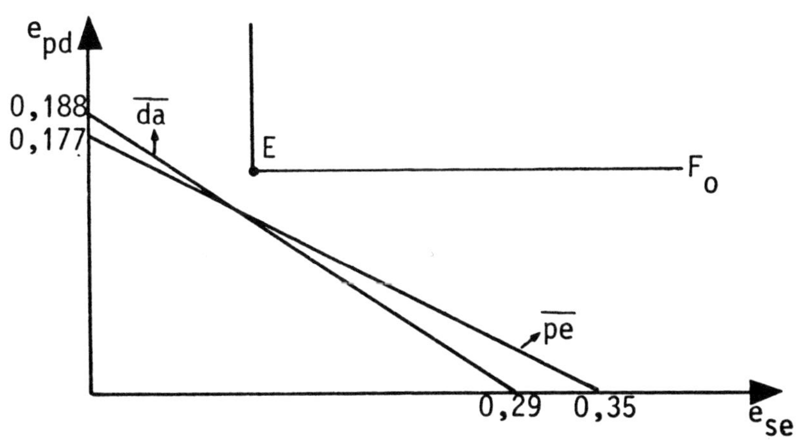

Figure 6.9.

It appears that both instruments have rather similar stabilisation effects and that they are not very effective when used in isolation (compare their frontiers with the 'no-information frontier' F_o).

Finally, figure 6.10 gives the uncertainty frontiers for the triplet (pd, se, $\overline{da}$) under the following informational constraints:

- F(o) : no information
- F(2+4) : ϵ_2 and ϵ_4 are observed
- F($\overline{dm}$) : $\overline{dm}$ is observed
- F(2+4 $\overline{dm}$) : ϵ_2, ϵ_4 and $\overline{dm}$ are observed
- F(2+4+9+$\overline{dm}$) : ϵ_2, ϵ_4, ϵ_9 and $\overline{dm}$ are observed
- F(Ω) : perfect information.

The shapes of these various frontiers can be easily compared with the previous decomposition of ex ante variances.

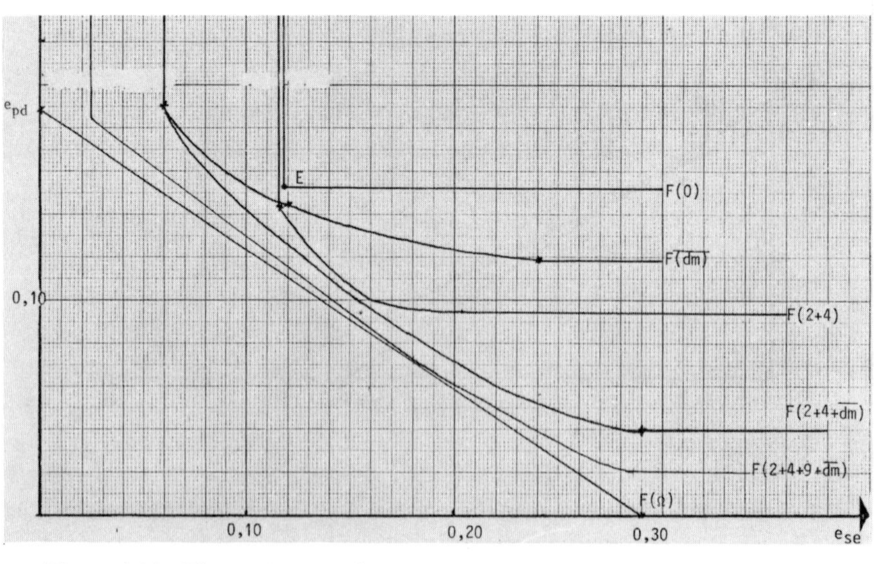

Figure 6.10. The static case: short run uncertainty frontiers

3.5 Long run uncertainty frontiers

We now turn to the dynamic state-variable representation of the linearised model. As noted above, a representation of order five can be obtained for the deterministic part of the model:

$$\begin{bmatrix} na \\ wa \\ i \\ p \\ k \end{bmatrix} = \begin{bmatrix} 0.709 & 0.063 & 0.036 & -0.035 & 0.122 \\ 0.259 & 1.023 & 0.013 & -0.013 & 0.044 \\ -0.255 & -0.199 & 0.792 & -0.106 & -0.098 \\ 0.616 & 0.597 & -0.039 & 0.997 & -0.184 \\ 0 & 0 & 0.084 & 0 & 0.916 \end{bmatrix} \begin{bmatrix} na_{-1} \\ wa_{-1} \\ i_{-1} \\ p_{-1} \\ k_{-1} \end{bmatrix} \tag{6.14}$$

The eigenvalues associated with this system are the following:

$$\left.\begin{aligned} \lambda_1, \lambda_2 &= 1.061 \pm 0.199\, i & |\lambda_1| &= 1.080 \\ \lambda_3, \lambda_4 &= 0.819 \pm 0.099\, i & |\lambda_3| &= 0.825 \\ \lambda_5 &= 0.676 & |\lambda_5| &= 0.676 \end{aligned}\right\} \tag{6.15}$$

The endogenous dynamics are thus unstable: a 'no-stabilisation' policy (constant action) would result in infinite variances. It can be checked, by means of sensitivity analysis, that the explosive eigenvalues are 'associated' with wage-price dynamics (wa, p), the cyclical ones with capital accumulation dynamics (i, k), and the monotonic eigenvalues with the productivity cycle (na). These features are indeed rather characteristic of a standard macroeconometric model.

In contrast with the static problem, an analytic computation of the uncertainty frontier is no longer possible as in the illustration section 2.3, since the relevant space here is of dimension 7: the two 'true' objectives, pd and se, which are not state variables, and the five state variables, which are 'indirectly' taken into account.

For this dynamic problem, the efficient vector of variances must be computed by an iterative application of the standard dynamic control formulae (6.10)–(6.11) (for more details see Taylor (1979)). Figure 6.11 displays uncertainty frontiers corresponding to two objectives, pd or p and se, one instrument, either $\overline{pe}$ or $\overline{da}$, and different informational constraints as follows:

- LR1 : objectives pd and se, instrument $\overline{pe}$, perfect information.
- LR2 : objectives pd and se, instrument $\overline{da}$, perfect information.
- LR3 : objectives p and se, instrument $\overline{da}$, perfect information.
- LR(0) : objectives pd and se, instrument $\overline{da}$, all uncontrolled variables observed with a one-period lag.

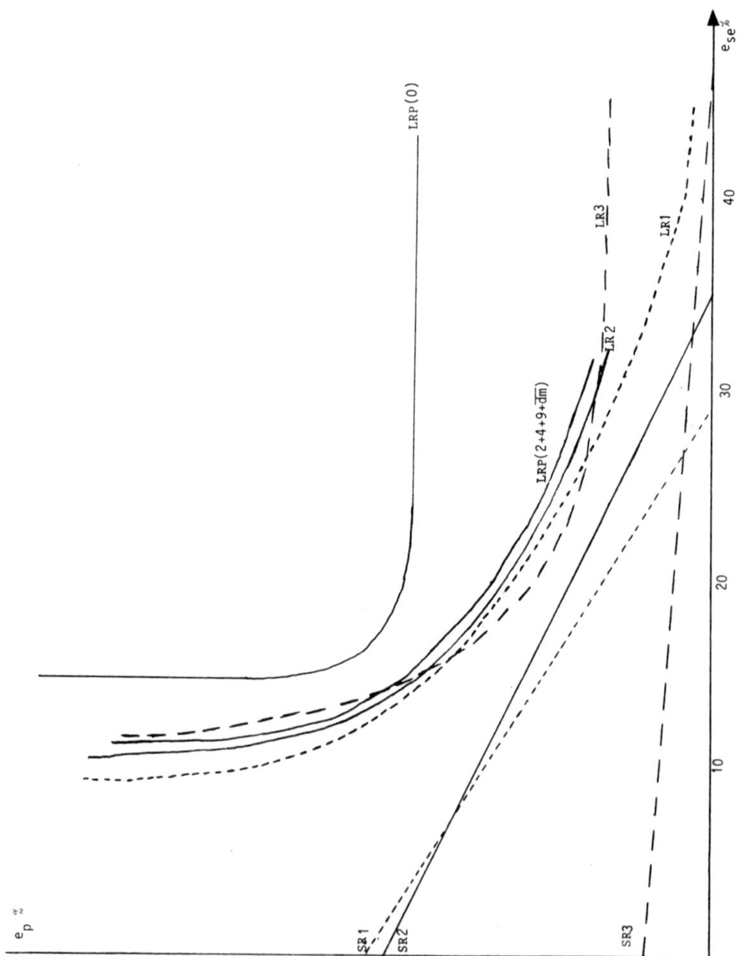

e_{pd} %
e_p %
30
20
10
SR1
SR2
SR3
LRP(0)
LRP(2+4+9+$\overline{dm}$)
LR1
LR2
LR3
10
20
30
40
e_{se}%

Figure 6.11.

- LRP(2+4+9+$\overline{\text{dm}}$) : objectives pd and se, instrument $\overline{\text{da}}$, perfect information about ϵ_2, ϵ_4, ϵ_9 and $\overline{\text{dm}}$.

Three short-run frontiers are also reproduced:

- SR1 : objectives pd and se, instrument $\overline{\text{pe}}$, perfect information.
- SR2 : objectives pd and se, instrument $\overline{\text{da}}$, perfect information.
- SR3 : objectives p and se, instrument $\overline{\text{da}}$, perfect information.

The following observations can be made:

- comparing SR_i and LR_i (i=1, 2, 3) shows how the dynamic feedbacks affect the stabilisation trade-offs. The modification is particularly important for p and se (from SR3 to LR3). Whereas in the short run prices are rigid, the wage-price dynamics, which are unstable, become relevant in the long run. Moreover, it can be checked that, in the dynamic case, it is not possible to reduce the variance of se beyond a certain limit without destabilising pd (or p).
- for dynamic stabilisation of pd and se, $\overline{\text{da}}$ is slightly more efficient than $\overline{\text{pe}}$.
- there is no big loss for these two objectives in taking into account ϵ_2, ϵ_4, ϵ_9 and $\overline{\text{dm}}$ only.
- a one period lag in information reduces noticeably the efficiency of stabilisation (from LR2 to LRP(0)), within a rather narrow angle.

4. CONCLUSION

With respect to previous studies which have been more concerned with analytical results, this chapter shows the applicability of the concept of uncertainty frontier to an estimated macroeconometric model which is small but with realistic properties. This concept provides a synthetic characterisation of the stochastic stabilisation short run and long run properties of the model, while allowing clear structural interpretations.

Further developments can be viewed in two directions. One concerns the applicability of our approach to large macroeconometric models. We think that it should be tractable. Despite their size and apparent diversity, it is now well recognised that the structures of such models are similar (Deleau, Malgrange and Muet (1981, 1982)) and can be, in fact, 'compacted' without noticeably altering their properties (for recent results about policy multipliers see Bureau and Norotte (1982, 1983) and Hughes Hallett and Rees (1983)). These homegeneity and simplicity characteristics should make feasible and interesting the application of previous techniques to large macroeconometric models, so as to get a synthetic characterisation of their stabilisation properties with possible structural comparative interpretations.

The other direction deals with applications to economic policy problems. It seems also that the concepts and techniques used in this chapter could be of help for analysing some actual economic policy questions, such as the coordination between medium-run objectives and short-run stabilisation measures. In this way, they could enlarge the application of optimisation methods (e.g. Gauron and Maurice (1980)) to macroeconometric models for decision making procedures.

NOTES

* We are indebted to the 'Service des Programmes' (INSEE) for permitting to make use of the MICRO-DMS model and of its data bank and to J.C. Brillet for his particular assistance.

1. If a zero-weight is put on some objectives, then mathematical 'peculiarities' may occur due to the fact that it does not matter if those objectives are not stabilised at all and they may even have an infinite variance (see Deleau and Malgrange (1979)). The uncertainty frontier, and the set of efficient stabilisation policies, are then not necessarily closed; for these problems see also Turnovsky (1974, 1977).
2. Recall that the ϵ_i's and $\overline{dm}$ are supposed to be independently distributed. Their standard errors are given in table 6.1.

REFERENCES

Brillet, J.L. (1982), 'L'Equation de Phillips: comparaison sur une maquette de plusieurs formulations alternatives', Working Paper, *INSEE,* Service des Programmes.

Bureau, D. and M. Norotte (1982), 'Quand l'analyse des données s'intéresse à la politique économique', Working Paper 79 C 32, *Direction de la Prévision.*

Bureau, D. and M. Norotte (1983), 'De METRIC à DMS', Working Paper 107 C 33, *Direction de la Prévision.*

Chow, G. (1975), *Analysis and Control of Dynamic Economic Systems,* John Wiley, New York.

Courbis, R. (1980), 'Une reformulation dynamique de la theorie des économies concurrencées', *Economie Appliquée,* Vol. 33, no. 1.

Deleau, M. and P. Malgrange (1972), 'Information et politiques dynamiques contraléatoires', *Annales de l'INSEE,* No. 9.

Deleau, M. and P. Malgrange (1979), 'Efficient stabilisation of economic systems: some global analytical results for the linear quadratic case', *European Economic Review,* No. 12.

Deleau, M., P. Malgrange and P.A. Muet (1981), 'Une maquette représentative des modèles économiques', *Annales de l'INSEE,* No. 42.

Deleau, M., P. Malgrange and P.A. Muet (1982), 'A study of short run and long run properties of macroeconometric dynamic models by means of an aggregative core model', in: P. Malgrange and P.A. Muet (eds.), *Contemporary Macroeconomic Modelling*, Basil Blackwell, Oxford (forthcoming).

Fair, R. (1980), 'Estimating the expected predictive accuracy of econometric models', *International Economic Review*, 21-2.

Fouquet, D., J.M. Charpin, H. Guillaume, P.A. Muet and D. Vallet (1978), 'Le modèle DMS', *Collections de l'INSEE*, Serie C.

Gauron, A. and J. Maurice (1980), 'Des politiques économiques pour le VIIIe Plan: exploration de l'ensemble des possibles', *Revue Economique*, 31-5.

Hughes Hallett, A.J. and H.J.B. Rees (1983), *Quantitative Economic Policies and Interactive Planning*, Cambridge University Press, Cambridge.

Le Van, C. (1983), 'Etude de la stabilité du sentier d'équilibre d'une maquette d'économie ouverte', *Annales de l'INSEE*, No. 50.

Malgrange, P. (1982), 'Steady growth path in a short run dynamic model: The case of the French quarterly model METRIC', Working-Paper, *CEPREMAP*.

Marschak, J. and R. Radner (1972), *Economic Theory of Teams*, Yale University Press, New Haven.

Taylor, J. (1979), 'Estimation and control of a macroeconomic model with rational expectations', *Econometrica*, 47-5.

Turnovsky, S. (1974), 'The stability properties of optimal economic policies', *American Economic Review*, 44-1.

Turnovsky, S. (1977), 'Optimal control of linear systems with stochastic coefficients and additive disturbances', in: J. Pitchford and S. Turnovsky (eds.), *Applications of Control Theory to Economic Analysis*, North-Holland, Amsterdam.

PART III

POLICY ANALYSIS AND DECISION MODELS

CHAPTER 7

INCOMES POLICY IN A POLITICAL ENVIRONMENT: A STRUCTURAL MODEL FOR THE U.K. 1961–1980

Meghad Desai, Manfred Keil and Sushil Wadhwani
London School of Economics, U.K.

1. INTRODUCTION

Incomes policies, meaning thereby policies designed to regulate the rate of growth of money wages (or earnings) and/or prices, have been frequently used in many countries as inflation control devices. They have been much discussed and currently seem to be out of favour both in left wing parties with their trade union supporters, and in right wing parties which believe instead in the market mechanism. Some trade unionists have taken the view that incomes policies are very effective in restraining the growth of nominal earnings, but not of prices, and hence lead to a cut in real wages; see Ormerod in Currie and Smith (1981) for a survey of the 'Left' views. The view of monetarist and market orientated economists is that incomes policies distort the labour market in the short run, and only postpone upward pressures on wages and prices which break through to render incomes policies potentially unpopular (Johnson (1972), Laidler (1980)). Our purpose in this chapter is to understand the decisions by governments to impose policies in the context of the political (electoral) as well as economic objectives of that government. Our model is set up in the U.K. context where incomes policies were used in two thirds of the period between 1961 and 1978; and where the electoral system, which allows for irregularly timed elections, makes the problem of integrating the political with the economic a challenging one.

We outline the econometric background of the incomes policy research in section 2 and point out the obvious gap in that area. Endogenising the decisions of a government seeking re-election yields a plausible rule for the behaviour of the con-

Hughes Hallett, A.J. (ed.) Applied Decision Analysis and Economic Behaviour

ISBN 90-247-2968-8. Printed in The Netherlands

trol variable we are interested in. This optimising rule is then used as a foundation for specifying and estimating an equation for incomes policies. We add to this the mutual dependence of these two variables. Our estimates are then given and their implications brought out in concluding remarks.

2. ECONOMETRIC MODELS OF INCOMES POLICIES

The pioneering work in this area was by Lipsey and Parkin (LP) who set the mould in which subsequent econometric debate about the efficacy of incomes policies has been carried out (Lipsey and Parkin (1970)). LP specified equations for wage and price inflation separately for periods when incomes policies were on and for periods when incomes policies were off. They also combined all the observations in a single equation by specifying a dummy variable taking 1 for 'policy-on' and 0 for 'policy-off' periods. They came to the conclusion that incomes policies were not very effective in controlling wage and/or price inflation.

While LP's equations were shown to suffer from dynamic misspecification as well as identification problems by K. Wallis (Wallis (1971), see also Desai (1976)), their substantive views about the inefficiency of incomes policies have been echoed by many economists (see Fallick and Elliott (1981), Chater, Dean and Elliott (1982)).

Our purpose in this chapter is to propose an alternative way of modelling the role of incomes policies. As we indicated above, in all econometric work to date, incomes policy episodes appear as exogenous dummy variables taking a value of 1 when the policy is on and 0 otherwise. While some attempt is made to distinguish between different episodes, there is no attempt to check whether the decision to impose or switch off incomes policy itself was not influenced by the prevailing economic environment (e.g. wages, price trends) as well as the political exigencies of the situation (the imminence of elections, by-election defeats, strikes). This is surprising as the plea to endogenise incomes policy decisions was originally made by Wallis in his critique of Lipsey-Parkin. As he put it, '. . . the decision to impose an incomes policy is not independent of the values of the variables of the model, and although treated as exogenous the policy itself must surely be a jointly dependent endogenous variable' (Wallis, op. cit., p. 309).

Once we decide to endogenise the *decision* to impose an incomes policy, we have to specify explicitly the information set available to the decision maker (the government). In particular, we have to model such a decision in *ex ante* terms. We also need to be aware that, in parliamentary democracies with periodic elections, economic (as well as other policies) are generally perceived by the government as instruments which enhance the re-election probabilities of the party in power. Thus we have to integrate the work on incomes policies with the recent work on the political business cycle (Alt (1980), Nordhaus (1975), McRae (1977), Minford and Peel (1981)).

3. A THEORETICAL MODEL OF ECONOMIC POLICY IN A POLITICAL CONTEXT

At the most general level, we can postulate that a party in power, having just been elected, would like eventually to be re-elected. It may have other purposes related to its social vision or its ideology which may embody its long run view, but we stick to the immediate goals. So the government must judge at each moment the number of votes it can get when elections come round again. Let us suppose that is specifies a voting function F giving the votes cast for it in terms of a set of variables. These could be economic objective variables (y) such as growth of real income, unemployment, foreign reserves. There would be the policy instruments (c) which can be seen as the cost of obtaining the y variables. These are variables such as the tax burden, the interest rate, incomes policy. But these variables do not exhaust the determinants of a government's popularity. The phase of the electoral cycle –how recently the elections have been held, how soon the next election must be held as well as the size of the majority will compromise the political variables (z). There are also social tension variables (s) such as strikes which affect government popularity.

We can thus define the 'present value' of votes obtained by the government at the date T of the next election as

$$V(T) = \int_0^T F(y(t), c(t), z(t), s(t)) e^{\mu(t-T)} dt \qquad (7.1)$$

In equation (7.1), μ denotes the discount factor which the government uses. It indicates the rate at which the citizen's memories decay or the extent to which the government chooses to ignore unpopularity in the period between elections. Thus if the government caters only for the votes obtained at the next election, it may choose a very high value for μ. Of course there is a critical value $\bar{V}$ which V must cross. Thus since the government has just got elected it must be true that $V(0) \geqslant \bar{V}$. The government's job is then to maximise V(T) in such a way that $V(T) \geqslant \bar{V}$.

This problem would be a straightforward problem in dynamic optimisation were it not for some further complications, such as the date of the next election T not being known with certainty. Thus in the U.S. case, the problem is straightforward. But we are interested in the U.K. case which being more complicated is also more general. It is easy enough to accommodate uncertainty into the dynamic optimisation framework and have the government maximise the expected value EV(θ) for the random variable θ whic determines the date of the next election. Elections are however discrete events with a specific calendar date and the government has to ensure that it gets sufficient votes on that date to be re-elected. Thus we need to combine a continuous time model with continuous constraints (the economic model) and a discrete constraint concerning votes on the unknown election date. Frey and Lau (1968) pose this problem but recognise the technical difficulties it poses.

An alternative is to cast the objective function and the model in a discrete stochastic framework and derive the control rule. Ginsburgh and Michel (1983) –GM– have done this with respect to Nordhaus' model. In terms of our notiation in equation (7.1) they write the maximand as the expected number of votes a party in power obtains on the election date. The function F is cast as a voting function in terms of unemployment (U) and inflation (π). The constraints are an expectations augmented Phillips curve and an adaptive expectations equation for expected inflation (π^e). It may be useful for our purposes to briefly lay out their discussion as it illustrates the difficulties of deriving an analytical rule in our case.

The government's problem is

$$\text{Max } E_{t=\tau}\ (V(0)) = \sum_{t=\tau}^{T-1} p_t F(U_t, \pi_t) \tag{7.2a}$$

where

$$p_t = \sum_{\theta=t+1}^{T} (1+\mu)^{t+1-\theta}\ p(R_\theta) \tag{7.2b}$$

Here $p(R_\theta)$ is the probability of the event that elections will take place in the period θ and $(1+\mu)$ is the discount rate. The other equations are

$$\pi_t = \alpha_0 - \alpha_1 U_t + \lambda \pi_t^e \tag{7.3a}$$

$$\Delta \pi_t^e = \gamma(\pi_t - \pi_t^e) \tag{7.3b}$$

$$F(U_t, \pi_t) = c - U_t^2 - \beta \pi_t \tag{7.3c}$$

Equation (7.3a) is the Phillips curve, and (7.3b) is the adaptive expectations equation where Δ is a forward difference operator. In equation (7.3c), c is a constant. Given equations (7.2a), (7.2b), (7.3a), (7.3b) and (7.3c), the lagrangean function is

$$\ell = \sum_{t=0}^{T-1} p_t(c - U_t^2 - \beta\pi_t) - \sum_{t=0}^{T-1} \psi_{t+1} \left[\gamma\left[\alpha_0 - \alpha_1 U_t + (\lambda-1)\pi_t^e\right] - \Delta\pi_t^e\right] \tag{7.4}$$

Deriving the usual first order conditions and solving out for the unobservable ψ, we get a simple stochastic control rule for the instrument U_t:

$$\Delta U_t^* = \left(\frac{\beta\alpha_1'}{2}\right)\left(\frac{\gamma(\lambda-1)}{1+\gamma(\lambda-1)}\right) - \frac{\gamma(\lambda-1)}{(1+\gamma(\lambda-1))} U_t^* - \frac{\gamma\alpha_1\beta\lambda}{2}\left(\frac{p_{t+1}}{p_t}\right) \tag{7.5}$$

(GM do not derive this rule explicitly but it can be shown to follow from the dynamic optimisation exercise).

Equation (7.5) summarises the essential character of a political business cycle model with uncertainty. Thus we have a rule for the optimal path of the control variable U_t^* which depends, apart from a constant and the previous level of the variable itself, on a term capturing the odds of elections happening in t + 1 as against t. The variable p_t follows a recursion relation as can be seen from (7.2b) and hence p_{t+1}/p_t can be approximated by $p(R_{t+1})/p(R_t)$. Thus the optimal path of the control variable depends on the odds of elections happening. Notice that if we have no money illusion ($\gamma = 1$), equation (7.5) collapses to a random walk in U^* with the random term depending on the odds of election occuring in t+1 as against t. The important thing is that governments may seek to lower U even in a world without money illusion. If we had longer lags in the structural equations (7.3a) – (7.3c) then we should get a term of the type (p_{t+k}/p_t) in equation (7.5) allowing for longer term intervention. By analogy one can extend this argument to a rational expectations world.

The simple structure of the Nordhaus problem, when extended to a discrete stochastic context, thus yields a specification for the control variable which connects it with electoral possibilities. In our case even if we keep to this simple framework of a single instrument, adaptive expectations and a single endogenous variable, there are further complications. The instrument which we seek to endogenise is of a discrete dummy variable of the 0 – 1 type, rather than a continuous real variable such as U_t. It is not easy to define F to be quadratic in such a variable. In the U.K. context also the government not only chooses a policy instrument such as U_t but also the date of election, θ.

For these reasons, while we specify an Incomes Policy equation in a simultaneous model along wigh a variable indicating the government's electoral position, we have not obtained the equation explicitly from an optimising framework. The discussion so far indicates however that if we do specify political variables in an Incomes Policy equation and vice versa, this is not an ad hoc procedure. Our aim in future work is to overcome the many technical difficulties involved in this area, but for the present we wish to concentrate on the endogenisation of the incomes policy variable. We sketch our model in non-formal terms below.

4. A MODEL OF INCOMES POLICY IN THE U.K. CONTEXT

At any point of time, the party in power in the U.K. has several indicators regarding the possibility of an election in the near future and if so, its chances of re-election. There is for instance its majority over the opposition in parliament (MAJ). If election has taken place recently, governments enjoy a honeymoon period and conditional on a sufficient majority, an early election can be ruled out. We specify as a 'New Government' dummy variable taking a value 8 in the quarter after the election, 7 The quarter following and so on for eight quarters following (NG8). A government which has to fight an election can also be sure of some support as a sitting tenant since it is a political truism that the opposition does not win elections, governments lose them. We capture this by a 'fear of change' variable, again a dummy variable taking a value 1, six quarters before a *'scheduled'* general election, rising to 6 in the end (i.e. an election is *scheduled* five years –20 quarters– after the last election). If there is an election in the meantime the dummy goes back to zero. This is labelled FC6.

The variables MAJ, NG8 and FC6 are exogenous variables not subject to government control. Their impact on the possibility of an imminent election, i.e. $p(R_{t+1})/p(R_t)$, is clear. The one variable which indicates the likely votes the government might get is measured by the Gallup Poll question 'If there were a General Election tomorrow which party would you support?' We use the end of quarter observations for this question. It measures what F(.) in equation (7.2a) stands for; the votes likely in t+1 given the variable values at t. This is labelled LEAD in our model. The government's re-election prospect depends on the difference between actual LEAD and the required LEAD* We take LEAD* to be U shaped, declining after an election and rising as the scheduled date approaches, and it is exogenously determined. The gap between LEAD and LEAD* is the popularity deficit of the government. The government then adjusts its control variable(s) to the size of the popularity deficit.

The actual LEAD depends on a variety of economic and political variables labelled as y, c, z, s in equation (7.1). Thus we postulate

$$\beta_1(L)\ \text{LEAD}_t = \beta_0 + \beta_2(L)y_t + \beta_3(L)c_t + \beta_4(L)z_t + \beta_5(L)s_t + u_{it} \qquad (7.6)$$

Among the variables we have real earnings, unemployment, tax burden, exchange rate and level of foreign exchange reserves. We also have the incomes policy variable itself affecting LEAD as is obviously implied by our model. The $\beta_i(L)$ are lag polynomials of an appropriate order.

The next step is to derive the government's decision as to whether to impose an incomes policy, or if there is an incomes policy already operating, whether to continue it. We envisage the government as making this decision at the beginning of each period. Thus its information set consists of the actual values of various variables as of the previous period, and the government then faces an *ex ante* decision. The decision once made becomes an *ex post* event. Being an *ex ante* decision, we formulate the question as one of predicting the conditional probability that the event in question –the imposition of an incomes policy– will occur. Let δ be the probability that the event IP (incomes policy) will occur. In the well known fashion, we model it as a logit process:

$$\delta \equiv P(\text{IP} = 1) = (1 + \exp(-x\theta))^{-1} \qquad (7.7)$$

The formulation in equation (7.7) enables us to use a dummy dependent variable. By partitioning the likelihood function in terms of those observations having a value of one (incomes policy on) and those having zero (incomes policy off), one can maximise the likelihood. We proceed to obtain estimates of the θ vector. The classification of the sample into one/zero categories is thus important. It also happens to be an area where there is much disagreement among different researchers. Thus, while some periods are classified as incomes policy on by one researcher, another may not use the same classification. In appendix 1, table 7.4, we have listed the classifications used by various authors and we can see that while some authors (e.g. Henry (1981)) use only the episodes of wage freeze as incomes policy, others use a looser criterion.

The appropriate way to approach this classification problem is to specify the underlying latent variables which determine the 0/1 outcome. As is now familiar, we need to specify the criterion in terms of a threshold or critical value y_1^* of variable y_1. Then if $y_{1t} > y_{1t}^*$ then the policy is switched on in t+1, and if $y_{1t} < y_{1t}^*$

the policy is switched off. We need to separate the decision to operate the policy from the decision on the degree of severity of that policy. The latter is itself another endogenously determined festure depending on a combination of economic and political variables. We must also separate this issue from the *ex post* effectiveness (or otherwise) of the particular policy episode. It is necessary therefore to examine the question of the threshold variable(s) determining the policy outcome.

The major, if not sole, purpose of incomes policy is to slow down the rate of price inflation by acting to cut the rate of wage (earnings) inflation. Since this is mostly done by aiming for a rate of wage inflation distinctly below the most recently observed rate of price inflation, it is also a policy for cutting real wages, at least in the short run. The long run promise being of course to bring both wage and price inflation down so as to bring real wage rises in line with productivity growth. Nevertheless, each policy has been announced in terms of the rate of nominal wage inflation thought desirable by the government of the day. Although a quantitative target has not always been announced, we have sufficient information to extract a quantitative signal. In table 7.1 we have indicated this as $\dot{e}_t^d$, the desired rate of earnings inflation. Beginning with the Selwyn Lloyd 'pause' $\dot{e}_t^d = 0$, we see a tremendous variation, as well as a trend, in $\dot{e}_t^d$.

To indicate the severity or mildness of each policy, we compare $\dot{e}_t^d$ to various measures of inflation. Thus one measure is to compare $\dot{e}_t^d$ to the most recent rate of inflation ($\dot{p}_{t-1}$). Looking at this we see how each wage freeze ($\dot{e}_t^d = 0$) has been quite severe in terms of past inflation. But once hyperinflation had got under way even a value of 10 per cent for $\dot{e}_t^d$, as in 1975.3 – 1976.2, meant a 13 per cent reduction in real earnings. Another measure is the rate of deceleration in earnings $\dot{e}_t^d - \dot{e}_{t-1}$. This measure follows $(\dot{e}_t^d - \dot{p}_{t-1})$ quite closely. A third measure is to compare $\dot{e}_t^d$ with the previous period's real earnings growth. This gives us some idea of the size of real earnings growth as a possible trigger for the introduction of an incomes policy. Thus it is clear that the Selwyn Lloyd pause was triggered off by a real earnings growth of nearly 5 per cent. Each other episode of wage freeze also shows a high rate of real earnings growth preceding it.

Another measure compares $\dot{e}_t^d$ with expectations of earnings growth, which are derived from the Financial Times – Taylor Nelson Survey which asks businessmen to state their expectations regarding wage inflation over the next 12 months; see Wadhwani (1982) for further details.

These indicators are a measure of the problem as faced by the government, and the severity of the solution which it thought necessary. These various indicators move quite closely together but, in a period of rising actual rates of inflation, the absolute values of $\dot{e}_t^d$ also rise. We therefore adopt a percentage rule to classify episodes as incomes policy *on* or *off*. If $\dot{e}_t^d$ is lower relative to $\dot{e}_{t-1}$, or equivalently if $(\dot{e}_t^d - \dot{e}_{t-1})/\dot{e}_{t-1}$ is negative, then we assume that implies that incomes policy is *on*. Thus episodes where the $\dot{e}_t^d$ indicated is high relative to $\dot{e}_{t-1}$, we take it as policy *off* even if some norm or 'binding agreement' may be said to have been in force. Of course there was a period when the government refused to signal any value for $\dot{e}_t^d$. This was in the 'Selsdon Man' period of the Heath government; 1970.3–1972.3. In this period, we take it that policy was *off*. Only in one case do we relax this rule. In the 1977.2 – 1978.2 period we take policy to be *on* since the equivalent measure in terms of the desired rate of price inflation $(\dot{p}_t^d - \dot{p}_{t-1})/\dot{p}_{t-1}$ was negative.

To summarise our criterion formally we can say that there is a desired value e_t^u (or $\dot{p}_t^d$) and an expected (i.e. forecast) value $\hat{\dot{e}}_t$ (or $\hat{\dot{p}}_t$). If the government forecasts an earnings (price) growth rate in excess of the desired growth rate, then it switches the policy on. It uses a naive extrapolative equation to forecast that earnings (price) growth $\hat{\dot{e}}_t = \dot{e}_{t-1}$ and $\hat{\dot{p}}_t = \dot{p}_{t-1}$. Combining the threshold value with the naive extrapolation we have

$$(\dot{e}_t^d - \dot{e}_{t-1})/\dot{e}_{t-1} \quad \begin{cases} < 0 \Rightarrow IP = 1 \\ \geqslant 0 \Rightarrow IP = 0 \end{cases} \tag{7.8}$$

For 1977.2 – 1978.2 we replace e by p.

One consequence of classifying all the periods for which the desired rate of acceleration of earnings was negative as policy *on* periods, is that we have very few observations when there is a policy switch from *on* to *off* or the other way round. In the eighteen years data 1961-1978, comprising 70 observations, there are only three instances of a policy being switched *off* (1963.2, 1970.3, 1974.1); two of which are periods when the party in power changed as a result of a General Election. Similarly there are three episodes when the policy is turned *on* from *off* (not counting the first observation when the policy came on). These are 1965.2, 1972.4 (the famous U-turn) and 1975.3 (TUC 'guidelines' being embodied in a White Paper). This lack of zeros in the sample and very few switches implies that our equation predicting the odds that the government will *introduce* an incomes policy is not tested very often since in most cases it is a decision to *continue* an incomes policy. We return to this point when we examine the predictive performance of our equation.

It is quite clear from table 7.1 that while $\dot{e}_t^d$ and $\dot{e}_t^d{-}1 - \dot{p}_{t-1}$ or $\dot{e}_t^d - \dot{e}_{t-1}$ show a tremendous range, the percentage deceleration measure $(\dot{e}_t^d - \dot{e}_{t-1})/\dot{e}_{t-1}$ is confined within quite narrow lines. Quite small variations in this measure imply great variations in the desired degree of deflation. Sometimes the degree of deflation even took the employers by surprise, as can be seen from the $\dot{e}_t^d - \dot{e}_{t-1}^e$ measure; see, for example, the enormous drop in 1972.4 or in 1975.3 and 1976.3. We use information on the degree of the desired wage deceleration as a further signal of the severity of the incomes policy. Thus we classified the episodes where $(\dot{e}_t^d - \dot{e}_{t-1})/\dot{e}_{t-1}$ was less than –0.5 as an indicator of a *severe* incomes policy. All other episodes of incomes policy were taken to be *mild.* Thus our classification of observations into policy on/off and into severe/mild is on the basis of the size of the variable measuring the desired degree of wage deceleration. Out of our total sample of 70 observations, there were 47 quarters when policy was on. There were fourteen episodes of incomes policy; nine of these were severe, taking up 28 quarters; and five episodes were mild, taking up 19 quarters. Thus two out of every five observations witnessed a severe incomes policy. Four of these nine severe episodes were wage 'freeze' cases with $\dot{e}_t^d = 0$. But such freezes lasted only a short time in each case; in all, nine quarters.

Before we turn to the specification of these equations, we may briefly look at some indicators of effectiveness of an incomes policy. In the very short run, an incomes policy aims to reduce the rate of wage (earnings) growth and/or price inflation. For each of the episodes we look therefore at the rate of earnings growth or price inflation in the beginning quarter of the episode, denoted $\dot{e}_0$ or $\dot{p}_0$. We then look at the same variable in the last quarter of each episode, $\dot{e}$ and $\dot{p}$. These measures are reported in table 7.2. In a rough sense, a policy is successful if $\dot{p} < \dot{p}_0$ and $\dot{e} < \dot{e}_0$. It is quite remarkable how many episodes in table 7.2 do fulfil this requirement. Of the nine severe episodes, five achieved a price growth deceleration and eight out of the nine achieved wage growth deceleration. As far as real wage growth deceleration is concerned, six out of nine episodes achieved that. For mild policies the breakdown was two out of five successful for price deceleration, wage deceleration, and for real wage deceleration. Thus we see that incomes policies are likely to slow down wage growth by more than price growth when they are severe. Incomes policies are more effective when they are severe rather than mild. As far as the idea that incomes policies *cut* real wages (i.e. achieve a negative growth rate of real wages) is concerned, this happened once in the 1967.1 – 1967.2 episode and again in the 1976.3 – 1977.2 episode. Both, let it be noted, were under Labour governments. But the 1974 – 1977 years were peculiar anyway because, even when the policy was off during 1974.1 to 1975.2 despite a 26 per cent growth in earnings, real wages declined. By and large, incomes policies achieved real wage growth deceleration (seven out of fourteen episodes) rather than a real wage cut.

In the light of this long discussion, it is obvious that the x variables in equation (7.7) will comprise: (a) economic variables – especially earnings and prices, as well as growth of productivity (Pr) and other target variables such as reserves or exchange rates; (b) political variables – the government's popularity deficit, its majority in parliament, its length in office (whether it is a new government enjoying a honeymoon period or an old government soon facing elections), etc. All these variables enter with a one period lag, so each decision is conditional upon information as of t–1. Obviously variables such as length in office or size of majority are assumed to be known in t.

Conditional upon having made the decision to impose (or continue) an incomes policy, a government has to decide upon the severity of such a policy. This would depend mainly on its perception of the seriousness of the problem it faces –i.e. the rate of wage or price inflation. But it will also depend on the political climate, the popularity of incomes policies, and the resistance which they may provoke. It takes the form

$$\Pr(\mu = 1 \mid \delta = 1) = (1 + \exp(-x\phi))^{-1} \tag{7.9}$$

5. ESTIMATION OF THE MODEL

Thus our three equations are the LEAD equation (equation (7.6)), the incomes policy equation (equation (7.7)) and the severity of incomes policy equation (equation (7.9)). The wage-price equations, which incorporate incomes policy variables as dummy variables have already been estimated by various authors, including ourselves, and nothing new can be said about them here (see Wadhwani (1982), Desai (1983)). At a future date, we hope to specify a model with other instruments, besides incomes policy and the macroeconomic variables such as wages, prices and unemployment, along with political variables. For the present we concentrate on the estimation of these three equations.

The LEAD equation (table 7.3a) says that the popularity of a government depends on growth of real earnings. ($\dot{e} - \dot{p}$) two quarters ago, the change in unemployment (DEVU) two quarters ago, the recent change in exchange rates (Ex), the level and change in the tax burden (T/Y), and the level or official reserves (or). In addition, there are two political variables – the 'honeymoon' variable for a newly elected government (NG8), and a fear of change in approach to imminent election (FC6) (see also the Data Definitions in the appendix). Notice that the incomes policy dummy enters with a positive sign (with one lag) and a negative sign with five lags. This crudely captures the notion that incomes policies are popular, initially, but become more unpopular as time goes on. (See also the evidence for this from Gallup surveys in table 7.5). This equation passes the various diagnostic tests and is satisfactory for our purposes.

The incomes policy equation (table 7.3b) is specified in terms of the log odds of policy being on as explained above. We see that the political factors all urge against an incomes policy. The honeymoon period variable NG8 has a negative sign and a large coefficient. This may seem paradoxical in the light of the view that if incomes policy were to be electorally unpopular governments would undertake them while they enjoy the extra boost during the honeymoon period. What it reflects is the practice whereby successive governments have come into power having criticised the other party's record in office and have exploited the electoral unpopularity of incomes policies of their predecessors (the previous policy had typically been on sufficiently long to engender unpopularity). The incoming governments have usually promised a miracle cure to the inflation problem when out of office and have foresworn the use of incomes policies. Upon coming to power they have reluctantly resorted to incomes policies. This was certainly true of the Heath government of June 1970 and the Wilson governments of February and October 1974.

The coefficient of LEAD entered as popularity deficit agrees with this. A government which is already popular does not worry about incomes policies. The coefficient on MAJ (majority) supports this. The popularity of incomes policies, as measured by Gallup Poll when a policy is on (hence the multiplicative variable), encourages the continuation of such policies. The coefficient on lagged incomes policy is also large and highly significant, indicating that it is easier to continue an incomes policy than to launch it.

The economic variables then give us the factors that push a government towards adopting an incomes policy. The most striking variables here are the growth rate of earnings and of prices, though $\dot{e}_{t-1}$ is non-significant and $\dot{p}_{t-1}$ has a t-value barely above one. Productivity growth has the expected negative sign. Reserves (or) and exchange rates (Ex) have again the expected sign and show that it would be signals such as loss of reserves or a falling pound or a high rate of inflation which makes a government switch on a policy. The level of real earnings is seen to be another signal. This may be a sign that, things having recently been going well as indicated by high real earnings, the hardship due to an incomes policy will not be resented too much. Another interpretation would be that a high value for real earnings may indicate a high share of labour in income and consequently a declining share of profits. It would then be seen by the government as requiring incomes policy to restore profitability.

The predictive performance of the equation is very heartening. We correctly predict 97 per cent of the on/off values. But a more stringent test is not the predictive ability of the equation in terms of all the observations, since sheer inertia makes governments continue an incomes policy once started, but the ability to predict switches from on to off and back again. Of the severn switches, we get five correct. We failed to predict the launching of incomes policy in April 1965 by the Wilson government, although this may be due to the large coefficient of NG8. The government was elected in October 1964, but with a tiny majority, and indeed had to seek re-election before the eight quarter period was up. This may imply that we should modify NG8 for shorter-lived governments (Wilson, October 1964 – April 1966; Wilson, February 1974 – October 1974).

The other episode we got wrong was the famous U-turn by the Heath government. The switch here between the predicted probability for 1972.3 (0.44) and 1972.4 (0.03) is puzzling. The policy switch came late in the fourth quarter (in November 1972) but it is still hard to believe that as of the beginning of October 1972 the probability of adopting an incomes policy was so much lower than as of the beginning of July 1972.

The influence of political factors is seen in the dramatic prediction for 1974.1. The change in government could not have been foreseen at the end of December 1973, though there was enough turmoil due to the 'Three Day Week'. It is still quite remarkable that our *ex ante* decision equation captures this major shift, as it also captures the subsequent U-turn by the Labour government in 1975.

The equation predicting the odds of a severe incomes policy (table 7.3c), as against a mild one, uses only a few variables. Strangely enough, once a government has decided to impose an incomes policy, a honeymoon period directs it to choose a severe rather than a mild policy, as does the size of its majority. The signs of $\dot{e}$ and ΔEx are similar to that in the incomes policy equation. The major new variable in this equation is SS_{t-1} which stands for a four quarter sum of strikes up to $t-1$. This indicates a government's reluctance to adopt a severe incomes policy in face of industrial unrest.

The predictive performance of this equation is similar to that of the previous one. We get 96 per cent of the observations correct but out of the eight switches from severe to mild, and vice versa, we again get two wrong. This may indicate that perhaps the governement could have (or should have!) chosen a severe policy when it chose a mild one. The two switches are 1967.3, where the predicted probability for imposing a severe policy is 0.913 but the Wilson government did not so choose. Devaluation came in the next quarter and after that the government relied on conventional deflationary measures to get inflation under control. This gamble did not succeed in June 1970. The other case interestingly enough is the Heath government's switch from severe to mild in 1973.2. In view of the tremendous problems it caused to the Heath government in controlling inflation in the face of rising employment, it may seem that the abandoning of the severe policy was unwise. There are obviously certain other pressures which make governments switch from a severe to a mild policy even when not required to do so by the observable political/economic environment which we have captured in our variables.

6. CONCLUSION

Our estimates here are only single equation estimates. Inasmuch as we have left the conventional economic variables such as earnings and prices unexplained, we have only an incomplete model. But it is in the endogenisation of the incomes policy variables that we see our contribution. Here we can claim that our objective has been achieved, although there is room for improvement. We have been able to model the decision by governments to impose an incomes policy in *ex ante* terms and our equations have demonstrated reasonably good predictive power. The separation of the severity of policy from its imposition has also been successful. The linking of these with the government's electoral lead both as cause and effect is another novel feature.

Obviously we are conscious of improvements that can be made. We need to specify the formal problem and derive an explicit dynamic equation. Here the combination of continuous and discrete variables presents a problem. But there need to be more instruments (money supply for instance) and more objective variables. We also need to explore the choice of the election date as an additional dimension. We hope to report on all these in the near future.

Table 7.1 Basic information for data classification

Date	Classification	$\dot{e}^d_t$	$\dot{e}^d_t - \dot{p}_{t-1}$	$\dot{e}^d_t - \dot{e}_{t-1}$	$\frac{\dot{e}^d_t - \dot{e}_{t-1}}{\dot{e}_{t-1}}$	$\dot{e}^d_t - (\dot{e}-\dot{p})_{t-1}$	$\dot{e}^d_t - \dot{e}^e_{t-1}$
61.3 – 62.1	on-severe	0	– 4.92	–9.80	–1.00	–4.88	NA
62.2 – 63.1	on-severe	2.25	– 1.52	–4.55	–0.66	–0.68	NA
63.2 – 65.1	off	3.25	1.15	0.70	0.18	1.39	NA
65.2 – 66.2	on-severe	3.25	– 2.63	–6.06	–0.65	–0.17	NA
66.3 – 66.4	on-severe	0	– 5.33	–9.53	–1.00	–4.19	NA
67.1 – 67.2	on-severe	0	– 4.29	–12.83	–1.00	–8.53	NA
67.3 – 68.1	on-mild	1.75	– 1.36	–1.21	–0.41	1.89	NA
68.2 – 68.4	on-mild	3.50	0.66	–3.14	–0.47	–0.30	–0.05
69.1 – 70.2	on-mild	3.50	– 1.98	–2.86	–0.45	–4.41	–0.57
70.3 – 72.3	off			'SELSDON MAN RULES O.K.'			
72.4 – 73.1	on-severe	0	– 7.58	–11.56	–1.00	–3.98	–10.2
73.2 – 73.4	on-mild	6.7	0	–2.80	–0.29	–9.50	–1.3
74.1 – 75.2	off	13.0	5.24	0.99	0.07	8.76	4.5
75.3 – 76.2	on-severe	10.4	–13.32	–15.43	–0.60	8.30	–11.1
76.3 – 77.2	on-severe	4.5	– 9.74	–12.63	–0.75	–1.61	–6.8
77.3 – 78.2	on-mild	10.0	– 3.32	3.09	0.24	16.41	–0.8
78.3 – 78.4	on-severe	5.0	– 4.45	–8.81	–0.64	–0.64	–7.5

Notes: – Lower case letters denote logarithm; upper case letters denote variables

– $\dot{x}_t = \Delta_4 \ln X_t$

– E = Earnings

– P = Prices

– d superscript denotes desired value on part of government as distilled by us from policy pronouncements

– e superscript denotes expected value as revealed in the Financial Times survey of employers

– Rules used: ON if $(\dot{e}^d_t - \dot{e}_{t-1})/\dot{e}_{t-1} < 0$; OFF otherwise (except for 1977.2 – 1978.2 where $(\dot{p}^d_t - \dot{p}_{t-1})/\dot{p}_{t-1} < 0$).

Severe if $(\dot{e}^d_t - \dot{e}_{t-1})/\dot{e}_{t-1} < -0.5$; mild otherwise.

Table 7.2 Indicators for effectiveness of incomes policy episodes

Date	Classification	$\dot{p}_\theta/\dot{p}$	$\dot{e}_\theta/\dot{e}$	$(\dot{e}-\dot{p})_\theta/(\dot{e}-\dot{p})$
61.3 – 62.1	on-severe	4.92/ 3.77	12.43/ 8.22	7.51/ 4.45
62.2 – 63.1	on-severe	5.61/ 2.66	4.73/ 3.95	–0.88/ 1.39
63.2 – 65.1	off	3.52/ 7.26	3.62/ 9.31	–0.10/ 2.05
65.2 – 66.2	on-severe	3.64/ 5.33	7.44/ 9.52	3.80/ 4.19
66.3 – 66.4	on-severe	4.12/ 4.30	8.92/ 5.84	4.80/ 1.54
67.1 – 67.2	on-severe	3.38/ 3.11	3.88/ 2.96	3.05/–0.15
67.3 – 68.1	on-mild	3.09/ 2.84	5.24/ 6.64	2.16/ 3.80
68.2 – 68.4	on-mild	3.44/ 5.48	6.44/ 6.39	3.00/ 0.91
69.1 – 70.2	on-mild	6.47/ 6.60	7.31/12.60	0.84/ 6.00
70.3 – 72.3	off	7.80/ 8.70	13.80/12.40	6.00/ 3.70
72.4 – 73.1	on-severe	3.72/ 6.70	12.98/ 9.50	9.28/ 2.80
73.2 – 73.4	on-mild	5.26/ 7.76	10.68/12.00	5.60/ 4.24
74.1 – 75.2	off	7.82/27.77	11.47/25.83	3.05/–1.94
75.3 – 76.2	on-severe	24.57/14.24	26.02/17.13	1.45/ 2.89
76.3 – 77.2	on-severe	17.69/13.22	12.30/ 6.91	–5.39/–6.41
77.3 – 78.2	on-mild	13.28/ 9.45	6.04/13.81	–7.24/ 4.36
78.3 – 78.4	on-severe	8.66/ 9.78	14.63/14.47	5.97/ 4.69

Table 7.3a The lead equation
Dependent variable – LEAD (estimated by OLS)

Independent variable	Coefficient estimate (t ratio)
$LEAD_{t-1}$	0.37 (3.07)
$LEAD_{t-2}$	–0.18 (1.71)
NG 8	1.83 (5.09)
FC 6	1.69 (2.90)
$\Delta_1(e-p)_{t-2}$	0.82 (2.08)
$\Delta_1(DEVU)_{t-2}$	–3.72 (1.79)
$\Delta_1 Ex_{t-2}$	0.10 (1.69)
$\Delta_1^2 Ex_t$	0.25 (2.85)
$\Delta_2(T/Y)_t$	–0.58 (2.69)
$(T/Y)_{t-3}$	–0.53 (3.49)
or_t	1.60 (2.25)
IPD_{t-1}	3.88 (2.26)
IPD_{t-5}	–4.81 (3.25)
DUML	1.87 (2.52)

Notes: Tests, S = 4.98; Chow (4,56) = 1.33; $\chi^2(4) = 9.47$; LM(4) = 2.08

$\chi^2(4)$ is a forecast test comparing the post sample residual variance for four observations with the within sample variance. LM(4) is the Lagrange Multiplier Test against fourth order residual correlation.

Sample period: 1961.3 – 1979.4 with 4 observations retained for forecasting

Table 7.3b The incomes policy equation

Dependent variable – Log odds of having incomes policy ON (IPD)

Independent variables	Coefficient estimates (t ratio)
NG 8	–3.63 (1.79)
or_{t-1}	–21.55 (1.52)
(LEAD–LEAD*).D1	–0.89 (1.68)
$POPIP.IPD_{t-1}$	1.45 (1.83)
IPD_{t-1}	8.66 (2.11)
$(e-p)_{t-4}$	19.57 (0.79)
$\dot{e}_{t-1}$	20.28 (0.35)
ΔEx_{t-1}	–20.45 (1.16)
MAJ	–0.062 (1.49)
ΔPr_{t-1}	–53.10 (1.49)
$\dot{p}_{t-1}$	59.86 (1.02)
Constant	169.20 (1.48)

$\hat{p} = 0.829$ % correct prediction 97.14

Switch point predictions

Date	Predictor probability	Actual Classification
1961.3	0.88	ON
1963.2	0.26	OFF
1965.2	0.41	ON
1970.3	0.30	OFF
1972.4	0.03	ON
1974.1	0.00	OFF
1975.2	0.90	ON

Thus we get 1965.2 and 1972.4 wrong. Note however that for 1972.3 the predicted probability was 0.44.

Note that $p = 1 - L(\hat{\theta})/L(\hat{\theta}^H)$, where $\hat{\theta}^H$ sets the parameter vector to zero, and is, therefore, a measure of goodness of fit.
Sample period: 1961.3 – 1979.4 with 4 observations retained for forecasting

Table 7.3c The severity of incomes policy equation

Dependent variable – Log odds of imposing a severe policy conditional on incomes policy being ON (IPS)

Independent variables	Coefficient estimates (t ratio)
IPS_{t-1}	7.93 (1.84)
ΔEx_{t-1}	−8.40 (0.67)
$\dot{e}_{t-1}$	270.60 (1.54)
NG 8	1.61 (1.34)
MAJ	0.118 (1.23)
SS_{t-1}	−12.35 (1.15)
Constant	54.44 (0.80)

$\hat{p} = 0.79$ % correctly predicted 95.74

Switch point predictions

Date	Predictor probability	Actual Classification
1961.3	0.999	severe
1965.2	0.611	severe
1967.3	0.913	mild
1972.4	0.791	severe
1973.2	0.629	mild
1975.3	1.000	severe
1977.3	0.011	mild
1978.3	0.996	severe

Thus we get 1967.3 and 1973.2 wrong

Sample period: 1961.3 –1979.4 with 4 observations retainded for forecasting

Table 7.4 Classification of incomes policy on/off by various authors

Date	Sargan (1980)	Parkin, Sumner and Ward	Henry (1981)	Desai, Keil and Wadhwani
61.3–62.1	ON	ON (up to 62.2)	N/A	ON–S
62.2–63.1	ON	OFF	N/A	ON–S
63.2–65.1	ON	OFF	OFF	OFF
65.2–66.2	ON	OFF	OFF	ON–S
66.3–66.4	ON	ON	ON	ON–S
67.1–67.2	ON	ON	ON	ON–S
67.3–68.1	ON	OFF	ON	ON–M
68.2–68.4	ON	OFF	ON	ON–M
69.1–70.2	ON (up to 69.4)	OFF	ON (up to 69.2)	ON–M
70.3–72.3	OFF (until 71.4) ON (from 72.1)	OFF	OFF	OFF
72.4–73.1	ON	N/A	ON	ON–S
73.2–73.4	ON	N/A	ON (up to 74.1)	ON–M
74.1–75.2	N/A	N/A	OFF	OFF
75.3–76.2	N/A	N/A	ON	ON–S
76.3–77.2	N/A	N/A	ON	ON–S
77.3–78.2	N/A	N/A	OFF	ON–M
78.3–78.4	N/A	N/A	OFF	ON–S

Table 7.5 Gallup surveys of the popularity of incomes policy

Year	QI	QII	Balance QIII	QIV
1961	–	–	+4.0	+1.5
1962	–1.0	–3.5	–6.0	–5.5
1963	–5.0	–4.5	–4.0	+1.0
1964	+6.0	+11.0	+16.0	+21.0
1965	+28.0	+36.0	+34.0	+33.0
1966	+32.0	+27.0	+28.0	+3.0
1967	+21.0	+11.0	+1.0	+1.3
1968	+1.5	+1.8	+2.0	+2.0
.	.	.	.	.
1972	–	–	–	+31.0
1973	+15.5	+19.0	+3.0	+9.5
1974	+3.5	–	–	–
.	.	.	.	.
1975	–	–	+32.0	+32.7
1976	+34.7	+34.3	+39.0	+17.0
1977	+10.0	+13.7	+21.0	+38.7
1978	+38.3	+35.7	+33.0	+33.7
1979	+18.3	–	–	–

Note: The observations refer to the balance of respondents who are favourable to incomes policy in answer to the following possible questions:

'Do you think that the Government's prices and incomes policy is a good thing or a bad thing?' (or variants thereof) in Nov. 1961 – July 1962
Jan. 1965 – Sept. 1968
Nov. 1972 – Feb. 1974
July 1975 – March 1979

Linear interpolation and quarterly averaging has been used.

APPENDIX 2: DATA DEFINITIONS

DEVU = $(U - \frac{1}{12} \sum_{i=1}^{12} U_{-i})$, where U is the percentage of the labour force wholly unemployed. Source: Department of Employment Gazette.

DUML = A dummy variable taking the value 1 when Labour is in power, and −1 when the Conservatives are in power.

E = This is an index of average hourly earnings in manufacturing industry, which is used in 'Wage Inflation in the U.K.' by S. Wadhwani (Centre for Labour Economics Discussion Paper No. 132).

Ex = Spot $/£ exchange rate. Source: Bank of England Quarterly Bulletin, quarterly averages.

FC 6 = A dummy variable taking the value 1 six quarters before a *scheduled* general election, 2 in the subsequent quarter, and so on until it reverts to zero when an election actually takes place.

IPD = A dummy variable which takes the value 1 when an incomes policy is regarded to have been on (See table 7.2).

IPM = A dummy variable which takes the value 1 when a mild incomes policy is regarded to have prevailed (see Table 7.2).

IPS = A dummy variable which takes the value 1 when a severe incomes policy is regarded to have prevailed (see Table 7.2).

LEAD = The government's percentage point lead over the main Opposition party, reported by Gallup from answers to the question 'If there were a General Election tomorrow, which party would you support?' and supplied by Gallup Polls Ltd., end-of-quarter observations.

LEAD* = A U-shaped variable between elections, which is postulated to reflect the government's desired lead.

MAJ = The parliamentary majority of the government over all other parties.

NG 8 = A dummy variable taking the value 8 in the quarter of a general election, 7 in the following quarter, and so on down to 0, or to the next general election, whichever comes first.

or = Stock of Official Reserves. Source: Bank of England Statistical Abstract 2, (1975), Bank of England Quarterly Bulletin.

P = GDP deflator, seasonally unadjusted. Source: Economic Trends, Annual Supplements.

Pf = Index of world prices, seasonally unadjusted.

Pr = Productivity (output per man employed), seasonally unadjusted. Source: Economic Trends, Annual Supplement.

POPIP = Balance of sample that approve of incomes policies. Source: Gallup Polls Ltd., average of quarterly observations (See Table 7.5).

SS = Number of industrial disputes (beginning in the period). Source: Ministry of Labour Gazette, Employment and Productivity Gazette, Department of Employment Gazette.

T = The ratio of the revenue from income and expenditure taxes to GDP, defined by (TE + GDP – YD/GDP), where TE is revenue from expenditure taxes, and YD disposable income, all seasonally unadjusted. Source: Economic Trends, Annual Supplement.

Y = GDP, seasonally unadjusted. Source: Economic Trends, Annual Supplement.

CONVENTIONS USED:

. denotes a fourth difference

Δ_j denotes a jth difference

Capital letters represent levels. Lower case letters represent logs.

NOTES

* We are grateful to Kathy Pick for her help in data collection, to Hugh Wills and Wiji Narendranathan for their help with the QUAIL program, and to Richard Layard and Jon Stern for discussion and early encouragement.
We would also like to thank SSRC for providing financial support.

REFERENCES

Alt, J. (1980), The Politics of Economic Decline, Cambridge University Press, Cambridge.

Chater, R., A. Dean and R. Elliott (1982), *Incomes Policy,* Oxford University Press, Oxford.

Currie, D. and R. Smith (1981), *Socialist Economic Review,* Merlin Press, London.

Desai, M. (1976), *Applied Econometrics,* Philip Allan, Oxford.

Desai, M (1983), 'Money, inflation and unemployment: An econometric model of the Keynes Effect', Londond School of Economics (unpublished manuscript).

Fallick, J. and R. Elliott (1981), *Incomes Policies, Inflation and Relative Pay,* Allen and Unwin, London.

Frey, B. and L. Lau (1968), 'Towards a mathematical model of government behaviour', *Zeitschrift für Nationalökonomie,* 28, pp. 355-380.

Frey, B. and F. Schneider (1978), 'A politico-economic model of the United Kingdom', *Economic Journal,* 88, pp. 245-253.

Ginsburgh, V. and P. Michel (1983), 'Random timing and the political business cycle', *Public Choice,* 37, pp. 155-164.

Goodhart, C. and R. Bhansali (1970),'Political economy', *Political Studies,* 18, pp. 43-106.

Henry, S.G.B. and P. Ormerod (1978), 'Incomes policy and wage inflation: Empirical evidence for the U.K. 1961-77', *National Institute Economic Review,* 85, pp. 31-39.

Henry, S.G.B. (1981), 'Incomes policy and aggregate pay', in Fallick and Elliott (1981).

Johnson, H. (1972), Memorandum to the Prime Minister.

Laidler, D. (1980), 'Memorandum to the Parliamentary Select Committee on Treasury and Civil Service', H.C. 720.

Lipsey, R. and M. Parkin (1970), 'Incomes policy: A reappraisal', *Economica,* 37, pp. 115-138.

MacRae, D. (1977), 'A political model of the business cycle', *Journal of Political Economy,* 85, pp. 239-266.

Middlemass, K. (1980), *Politics in an Industrial Society,* A. Deutsch, London.

Minford, P. and D. Peel (1982), 'The political theory of the business cycle', *European Economic Review,* 17, pp. 253-271.

Nordhaus, W. (1975), 'The political business cycle', *Review of Economic Studies,* 42, pp. 169-190.

Ormerod, P. (1981), 'Inflation and incomes policy', in Currie and Smith (1981).

Parkin, J.M., M. Sumner and R. Ward (1976), 'The effects of excess demand, generalised expectations and wage price controls in wage inflation in the U.K.', in K. Brunner and A. Meltzer (eds.), *The Economics of Price and Wage Controls,* North-Holland, Amsterdam.

Pissarides, C. (1980), 'British government popularity and economic performance', *Economic Journal,* 90, pp. 569-581.

Sargan, J.D. (1980), 'A model of wage price inflation', *Review of Economic Studies,* 47, pp. 97-117.

Wadhwani, S. (1982), 'Wage inflation in the U.K.', London School of Economics, Centre for Labour Economics, Discussion Paper No. 132.

Wallis, K. (1971), 'Wages, prices and incomes policies: Some comments', *Economica,* 38, pp. 304-310.

CHAPTER 8

MULTIPERIOD PREDICTION FROM DYNAMIC MODELS WITH AUTOCORRELATED ERRORS CONDITIONAL ON FEEDBACK RULES FOR THE FUTURE POLICY VARIABLES

Ralph Friedmann
University of Bielefeld, Germany

1. INTRODUCTION

The dynamic simulation of an econometric model produces predictions over several periods ahead which are conventionally taken as conditional on given values of the policy instrument variables and non-controlled exogenous variables. For such multiperiod predictions, Schmidt (1974) derived the asymptotic distribution of the prediction error where the model disturbances are serially uncorrelated. For the model with autocorrelated errors, Yamamoto (1980) developed the optimal multiperiod prediction scheme and its asymptotic distribution.

This chapter is concerned with the error of predictions conditional on feedback functions –instead of exogenously fixed values– for the future policy instrument variables. That is, we suppose that the policy maker will react to future observations of endogenous variables according to some specified feedback functions. Of course we obtain the conventional situation as a special case if we consider 'feedback functions' which are restricted to constants. In general, however, the multiperiod prediction error is different depending on whether the policy instrument variables will be set equal to some prespecified values without regard to future events or whether they will be fixed in response to observations yet to be made.

For the linear dynamic model with uncorrelated disturbances, the multiperiod prediction errors conditional on feedback rules for the future policy variables has recently been analysed; see Friedmann ((1981), p. 421-426). In the present chapter we shall allow for autocorrelation of the model disturbances. Under this generalised assumption we derive the asymptotic distribution of the multiperiod prediction

Hughes Hallett, A.J. (ed.) Applied Decision Analysis and Economic Behaviour

ISBN 90-247-2968-8. Printed in The Netherlands

error conditional on feedback rules for the policy variables. In particular we consider the application of the optimal control equations derived by Pagan (1975), but our results can also be applied to other feedback rules.

The structure of the chapter is as follows. In section 2 we review the treatment of autocorrelated errors in multiperiod control and prediction. As a result we find that the optimal control equations derived by Pagan (1975) are not really operational until the autocorrelation representation suggested by Pagan is complemented by the backward representation introduced by Yamamoto (1980) in the context of multiperiod prediction analysis. In section 3 we consider multiperiod prediction of the controlled model with known coefficients. In this connection we examine the gain in predictive accuracy due to the implementation of optimal feedback rules instead of a deterministic policy. Section 4 concentrates on multiperiod prediction of the controlled model with estimated coefficients. After introducing a state variable representation of the system with feedback policy rules being implemented we derive the asymptotic distribution of the multiperiod prediction error.

2. TREATMENT OF AUTOCORRELATED ERRORS IN MULTIPERIOD PREDICTION AND CONTROL

2.1 The model

Consider the reduced form of a linear dynamic econometric model with state variables and identities being introduced to eliminate second and higher order lagged endogenous variables, i.e.

$$y_t = Ay_{t-1} + Cx_t + Bz_t + u_t = \Pi w_t + u_t \tag{8.1}$$

where y_t is a px1 vector of state variables; x_t a qx1 vector of control variables; z_t an sx1 vector of non-controlled exogenous variables; $w_t = (y'_{t-1}, x'_t, z'_t)'$; A, C, B are pxp, pxq, and pxs matrices of reduced form coefficients; and $\Pi = (A, C, B)$. Finally, u_t is a px1 vector of disturbances obeying either the r-th order AR process

$$u_t = \phi_1 u_{t-1} + \ldots + \phi_r u_{t-r} + e_t, \tag{8.2}$$

or the MA process

$$u_t = e_t + \phi_1 e_{t-1} + \ldots + \phi_r e_{t-r}, \tag{8.3}$$

where $\phi_1, \ldots, \phi_r$ are pxp matrices of coefficients, and the e_t's are serially independent with $E[e_t] = 0$ and $E[e_t e_t'] = \Omega$. For stability and invertibility it is assumed that all eigenvalues of A lie inside the unit circle and that all roots of the characteristic equation $\phi(z)$ of the AR process or MA process lie outside the unit circle; where $\phi(z) = I - \phi_1 z - \ldots - \phi_r z^r$ for the AR case, and $\phi(z) = I + \phi_1 z + \ldots + \phi_r z^r$ for the MA case.

Pagan (1975) showed that the system (8.1) may be converted to one with serially uncorrelated errors in the following way. First, an autocorrelation representation which incorporates both (8.2) and (8.3) is given with

$$u_t = \phi v_{t-1} + e_t \tag{8.4}$$

$$v_t = F v_{t-1} + L e_t \tag{8.5}$$

where

$$\phi = (\phi_1, \ldots, \phi_r) \tag{8.6}$$

$$v_t = \begin{cases} (u_t', \ldots, u_{t-r+1}')' & \text{for AR} \\ (e_t', \ldots, e_{t-r+1}')' & \text{for MA} \end{cases} \tag{8.7}$$

$$F = \begin{cases} \left[\begin{array}{c|c} \phi_1 \cdots \phi_{r-1} & \phi_r \\ \hline I_{p(r-1)} & 0 \end{array}\right] & \text{for AR} \\ \left[\begin{array}{c|c} 0 \cdots 0 & 0 \\ \hline I_{p(r-1)} & 0 \end{array}\right] & \text{for MA} \end{cases} \tag{8.8}$$

$$L = \begin{bmatrix} I_p \\ 0 \end{bmatrix} \qquad \text{(prxp) matrix)}, \tag{8.9}$$

and I_k is the identity matrix of rank k.

By substituting (8.4) into (8.1) and combining the result with (8.5) we then have a first-order system with serially uncorrelated errors,

$$\begin{bmatrix} y_t \\ v_t \end{bmatrix} = \begin{bmatrix} A & \phi \\ 0 & F \end{bmatrix} \begin{bmatrix} y_{t-1} \\ v_{t-1} \end{bmatrix} + \begin{bmatrix} C \\ 0 \end{bmatrix} x_t + \begin{bmatrix} B \\ 0 \end{bmatrix} z_t + \begin{bmatrix} I_p \\ L \end{bmatrix} e_t ,$$

or

$$y_t^* = A^* y_{t-1}^* + C^* x_t + B^* z_t + e_t^* . \qquad (8.10)$$

In principle the well known results for multiperiod prediction (Schmidt (1974)), as well as those for optimal control problems (e.g., Chow (1975)), apply to that system. A difficulty arises, however, due to the unobservability of the augmented part of the state vector, v_t. The unobservability of v_t matters to the application of the prediction formulae as well as to the application of the optimal feedback rules derived from (8.10) with a quadratic criterion.

2.2 Multiperiod prediction

We first review the problem of predicting the model (8.1) over h periods. That is, starting at some initial time zero, consider the predictor of y_h. Assume for the present that the policy variables, as well as the non-controlled variables, are exogenously given. Using the converted system (8.10), the predictor of y_h is given by the corresponding subvector of the predictor of y_h^*. This h-period predictor of y_h^* is typically taken as conditional on the initial vector $y_0^* = (y_0', v_0')'$. Now that v_0 is unobservable it has to be expressed in terms of past observations, where we assume that the past observations y_j, x_j, z_j, $j = 0, -1, -2, \ldots$ belong to the information set prevailing at time zero. To express v_t in terms of past observations is exactly the issue of the backward representation of the complete model (8.10) raised by Yamamoto (1980). Concentrating on the representation of the critical subvector v_t will point out the relationship between this backward representation and the state variable representation, (8.5), of v_t.

Notice that the problem with (8.5) is that e_t cannot be expressed in terms of observations as simply as could the original disturbance vector u_t. Using (8.1), the latter may be written as

$$u_t = y_t - (Ay_{t-1} + Cx_t + Bz_t) = y_t - \Pi w_t . \qquad (8.11)$$

The state variable representation (8.5) of v_t is transformed into the backward representation by replacing e_t in (8.5) with $e_t = u_t - \phi v_{t-1}$ from (8.4). Hence, (8.5) is rewritten in the backward representation by

$$v_t = Fv_{t-1} + L(u_t - \phi v_{t-1}) ,$$

that is

$$v_t = Hv_{t-1} + Lu_t , \qquad (8.12)$$

with

$$H = F - L\phi = \begin{cases} \left[\begin{array}{ccc|c} 0 & \dots & 0 & 0 \\ \hline & I_{p(r-1)} & & 0 \end{array}\right] & \text{for AR} \\ \\ \left[\begin{array}{ccc|c} -\phi_1 & \dots & -\phi_{r-1} & -\phi_r \\ \hline & I_{p(r-1)} & & 0 \end{array}\right] & \text{for MA} \end{cases} \tag{8.13}$$

By repeatedly employing (8.12) we find

$$v_t = \sum_{j=0}^{m} H^j L u_{t-j} , \tag{8.14}$$

with $m = r-1$ for AR and $m = \infty$ for MA. Hence, using (8.11) to substitute for u_{t-j}, we have v_t expressed solely with observations up to period t. It should be noted that in case of AR disturbances (8.14) reduces to the original definition (8.7), that is $v_t = (u_t', \dots, u_{t-r+1}')'$.

Now the complication due to the unobservability of v_0, which arises in the h-period prediction of y_h by (8.10), can be handled by use of (8.14). If the true parameter values are known, v_0 may be calculated from (8.14) and thus v_0 can in fact be treated as if it was observable at time zero. In particular the prediction error is not affected by the unobservability of v_0 in the case of known coefficients. If on the other hand the values of the coefficients are unknown and consistent estimates of the parameters are given, v_0 has to be substituted by $\tilde{v}_0$ in the predictor of y_h, where

$$\tilde{v}_0 = \sum_{j=0}^{m} \tilde{H}^j L(y_{-j} - \tilde{\Pi} w_{-j}) \tag{8.15}$$

is derived by (8.14) with the consistent estimates replacing the unknown parameters of (8.11) and (8.13). Clearly in this case the estimation of v_0 will contribute to the (asymptotic) prediction error.

2.3 Multiperiod control

Now let us review the optimal feedback policy derived from (8.10) with the quadratic criterion

$$W = E\left[\sum_{t=1}^{T} (y_t^* - a_t^*)' K_t^* (y_t^* - a_t^*) \right] , \tag{8.16}$$

where a_t^* denotes a vector of desired values and K_t^* a symmetric positive semi-definite matrix of weights, t = 1, . . . , T. Notice that the quadratic criterion W is originally formulated with respect to system (8.1); that is

$$K_t^* = \begin{bmatrix} K_t & 0 \\ 0 & 0 \end{bmatrix}, \qquad a_t^* = \begin{bmatrix} a_t \\ 0 \end{bmatrix},$$

where the partitioning correponds to the partitioning of $y_t^* = (y_t', v_t')'$.

Assuming non-stochastic parameter matrices for the augmented system (8.10), Pagan derived the optimal controller by the application of well known results from standard linear quadratic control problems:

$$x_t = G_t y_{t-1} + G_{vt} E_{t-1} [v_{t-1}] + g_t, \qquad t = 1, \ldots, T,$$

where E_{t-1} denotes that the expectation conditional on information at time t−1, and the matrices G_t, G_{vt}, g_t are derived from the parameters of the system (8.10) and of the quadratic criterion function (see Pagan (1975)). This feedback function becomes operational, however, only if it is supplemented by some device for the calculation of $E_{t-1}[v_{t-1}]$. Notice that with non-stochastic parameters and with the observations up to period t−1 given at time t−1, we obtain $E_{t-1}[v_{t-1}] = v_{t-1}$ by (8.14) and (8.11). Then v_{t-1} is conveniently expressed by the backward representation (8.12). Thus the optimal control rule to be applied at time t is composed of two equations,

$$x_t = G_t y_{t-1} + G_{vt} v_{t-1} + g_t, \qquad t = 1, \ldots, T, \qquad (8.17)$$

$$v_{t-1} = H v_{t-2} + L(y_{t-1} - \Pi w_{t-1}), \qquad t = 2, \ldots, T, \qquad (8.18)$$

with the initial condition $v_0 = \sum_{j=0}^{m} H^j L(y_{-j} - \Pi w_{-j})$.

The recursive computation of the unobservable disturbance vector v_{t-1} by (8.18) clearly requires the model parameters to be known. Notice that the parameters were also treated as given in deriving the optimal controller (8.17). However, to treat the parameters of an econometric decision model as given usually means that in deriving the optimal controller some numerical values, say the estimates from a given sample, will be substituted for the unknown parameters. In that case, numerically specified matrices A^0, B^0, C^0, and ϕ^0 serve as substitutes for A, B, C, and ϕ respectively, and the unobservable disturbance vector is no longer exactly computable.

Then the feedback function gives the control vector x_t in response to y_{t-1} and to v^0_{t-1}, the latter being a well defined substitute for the unobservable v_{t-1}.

Thus when we consider the prediction error where the prediction is conditional on control rules as given by (8.17), (8.18), we must carefully distinguish two cases:

(a) First we assume that the true coefficients are known in the prediction as well as in the specification of the control rules. Accordingly we assume that the control vector x_t will be specified as a function of y_{t-1}, and of the unobservable but computable v_{t-1}, in the form of (8.17). This case will be considered in section 3.

(b) In section 4 we consider the more realistic situation where the coefficients have to be estimated. There we assume that the control vector x_t follows a function of y_{t-1} and v^0_{t-1}, where v^0_{t-1} depends on observations in a well defined way using matrices A^0, B^0, C^0, and ϕ^0 as substitutes for the unknown coefficients in (8.18). The complication due to the use of v^0_{t-1} instead of v_{t-1} will be handled by an appropriate state variable representation of the system. With respect to the prediction error it should be noted that while the model estimation clearly contributes to the predictive uncertainty, we may still consider the prediction error conditional on known control rules for the policy variables. Although the matrices A^0, B^0, C^0, and ϕ^0 will generally result from estimating the model, it is reasonable to consider the policy variables to be subject to exact rules (once they have been selected) whatever their origin may be.

3. MULTIPERIOD PREDICTION OF THE CONTROLLED MODEL WITH KNOWN COEFFICIENTS

Starting from time zero, we consider the prediction of y_h, $h \leqslant T$, given y_0, v_0, the non-controlled exogenous variables z_t, $t = 1, \ldots, h$, and the policy variables x_t subject to the control rule (8.17), i.e. $x_t = G_t y_{t-1} + G_{vt} v_{t-1} + g_t$ for $t = 1, \ldots, h$, when the true parameter values are known. It should be noted that we assume that the unobservable v_{t-1} will be computed exactly by (8.18) when the policy is implemented. With v_0 taken as given we obviously suppose that past observations are known, because by (8.11) and (8.14) we have $v_0 = \Sigma_o^m H^j L(y_{-j} - \Pi w_{-j})$. Rewriting the control rule as

$$x_t = G_t^* y_{t-1}^* + g_t, \qquad t = 1, \ldots, h \tag{8.19}$$

where $G_t^* = (G_t, G_{vt})$, we obtain a representation of the controlled system by substituting (8.19) for x_t in the system (8.10); i.e.

$$y_t^* = R_t^* y_{t-1}^* + r_t^* + e_t^*, \qquad t = 1, \ldots, h, \qquad (8.20)$$

where $R_t^* = A^* + C^* G_t^* = \begin{bmatrix} A + CG_t & \phi + CG_{vt} \\ 0 & F \end{bmatrix}$

and $r_t^* = B^* z_t + C^* g_t = \begin{bmatrix} Bz_t + Cg_t \\ 0 \end{bmatrix}$,

For convenience let us first consider the predictor of the controlled state vector y_h^* conditional on y_0^* and $r_1^*, \ldots, r_h^*$, although ultimately we will be interested in the predictor of y_h rather than of y_h^*.

The predictor of y_h^* conditional on y_0^* and $r_1^*, \ldots, r_h^*$, which will be denoted by $\bar{y}_h^*$, is given recursively by

$$\bar{y}_t^* = R_t^* \bar{y}_{t-1}^* + r_t^*, \qquad t = 1, \ldots, h, \qquad (8.21)$$

where $\bar{y}_0^* = y_0^*$. The corresponding prediction error $\epsilon_t = y_t^* - \bar{y}_t^*$ is written recursively as

$$\epsilon_t = R_t^* \epsilon_{t-1} + \xi_t^*, \qquad t = 1, \ldots, h \qquad (8.22)$$

where $\epsilon_0 = 0$. Thus we obtain the mean square prediction error, $V_h^* = E[\epsilon_h \epsilon_h']$, as

$$V_t^* = R_t^* V_{t-1}^* R_t^{*\prime} + \Omega^*, \qquad t = 1, \ldots, h, \qquad (8.23)$$

where $V_0^* = 0$, and Ω^* is the covariance matrix of e_t^* given by $\Omega^* = (I_p, L')'\Omega(I_p, L)$.

Once we have $\bar{y}_h^*$ by (8.21), we immediately obtain the predictor $\bar{y}_h$ as the upper px1 subvector of $\bar{y}_h^* = (\bar{y}_h', \bar{v}_h')'$. The mean square prediction error of $\bar{y}_h$ is given by the upper left pxp submatrix of V_h^*, say V_h, where V_h^* is obtained from (8.23). It is easily verified that the predictor $\bar{y}_h$ is optimal in the sense of the mean square prediction error, provided that the disturbances e_t^* in (8.20) are serially uncorrelated.

To conclude this section, let us consider the impact of using optimal feedback rules on the prediction error. Notice that in the optimal control framework the prediction error ϵ_t from (8.22), i.e. the deviation of the state vector y_t^* from its mean $\bar{y}_t^*$, is the stochastic part of the deviation of desired from realised state variables. The optimal feedback rule minimises the corresponding part of the expected welfare loss (8.16),

$$E[\sum_{t=1}^{T} \epsilon_t' K_t^* \epsilon_t] = \sum_{t=1}^{T} tr(K_t^* V_t^*) = \sum_{t=1}^{T} tr(K_t V_t),$$

where the last equation holds by definition of K_t^*. Hence, if the predictive accuracy over the planning horizon is measured by the same weights as in the welfare loss function, then we have a gain in predictive accuracy from implementing the optimal feedback rules rather than an open loop policy. For comparison, consider the prediction error of the optimal predictor conditional on an open loop policy. With known parameters that prediction error, say $\epsilon_t|OL$, is independent of the values being selected for the policy variables, and we have

$$\epsilon_t|OL = A^* \epsilon_{t-1}|OL + e_t^*, \qquad t = 1, \ldots, T \tag{8.24}$$

with $\epsilon_0|OL = 0$. Thus the corresponding mean square prediction error matrix, say $V_t^*|OL$, is given by

$$V_t^*|OL = A^*(V_{t-1}^*|OL)A^{*\prime} + \Omega^*, \qquad t = 1, \ldots, T, \tag{8.25}$$

where $V_0^*|OL = 0$ and Ω^* is defined in (8.23). Let $V_t|OL$ denote the upper left pxp submatrix of $V_t^*|OL$. From (8.23) we have the mean square prediction error matrix under the optimal feedback rules, say $V_t^*|FB$, with upper left pxp submatrix $V_t|FB$. Then, by definition of the optimal feedback rules, it follows that

$$\sum_{t=1}^{T} tr(K_t V_t|OL) - \sum_{t=1}^{T} tr(K_t V_t|FB) \geq 0 . \tag{8.26}$$

The gain in predictive accuracy as measured in (8.26) is due to the fact that the optimal feedback policy damps down the dynamic effects of the prediction error whereas under an open loop policy, where the policy variables are fixed with respect to future observations, the dynamic structure of the (uncontrolled) system is unchanged in generating the prediction error by (8.24). That is, the gain in reducing the variances of the prediction errors is produced by choosing the optimal feedback matrix G_t^* in a way that makes the matrix $R_t^* = A^* + C^*G_t^*$ 'small' compared to A^*. In fact, G_t^* is defined as $-(C^{*\prime}H_t^*C^*)^{-1}C^{*\prime}H_t^*A^*$, and moreover it minimises $tr(R_t^{*\prime}H_t^*R_t^*)$, where the weighting matrix H_t^* is determined by the Riccati equation $H_t^* = K_t^* + R_{t+1}^{*\prime}H_{t+1}^*R_{t+1}^*$ with $H_T^* = K_T^*$. Through that weighting matrix, the minimisation of $tr(R_t^{*\prime}H_t^*R_t^*)$ takes into account the current prediction error ϵ_t as well as the prediction error dynamics up to the end of the planning horizon.

A formal analogy between the calculation of G_t^* and generalised least squares regression indicates what the gains from applying optimal feedback rules depend on. Let us write (see Chow (1975) for a similar treatment)

$$A^* = -C^*G_t^* + R_t^*$$

where the j-th column of G_t^* plays the role of the 'generalised least squares estimator' in the regression of the j-th column of A^* on the matrix of 'explanatory variables' $-C^*$, and the j-th column of R_t^* plays the role of the 'regression residuals'; the index t refers to the weighting matrix H_t^* used in the 'generalised least squares estimation'. Clearly the gain from using the matrix R_t^*, rather than the matrix A^* itself in the process that generates the prediction error, depends on the 'explanatory power' of the matrix $-C^*$ with respect to the columns of A^*; hence, in particular, it depends on the number of policy instrument variables.

A final remark may be in order to prevent misunderstanding: The gain in predictive accuracy from applying the optimal feedback rules is guaranteed only if it is measured by (8.26), that is, by use of the weights from the welfare loss function. It cannot be proved that the difference between the two prediction error covariance matrices, $V_t|OL - V_t|FB$, is positive semi-definite.

4. MULTIPERIOD PREDICTION OF THE CONTROLLED MODEL WITH ESTIMATED COEFFICIENTS

4.1 Representation of the controlled model

For convenience let us first rewrite the system (8.10) as

$$\begin{bmatrix} y_t \\ \\ v_t \end{bmatrix} = \begin{bmatrix} A & \phi \\ \\ 0 & F \end{bmatrix} \begin{bmatrix} y_{t-1} \\ \\ v_{t-1} \end{bmatrix} + \begin{bmatrix} C \\ \\ 0 \end{bmatrix} x_t + \begin{bmatrix} B \\ \\ 0 \end{bmatrix} z_t + \begin{bmatrix} I_p \\ \\ L \end{bmatrix} e_t \tag{8.27}$$

From now on we assume that for t = 1, . . . , T the control vector x_t follows a given feedback function in the form of (8.17) and (8.18):

$$x_t = G_t^0 y_{t-1} + G_{vt}^0 v_{t-1}^0 + g_t^0 , \tag{8.28}$$

$$v^0_{t-1} = H^0 v^0_{t-2} + L(y_{t-1} - \Pi^0 w_{t-1}), \tag{8.29}$$

with the initial condition v^0_0. Notice that the functional form of this feedback policy covers the first order certainty equivalent rules as well as stochastic control rules without learning. In the first case certainty equivalents serve as substitutes for unknown parameters in deriving the control rule (8.28) and (8.29) inclusive of the computation of the initial condition v^0_0 by the backward representation. In the second case the computation of G^0_t, G^0_{vt}, and g^0_t involves the parameter uncertainty expressed in terms of the variances and covariances of the parameters, whereas the calculation of v^0_{t-1} by (8.29) remains unchanged.

In deriving a state variable representation of the controlled model we have to incorporate the development of v^0_t which is no longer equal to the unobservable disturbance vector v_t. By (8.29) v^0_{t-1} depends on the contemporary observation of y_{t-1} which we assume is available when x_t is to be implemented. Thus (8.29) is convenient for computing v^0_{t-1} at the same time. It has to be written in reduced form, however, for the purpose of augmenting system (8.27) by v^0_t. Shifting the time index in (8.29), and substituting for the contemporary endogenous variables at the right hand side of (8.29), we obtain the reduced form equation

$$v^0_t = H^0 v^0_{t-1} + L\left\{(\Pi - \Pi^0)w_t + \phi v_{t-1} + e_t\right\}. \tag{8.30}$$

Hence, the augmented system may be written as

$$\mathcal{y}_t = \mathcal{A}\mathcal{y}_{t-1} + \mathcal{C}x_t + \mathcal{B}z_t + \mathcal{e}_t, \tag{8.31}$$

where

$$\mathcal{y}_t = \begin{bmatrix} y_t \\ v^0_t \\ v_t \end{bmatrix}, \qquad \mathcal{A} = \left[\begin{array}{c:c:c} A & 0 & \phi \\ L(A-A^0) & H^0 & L\phi \\ 0 & 0 & F \end{array}\right]$$

$$\mathcal{e}_t = \begin{bmatrix} I_p \\ L \\ L \end{bmatrix} e_t, \qquad \mathcal{C} = \begin{bmatrix} C \\ L(C-C^0) \\ 0 \end{bmatrix}, \qquad \mathcal{B} = \begin{bmatrix} B \\ L(B-B^0) \\ 0 \end{bmatrix}$$

Rewriting the control equation (8.28) in terms of the augmented state vector $\mathcal{y}_{t-1}$, we get

$$x_t = G_t^0 y_{t-1} + g_t^0 \tag{8.32}$$

where $G_t^0 = (G_t^0, G_{vt}^0, 0)$. Now substituting (8.32) into (8.31), we derive the representation of the controlled model as

$$y_t = R_t y_{t-1} + r_t + e_t, \qquad t = 1, \ldots, T \tag{8.33}$$

where

$$R_t = A + CG_t^0,$$

$$r_t = Bz_t + Cg_t^0.$$

4.2 Prediction scheme with estimated coefficients

Starting at time zero we assume that the components y_0 and v_0^0 of y_0 are known. For v_0 we again use the backward representation $v_0 = \Sigma_o^m H^j L(y_{-j} - \Pi w_{-j})$, where we suppose that the observations occuring at the right hand side are given. Let $\tilde{\Pi}$, $\tilde{\phi}$ denote consistent estimates of the respective parameter matrices. Substituting the estimates for the unknown parameters in the backward representation of v_0 we obtain $\tilde{v}_0$. Then our predictor of y_h, $h \leqslant T$, will be based on the initial vector $\tilde{y}_0 = (y_0', v_0^{0'}, \tilde{v}_0')'$. Assuming further that the conditioning information comprises expected future values of the non-controlled exogenous variables as well as the parameter values of the control rule (these will be the certainty equivalent matrices indicated by ^{0}), we consider the predictor $\tilde{y}_h$ of y_h given by the recursive equation

$$\tilde{y}_t = \tilde{R}_t \tilde{y}_{t-1} + \tilde{r}_t, \qquad t = 1, \ldots, h, \tag{8.34}$$

with $\tilde{y}_0 = (y_0', v_0^{0'}, \tilde{v}_0')'$, and $\tilde{R}_t$, $\tilde{r}_t$ given by substituting the estimates $\tilde{\Pi}$, $\tilde{\phi}$ for the unknown parameters in (8.33). Finally, the predictor of the px1 vector y_h can be obtained by (8.34) as the upper px1 subvector of $\tilde{y}_h = (\tilde{y}_h', \tilde{v}_h^{0'}, \tilde{v}_h')'$.

The policy vector x_t, from (8.32), is predicted by replacing y_{t-1} with its predictor (8.34)

$$\tilde{x}_t = G_t^0 \tilde{y}_{t-1} + g_t^0, \qquad t = 1, \ldots, h. \tag{8.35}$$

It should be noted that, in the prediction scheme (8.34), discriminating between $\tilde{v}_t^0$ and $\tilde{v}_t$ is useful above all for the analysis of prediction errors due to parameter estimation. Here we have to distinguish between the estimates of the unknown but effective system parameters and the certainty equivalents which we assume to be actually applied in determining the policy variables. With respect to the point prediction, however, the prediction scheme may be simplified if the estimates used in prediction numerically coincide with the certainty equivalents. In that case we may obtain the point prediction of y_h by the recursive system with reduced dimension given by

$$\begin{bmatrix} \tilde{y}_t \\ \\ \tilde{v}_t \end{bmatrix} = \begin{bmatrix} \tilde{A} + \tilde{C}G_t^0 & \tilde{\phi} + \tilde{C}G_{vt}^0 \\ \\ 0 & \tilde{F} \end{bmatrix} \begin{bmatrix} \tilde{y}_{t-1} \\ \\ \tilde{v}_{t-1} \end{bmatrix} + \begin{bmatrix} \tilde{B}z_t + \tilde{C}g_t^0 \\ \\ 0 \end{bmatrix}, \quad t=1,\ldots,h. \tag{8.36}$$

4.3 Asymptotic distribution of the prediction error

The prediction error can be expressed as

$$\tilde{y}_h - y_h = \tilde{y}_h - \bar{y}_h - d_h \tag{8.37}$$

where

$$d_h = y_h - \bar{y}_h \ ,$$

and $\bar{y}_h = \text{plim}\, \tilde{y}_h$ can be recursively obtained by

$$\bar{y}_t = R_t \bar{y}_{t-1} + r_t \ , \qquad t = 1, \ldots, h \ , \tag{8.38}$$

with $\bar{y}_0 = y_0$, and R_t, r_t as given by (8.33).

4.3.1 Prediction error due to future disturbances

The error due to future disturbances, that is $d_h = y_h - \bar{y}_h$, follows from (8.33) and (8.38) as

$$d_t = R_t d_{t-1} + e_t \ , \qquad t = 1, \ldots, h \ , \tag{8.39}$$

Hence the covariance matrix $D_t = \text{E}[d_t d_t']$ is given by

$$D_t = R_t D_{t-1} R_t' + (I_p, L', L')'\Omega(I_p, L, L) \ , \qquad t = 1, \ldots, h \ , \tag{8.40}$$

where $D_0 = 0$. Let us denote the upper px1 subvector of d_h by δ_h, and the corresponding pxp submatrix of D_h by Δ_h. Then we can state the following theorem.

Theorem 1

The h-period prediction error due to the future disturbances, $\delta_h = y_h - \bar{y}_h$ has covariance matrix

$$\Delta_h = (I_p, 0)\, R_h D_{h-1} R_h' (I_p, 0)' + \Omega$$

where D_{h-1} is given by (8.40).

Notice that if the certainty equivalents coincide with the true parameters, then Δ_h is equal to the matrix V_h and hence may be easier obtained from the upper left pxp matrix of V_h^* in (8.23).

Now let us consider the prediction error due to the estimation of the unknown parameters from a finite sample of size n.

4.3.2 *Prediction error due to parameter estimation*

By use of the vec operator, which stacks the columns $p_1, \ldots, p_m$ of any kxm matrix P to the mkx1 vector $\text{vec}(P) = (p_1', \ldots, p_m')'$, we obtain the reduced form parameters Π, and the disturbance process parameters ϕ, in vectorised form, ordered equation by equation, as

$$\pi = \text{vec}(\Pi'), \qquad \varphi = \text{vec}(\phi'), \tag{8.41}$$

where the length of π and φ is p(p+q+s) and p^2r, respectively. Let $\psi = (\pi', \varphi')'$, with the consistent estimator $\tilde{\psi} = (\tilde{\pi}', \tilde{\varphi}')'$. Teh following theorem provides a useful representation of the difference $\tilde{y}_h - \bar{y}_h$ in terms of the difference $\tilde{\psi} - \psi$.

Theorem 2

For t = 1, . . . , h, $h \leqslant T$, we have

$$\tilde{y}_t - \bar{y}_t = \tilde{Q}_t(\tilde{\psi} - \psi) + R_t(\tilde{y}_{t-1} - \bar{y}_{t-1}) \tag{8.42}$$

and

$$\tilde{y}_0 - \bar{y}_0 = \tilde{Q}_0(\tilde{\psi} - \psi). \tag{8.43}$$

Here the matrices $\tilde{Q}_t$ (t = 1, . . . , h) are defined by $\tilde{Q}_t = [M \otimes \tilde{w}_t', N \otimes \tilde{v}_{t-1}']$, where $\tilde{w}_t' = (\tilde{y}_{t-1}', \tilde{x}_t', z_t')$ and $\tilde{v}_{t-1}'$ are given by (8.34) and (8.35); and M, N are matrices of order p(2r+1)xp defined by $M = (I_p, L', 0)'$ and $N = (I_p, L', L')'$ for AR disturbances, and N = M for MA disturbances.

For the matrix $\tilde{Q}_0$ we have $\tilde{Q}_0 = (0, I_{pr})' Q_0$, where

$$Q_0 = \begin{cases} \left[-\sum_{j=0}^{r-1} H^j L(I_p \otimes w'_{-j}) \;\middle|\; 0 \right] & \text{for AR} \\ \left[-\sum_{j=0}^{\infty} H^j L(I_p \otimes w'_{-j}, I_p \otimes \tilde{v}_{-j-1}) \right] & \text{for MA} \end{cases}$$

and $\tilde{v}_i$, $i \leqslant 0$, may be obtained by

$$\tilde{v}_i = \tilde{H} \tilde{v}_{i-1} + L(y_i - \tilde{\Pi} w_i) = \sum_{j=0}^{\infty} \tilde{H}^j L(y_{i-j} - \tilde{\Pi} w_{i-j}).$$

Proof

By (8.34) and (8.40) we have

$$\tilde{y}_t - \bar{y}_t = (\tilde{R}_t - R_t)\tilde{y}_{t-1} + \tilde{r}_t - r_t + R_t(\tilde{y}_{t-1} - \bar{y}_{t-1}). \tag{8.44}$$

Let us denote the expression $(\tilde{R}_t - R_t)\tilde{y}_{t-1} + \tilde{r}_t - r_t$ at the right hand side of (8.44) by q_t. To prove (8.42) we have to show that q_t can be written as $\tilde{Q}_t(\tilde{\psi} - \psi)$. Using the definitions of R_t, r_t we begin with

$$q_t = (\tilde{A} - A)\tilde{y}_{t-1} + (\tilde{C} - C)(G_t^0 \tilde{y}_{t-1} + g_t^0) + (\tilde{B} - B)z_t,$$

where A, C, and B are defined in (8.31). Substituting $\tilde{x}_t$ from (8.35), q_t can be rewritten, using the matrix M defined in the theorem,

$$q_t = M(\tilde{\Pi} - \Pi)\tilde{w}_t + \left\{ M(\tilde{\phi} - \phi) + \begin{bmatrix} 0 \\ 0 \\ \tilde{F} - F \end{bmatrix} \right\} \tilde{v}_{t-1}.$$

Notice that $\tilde{F} - F = 0$ for MA disturbances and $\tilde{F} - F = L(\tilde{\phi} - \phi)$ for the AR case. Thus, using the matrix N as defined in the theorem, we find

$$q_t = M(\tilde{\Pi} - \Pi)\tilde{w}_t + N(\tilde{\phi} - \phi)\tilde{v}_{t-1},$$

or

$$q'_t = \tilde{w}'_t(\tilde{\Pi} - \Pi)' M' + \tilde{v}'_{t-1}(\tilde{\phi} - \phi)' N' .$$

Applying the stacking operator to the matrix products at the right hand side of the equation of q'_t, according to the rule vec(UVW) = (W′ ⊗ U)vec(V) (see Nissen 1968)), we conclude

$$q_t = \mathrm{vec}(q'_t) = (M \otimes \tilde{w}'_t)(\tilde{\pi} - \pi) + (N \otimes \tilde{v}'_{t-1})(\tilde{\varphi} - \varphi) = \tilde{Q}_t(\tilde{\psi} - \psi).$$

Substituting this expression for q_t in (8.44) we obtain (8.42). To prove the second part of the theorem, i.e. the initialisation of (8.42) by (8.43), we start by noting that at the initial time zero we have

$$\tilde{y}_0 - y_0 = (y'_0, v_0^{0\prime}, \tilde{v}'_0)' - (y'_0, v_0^{0\prime}, v'_0)' = (0, I_{pr})'(\tilde{v}_0 - v_0) .$$

By the backward representation $v_j = Hv_{j-1} + L(y_j - \Pi w_j)$ we derive

$$\tilde{v}_j - v_j = -L(\tilde{\Pi} - \Pi)w_j + (\tilde{H} - H)\tilde{v}_{j-1} + H(\tilde{v}_{j-1} - v_{j-1}) .$$

Starting with j = 0 and repeatedly employing that equation we find

$$\tilde{v}_0 - v_0 = \sum_{j=0}^{m} H^j \left\{ -L(\tilde{\Pi} - \Pi)w_{-j} + (\tilde{H} - H)\tilde{v}_{-j-1} \right\} .$$

By definition (8.13) of H we have $\tilde{H} - H = 0$ for AR disturbances and $\tilde{H} - H = -L(\tilde{\phi} - \phi)$ in case of an MA process. Thus we derive

$$\tilde{v}_0 - v_0 = \begin{cases} -\sum_{j=0}^{r-1} H^j L(\tilde{\Pi} - \Pi)w_{-j} & \text{for AR} \\ \\ -\sum_{j=0}^{\infty} H^j L \left\{ (\tilde{\Pi} - \Pi)w_{-j} + (\tilde{\phi} - \phi)\tilde{v}_{-j-1} \right\} & \text{for MA} \end{cases}$$

Applying the stacking operator in the same way as above we finally obtain $\tilde{v}_0 - v_0 = \tilde{Q}_0(\tilde{\psi} - \psi)$. Hence we have shown (8.43), thereby concluding the proof of the theorem.

Given the asymptotic distribution of $\sqrt{n}(\tilde{\psi} - \psi)$, Theorem 2 immediately implies the asymptotic distribution of $\sqrt{n}(\tilde{y}_h - \bar{y}_h)$.

Theorem 3

If the asymptotic distribution of $\sqrt{n}(\tilde{\psi} - \psi)$ is $N(0, \Sigma)$, then the asymptotic distribution of $\sqrt{n}(\tilde{y}_h - \bar{y}_h)$ is $N(0, E_h \Sigma E_h')$, where $E_h = (I_p, 0)\, E_h$, and E_h is recursively defined by

$$E_0 = Q_0$$

$$E_t = Q_t + R_t E_{t-1} \,, \qquad t = 1, \ldots, h\,.$$

Here Q_0 and Q_t, $t = 1, \ldots, h$, are given by substituting the true parameter values for the estimates in $\tilde{Q}_0, \tilde{Q}_t$.

Proof

Clearly by Theorem 2 we have $\sqrt{n}(\tilde{y}_h - \bar{y}_h) = \tilde{E}_h \sqrt{n}(\tilde{\psi} - \psi)$ for $h \leqslant T$, where $\tilde{E}_h$ is recursively defined by

$$\tilde{E}_0 = \tilde{Q}_0 \,, \quad \text{and} \quad \tilde{E}_t = \tilde{Q}_t + R_t \tilde{E}_{t-1}, \qquad t = 1, \ldots, h.$$

Further we obtain the upper px1 subvector of $\tilde{y}_h - \bar{y}_h$ by the choice matrix $(I_p, 0)$ of order pxp(2r+1), hence, $\sqrt{n}(\tilde{y}_h - \bar{y}_h) = \tilde{E}_h \sqrt{n}(\tilde{\psi} - \psi)$, where $\tilde{E}_h = (I_p, 0)\tilde{E}_h$. Noting that the probability limit of $\tilde{E}_h$ is E_h as defined in the theorem, the proposition is an immediate consequence of the well known result that if ξ is a vector with asymptotic distribution $N(0, \Sigma)$, and if $\tilde{E}$ is a matrix with probability limit E, then $\tilde{E}\xi$ has asymptotic distribution $N(0, E\Sigma E')$.

4.3.3 Aysmptotic mean square prediction error

In the preceding two sections we have analysed the two parts of the h-period prediction error $\tilde{y}_h - \bar{y}_h$ of the controlled model. Because we consider predictions outside of the sample used to estimate the parameters, the error $y_h - \bar{y}_h$, depending on the future disturbances $e_1, \ldots, e_h$, is independent of the error due to parameter estimation, $\tilde{y}_h - \bar{y}_h$. Thus the asymptotic mean square error of prediction is given by the results of Theorem 1 and Theorem 3 as

$$\Delta_h + (1/n)\, E_h \,\Sigma\, E_h' \,. \tag{8.45}$$

Notice that the asymptotic covariance matrix of the reduced form estimates Σ can be derived from the asymptotic covariance matrix of the structural form estimates, say θ, by $\Sigma = P\,\theta\,P'$, where the transformation matrix P follows by straightforward application of the method proposed in Dhrymes (1973). The covariance matrix θ of the structural form estimator is given in Dhrymes and Erlat (1974) or Hatanaka (1976) for AR disturbances.

Obviously (8.45) depends on unknown parameters. However, these parameters can be estimated, so the above covariance matrix can be estimated.

5. CONCLUSION

We have derived the asymptotic mean square prediction error for the h-period prediction of a linear dynamic model with autocorrelated disturbances, where we assume that the future policy variables follow given feedback rules. The prediction error conditional on an open loop policy, as analysed in Yamamoto (1980), may be obtained as a special case by setting $G_t = 0$. That is equivalent to replacing the matrix R_t with A in Theorem 1, 2 and 3. Furthermore, the computation in that case can be simplified by deleting the subvector v_t^0 from the system because y_t will no longer depend on v_{t-1}^0.

All the major results are given by recursive equations which are particularly convenient for computational purposes. It should be noted, however, that we were only concerned with the *transformation* of uncertainty due to the disturbances and the estimates into predictive uncertainty, and hence for the application of the results we basically require the (estimated) covariance matrix of the parameter estimates. Further research is required with respect to the estimation problem itself, if we not only propose some feedback rules to be applied in the future but assume that the policy instrument variables also depend upon endogenous variables in the estimation period.

In section 3 we have shown that in the case of known coefficients the predictive accuracy measured by the welfare loss criterion will be improved by implementing optimal feedback rules rather than an open loop policy. For the prediction with estimated coefficients we might also expect a gain in predictive accuracy from applying, say, the first order certainty feedback rules. The situation however becomes more complicated when we consider the predictive uncertainty from the disturbances as well as from the estimated coefficients and at the same time take the coefficients as given in deriving optimal feedback rules. Further investigations will have to clarify if and in what sense the prediction error due to the disturbances and to the estimation is reduced by applying optimal feedback rules instead of an open loop policy.

REFERENCES

Chow, G.C. (1975), *Analysis and Control of Dynamic Economic Systems*, Wiley, New York.

Dhrymes, P.J. (1973), 'Restricted and unrestricted reduced forms: Asymptotic distribution and relative efficiency', *Econometrica*, 41, pp. 119-134.

Dhrymes, P.J. and H. Erlat (1974), 'Asymptotic properties of full information estimators in dynamic autoregressive simultaneous equation models', *Journal of Econometrics*, 2, pp. 247-259.

Friedmann, R. (1981), 'The reliability of policy recommendations and forecasts from linear econometric model', *International Economic Review*, 22, pp. 415-428.

Hatanaka, M. (1976), 'Several efficient two-step estimators for the dynamic simultaneous equation models with autoregressive disturbances', *Journal of Econometrics*, 4, pp. 189-204.

Nissen, D. (1968), 'A note on the variance of a matrix', *Econometrica*, 36, pp. 603-604.

Pagan, A. (1975), 'Optimal control of econometric models with autocorrelated disturbance terms', *International Economic Review*, 16, pp. 258-262.

Schmidt, P. (1974), 'The asymptotice distribution of forecasts in the dynamic solution of an econometric model', *Econometrica*, 42, pp. 303-309.

Yamamoto, T. (1980), 'On the treatment of autocorrelated errors in the multiperiod prediction of dynamic simultaneous equation models', *International Economic Review*, 21, pp. 735-748.

CHAPTER 9

THE EVALUATION OF HISTORICAL POLICY VIA OPTIMAL CONTROL TECHNIQUES

C.F. Baum
Boston College, USA

1. INTRODUCTION

Economists and policymakers have been concerned with the evaluation of historical policies in the macroeconomy since the development of macroeconomics. Although it is possible to 'evaluate' policies in an informal, purely descriptive sense, any formal evaluation must include the specification of targets, or goals, and a scheme for assessing performance toward those goals.

The theoretical development of macroeconomics and quantitative methods has led to a formalised theory of economic policy, in which the selection of policies is the outcome of an optimisation procedure. This introduction of optimisation into the policy selection problem is fortuitous for those concerned with policy evaluation, for the specification and weighting of goals mentioned above is analogous to the construction of an objective function for policy selection. Therefore, many of the mathematical tools adapted for policy selection may also be used to good advantage in policy evaluation. The solution of a policy selection problem as a multi-period dynamic optimisation, or optimal control problem, suggests that historical policies may be judged *ex post* by using the same apparatus.

The application of optimal control techniques to policy evaluation has several advantages over the more common procedures based upon dynamic simulation methods. First of all, to enable comparability any multi-dimensional evaluation of realised versus target values must be reduced to a scalar measure, such as the scalar expected loss in an optimal control problem. The practitioners of simulation methodology have used the point estimates generated by a deterministic simulation to calculate a scalar measure of weighted loss, without any explicit optimisation over targets. This allows modellers to state that the policy settings of one simulation are to

Hughes Hallett, A.J. (ed.) Applied Decision Analysis and Economic Behaviour
©1984, Martinus Nijhoff Publishers. Dordrecht/Boston/Lancaster
ISBN 90-247-2968-8. Printed in The Netherlands

be preferred to those of another, given a target set. However, this approach either treats the observed residuals as known exogenous variables, or ignores them completely —neither alternative doing justice to the considerable information gained in the construction and operation of a macroeconometric model. Thus, as a second principle, we suggest that any reasonable method of policy evaluation should take the probability distributions of the disturbances into account, rather than their realisations. Otherwise, the policy evaluation problem unjustly penalises the policymaker for disregarding information which was not available at the time his decisions were made.

A similar (and perhaps even stronger) argument may be made for the consideration of policymakers' uncertainty about the econometric model's parameters. We have known since Brainard's classic article (1967) that optimal policy settings, or rules, will be affected by the degree of uncertainty expressed by each parameter's interval estimate. Nevertheless, policy selection exercises have often been (informally) conducted without any concern for this factor. For instance, stochastic simulations have often considered only the degree of additive uncertainty facing policymakers, and ignored the more damaging multiplicative uncertainty derived from estimated parameters. Policy evaluation exercises should be performed with the same techniques as those applicable for policy selection —including optimisation over the probability distributions of the model's unknown parameters.

This paper presents a framework for the evaluation of historical policy, applying both 'standard' optimal control techniques (in section 2) and 'suboptimal control' techniques, explicitly designed to act as a benchmark in the comparison of a suboptimal policy against its optimal counterpart (in section 3). These techniques are designed to provide a consistent scalar measure for historical policies, which takes into account both the additive and multiplicative scources of uncertainty about the structure of the macroeconometric model. An application of these sets of techniques to a familiar macroeconometric model —Klein's Model I— is presented in section 4. Section 5 presents some concluding remarks.

2. STANDARD OPTIMAL CONTROL TECHNIQUES

It is not the purpose of this paper to survey all types of control-theoretic solutions to policy selection and evaluation problems. Rather, the subsequent development will be focused upon one particular technique: closed loop, feedback control in the presence of uncertainty. The solution of the closed loop (feedback control) problem expresses the future policy settings as functions of the observed state of the economic system at that point, so that as disturbances occur, a feedback law or control rule applies the optimal 'course correction' to offset their effects. The most concise statement of the closed loop approach is probably that of Chow (1975). The alternative approach involves the open loop control technique, as exemplified by Theil (for instance, in Theil (1964)). It should be noted that a first period equivalence of the two approaches was demonstrated by Norman (1974). But it does not generalise (as demonstrated by Holbrook and Howrey (1978)) to cases with parameter uncertainty when the two approaches become not merely computational alternatives, but solutions to quite separate optimisation problems. The open loop approach has found favour with the proprietors of large econometric models, for it is a straightforward extension of the computational methodology required for simulation of those structures; see, for example, Fair (1974, 1978, 1983), Holbrook (1974), and Hirsch et al. (1978).

With these caveats aside, let us briefly describe the fundamental technique to be considered in this study. We wish to solve a finite horizon (T-period) stochastic optimal control problem in discrete time. All economic variables of interest are contained in the system's state vector, y_t, with conformable target vector a_t. A weighting matrix K_t, usually assumed diagonal and time varying, expresses the policymaker's preferences. The objective function is thus a quadratic form,

$$L = E_0 \Sigma (y_t - a_t)' K_t (y_t - a_t) \tag{9.1}$$

which is to be minimised subject to the set of constraints posed by the reduced form econometric model:

$$y_t = Ay_{t-1} + Cx_t + Pw_t + u_t \tag{9.2}$$

in which the coefficient matrices (A, C, P) are assumed unknown but time invariant. The elements of x_t are the policy variables, while the truly exogenous variables are contained in w_t. The error process u_t is assumed to be Gaussian. The expectations operator in the objective function, E_0, denotes that the problem is to be solved conditional upon the information available in period zero (summarised by the state vector y_0). In the presence of learning, or adaptive control, the expectation of an element of A, say, would be updated as the relevant information is acquired. In our scheme, this updating is not performed.

The solution to this multiperiod control problem is thus a constrained optimisation, which may be constructed via Lagrangean techniques (see Chow (1975, Ch. 7)) or via the more customary dynamic programming techniques (see Chow (1975, Ch. 8, 10)). As the latter reference develops in considerable detail, a solution is the sequence of feedback rules:

$$x_\tau = G_\tau y_{\tau-1} + g_\tau \qquad \tau = 1, \ldots, T \tag{9.3}$$

with optimal policy settings expressed as linear functions of the most recently observed state of the system. This suggests that a number of alternative (non-optimal, or arbitrary) policies may be considered not as policy settings, but as alternative policy rules. For instance, a non-feedback policy may be represented as a null matrix G_t, with vector g_t equal to the historical policy values. Any sequence of observed policy settings may be analysed, *ex post*, as a time varying feedback rule; and regression techniques may be used to determine whether observed policies represent a policy-maker's stable set of choices of G_t and g_t. The minimal expected loss achieved by the optimal settings may then be compared, on a scalar basis, with that presented over the same horizon by the G_t, g_t sequence. Section 3 describes the modifications made to the optimal policy algorithm to facilitate the 'costing' of such an arbitrary sequence, and the ramifications of doing so.

3. 'SUBOPTIMAL CONTROL' TECHNIQUES

Evaluation of historical policies for the macroeconomy within a consistent framework may be performed with 'suboptimal control' methods: essentially, those modifications to the standard Chow-type dynamic programming algorithm which enable the 'costing' of any arbitrary set of feedback rules, and comparison of that cost with a measure associated with the optimal solution to the policy selection problem. These modifications (described in more detail in Baum (1977, 1983)) involve purely analytical extensions to Chow's formulae (1975, p. 231) for what has been generally termed the 'cost-to-go' – that is, the expected loss associated with policy selection from this point onward.

The backward recursion of the dynamic programming algorithm must be made capable of calculating the 'cost-to-go' associated with an arbitrary G_t and g_t. When this is achieved, the optimal control software can compare the characteristics of the optimum versus that of any suboptimum, including that which is taken to represent the effects of historical policy. It should be stressed that this approach, involving the calculation of expected loss for the suboptimum, is not equivalent to that computed by inserting the historical (realised) values of the endogenous variables in the loss function. That latter approach, effectively that chosen by the NBER/NSF Model Comparison Seminar (see Hirsch et al. (1978)), focuses upon the outcomes – the outputs of the economic system – rather than the policy inputs, and ignores all issues of policymakers' uncertainty about the efficacy of their instruments. This approach was also that used by Fair (1978) in his evaluation of U.S. presidential administrations' economic performance via open loop control techniques.

A contemporaneous study by Chow (1978) utilised the closed loop methodology, but failed to confront the multiplicative uncertainty emanating from the model's parameter estimates. Chow's approach considered that a suboptimal (arbitrary) policy affects the initial conditions for future policy choices. In each period, the marginal loss associated with that period's suboptimal policy could be then calculated as an increase in the cost-to-go, assuming that all future policies were optimal. Thus, Chow constructed a measure of loss in each period, and summed that loss over the suboptimal horizon. In the absence of multiplicative uncertainty, this approach is well founded; however, it rests upon a certainty equivalence argument which does not carry over to the unknown parameter case.

In this development, we must note that no unique representation of historical policy exists in terms of an arbitrary feedback rule. One alternative has already been mentioned – that we might represent historical policy as:

$$x_t = G_t y_{t-1} + x_t(h) \qquad \text{with } G_t \text{ null} \tag{9.4}$$

That is, the arbitrary 'feedback rule' representing historical policy is not a feedback rule at all, but merely a passive echo of the historical policy settings. This representation is straightforward, but probably should not be compared directly with the optimal policy set's expected loss. The latter is essentially the outcome of examining the dynamics of a time varying system:

$$y_t = (A+CG_t)y_{t-1} + Cg_t + Pw_t + u_t \tag{9.5}$$

where policy variables have been endogenised. The dynamic properties of this model differ from those of the original econometric model, which has a fundamental dynamic matrix A rather than $(A+CG_t)$. If we wish to examine historical policy settings for x_t on a consistent basis, we might define the benchmark:

$$x_t = G_t y_{t-1} + \hat{x}_t \qquad \text{with } G_t \text{ null} \tag{9.6}$$

where $\hat{x}_t$ is the expected policy setting for the true optimum. This model will have the same dynamic properties as that constructed from (9.4) above. The shortcoming, of course, is that we are now making use of the optimal expected (E_0) settings for policy variables. A policymaker performing closed loop control generally would not make use of $\hat{x}_2$, $\hat{x}_3$ and the rest, but would follow the optimal rule defining those policy settings in terms of the most recently observed state variables. Nevertheless, the comparison of the expected loss associated with (9.6) *vis-a-vis* that associated with (9.7) from historical policy, is a reasonable comparison.

In addition to conducting a comparison of the expected loss function's magnitudes for these two alternatives, both suboptimal, we may also compare the expected trajectories of state variables, both targets and controls. The benchmark solution's expected trajectories should not differ from those generated by the fully optimal solution; only the stochastic components of expected loss should be affected. In the historical case, the expected trajectories of targets may differ from historical values; the system's inputs are identical to those used in history, but the outputs –endogenous variables– will be those generated by the econometric model, which will not reproduce history perfectly. In the following section's application of these techniques, we shall denote these alternatives as 'fully optimal', 'suboptimal benchmark' (as in (9.6)) and 'historical' (as in (9.4)).

4. AN APPLICATION OF OPTIMAL CONTROL TO KLEIN'S MODEL I

In this section, we apply the techniques discussed above to a policy selection and evaluation problem based upon the behaviour of the U.S. economy during the Great Depression. The macroeconometric model utilised for this purpose is Klein's celebrated interwar model, 'Model I' (Klein (1950)). It must be stressed that the purpose of this exercise is not to demonstrate the superiority of this particular model for evaluation of the period, or indeed to claim that large-scale structural models are generally necessary for policy evaluation and selection. We merely apply the well known Klein's Model I to illustrate the usefulness of the optimal control methodology, given an econometric model and loss function. The use of this extremely simple, well known model permits us to introduce it in an abbreviated fashion and proceed to the control exercise.

The model contains three stochastic equations and three identities:

$$C_t = \underset{(1.3197)}{16.5548} + \underset{(0.1179)}{0.0173}\, P_t + \underset{(0.1072)}{0.2162}\, P_{t-1} + \underset{(0.0402)}{0.8102}\, (W_{1t}+W_{2t}) + u_{1t}$$

$$I_t = \underset{(7.5225)}{20.2782} + \underset{(0.1728)}{0.1502}\, P_t + \underset{(0.1624)}{0.6159}\, P_{t-1} - \underset{(0.0360)}{0.1578}\, K_{t-1} + u_{2t}$$

$$W_{1t} = \underset{(1.1471)}{1.5003} + \underset{(0.0356)}{0.4389}\, (Y_t+T_t-W_{2t}) + \underset{(0.0388)}{0.1467}\, (Y_{t-1}+T_{t-1}-W_{2t-1}) + \underset{(0.0291)}{0.1304}\, t + u_{3t}$$

$$Y_t = C_t + I_t + G_t - T_t$$
$$P_t = Y_t - W_{1t} - T_t$$
$$K_t = K_{t-1} + I_t$$

where C is consumption, P is profits, W_1 is the private wage bill, W_2 is the government wage bill, I is net investment, K is the end-of-period capital stock, Y is (net) national income, T is business taxes, t is time measured from 1931, and G is government expenditures (other than wages). The model's estimated parameters and standard errors given above were calculated via two-stage least squares from annual observations for 1921-1941 by Kloek and Mennes (1960), as reported by Goldberger et al. (1961).

The model is an extremely simple, fixed price Keynesian representation of the interwar macroeconomy. It contains rudimentary dynamic elements, in the form of once-lagged profits in the consumption and investment equations, the lagged capital stock in the investment equation, and once-lagged business gross revenues in the private wage bill equation. Three of the four remaining predetermined variables are government policy instruments (G, T, W_2); the fourth is the time trend.

To prepare the model for a policy selection and evaluation problem, we must first derive its restricted reduced form. Since the model is linear in parameters, this involves only matrix manipulations. Point estimates of the reduced form parameters were taken from Goldberger et al. (1961, p. 566). The derivation of the estimated asymptotic covariance matrix of those reduced form coefficients may be performed via the Goldberger-Nagar-Odeh approximation (1961); the covariance matrix used below was taken from their Table III. (The covariance matrix of reduced form disturbances was taken from their equation (7.4) p. 571).

With the model put into a form amenable for optimal control, the policymaker's objective function must be specified. We have three independent policy instruments; in the context of a fully stochastic (unknown parameter) control problem, we could specify any number of objectives, selecting some or all of the six endogenous variables, plus some or all of the three policy variables as targets. A simple optimisation exercise was performed for this model by van den Bogaard and Theil (BT) (1959), who took President Roosevelt's first term (1933-1936) as the policy horizon. Their general goal was that of ending the Depression by 1936. This took the specific form of restoring consumption per capita to its 1929 level; restoring net investment to ten percent of consumption; and restoring the ratio of business profits to the private wage bill to fifty percent, each goal to be achieved by 1936. Intermediate targets, for 1933-1935, were linear interpolations between realised 1932 values and the goals for 1936. Goals were also set (less realistically) for the three policy variables, requiring them to grow along linear trends estimated from 1920-1932 data. This exercise in 'macrodynamic policy making' was solved by the Theil open loop certainty equivalence approach, essentially ignoring all uncertainty associated with Klein's estimated model.

The policy exercise to be performed here adopts two of BT's goals: the restoration of per capita consumption to its 1929 level, and the restoration of investment to ten percent of that value, for each year of the policy horizon. The horizon is taken to be 1933-1940 –Roosevelt's first two terms– to reduce the danger of policy being adversely affected by the proximity of the terminal period. Given an approximate one percent population growth rate, we constructed target consumption as $C_{1929}(1.01)^{\tau}$ where τ=4 in 1933. This posed a much more ambitious goal than BT's interpolation between 1932 actual and 1936 target values. We placed weight upon these two goals so as to equalise the loss from one unit's deviation from its desired value.

To specify desired values for the policy instruments, we formed target trajectories at a six percent growth rate from their 1929 values. This suggests that the public sector's desired growth rate considerably exceeds that of the private sector. Nevertheless, this is consistent with the behaviour of those policy tools throughout the 1920's, in a period when the government's presence in the economy doubled. Equal weight was placed on each of the policy variables' deviations from desired values, the common value set at ten percent of the endogenous targets' values. This relative weight placed primary emphasis on achievement of the consumption and investment goals, with secondary emphasis on stabilisation of instruments' trajectories.

The eight-year horizon stochastic optimal control solution for this policy selection problems was calculated, and its salient features are reported in Table 9.1.

Table 9.1. Optimal policy, 1933-1940, for Klein's Model I

1933-1940 Average	Optimal Path	Target Path	Deviation (Opt-Tgt)	Historical Path	Deviation (Opt-Hist)
Consumption	63.29	62.29	1.00	55.88	7.42
Investment	2.53	6.23	–3.70	– 0.33	2.86
Private Wage Bill	46.13	–	–	36.86	9.27
Profits	22.38	–	–	15.98	6.41
National Income	73.43	–	–	59.75	13.68
Capital Stock	226.23	–	–	200.74	25.49
Business Taxes	6.72	6.25	0.47	7.54	–0.82
Gov't Purchases	14.32	12.95	1.67	11.74	2.58
Gov't Wage Bill	4.93	6.25	–1.32	6.91	–1.98

Total Expected Loss : 4082.74
Deterministic ('bias-squared') : 3804.01
Stochastic ('variance') : 278.73

The overall expected loss is 4083 units, of which 93% are due to deterministic components: i.e. the degree to which targets are not achieved even in an expected sense (akin to an econometric concept of bias-squared). The problem is a five target, three instrument exercise, so that even in the absence of parameter uncertainty the expected deterministic loss would be nonzero. The optimal and historical paths for the two targeted endogenous variables, national income, and the three instruments are given in Figures 9.1-9.6, respectively. We may note that the proximity of the terminal period markedly affects the last period policy; a longer policy horizon would reduce this effect. Optimal consumption exceeds its targeted path by an average of one billion (1934) dollars, with a large overshoot in the 1937-40 period. Its average level exceeds the historical counterpart by $7.42 billion, Net investment, on the other hand, is less successfully controlled; its optimal path lies $3.7 billion below the targeted path of $6.0-6.7 billion, on average. However, its optimal values are uniformly positive, while the historical values for 1933-35 and 1938 are negative. Investment is increased $2.86 billion from the historical average. National income, which is not targeted, is increased by an average of $13.68 billion over its historical path.

Turning to the instruments, optimal business taxes are on average within $0.5 billion of the desired trajectory, but their timc form is inverted –with optimal taxes declining (rather than steadily growing) until the 1940 setting. Even with the sizeable (and unrealistic) 1940 value, optimal taxes are $0.8 billion less than actual taxes over the period. Government spending is utilised more vigorously than its target trajectory would indicate, and on average at a $2.5 billion higher rate than in the historical period. The government wage bill, on the other hand, is decreased in the optimal solution (until the anomalous 1940 value), and deviates almost $2 billion on average below its historical path.

Analysis of this optimal policy selection exercise points out that even a small, relatively uncomplicated econometric model, possessing minimal dynamic linkages, can generate quite intriguing interactions of policy and outcome. In a fully stochastic setting, the result that some targets are more readily achieved than others is indicative of the difference that parameter uncertainty has made in the policy selection problem. An artificially optimistic result would be generated by an optimal control exercise devoid of such uncertainty –or in a simulation context, for that matter– where both consumption and investment targets might be achieved. Such a result, in the presence of extremely tenuous stochastic linkages between government policy instruments and private sector targets, suggests that the more pessimistic conclusions reached above are more realistic.

We now proceed to the policy evaluation exercise, using the expected optimal

Figures 9.1-9.6.

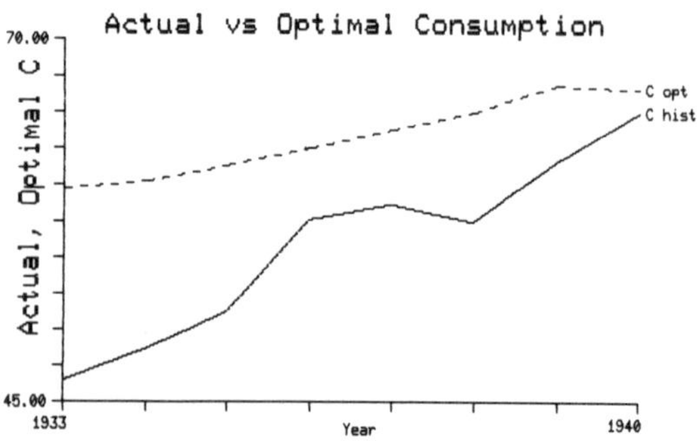

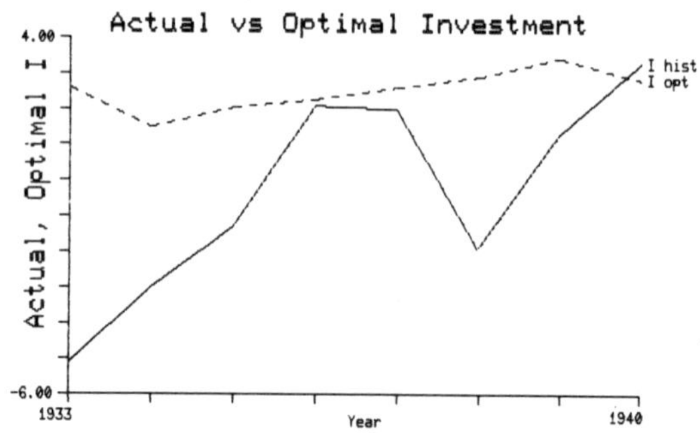

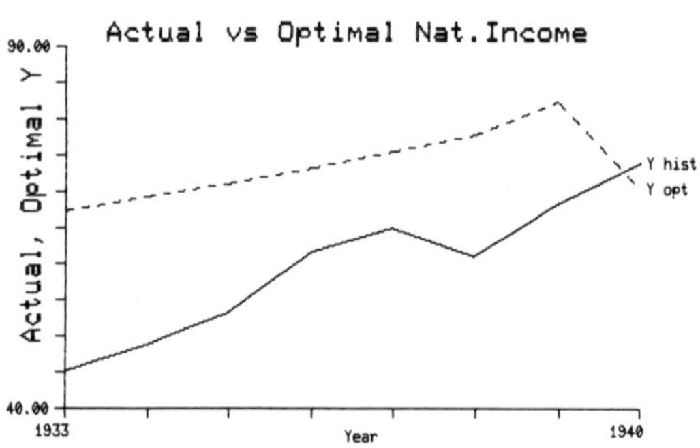

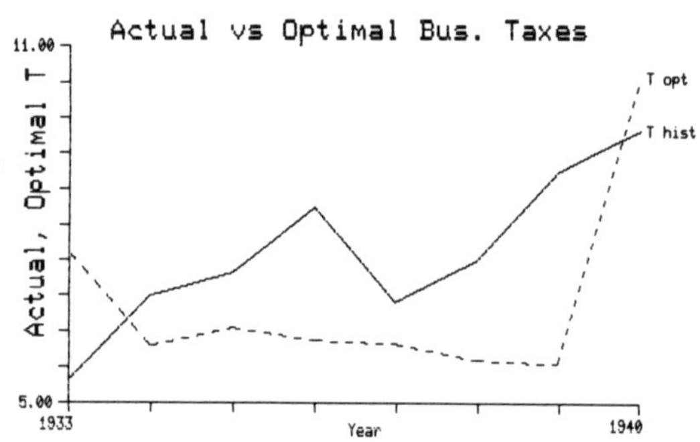

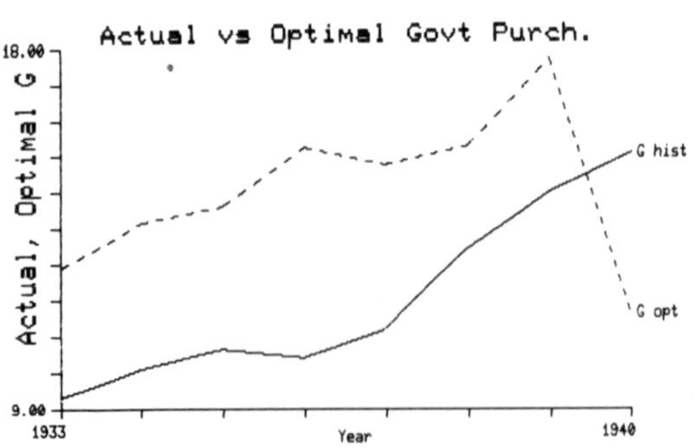

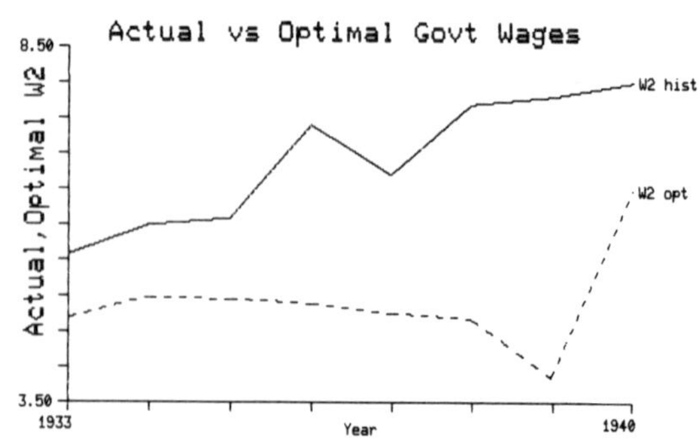

policy settings generated in the above solution to the benchmark historical –'sub-optimal'– policy. The horizon for such a comparison was shortened to four years: the 1933-1936 period. This was necessitated by the abrupt swings in optimal policy in the terminal year (1940). This seeming instability in the instruments has no economic rationale, but is merely the result of approaching the end of the policy horizon (the transversality problem). In a dynamic model of low order –such as Klein's model, which contains only first order lags– optimal policy rules in period τ are constructed taking account of contemporaneous and lagged effects. When the terminal period's policy rule is constructed, there is no loss associated with the lagged effects of that policy. One step back in the dynamic programming recursion, lagged effects become important, and the vigour of planned policy is altered accordingly. Thus, as in other work judging historical versus optimal policy, we have chosen an evaluation horizon shorter than the selection horizon.

The policy evaluation exercise was thus conducted (as was van den Bogaard and Theil's) over the first term of President Roosevelt. The historical settings for the three fiscal instruments were introduced into an 'historical suboptimal' control run, where the eight year optimum was calculated in the first 'pass' over the horizon; then, a second 'pass' was made, with the historical 'rules' (defined in (9.4) above) substituted for the optimal rules for the 1933-1936 period. The computations of expected loss then compare an eight year optimum with an eight year suboptimum, the first four of which refer to historical policy.

The appropriate benchmark against which to judge these historical policy settings, as discussed above, is the 'suboptimal benchmark' control run, where the second pass makes use of the expected optimal policy settings for 1933-1936. Thus, another eight year suboptimum is calculated, with the expected loss reflecting four years of optimal policy settings. This measure of loss may then be compared directly with that derived from the historical suboptimum. These measures are presented in Table 9.2.

Making the proper comparison –between Suboptimal Benchmark and Historical Suboptimal columns– we see that the expected loss from historical policy is 4.22 times that of the suboptimal counterpart. As illustrated in the examination of optimal versus historical policy settings, taxes and government employment were too high in the 1933-36 period, and government spending was too low. The overall fiscal impact of the government sector may have been more contractionary than was necessary to achieve the stated private sector goals. To some degree, the historical government surplus may have been in a reasonable range; but given the differential impacts in the model of government purchases versus government wages, the mix of expenditures was inappropriate. In any case, taxes were too high, and were

Table 9.2. Optimal and suboptimal policy measures for Klein's Model I

	Optimal 1933-40	Suboptimal Benchmark	Historical Suboptimal
Total Expected Loss	4082.74	8479.06	35,807.57
Deterministic	3804.01	8165.00	35,493.45
Stochastic	278.73	314.06	314.12

Notes: The Suboptimal Benchmark consists of optimal settings for 1933-36, optimal rules thereafter.
The Historical Suboptimum consists of historical settings for 1933-36, optimal rules thereafter.

increased rather than reduced in the early years. To some degree, this may reflect the increase in the tax base with tax rates held constant, since the variable measures collections; but a reduction in rates would have achieved the reduction indicated. (Arthur Laffer's prescriptions would have been quite fitting).

The increase in expected loss due to historical policy is seen to be almost exclusively due to the deterministic component. Both historical and suboptimal benchmark policy settings' loss take into account the uncertainty associated with policy linkages. But the settings utilised for the historical period were, in retrospect, quite inappropriate to achieve our private sector targets. In addition, although the number of historical observations is not adequate for sophisticated tests (such as spectral variance decompositions), the figures show that historical policy was considerably more variable than the expected optimal settings. This is not surprising, given that stabilisation of the instruments was an explicit part of the optimisation; but the observed stability of optimal expected consumption, investment and national income reflects the steadier courses taken by optimal fiscal instruments.

5. CONCLUSIONS

In summary, this paper has argued for the utilisation of stochastic closed loop optimal control techniques for historical policy evaluation. The application of these techniques, and the resulting comparison of historical policies with appropriate benchmarks is performed in a fully stochastic setting, wherein all sources of uncertainty faced by the econometric model builder are taken into account. An application of these methods to Klein's Model I illustrated how U.S. fiscal policies during the Great Depression were quite inappropriate to achieve reasonable levels of private aggregate demand.

REFERENCES

Baum, C.F. (1977), 'Applications of optimal control theory to macroeconomic stabilisation policy', unpublished doctoral dissertation, The University of Michigan, Ann Arbor.

Baum, C.F. (1983), 'Evaluating macroeconomic policy: optimal control solutions versus sub-optimal alternatives', in J. Gruber (ed.), *Notes in Economics and Mathematical Systems 208: Econometric Decision Models*, Springer Verlag, Berlin.

Brainard, W. (1967), 'Uncertainty and the effectiveness of policy', *American Economic Review*, 62, 2, pp. 411-425.

Chow, G.C. (1975), *Analysis and Control of Dynamic Economic Systems*, Wiley, New York.

Chow, G.C. (1978), 'Evaluation of macroeconomic policies by stochastic control techniques', *International Economic Review*, 19, 2, pp. 311-320.

Chow, G.C. (1981), *Econometric Analysis by Control Methods*, Wiley, New York.

Fair, R.C. (1974), 'On the solution of optimal control problems as maximisation problems', *Annals of Economic and Social Measurement*, 3, pp. 135-154.

Fair, R.C. (1978), 'The use of optimal control techniques to measure economic performance', *International Economic Review*, 19, pp. 289-309.

Fair, R.C. (1983), *Specification, Estimation and Analysis of Macroeconometric Models*, Harvard University Press, forthcoming.

Gandolfo, G. (1981), *Qualitative Analysis and Econometric Estimation of Continuous Time Dynamic Models*, North Holland, Amsterdam.

Goldberger, A., A. Nagar and H. Odeh (1961), 'The covariance matrices of reduced form coefficient and of forecasts for a structural econometric model', *Econometrica*, 29, 4, pp. 556-573.

Hirsch, A., S. Hymans and H. Shapiro (1978), 'Econometric review of alternative monetary and fiscal policies, 1971-1975', *Review of Economics and Statistics*, 60, pp. 334-345.

Holbrook, R. (1974), 'A practical method for controlling a large non-linear stochastic system', *Annals of Economic and Social Measurement*, 3, pp. 155-175.

Holbrook, R. and E.P. Howrey (1978), 'A comparison of the Chow and Theil optimisation procedures in the presence of parameter uncertainty', *International Economic Review*, 19, 3, pp. 749-759.

Kendrick, D.A. (1981), *Stochastic Control for Economic Models*, McGraw-Hill, New York.

Klein, L.R. (1950), *Economic Fluctuations in the United States 1921-1941*, Wiley, New York.

Kloek, T. and L. Mennes (1960), 'Simulations equations estimation based upon principal components of predetermined variables', *Econometrica*, 28, pp. 45-61.

Norman, A.L. (1974), 'On the relationship between linear feedback control and first period certainty equivalence', *International Economic Review*, 15, 1, pp. 209-215.

Theil, H. (1964), *Optimal Decision Rules for Government and Industry*, North Holland, Amsterdam.

Theil, H. and P.J.M. van den Bogaard (1959), 'Macrodynamic policy making: an application of strategy and certainty equivalence concepts to the economy of the United States, 1933-1936', *Metroeconomica*, 11, pp. 149-167.

PART IV

MARKET MANAGEMENT

CHAPTER 10

ENDOGENOUS VERSUS EXOGENOUS PRICE TARGETS FOR COMMODITY MARKET STABILISATION

Bruce L. Dixon *University of Illinois, USA*
Wu-Hsiung Chen *Ministry of Economic Affairs, Taiwan*

1. INTRODUCTION

Because of the inherent instability of the supply of agricultural commodites due to weather variations, farmer income is subject to constant fluctuation. Because farmer populations can be politically powerful and tend also to constitute a sizeable proportion of many countries' populations, many governments seek to stabilise commodity prices or farm income in some way. Examples of such support plans are minimum prices for commodities, acreage limitations on production and subsidies for various inputs such as fertilizer, seed, operating capital, etc. A currently popular proposal is the use of buffer stock operations where a government acts as a buyer and seller of a commodity to smooth out price variation due to short term fluctuations in supply; see, for example, Burt, Koo and Dudley (1980) or Taylor and Talpaz (1979). It has been argued that overall welfare benefits can result from price stabilisation (Turnovsky (1978)). Klein (1978) has argued that optimal control methods might provide some promising methodological approaches to the problem of buffer stock management.

Dixon and Chen (1982) investigate the use of both deterministic and stochastic control techniques for generating a solution to the problem of stabilisation in the rice market in Taiwan. This market is competitive, although only the government can participate in international trade. Demand is modelled on a monthly basis with an annual supply model having two crops. The control problem formulated by Dixon and Chen is one where the supply and demand models are linear, and the objective is to minimise the squared deviation of farmer and consumer prices from a specified rice price trajectory Two types of targets are formulated: in the first type the target trajectory for the farm price of rice is set according to a price trajectory generated

Hughes Hallett, A.J. (ed.) Applied Decision Analysis and Economic Behaviour

ISBN 90-247-2968-8. Printed in The Netherlands

by the government. In the second type the objective is to keep period-to-period price changes at a constant level. That is, letting PF_t be the farm price of rice in period t, they define a new endogenous variable Δ_{1t} as

$$\Delta_{1t} = FP_t - FP_{t-1} .$$

The target for Δ_{1t} is the amount by which the price is targeted to change each period. Since inflation is anticipated and the model is in nominal terms, it is expected the farm price of rice will rise over time. The planning horizon for the optimal control experiments is 48 months.

Dixon and Chen conduct two sets of experiments, one in which all the behavioural equations of the model are assumed deterministic and another set in which supply is stochastic with yield variations induced by a random number generator. In the deterministic case there is really no distinction between the two types of targets since once the initial farm price is known, the target farm price for all 48 months can be determined. This follows because there is one control variable, government purchases, and one target, the change in farm price.[1] Thus the target price trajectory for the entire planning horizon is known at the beginning of the problem and this trajectory could just as easily be used for absolute price targets.

For problems that seek to minimise period-to-period changes around a target level for change, the absolute price targets are no longer known at t = 0 in a stochastic environment. That is, as stochastic shocks occur, the action taken by the government no longer exactly meets targets and the actual price will usually be different from the target price implied by having prices change by a fixed amount each period. Since the objective is to keep period-to-period price changes at a given level, the absolute price target in the next period will be the current price plus some increment. In such a process it is not possible to state with certainty at the beginning of the planning horizon what the absolute price targets will be over the horizon.

The central question this chapter addresses is whether there is a difference in the performance of a system as a function of the way the price targets are formulated and to assess the attributes of system performance under the alternative price target trajectories. The study by Dixon and Chen suggests several hypotheses for investigation. For a point of reference they compute a 'free market' solution in which there are no government purchases or sales of rice. Then they compute nine different optimal control solutions under varying price target trajectories. All of the price trajectories for the control simulations are much smoother than the free market solution, see the examples in Figure 10.1. Using thirty stochastic simulations of each of the ten different problems, the free market solution displayed significantly less variation in aggregate farmer income and aggregate demand (consumer) expenditures on rice over the planning horizon.[2] This raises two interesting questions: is there a tradeoff between price stability on the one hand, roughly defined as prices not varying much from period-to-period or only changing at relatively few points in time, and stability in the aggregate expenditure and income levels, on the other, over the whole planning horizon? The second question is whether a target trajectory, which is the deterministic price trajectory for the free market solution, would be the most desirable target trajectory to track using stochastic control. In this case 'desirable' is defined as a minimal deviation of prices from target levels and a minimum variation in consumer expenditures and producer income.

The second question raises the issue of what is meant by price stability. It is hard to imagine defending prices changing slowly over time solely on the grounds that such a trajectory is beneficial in and of itself. Usually it is desired to stabilise both producer income and expenditures by consumers, as well as quantity supplied. An alternative view of price stability is to minimise price fluctuations from anticipated levels. With this in view, the idea of governments entering the market to move prices toward the deterministic free market levels would by a type of price stability. One off-shoot of such a policy is that government expenditures might tend to be smaller since the government would possibly not have to store the commodity for as long a period as with a smooth price target trajectory. Additionally, there may be a goal of increasing producer income or decreasing consumer expenditures. Then it becomes important to determine the buffer stock actions that would achieve these goals with a minimum of variability in demand expenditures and producer income. Thus it could be that, if the goal were to increase farmer income over what it would be in a free market solution, then the best target trajectory for the planning horizon might be a five or ten percent increase in prices over the deterministic free market trajectory. Likewise, if the objective were to decrease consumer expenditures, then a plausible set of targets might be to decrease the free market targets by a given percent and use them as an optimal target trajectory.

An aspect that was not explored in Dixon and Chen is whether first differences on prices are the best lag structure for generating price targets endogenously. As noted earlier, a sudden shock to supply would make the price change abruptly and thus cause the absolute price target level to shift markedly. It seems reasonable that a price trajectory, which produces both more stable prices in the sense of small period-to-period variation and stability of income and expenditure aggregates, can be obtained by defining the current target price as a weighted average of a number of past prices plus a small increment. Alternatively, the objective function could be specified to minimise both first and second order differences in price changes. Sarris (1973) gives examples showing the comparative stability of second order stochastic processes with first order processes. Clearly there is no reason why an objective function could not include even third or higher order terms.

A final aspect is whether a preferred price target trajectory can be derived in an endogenous manner, such as using first or second differences, and then used as exogenous targets for the buffer stock agent in the actual control of the system. As noted earlier, in a deterministic setting the price target trajectory under a first difference target scheme is completely determined once the initial price is known. If these absolute prices were used as targets, the results would be the same for the deterministic control solutions as for minimising the first differences. Our conjecture is that the deterministic price trajectory from a perhaps elaborate endogenous price generating process might give a target trajectory to be tracked in the real time control of the system that would generate an overall desirable system performance. If such a process generated real time prices that closely followed the targeted price and other performance criteria, then planning for future activities could be done on a more certain basis.

Given the previous discussion, the following hypotheses are investigated:

1. There is no tradeoff between a smooth price trajectory and the variability of demand expenditures and producer income.
2. The variation of actual price from its targeted level is no different for a target trajectory set by a deterministic free market solution than for a smooth target price trajectory.
3. There is no difference in stablility of prices, expenditures, and income, when prices are set exogenously as opposed to having price targets generated endogenously as the system evolves through time.

In investigating the above hypotheses, the solutions using endogenously generated prices use three different methods of target determination: first differences, first and second differences, and a six-month moving average. The relative performance characteristics of these methods are also considered.

In the following section the methodology for testing these hypotheses is discussed. Then a brief description of the estimated econometric model of the Taiwan rice market is presented and in the final section the results of the stochastic control simulations are presented as a means of testing the hypotheses.

2. METHODOLOGY

2.1 The control problem and solution

Stochastic optimal control is used to investigate the above hypotheses. The control problem is framed as one with a quadratic objective function of the form:

$$J = \sum_{t=1}^{T} (y_t - a_t)' K (y_t - a_t) \tag{10.1}$$

where J is a scalar, y_t is a vector of endogenous (state) variables, a_t is a vector of target levels for the endogenous variables and K is a positive semi-definite matrix of weights giving the relative loss of not meeting one target relative to another. In this investigation the targets of interest are prices although the model could certainly be framed to control the level of other state variables, if desired. Since the endogenous variables are specified to be stochastic, the goal of the control problem is to minimise the expected value of J.

The expected value of the objective function in (10.1) is minimised with respect to a set of first-order, stochastic difference equations given as:

$$y_t = A_t y_{t-1} + B_t u_t + C_t x_t + e_t \tag{10.2}$$

where y_t is the vector of endogenous variables, u_t is a vector of controls (exogenous variables subject to control), and x_t is a vector of uncontrollable exogenous variables. The vector e_t represents stochastic disturbances with mean zero and is assumed to be a white noise process. The parameter matrices A_t, B_t and C_t are coefficient matrices and in this study they are the reduced form coefficients of an econometric model.

Because the coefficients are derived from an econometric model, they clearly are not known with certainty. However, in the simplest control strategies the coefficients are assumed to be known constants and set equal to their point estimates. Given this assumption the optimal levels of u_t, for minimising the expected value of (10.1) subject to (10.2), are given by the linear feedback rule

$$u_t = G_t y_{t-1} + g_t \tag{10.3}$$

as derived in Chow (1975). More complex control strategies acknowledge the uncertainty about the parameters of (10.2) and employ strategies to learn about the unknown parameters; see, for example, Rausser and Freebairn (1974) or Chow (1975). This is not an important concern for the present study. The major source of uncertainty in the Taiwan rice market is weather (implying yield) variability. There is likely to be little information to be gained about weather patterns in Taiwan by the government perturbing its buffer stock actions.

In our investigation both deterministic and stochastic solutions are computed. For both types of solutions the control rule (10.3) is utilised. In the deterministic environment the controls, u_t, can be computed for the entire time horizon at $t = 0$. For stochastic simulations the yield variability for each crop is represented by a random number generator and then the optimal control for period t can be computed as a function of the observed value of y_{t-1}.

Optimal control is certainly not the only method of examining the outcomes of buffer stock operations or other methods of commodity market stabilisation. Chen (1980) investigates a number of methods using a variety of rules to determine government buying and selling activities. Optimal control has an advantage over simulation because by formulating an objective function, the decision maker states explicitly what the goals are of the commodity market manipulation. In our problem that goal is specifically some form of price stability. However, one could just as easily have total consumer expenditure and/or farmer income as goals, or a combination of these monetary aggregates with price levels.[3] By virtue of the explicit optimisation executed by solving the control problem, the system comes as close as possible to obtaining that level of the targeted variable(s). In a simulation process without an explicit statement of an objective function, the search for an optimal policy is ambiguous. In relation to using simulation to obtain price stability as the only goal, optimal control is a superior method because it directly obtains the most stable price trajectory given the parameters of the problem.

2.2 Specification of the stochastic control experiments

The hypotheses given above are tested using a variety of methods. First optimal control simulations are executed under several different objective function specifications, as indicated in table 10.1 below. The first of these, E1, is a free market solution where the government refrains from any selling or purchasing activity. In the next objective function specification, E2, absolute levels for the farm price targets were set based on target prices formulated by the government in Taiwan. The prices are generated with the intent of supporting farmer income, and the particular price shifts are designed to accomodate general price increases as shown in Figure 10.1. In the third specification, E3, the objective is to minimise deviations from prices favourable to consumers. In E4 the change in farm price from month-to-month, Δ_{1t}, is targeted at NT$ 0.046 (NT$ means New Taiwanese dollars) and the objective is to minimise deviations from this target. The initial farm price is increased NT$ 0.25 over the ini-

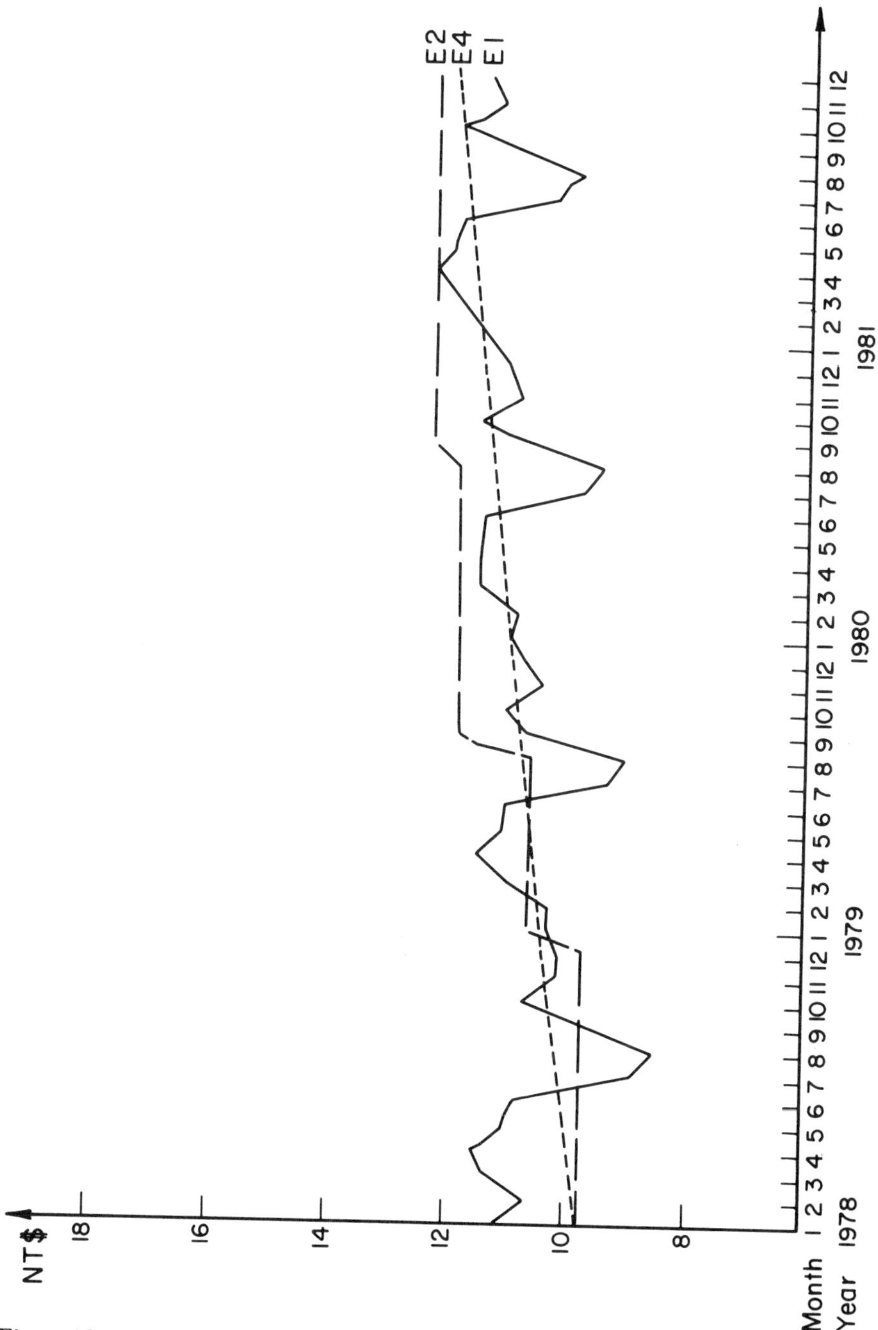

Figure 10.1. Deterministic farm price trajectories for simulations E1, E2 and E4. E1 is the free market trajectory, E2 is based on government plans and E4 portrays constant increase per period.

tial farm price in E1 to give a deterministic price trajectory more favourable to producers than in E1. Then E5 is identical to E4 except the initial price is NT$ 9.25. This gives a deterministic trajectory that favours consumers more than in E1. In general the experiments are structured in pairs like E2, E3, and E4, E5 so that each type of objective function is used to favour consumers in one experiment and producers in the other. The point of reference for these comparisons is E1 because it has no government buying or selling.

In the sixth experiment, E6, the targets for E2 and E4 are combined. As shown in figure 10.1, the absolute price targets in E2 remain constant for a number of months and then shift upwards abruptly. The effect of combining the objectives of E2 and E4 should smooth the abruptiness of the change. The deterministic price trajectories are displayed in figure 10.1 for E1, E2 and E4. Technically E6 is a combination of both exogenous and endogenous target price generation and should therefore be considered as an endogenous method of price generation.

As noted earlier, a criterion of minimising deviations from a target level for first differences for prices may induce considerable noise into the price trajectory. To reduce this possibility, two alternatives are examined. In E7 and E8 first and second order differences are tracked with deviations being weighted equally. In this trajectory the second order price difference is defined as

$$\Delta_{2t} = FP_t - FP_{t-2} \tag{10.4}$$

The targets for the first and second differences are such that the deterministic trajectory is still a straight line, i.e., the first order target is NT$ 0.046 and the second order target is NT$ 0.092. As an alternative to the second order scheme, experiments E9 and E10 specify current farm price less the average of the last six farm prices to grow by a constant amount, NT$ 0.046, each period.[4] Because the initial lagged six prices follow no particular pattern, the deterministic target trajectory is neither linear nor rising constantly.

For the experiments involving the tracking of price changes instead of absolute prices, new endogenous variables are defined and they become the object of control. For example, in E4 and E5 we declare a new endogenous variable Δ_{1t} with a target level in each period of NT$ 0.046. Thus, for E4 and E5, only Δ_{1t} is controlled by the buffer stock actions.

In the final five experiments, E11-E15, the third hypothesis is tested directly. The deterministic target trajectories of E1, E4, E5, E9, and E10 are set as target trajectories in E11-E15, respectively. The objective is then to use government buffer stock operations to keep farm prices as close as possible to these target prices. For the experiments E1-E15, 30 stochastic simulations are performed with yield variability simulated using a random number generator.

2.3 Statistical evaluation of the hypotheses

Given the observations on the endogenous variables, the first hypothesis, that there is a tradeoff between price stability and the variation of demand expenditures and producer income, can be evaluated. This evaluation demands an explicit definition of price stability. A very simple approach for defining price stability is to acknowledge that the model assumes a gradual price rise over time and thus define price stability as the simulated prices rising smoothly over time. This kind of price stability can be measured by regressing the simulated prices on time defined as a variable increasing monotonically from 1 to 48. Clearly, for the deterministic simulations in E4 or E5, the coefficient of determination, R^2, would be equal to one. The estimated variance of the error term in the regression

$$FP_t = a + b_t + e_t \qquad e_t \sim N(0, \sigma^2), \qquad (10.5)$$

where FP_t is the simulated value of farm price in month t, measures the variance of observed prices from a smooth trajectory. Aggregate demand expenditures are defined as the sum of demand expenditures over the 48-month planning horizon of the control problem. Aggregate farmer income is defined similarly. By computing the variance of these aggregates for the 30 simulations for each experiment, the variability of these aggregates for different experiments can be measured. It is then possible to determine if there is a tradeoff between price stability and the variability of aggregate demand expenditures and producer income.

In our earlier discussion it was suggested the above concept of price stability is narrow and confining. A more flexible concept of price stability might require prices staying close to their deterministic target levels even though these levels do not rise smoothly or stay constant over time. To measure this kind of variability another regression model of the form

$$FP_t = a + bFP_t^* + e_t \qquad e_t \sim N(0, \sigma^2) \qquad (10.6)$$

is utilised where FP_t^* is the deterministic target farm price in period t. By deterministic targets it is meant those targets that are imposed on the system as in E2 and E3 or those generated by a deterministic solution of the control model. That is, the FP_t^* for E1 and E4-E15 are those obtained from deterministic solutions. For example, for E4, E5, E7, E8, E12 and E13, the targets all rise by NT$ 0.046 each period. For E9, E10, E14 and E15, the FP_t^* are computed as a deterministic solution of the moving average method of controlling price changes. Again, the level of the variance of the error term is a measure of the average variation of a stochastically simulated price from its target level. The coefficients a and b in (10.6) are also of interest. If the simulated farm price, FP_t, is distributed randomly around its target price, FP_t^*, then it would be expected that the intercept, a, would equal zero and the slope coefficient, b, would equal one. These specific hypotheses are tested to see if there is any systematic bias in the deviations from the desired targets. The existence of such a bias is clearly of major concern to policy makers.

The regression results from the estimates of (10.6) will give direct evidence on the second hypothesis. That is, the results of E11 for the regression (10.6) are compared with those of E12 and E13. In addition, the target trajectories of E14 and E15 are also relatively smooth so that they serve as somewhat of a compromise between the ragged trajectory of E11 and the perfectly smooth trajectories of E12 and E13. The estimates of (10.5) and (10.6) for all the simulations provide necessary evidence to evaluate the other two hypotheses since neither of these hypotheses defines price stability exactly.

3. DESCRIPTION OF THE ESTIMATED TAIWAN RICE MODEL

A model specified by Chen (1980) is used as the basis for modelling the rice market in Taiwan. The model is divided into two blocks, the first being an annual supply model of rice in Taiwan. The model has harvesting activities occurring in eight months of each year. The scheduling of the harvesting for a given month is indicated by weather patterns and is thus exogenous to the model. Within the supply model, two rice crops per year are planted; the first has harvesting occurring in the months of May through August, and the second has harvesting occurring in September through December. Rice comes out of government or privately held stocks during the other four months. The demand model is specified on a monthly basis. Data were obtained from surveys of rice consumption for three months out of the year over a twelve-year period. Because of the monthly nature of the demand model it is possible to explicitly incorporate the seasonal variation of rice consumption due to variation in weather.

3.1 The supply model

The supply model has two equations predicting yield for each crop and two additional equations predicting acreage planted for each crop. These equations are specified as:

$$AR1_j = f(APF2_{j-1}, PSGY_j, AP1_j)\,, \tag{10.7}$$

$$AR2_j = f(APF1_j, PSGY_j, AP2_j)\,, \tag{10.8}$$

$$YD1_j = f_1(j,j^2)\,, \tag{10.9}$$

$$YD2_j = f_2(j,j^2)\,, \tag{10.10}$$

where the notation is defined as:

$AR1_j$, $AR2_j$ – planted area of first and second crop in year j (hectares),

$APF1_j$ – average farm price of rice, January through June of current year in New Taiwanese dollars (NT\$) per kilogram (Kg),

$APF2_{j-1}$ – average farm price of rice, June through December of previous year,

$YD1_j$, $YD2_j$ – average yield of husked rice per hectare, first and second crop,

$PSGY_j$ – guaranteed price for sugar (NT\$/Kg),

$AP1_j$, $AP2_j$ – irrigated paddy land available, first and second crop (hectares),

j – trend variable, at year = 1953, j = 1 and increases monotonically.

The total yield in any month is then computed as

$$QP_{i,j} = \begin{cases} AR1_j \times YD1_j \times HR_{i,j} & i = 5, 6, 7, 8 \\ AR2_j \times YD2_j \times HR_{i,j} & i = 9, 10, 11, 12 \end{cases} \tag{10.11}$$

where

$QP_{i,j}$ – production in ith month of jth year, husked rice in metric tons (m. Tonnes),

$HR_{i,j}$ – harvest rate of rice fields in ith month of jth year assumed to be known constants.

The guaranteed price for sugar, $PSGY_j$, is included because sugar cane is a major competitor for rice paddy land. The monthly harvest rate, $HR_{i,j}$, is variable over the subscript i, that is the rate within a year, but is assumed constant over years since this level is determined by weather patterns and exhibits little annual variation. The yield equations are solely a function of time and reflect the fact that yield per hectare has been increasing over time. While equation (10.11) is clearly nonlinear in the endogenous variables, given the fact that the harvest rate and yield are determined exogenously of any other variables in the model, they can be computed as parameters. Hence, quantity produced in any month becomes a linear function of the area planted equations, (10.7) and (10.8). It is therefore a straightforward matter to incorporate supply linearly into the rice model.

3.2 The demand model

In the demand model, rice is demanded essentially for personal consumption and for storage. Exports of rice, which constitutes a small percentage of production, are not handled explicitly by the model and come out of government stocks. The model consists of four stochastic equations and one identity. Endogenous variables are rice consumed, reported private stocks, nonreported private stock and the farm and retail prices of rice. Algebraically, the model is specified as:

$$QES_{i,j} = f(PR_{i,j}, INXY_{i,j}, PFF_{i,j}, TM_{i,j}, NT_{i,j}), \qquad (10.12)$$

$$SPR_{i,j} = f(QP_{i,j}\ SPR_{i-1,j}) \qquad (10.13)$$

$$SPF_{i,j} = f(PR_{i,j}, DPR_{i-11,j}, QP_{i,j}, SPF_{i-1,j}, NSGD_{i,j}), \qquad (10.14)$$

$$QES_{i,j} + SPR_{i,j} + SPF_{i,j} = QP_{i,j} + SPR_{i-1,j} + SPF_{i-1,j} - NSGD_{i,j}, \qquad (10.15)$$

$$PF_{i,j} = f(Pr_{i,j}, WF_{i,j})\,. \qquad (10.16)$$

Letting i denote month and j denote year, those variables not defined in the supply model are defined as

- $QES_{i,j}$ – rice for food consumption, husked rice (m. Tonnes),
- $SPR_{i,j}$ – reported private stock, end of current month, husked rice (m. Tonnes),
- $SPF_{i,j}$ – non-reported private stock, end of the current month, husked rice (m. Tonnes),
- $PR_{i,j}$ – retail price of white rice (NT\$/Kg),
- $INXY_{i,j}$ – per capita income (NT\$),
- $PFF_{i,j}$ – retail price of fish in rural area (NT\$/Kg),
- $TM_{i,j}$ – monthly average temperature in centigrade,
- $NT_{i,j}$ – population (thousands of persons),

$NSGD_{i,j}$	– net purchase of rice from domestic market by government, husked rice (m. Tonnes),
$DPR_{i-11,j}$	– retail price difference of two adjoining months, lagged 11 months (i.e., $PR_{i-11,j} - PR_{i-12,j}$), white rice (NT$/KG),
$PF_{i,j}$	– farm price of rice, unhusked rice (NT$/Kg),
$WF_{i,j}$	– wage rate at firm (NT$/day/male labourer).

Rice consumption is specified to be a function of price, per capita income, population level and the price of fish. It is also important to have the monthly temperature since rice consumption rises as temperatures decline. The stock equations show how current production is stored for sale in later periods and greater elaboration on the theoretical justification of the specification can be found in Chen (1980). The last equation recognises that the retail and farm prices of rice are closely related since the marketing cost is essentially a function of the price of labour. This has the implication for the control model results that controlling either the farm price or the retail price implies control of the other price.

3.3 Estimation and validation

The data for the production model span from 1953 to 1977. Because of technological change in farm practices the acreage equations were estimated using data from 1966 to 1977. Because of the different units of time for the supply and demand data and the fact that the demand and supply models are block recursive in the endogenous variables, the parameters of the two sub-models are estimated separately. As shown in table 10.1, the equations of the supply model which are estimated by ordinary least squares give a very good fit. This is indicated by the coefficients of determination, and the signs of the variables being consistent with expectations and the coefficients being statistically significant. Both the supply and demand equations are characterised by being inelastic with respect to own price.

Originally the demand model was estimated by two stage least squares. Because optimal control simulations require reduced form parameters, the two stage least squares were used to derive the restricted reduced form parameters. In general, the resulting reduced form estimates gave poor ex-post forecasts. By using the unrestricted reduced form estimate of the retail price equation, the overall model demonstrated a much better ex-post forecasting performance. Hence this estimate of retail price is subsituted into the other demand equations estimated by two stage least

Table 10.1. Structural coefficients of the model and the unconstrained estimates of the reduced form of the retail price*

Supply submodel

$$AR1_j = \underset{(-0.588)}{-46241.54} + \underset{(5.402)}{3576.23^{****}}APF2_{j-1} - \underset{(-3.547)}{3751.51^{***}}PSGY_j$$

$$+ \underset{(4.657)}{1.0976^{***}}AP1_j$$

$R^2 = 0.9408$ DW = 2.6819 (–0.4133)

$$AR2_j = \underset{(-7.961)}{-848101.39^{***}} + \underset{(6.036)}{3966.84^{***}}APF1_j - \underset{(-4.147)}{2927.78^{***}}PSGY_j$$

$$+ \underset{(12.095)}{2.4578^{***}}AP2_j$$

$R^2 = 0.9515$ DW = 2.7367 (–0.4577)

$$YD1_j = \underset{(28.081)}{2047.18^{***}} + \underset{(9.547)}{126.02^{***}}j - \underset{(-4.556)}{2.1938^{***}}j^2$$

$R^2 = 0.96$ DW = 1.5759 (0.2445)

$$YD2_j = \underset{(18.244)}{1847.21^{***}} + \underset{(3.923)}{70.281^{***}}j - \underset{(-1.64)}{1.1006^{*}}j^2$$

$R^2 = 0.81$ DW = 1.5823 (0.1816)

Demand submodel

$$QES_{i,j} = \underset{(4.631)}{67177.99^{***}} - \underset{(-4.858)}{593.847^{***}}PR_{i,j} - \underset{(-5.045)}{2.0084^{***}}INXY_{i,j}$$

$$= \underset{(4.963)}{301.5685^{***}}PFF_{i,j} + \underset{(7.944)}{11.4526^{***}}NT_{i,j} - \underset{(16.847)}{891.0583^{***}}TM_{i,j}$$

$R^2 = 0.8756$ DW = 0.7114 (0.6346)

$$SPR_{i,j} = \underset{(-0.160)}{-2709.1833} + \underset{(15.576)}{0.33815^{***}}QP_{i,j} + \underset{(14.585)}{0.75847^{***}}SPR_{i-1,j}$$

$R^2 = 0.7790$ DW = 1.8050 (0.0849) H = 0.9667

$$SPF_{i,j} = \underset{(-0.124)}{-5017.1838} - \underset{(-2.574)}{3956.55^{**}}PR_{i,j} + \underset{(33.911)}{0.92002^{***}}SPF_{i-1,j}$$

$$\underset{(-6.806)}{-0.79158^{***}}NSGC_{i,j} + \underset{(2.194)}{16193.99^{***}}DPR_{i-11,j} + \underset{(24.439)}{0.5817^{***}}QP_{i,j}$$

$R^2 = 0.9688$ DW = 1.7662 (0.1000) H = $1.0164PF_{i,j}$

$$PF_{i,j} = \underset{(3.655)}{0.48876^{***}} + \underset{(14.269)}{0.62937^{***}}PR_{i,j} - \underset{(-1.449)}{0.005585}\ WF$$

$R^2 = 0.9707$ DW = 1.2544 (0.3723)

$$PR_{i,j} = \underset{(-1.372)}{-23.16429} - \underset{(-3.813)}{0.001324^{***}}INXY_{i,j} + \underset{(8.089)}{0.34217^{***}}PFF_{i,j}$$

$$+ \underset{(3.441)}{0.004387^{***}}NT_{i,j} - \underset{(4.665)}{0.43762^{***}}TM_{i,j} - \underset{(-4.175)}{0.00000425^{***}}QP_{i,j}$$

$$\underset{(-2.643)}{-0.00000857^{***}}SPR_{i-1,j} - \underset{(-3.543)}{0.00000706^{***}}SPF_{i-1,j}$$

$$+ \underset{(3.389)}{0.0000262^{***}}NSGD_{i,j} + \underset{(0.102)}{0.026363}\,DPR_{i-11,j}$$

$R^2 = 0.89$ DW = 0.4917 (0.7489)

* The figures in parentheses below the estimates are the ratios of the estimates to their estimated standard errors. R^2 is the coefficient of determination. DW is the Durbin-Watson statistic and H is the statistic in Johnston (1972) for testing for autocorrelation in the presence of a lagged endogenous variable. The figure in parentheses next to the Durbin-Watson statistic is the estimated first order autocorrelation coefficient.

Source: Chen (1980).

squares. Once the substitution is made, the equations are in their reduced form since retail price is the only endogenous variable appearing as an explanatory variable. More results of the estimation and validation are given in table 10.1.[5]

4. SIMULATION RESULTS AND ANALYSIS

4.1 General observations

Before reviewing the evidence generated by the simulations about the three hypotheses, it is useful to make some general remarks about the simulation results as a whole. Table 10.3 displays the results of the simulations in terms of mean, aggregate demand, and government expenditure totals, over the four year horizon; as well as mean, aggregate producer incomes, and production levels. A surprising finding is that there is very little variation in production levels regardless of the policy pursued. This table also reflects the general strategy in setting up the various experiments. The free market solution, E1, was regarded as the benchmark solution and the other experiments were set to vary from this solution in ways that would alternate between being favourable to consumers and to producers.

An important characteristic of the results is that the level of government expenditures is very much a function of either the absolute level of the targets for the exogenous target experiments or the level of the initial prices for the endogenous experiments. For example, the deterministic target levels are the same for E4, E7 and E12 and the expenditure levels are not statistically different pairwise from each other. The same is true for E5, E8 and E13. Thus, the way in which a particular objective is pursued does not appear to affect the mean level of costs to the government.

A surprising result is the stability of the demand expenditures and farmer incomes in the free market solution, E1. Assuming the various aggregates in table 10.3 to have a normal distribution,[6] it is possible to test if the variances are significantly different from each other. This is done by taking the ratio of two variances which has an F distribution with eqùal numerator and denominator degrees of freedom. The critical value of the F distribution for 29 numerators and denominator degrees of freedom is approximately 1.84 at a 95 percent level of confidence and approximately 2.39 at the 99 percent level. The variance of demand expenditures is at least twice that of E1 in all the experiments except E7 and E10. Likewise for producer incomes in comparison to the free market solution. And for both aggregate figures their variability is the least in comparison to the variances in E7 and E10.

Those simulations with the largest variances in farmer incomes, demand, and

Table 10.2. Experimental design: specification of the objective function for the stochastic control simulations

Experiment	Description
E1	Free market solution. No endogenous variables are tracked and there are no government purchases or sales.
E2	Minimise squared deviations of farm price, $PF_{i,j}$, from target levels based on a government trajectory that would favour farm income.
E3	Minimise squared deviations of retail price, $PR_{i,j}$, from prices favourable to consumers.
E4	Minimise squared deviations of period-to-period changes in farm price, i.e., Δ_{1t}, from a target of NT$ 0.046 with initial price of NT$ 9.75.
E5	Same as E4 except initial price in NT$ 9.25.
E6	Combine objectives of E2 and E4 except initial price is NT$ 9.50.
E7	Minimise squared deviations of first and second order price changes, Δ_{1t} and Δ_{2t}, for price to change by NT$ 0.046 per period with initial price NT$ 9.75.
E8	Same as E7 except initial price is NT$ 9.25.
E9	Minimise squared deviations of period-to-period changes of current price less average of last six farm prices from a target of NT$ 0.046 and initial price NT$ 9.75.
E10	Same as E9 except initial price is NT$ 9.25.
E11	Minimise squared deviations of farm prices from the deterministic trajectory of farm price for E1.
E12	Minimise squared deviations of farm prices from the deterministic trajectory of farm prices for E4.
E13	Minimise squared deviations of farm prices from the deterministic trajectory of farm prices for E5.
E14	Minimise squared deviations of farm prices from the deterministic trajectory of farm prices for E9.
E15	Minimise squared deviations of farm prices from the deterministic trajectory of farm prices for E10.

Table 10.3 Four year mean totals of consumer expenditure, farmer income, government expenditures and production for the experiments*

	Demand Expenditures	Farmer Income	Government Expenditures	Production
E1	165.1 (1.79)	138.9 (1.46)	0 (0)	10,090 (265)
E2	178.8 (4.53)	151.4 (3.80)	6.250 (1.92)	10,150 (283)
E3	149.2 (3.51)	124.6 (2.89)	−7.851 (1.541)	9,886 (260)
E4	171.9 (3.88)	145.2 (3.51)	2.218 (2.00)	10,040 (267)
E5	163.9 (3.59)	137.8 (3.23)	−2.084 (1.62)	10,050 (261)
E6	178.8 (4.33)	151.4 (3.61)	6.266 (1.69)	10,140 (284)
E7	170.5 (2.49)	144.0 (2.06)	1.767 (0.940)	9,984 (317)
E8	163.5 (2.97)	137.6 (2.68)	−2.040 (1.169)	9,965 (239)
E9	173.1 (2.79)	146.2 (2.25)	1.342 (0.854)	10,130 (254)
E10	152.6 (2.44)	127.6 (1.92)	−8.322 (9.46)	9,902 (267)
E11	165.0 (3.81)	138.9 (3.17)	−0.283 (1.56)	10,003 (251)
E12	170.7 (4.34)	144.2 (3.62)	1.484 (2.02)	10,010 (286)
E13	162.9 (4.85)	137.0 (4.03)	−2.398 (2.05)	9,967 (330)
E14	172.8 (4.27)	146.0 (3.57)	1.396 (1.81)	10,100 (280)
E15	152.5 (3.08)	127.6 (2.54)	−8.244 (1.51)	9,934 (229)

* Dollar figures in billions of New Taiwanese dollars. Production figures are thousands of metric tons. Estimated standard deviations of the totals are in parentheses.

Source: Computed.

government expenditures, are almost always associated with fixed targets for the absolute price levels. Experiments E2, E3, and E11-E15 have fixed price targets although the method of target generation varies. Also, the variances in E4 and E5, which control the first difference in price change, are fairly large. Experiments E7-E10 display smallest variances of aggregate dollar totals of all the experiments except E1. Experiments E7 to E10 use comparatively more sophisticated methods of price target generation. E7 and E8 are the first and second order differences and E9 and E10 are moving averages. It is important to observe that E7 and E8 produce essentially the same respective aggregates as E4 and E5 but with less variability. This suggests second order and perhaps higher order differences might be desirable in terms of stabilisation of prices and expenditures and income. Evidence on price stability is given shortly. Note that government expenditures are also less variable in these more sophisticated target schemes.

One further characteristic of the comparisons between endogenous versus exogenous targets emerges from table 10.3. The means in E11-E15 are not significantly different from their corresponding figures in the upper portion of the table.[7] This simply implies that using control around the deterministic targets does not bias the solution in terms of expenditure or income aggregates in favour of consumers over producers, or vice versa.

The evidence in table 10.3 suggests there may be a tradeoff between a smooth price trajectory and the variability of government, consumer and producer aggregates. The table shows the free market solution to be clearly superior in terms of minimum variance of demand, incomes, and government expenditures; but the question of price stability still remains to be answered (see below). The evidence does suggest having a set trajectory of target prices in absolute terms leads to greater variability of the aggregates. The endogenously set price experiments tend to give greater stability of the aggregates. This appears to be true for the more sophisticated methods of setting endogenous prices, such as E7-E10.

4.2 Examining price stability

The extent of price stability can be evaluated by considering the regression results in tables 10.4 and 10.5. In table 10.4 the simulated prices are regressed on their deterministic price levels, and in table 10.5 the simulated prices are regressed on time, a variable increasing monotonically from 1 to 48.

Some general patterns in table 10.4 should be discussed. In all the experiments for which the target trajectory prices are set exogneously, almost all the intercept terms are not significantly different from zero and the slope coefficients are not sig-

Table 10.4. Regressions of simulated prices on deterministic price levéls for the stochastic simulations

Experiment	Intercept	Slope	Standard Error	R^2
E1	–0.0069 (0.126)	0.995 (0.012)	0.375	0.834
E2	0.048 (0.020)	0.996 (0.0018)	0.070	0.995
E3	0.051 (0.018)	1.01 (0.0019)	0.065	0.995
E4	–0.539 (0.210)	1.05 (0.019)	0.467	0.674
E5	0.424 (0.182)	0.957 (0.018)	0.425	0.674
E6	0.022 (0.026)	0.998 (0.002)	0.090	0.992
E7	–0.790 (0.158)	1.07 (0.015)	0.351	0.792
E8	–0.620 (0.153)	1.06 (0.015)	0.356	0.784
E9	–0.013 (0.202)	1.00 (0.018)	0.140	0.673
E10	–1.02 (0.19)	1.11 (0.020)	0.147	0.692
E11	0.019 (0.023)	0.998 (0.002)	0.067	0.994
E12	–0.033 (0.032)	1.00 (0.003)	0.070	0.988
E13	–0.021 (0.028)	1.00 (0.003)	0.065	0.990
E14	0.160 (0.105)	0.985 (0.010)	0.073	0.880
E15	–0.105 (0.086)	1.01 (0.009)	0.066	0.902

Estimated standard errors are in parentheses directly below the estimated coefficients.

Source: Computed.

Table 10.5. Regressions of simulated prices on time for the stochastic simulations

Experiment	Intercept	Slope	Standard Error	R^2
E1	10.2 (0.046)	0.022 (0.0017)	0.870	0.108
E2	9.58 (0.021)	0.070 (0.0007)	0.387	0.863
E3	8.34 (0.026)	0.057 (0.001)	0.491	0.721
E4	9.74 (0.025)	0.048 (0.001)	0.467	0.674
E5	9.28 (0.023)	0.044 (0.001)	0.425	0.674
E6	9.56 (0.019)	0.070 (0.001)	0.350	0.886
E7	9.69 (0.019)	0.049 (0.001)	0.351	0.792
E8	9.23 (0.019)	0.049 (0.001)	0.356	0.784
E9	10.62 (0.008)	0.014 (0.0003)	0.148	0.637
E10	9.40 (0.008)	0.016 (0.0003)	0.153	0.664
E11	10.30 (0.042)	0.022 (0.001)	0.788	0.132
E12	9.75 (0.004)	0.046 (0.0001)	0.070	0.988
E13	9.25 (0.003)	0.046 (0.0001)	0.065	0.990
E14	10.63 (0.005)	0.014 (0.0001)	0.089	0.823
E15	9.40 (0.004)	0.014 (0.0002)	0.079	0.859

Estimated standard errors are in parentheses directly below the estimated coefficients.

Source: Computed.

nificantly different from one. This appears to indicate that the stochastic control technique tracks a given set of price targets quite accurately regardless of whether it is a smooth trajectory of target prices or a jagged one as in E1.[8] This relative accuracy of the exogenous targets is also indicated by comparing the estimated standard errors for the fixed trajectory with those having endogenous trajectories. Thus if price stability is defined in terms of being able to hit desired absolute price levels, a buffer stock operation using stochastic control appears an efficient methodology. Alternatively, the simulations that have endogenous price targets display significant bias in deviating from the deterministic trajectory. This suggests it would be unwise to publicise the deterministic trajectory as that to be tracked if endogenous price targets are actually going to be used.

When price stability is defined as not deviating from price targets generated by the deterministic experiments, even though those targets are not smooth over time, the experiments with endogenously generated targets not surprisingly have an inferior performance to those methods which set targets exogenously, i.e., E2, E3, E11-E15, as shown in table 10.4. It is interesting to note that the inferiority of E1 to the other methods as measured by the coefficient of determination, R^2, is greatly reduced and, in fact, it comes closer to its deterministic trajectory than some of the endogenous methods such as E4 and E5.

Table 10.5 shows the free market trajectory to be clearly more variable than any of the other price trajectories. When regressed on time the trajectories of E1 have substantially greater variability both in terms of low R^2 and the standard error of the regression. The best way to get a smooth price trajectory over time is to track a set of absolute targets which increase smoothly over time, as in E12 and E13. Note this method gives much different results in terms of smoothness of the overall trajectory than trying to minimise first or second differences in price changes. Interestingly, the second order and moving average schemes come closer to a smooth trajectory than the first order scheme. This suggests that even more sophisticated endogenous schemes might yield a smooth price trajectory. The small standard errors of E9 and E10 means the overall variability of prices from a trend line over the 48 period horizon is smaller than those for E1-E8.

4.3 Evaluating the hypotheses

It is now possible to address the three hypotheses directly. The first hypothesis claims there is no tradeofff between having a smooth price trajectory and low variability in the aggregate expenditure and income figures. This hypothesis must be rejected. From table 10.3 it is clear that E1 has a lower variability of the aggregate money measures than any of the other experiments and this difference in variance is significant in all but two of the other experiments. It is also the most variable trajectory over time, as well as one which varies substantially from its deterministic price trajectory but not in any systematic way. Tracking the deterministic trajectory tends to combine two possibly negative features. The monetary aggregate figures vary considerably and prices do not change smoothly over time. The one positive aspect is that the buffer stock operation can be used to track the deterministic trajectory very closely (E11), but such tracking creates considerable variability in the aggregates with the added burden of the government financing the buffer stock operation. While the net cost to the government is not significantly different from zero, there are still the transaction costs of the operations to be covered.

A compromise between a smooth trajectory of prices and low variability of the financial aggregates is offered by the moving average scheme. As the regressions in table 10.5 show, prices change comparatively smoothly over time. The lower levels of variability of E7-E10 for the monetary aggregates suggests that more complex methods of generating endogenous targets might lead to lower variability of the aggregates, so that the aggregates would have lower variances and smoother price trajectories. This is a particularly important point if the government takes the view that the outcome under the free market is not desirable. If it wanted to transfer income to farmers above the free market level, say, it might want to do so with minimum price and income variability. More research is required for exploring and refining this type of target generation.

The second hypothesis is evaluated in a straightforward manner. The evidence shows that, whether or not the absolute price targets are set by endogenous or exogenous methods, their absolute levels can be tracked equally well. This result is seen clearly in table 10.4 for experiments E11-E15. In E11 the targets were set by the deterministic market solution and in E12-E15 other endogenous methods were used. Although the R^2 is somewhat lower for E14 and E15, the standard errors are about the same as for E11-E13. Thus, the results suggest that targets, in absolute terms, can be tracked closely regardless of how they are generated.[9] Earlier we conjectured that tracking the free market trajectory raised or lowered by some proportion might be an efficient means of subsidising producers or consumers. The variability associated with tracking any exogenous trajectory suggest such a plan would not yield low variability of the monetary aggregates.

The third hypothesis asks whether the method of target generation makes a difference in terms of the stability of prices and the monetary aggregates. If price stability is defined in terms of a constant increment in each period, table 10.5 shows that the way to achieve the minimum price deviations is by having absolute price targets grow by a constant amount over time. E12 and E13 have the lowest standard errors of regression indicating the smallest average deviation. If price stability is defined in terms of tracking its deterministic target value, then it is also clear that having fixed targets gives better price stability. All the exogenous target experiments have higher R^2's, and lower standard errors, than any of the endogenous methods. Thus the first part of the hypothesis must be rejected: absolute price targets give greater price stability by either of the two definitions chosen than by endogenous methods. With reference to stability of the monetary aggregates, the earlier evaluation of table 10.3 indicated that the endogenous target methods displayed less variability of the aggregates than the exogenous methods. Thus the second part of the third hypothesis is also rejected: the method of target generation does appear to have an effect on the variability of aggregates. It seems the free market solution is the most stable but the more complex endogenous methods of target generation also tend to generate more stable values of the aggregates than the exogenous methods.

An important caveat should be noted in evaluating the results above. Demand expenditure is defined as aggregate demand, including demand for food consumption and demand for storage. As can be seen in the consumer demand equation in table 10.1, once price is fixed the quantity demanded for consumption is then only a function of other variables which are essentially unaffected by supply uncertainty. Therefore, in those experiments that track an absolute price level over the planning horizon, i.e. E2, E3, E6 and E11-E15, the sum of rice for food consumption, $QES_{i,j}$, times its price over the horizon is very stable compared to its variability for the endogenous methods. This is a result due to the ability of fixed targets to be tracked, as evidenced in table 10.4. Thus it could be argued that stabilising around a fixed target trajectory will give the consuming public price stability and that their overall expenditure aggregate will experience little variability regardless of supply uncertainty.

5. CONCLUSIONS

The stochastic simulations show the free market solution to have the lowest variability in terms of demand expenditures and producer income. It also has the least stability of the price trajectory of any of the experiments. However, the deterministic free market trajectory, when treated itself as a set of targets, displays the same variability of aggregates as the other absolute price target trajectories. Simple methods of trying to obtain price stability such as tracking first differences do not appear to be effective in yielding price stability or in stabilising the monetary aggregates. However, the more complex endogenous methods appear to offer some gain in terms of price stability and stability of the money aggregates.

The best approach to controlling a system is very much a function of the desired system performance. That is, depending on how price stability is defined, various types of targets can be used. It would appear, for example, that to achieve a constantly increasing price over time, it is better to track a target trajectory of constantly increasing prices than to use an endogenous method of minimising first differences on a period-by-period basis.

This result indicates a general finding of the study. The selection of a desired target trajectory is not independent of how that trajectory is tracked by an optimal control model. Because of this result, a question for further research is that given a desired set of targets, what is the best means of achieving them? Should absolute targets be tracked as in E11-E15, or are there other methods of control such as tracking third or higher order schemes that would be more efficient? Would more or less elaborate moving average schemes be desirable?

Because of the very specific nature of the model and the limited experimental design, it is not possible to claim any universality for the results. The results do indicate that in terms of commodity price stabilisation, and perhaps for the stabilisation of other economic models, the selection of the targets is not arbitrary and that the method of tracking the desired trajectory will have a noticeable impact on the performance of the system.

NOTES

* The authors thank North-Holland Publishing Co. for permission to use some material previously published in Dixon and Chen (1982).

1. See Chow (1975) for proof that when there is only one target and one control in a linear quadratic control model the target will be met exactly in each period in a deterministic environment. Tinbergen's (1967) theory of economic policy considered the case of equal numbers of targets and instruments.
2. Demand expenditures are defined to be the aggregate value of demand for rice produced, i.e. actual consumption, storage and government purchases at the time of harvest.
3. Using a linear econometric model in which both price and quantity are endogenous presents a problem for using a linear quadratic control model to control income or expenditures. Targets are set for individual endogenous variables and not for their product. However, a Taylor series linear approximation would

probably yield a reasonably accurate model allowing such variables to be included and controlled.

4. In order to give comparisons that are meaningful to the experiments E1-E6, the initial lagged six prices are adjusted upwards by a proportional factor. A six period average is used because farmers are specified to determine acreage planted as a function of the average of the past six and seven months prices for the second and first crops, respectively.
5. By using both unconstrained reduced form estimates and the two stage least squares estimate there is no guarantee that the equilibrium condition (10.14) will be satisfied. Simulation experiments in Chen (1980) showed the difference between aggregate quantity demanded and supplied to be less than 5 percent.
6. Even though a normally distributed random number generator is used for the yield variability simulation, the totals themselves in table 10.3 are not exactly normally distributed because the yield variability enters the reduced form equations multiplicatively through the matrices A_t. However, samples of the totals selected for inspection appeared to be very close to a normal distribution.
7. E11 should be compared with E1, E12 with E4, E13 with E5, E14 with E9 and E15 with E10.
8. Earlier, it was observed that E6 was technically an endogenous method of price generation since it combines E2 and E4. However, in tables 10.3, 10.4 and 10.5, it is clear that it performs much more like E2 than E4. We interpret this as meaning the predetermined target trajectory dominates in terms of influencing the path followed by the simulated endogenous variables and, hence, is empirically more of an exogenous target experiment than endogenous.
9. A question for further research would be to examine how these results hold up if there are more targets per period than controls.

REFERENCES

Burt, O.R., W.W. Koo and N.J. Dudley (1980), 'Optimal stochastic control of U.S. wheat stocks and exports', *American Journal of Agricultural Economics*, 62, pp. 172-187.

Chen, W.H. (1980), 'An economic study of government rice stock operation in Taiwan', unpublished Ph.D. dissertation, University of Illinois, Urbana, Illinois.

Chow, G.D. (1975), *Analysis and Control of Dynamic Economic Systems*, Wiley-Interscience, New York.

Dixon, B.L. and W.H. Chen (1982), 'A stochastic control approach to buffer stock management in the Taiwan rice market', *Journal of Development Economics*, 10, pp. 187-207.

Klein, L.R. (1978), 'Potentials of economics for commodity stabilisation policy analysis', in: F.G. Adams and S.A. Klein (eds.), *Stabilising World Commodity Markets*, Lexington Books, Lexington, Massachussets, pp. 105-116.

Rausser, G.C. and J.W. Freebairn (1974), 'Approximate adaptive control solutions to beef trade policy', *Annals of Economic and Social Measurement,* 3, pp. 177-203.

Sarris, A.H. (1973), 'A Bayesian approach to estimation of time-varying regression coefficients', *Annals of Economic and Social Measurement,* 2, pp. 501-524.

Taylor, C.R. and H. Talpaz (1979), 'Approximately optimal carryover levels for wheat in the United States', *American Journal of Agricultural Economics,* 61, pp. 32-40.

Tinbergen, J. (1967), *Economic Policy: Principles and Design,* North-Holland, Amsterdam.

Turnovsky, S.J. (1978), 'The distribution of welfare gains from price stabilisation: A survey of some theoretical issues', in: F.G. Adams and S.A. Klein (eds.), *Stabilising World Commodity Markets,* Lexington Books, Lexington, Massachussets, pp. 119-148.

CHAPTER 11

SIMPLE AND OPTIMAL CONTROL RULES FOR STABILISING COMMODITY MARKETS

S. Ghosh *University of Oxford, UK*
C.L. Gilbert *University of Oxford, UK*
A.J. Hughes Hallett *Erasmus University, Rotterdam, the Netherlands*

1. INTRODUCTION

For a decade there has been pressure, particularly within UNCTAD, to set up stabilisation agreements for the world's major commodity markets. But issues such as the desirability and the best method of intervening in these markets raise sharp disagreements, as shown by the opposite positions taken by the Brandt commission and the Reagan administration and by different commodity producers in the third world. Such disagreements were highlighted at the Cancun 'North-South' summit meeting (Goldstein (1982)). The main difficulty has been to provide a yardstick for measuring the potential effectiveness of such an agreeement, while at the same time identifying those elements which are essential to successful intervention and hence essential to the design of the agreement's operation. To do that requires an analysis of both the structure and the performance of optimal intervention rules.

There appear to be two reasons why stabilisation agreeements are not usually analysed as a dynamic optimisation problem. Commodity producers and UNCTAD tend to argue that price volatility itself constitutes a prima facie case for stabilisation (UNCTAD (1976)); a view sometimes echoed in the developed world (Brandt (1980)). But they have been unable to specify their objectives more precisely, with the result that it is not clear what they expect from such stabilisation agreements, nor how they intend them to be operated in practice. The main UNCTAD proposal (the 1976 Integrated Programme for Commodities) never made clear whether stabi-

Hughes Hallett, A.J. (ed.) Applied Decision Analysis and Economic Behaviour

ISBN 90-247-2968-8. Printed in The Netherlands

lised prices, or improvements in the terms of trade, was to be the means by which wealth was to be redistributed between 'North' and 'South'. This ambiguity is evident from 'Commodity prices should be stabilised at a remunerative level to become les vulnerable to market fluctuations' (Brandt (1980)) and similar statements in many UNCTAD documents, There has been no clear view on what intervention schemes are best, nor on whether intervening could achieve the desired goals at acceptable financial costs.

Secondly, an optimal decision rule often gives the impression that decisions are made automatic, leaving no place for discretionary or judgemental inputs from the policy maker himself. While it is not clear that policy makers always have access to a fully specified model of all noncontrollable variables which influence the economy, they are subject to the many forecasts which are generated in the financial and government communities. They also tend to have more accurate information on likely reactions of other decision makers, or events which cannot be captured by an econometric model that is necessarily restricted in its scope. Hence policy makers are likely to have access to a wider (or at least different) information set from that incorporated in an automatic decision rule. It might be wise to concentrate judgement on the problem of specifying the objectives, model, or expectations of exogenous events properly. In the same way there may be merit in rules which policy makers can use without having to gather detailed information for a precise specification of their preferences and all the variables in the market, and without having to create and operate a complicated dynamic econometric model. It may be profitable to accept a limited degree of sub-optimality for economy of information, simplicity of operation, and robustness to errors.

The purpose of this chapter is first to examine the best form of intervention rule for stabilising a commodity market and the extent to which conventional buffer stock schemes compare to optimal schemes. Second, various simple intervention rules are built up from the components of an optimal rule in order to identify the elements which are essential for successful intervention and to examine the role played by discretionary information (in this case, expectations of market developments) in particular.

We have chosen to investigate copper as a prime candidate for a stabilisation agreement. It is one of the 10 'core commodities' proposed by UNCTAD, being both particularly suited to stockpiling and one of the most important commodities in world markets. The free market (London Metal Exchange) price, at which the bulk of metal outside the communist block countries now exchanges, is notoriously volatile. The metal is substantially produced in developing countries, and for many of them (Zambia, Zaire, Chile, and Papua New Guinea) it contributes over 50 percent of export earnings. Both UNCTAD and CIPEC (Conseil Intergouvernementtal des Pays Exporteurs de Cuivre) have pressed for a marketing system which is both less uncertain and more favourable to producers in the third world.

2. SIMPLE AND OPTIMAL CONTROL STRATEGIES

Bandwidth intervention rules are the decision rules most commonly proposed (and studied) for commodity stabilisation agreements, both at the level of UNCTAD discussions and in negotiating agreements for the stabilisation of individual markets. They conventionally operate in terms of stabilisation within an agreed price range. In the simplest schemes the agency is required to buy into a buffer stock when the price reaches the 'floor' of that price range, and to sell at the 'ceiling'; and to do both of these without limit so long as funds or stocks permit. Commodity markets are obvious candidates for control of this kind, but there are many other important applications. Domestic agricultural support schemes typically operate in this way, and since 1979 the European Monetary System has been operated as an explicit bandwidth intervention system. In practice purchases may be allowed at prices above the floor, and sales at prices below the ceiling, so that within the range (but not beyond) the buffer stock manager may exercise some discretion. We will try to capture this discretion in the two-tier bandwidth schemes described below.

2.1 Bandwidth intervention rules

A bandwidth control may be defined either by the floor or ceiling prices, or by the central price and the 'bandwidth'. The latter parametisation is convenient since it focusses on two quite separate questions. The central price may be set at the approximate free market equilibrium price at which production and consumption will tend to balance. A decision about the bandwidth, on the other hand, reflects a judgement about the degree of stabilisation which is desirable: the tighter the bandwidth the less price variability, but that implies lower profits and a more costly scheme.

General considerations, on the other hand, demonstrate that no bandwidth rule will be optimal within a wider class of decision rules. For example, the non-discretionary nature of the rule, particularly at the ceiling, is clearly sub-optimal. In fact the optimal stockpiling rule for a commodity depends only on the total supply in the market, and not on the price (Gustafson (1958), Newberry and Stiglitz (1981, 1982)). Therefore the instrument available to the stabilisation agency in these stabilisation exercises will be buffer stock purchases or sales. The target variables are deviations of the free market (LME) price from some predetermined trend. One difficulty with such intervention rules in practice is that they presuppose knowledge of the path about which prices would best be stabilised.[1] The choice of that path appears to present serious problems (Ghosh, Gilbert and Hughes Hallett (1982)) but, since it is present in simple or bandwidth as well as optimal rules, comparisons may still be made on the basis of a predetermined path.

A stabilisation authority will typically wish to impose further restrictions on the use of instruments. It cannot in any case allow its intervention stock to fall below zero; and it is unlikely to wish to hold unreasonably large stocks for extended periods if only because the funds it can raise to finance the necessary stabilisation operations will be limited. For these reasons we included penalties on buffer stock holdings (as a target) and its purchases or sales (the instrument) in the optimal control exercises. But such restrictions cannot be accommodated directly in simulating a bandwidth rule. To overcome that we incorporate a trap in the decision rule to prevent the cumulative buffer stock turning negative. Similarly we undertake a number of exercises in which the finance available is restricted, so that the corresponding buffer stock accumulations are also limited.

2.2 Optimal intervention rules

In this chapter, optimal decision rules will be used as a benchmark against which other simpler decision rules can be compared. This benchmark will be used to indicate the absolute and relative success of alternative decision rules in a specified decision problem.

Suppose a decision problem concerns a vector of n instrument variables x_t; m target variables y_t; and a vector of uncontrollable and uncertain variables s_t. The decision variables will be written as $z_t' = (y_t', x_t')$ at each period of the planning interval $t = 1, \ldots, T$. Let y_t^d and x_t^d, for $t = 1, \ldots, T$, describe a set of ideal (but infeasible) paths for the target and instrument variables. Then $\tilde{z}_t' = (\tilde{y}_t', \tilde{x}_t')$, where $\tilde{y}_t = y_t - y_t^d$ and $\tilde{x}_t = x_t - x_t^d$, denotes the decision failure of each period. We aim to pick each x_t to minimise a weighted sum of squared decision failures:

$$w = \tfrac{1}{2} \sum_{t=1}^{T} \left\{ \tilde{y}_t' B_t \tilde{y}_t + \tilde{x}_t' A_t \tilde{x}_t \right\} = \tfrac{1}{2} \sum_{t=1}^{T} \tilde{z}_t' Q_t \tilde{z}_t \qquad (11.1)$$

where Q_t is a positive semi-definite and symmetric matrix with rank $\geqslant$ n. In stabilisation exercises, (11.1) is usually specifed to penalise deviations fo the targets from some preassigned trend path; and to penalise large deviations of the instruments from some acceptable levels represented by x_t^d.

The decision variables are linked through a model of the market, which contains y_t as a subset of the set of all endogenous variables Y_t. The minimisation of (11.1) is thus constrained by the econometric model

$$Y_t = \pi_1 Y_{t-1} + \pi_2 x_t + \pi_3 N_t + V_t \tag{11.2}$$

where Y_t is the set of all endogenous variables, N_t are uncontrollable exogenous variables, and V_t are random disturbances. This model can of course be a reparameterisation of a model containing many lags in Y_t and x_t (Chow (1975), p. 153).

Optimal decision *rules* are usually derived by solving

$$\min_{\substack{x_t \\ t=1\ldots T}} \left\{ \tfrac{1}{2} \Sigma \tilde{z}_t' Q_t \tilde{z}_t \mid \; Y_t - \pi_1 Y_{t-1} - \pi_2 x_t - a_t \right\} \tag{11.3}$$

where $a_t = \pi_3 N_t + V_t$. The solution to (11.3) by dynamic programming yields optimal feedback rules (see Chow (1975), pp. 176-179)

$$x_t^* = G_t Y_{t-1} + g_t \tag{11.4}$$

where G_t is obtained recursively as a function of Q_t, π_1, π_2 and G_{t+1}. Hence G_t depends on π_1, π_2, and Q_k for $k = 1 \ldots T$. Similarly g_t is a function of Q_t, π_1, π_2, G_{t+1}, and also a_t, z_t^d and g_{t+1}. Thus g_t depends on a_k and z_k^d (in addition to π_1, π_2, and Q_k) for $k = t \ldots T$. But a_k, $k = t \ldots T$, are random variables and cannot be known at t. So in practice $E_t(a_k)$ is used in the backwards recursions which generate g_t, because, by the certainty equivalence theorem, (11.4) then minimises $E_t(w)$ for each t. Here $E_t(.) = E(. \mid \Omega_t)$ denotes an expectation conditioned on Ω_t, the set of information available at the start of period t. The optimal decisions x_t^*, as computed using a given information set, say Ω_t, are therefore dependent of the other anticipated optimal decisions through their expected consequences Y_{t-1} (containing x_k, $k<t$) and through G_k, g_k for $k>t$ which imply the remaining (currently expected) x_k^* values.

Alternatively we may derive optimal decision *values*, using a technique set out in Theil (1964) which explicitly shows the mutual dependence of current and anticipated decisions. The decision variables can be stacked, targets before instruments, over the whole planning interval as: $z' = (y', x') = (y_1' \ldots y_T', x_1' \ldots x_T')$. Let $\tilde{z} = z - z^d$, where z^d contains the ideal values ordered as z. Then the objective can be written as

$$w = \tfrac{1}{2} \tilde{z}' Q \tilde{z} \tag{11.5}$$

where Q is the permutation of $\underset{t=1...T}{\text{diag}} \{Q_t\}$ which order target penalties before instrument penalties. Now by backsubstituting and then deleting all equations corresponding to the nontargets in Y_t, the constraints (11.2) can be condensed to

$$y = Rx + s \tag{11.6}$$

where $R = \begin{bmatrix} R_1 & & 0 \\ \vdots & \ddots & \\ R_T & \cdots & R_1 \end{bmatrix}$ and $s = \begin{pmatrix} s_1 \\ \vdots \\ s_T \end{pmatrix}$ respectively contain the relevant dynamic multipliers from $R_t = \pi_1{}^{t-1} \pi_2$, and noncontrollable elements from $s_t = \pi_1^t y_o + \sum_{j=0}^{t-1} \pi_1^j(\pi_3 N_{t-j} + V_{t-j})$. Substituting

$$\tilde{y} = R\tilde{x} + b \qquad \text{where} \qquad b = s - y^d + Rx^d \tag{11.7}$$

into (11.5) yields the optimal decisions

$$x^* = x^d - (H'QH)^{-1} H'Q\left(\begin{smallmatrix} b \\ 0 \end{smallmatrix}\right) \tag{11.8}$$

where $H' = [R' \vdots I]$. If the only uncertainties are additive, then s is known in advance only in a probabilistic sense.[2] By certainty equivalence, replacing w by $E_t(w)$ leads to (11.8), with $E_t(b)$ for b, as the optimal decision values. So we start with (11.8) and $E_1(b)$. At $t \geq 2$, we can reoptimise $x_t \ldots x_T$ conditioned on Ω_t. So updating the remaining expectations, inserting realisations for y_{t-j} and x_{t-j} (for $1 \leq j \leq T-t$), and making certain adjustments to H, Q, and b to allow for the reduced horizon, gives the closed loop (or implemented) decision sequence as x_t^* each one from the reevaluation of (11.8) based on Ω_t.[3]

In this framework, the optimal feedback rule (11.4) supplies identical decisions to those derived from repeatedly reevaluating (11.8) using the same sequence of information sets (Norman (1974)). The point here is (11.8) shows explicitly that x_t^* is jointly dependent on x_k^*, $k \neq t$. Moreover, because the constraints have been condensed onto just the target variables, (11.8) usually provides substantial computational savings over (11.4) (Brandsma, Hughes Hallett and van der Windt (1983)).

2.3 Simple feedback intervention rules

The other group of simple intervention rules considered in this chapter are simple –and possibly fixed– policy rules. There is a powerful body of opinion among economists that optimal rules are too complex to be evaluated and operated sucessfully by policy makers. There is the further, and potentially more serious, objection that such highly developed rules are not robust enough to be reliable in the face of the inevitable uncertainties introduced by the model specification and estimation errors, or by the difficulties of accurately specifying relative priorities, or the impact of speculative behaviour, and so on. Indeed these objections have led a number of authors to advocate simplified feedback rules in place of the optimal decision rules. Kydland and Prescott (1977), for example, argue that the difficulty of allowing correctly for the impact of anticipated future decisions on current outcomes warrants a simplified decision rule. Lucas (1976) suggests simplified decision rules to reduce the errors caused by selecting decisions conditional on fixed reaction parameters for other agents when those parameters are actually dependent on those selected decision values. In a similar vein, Friedman (1953) recommends simple decision rules because sufficient uncertainty over policy impacts can actually increase uncertainty about the target outcomes. Mirrlees and Stern (1972) propose simple rules to reduce the errors caused by misspecified preferences.

In general, decision rules suitable for controlling a dynamic system will be of the servo-mechanism type (Philips (1954, 1957)): [4]

$$x_t = \sum_{j=1}^{p} F_j y_{t-j} + f \qquad (11.9)$$

This rule is a simplification of the optimal feedback rule (11.4). For $p \geqslant 2$ and suitable choices of F_j it contains proportional, differential and integral control elements; and, provided p is large enough, it is a sufficiently powerful 'error correction mechanism' to steer (11.2) along a given path (Salmon (1982)). Moreover (11.9) is fixed in the sense of time invariance. If $F_j = 0$ it is further simplified to be fixed in the neoclassical sense of not reacting to the events in the market. A more elaborate rule would be

$$x_t = \sum_{j=1}^{p} F_{tj} y_{t-j} + f_t \qquad (11.10)$$

In both (11.9) and (11.10), the value of p might be determined by experimentation. The remaining paramters could be determined by ordinary least squares applied to the x_t and y_{t-j} values obtained from stochastically simulating the information sets within a preliminary optimal control exercise. The object here is to develop simple feedback rules to find one which copies the optimal rule adequately and reproduces most of its stabilising power.

2.4 Anticipations and innovations dependent rules

A development of (11.10) is to split the deterministic elements (foreseen in Ω_1) from the subsequent innovations in Ω_t which introduce policy revisions:

$$x_t = \sum_{j=1}^{p} D_{tj} y_{t-j|1} + \sum_{j=1}^{p} F_{tj}(y_{t-j} - y_{t-j|1}) + f_t \tag{11.11}$$

where $y_{t-j|1} = E(y_{t-j}|\Omega_1)$. The information set used in forming these expectations could be quite restricted, and does not have to be the same as that used in generating optimal decision rules.

All these rules are strictly backwards looking whereas the optimal decision rule (11.4) contains elements reflecting expectations of future events in g_t, which depends on $E_t(a_k)$ for $k = t \ldots T$. The main benefit of optimisation may be the opportunity to anticipate the effects of unwelcome future events and to set x_t so as to be in the best position to counteract their predicted consequences. If that is the case (and our numerical results for the copper market suggest that it is) then the simple rules such as (11.9) – (11.11) will be rather ineffective. An improvement would be

$$x_t = \sum_{j=1}^{p} A_{tj} y_{t-j} + \sum_{j=0}^{q} B_{tj} y_{t+j|t} + a_t \qquad \text{for } t = 1 \ldots T \tag{11.12}$$

To use (11.12) of course requires a specification of either Ω_t, or of a simple mechanism for forming the expectations $y_{t+j|t}$ which is both suitable and informationally feasible. However, (11.12) is both a forward and a backwards looking decision rule. Its success depends not only on how effective it is as a rule but also on how accurate the policy maker's expectations process $y_{t+j|t}$ proves to be. The expectations of some variables are easily formed. For prices, there are forward prices. For others, experience or naive forecasts (e.g. the same change as last time) could be used. But to use a complete econometric model to generate $y_{t+j|t}$ exactly implies that the policy maker may as well accept the optimal decision rules at the same time. Indeed, strictly speaking, $y_{t+j|t}$ should account for the values set for x_t, while y_t should likewise be conditioned on the values of $y_{t+j|t}$.

The objective here, then, is to see whether any of the rules (11.9) – (11.12) can supply good stabilisation results (for a reasonable financial commitment) when judged against optimal rules. If so, how far can we simplify (from (11.12) down to (11.9)) before the degree of stabilisation lost becomes unacceptable?

A second purpose is to use these estimated rules to identify which elements play the biggest role in the stabilisation problem. Is it the feedback control, the time varying parameters, or the size of p, which is important? Or is it the innovations terms (i.e. the ability to revise policies en route), or the forward looking anticipations, which are the most important? Of course by varying the list of variables in y_t we can also see which are the most important indicators, and by varying the coverage of Ω_t in (11.12) we can see the importance of different elements of information about the market's performance for successful decision making. In particular one can test the importance of a sophisticated rule with simple information inputs, versus a fixed rule with sophisticated information. The issue here is whether it is the design of the intervention rule or the contents of the information set which is crucial to successful market stabilisation.

3. COMMODITY MARKET STABILISATION: THE COPPER MARKET CASE

3.1 Commodity market models

The main variable of interest in any commodity market model is the price at which the commodity is exchanged. Models of commodity markets therefore have a simple structure reflecting the determination of price through the familiar 'Marshallian cross':

$$\begin{aligned} Q_t &= f(\alpha(L)P_t, X_t) \\ C_t &= g(\beta(L)P_t, X_t) \\ S_t &= h(\gamma(L)P_t, P_t^e, X_t) \\ \Delta S_t &= Q_t - C_t \end{aligned} \qquad (11.13)$$

where Q_t is production, C_t consumption, and S_t stock holdings in period t. Here P_t is the market price; P_t^e is a vector of expectations, formed at t, of prices up to some specified horizon; and X_t is a vector of exogenous variables. Finally $\alpha(L)$, $\beta(L)$ and $\gamma(L)$ contain the parameters of distributed lags in the lag operator L. This model is complete once the expectations mechanism is specified. If we assume that stock-holders form mechanistic expectations –say from some adaptive scheme in past prices and X_t values— then we can reformulate this stock relationship as

$$S_t = h^*(\gamma^*(L)P_t, \delta(L)X_t) \tag{11.14}$$

and the price will clear the market period by period.

The model (11.13), but with stocks explained by (11.14), contains no explicit price equation. It is generally found that the prices predicted from a model of this structure are significantly more variable than the corresponding historical series. Not only is this an awkward result militating against the simple structure of (11.13) with (11.14), but it also contradicts the result that the variance of the predictions from an estimated, but correctly specified, dynamic model will understate that of the realisations (Granger and Newbold (1977)).

Two explanations of this predictive failure in prices are possible. The orthodox view has been that the additional variability is due to an incomplete coverage of stockholdings in the statistical sources. Since a rise in prices in response to excess demand for the commodity will generally lead to a reduction of the stocks held, an incomplete coverage would typically lead to prices having the play too large an equilibriating role in the estimated model. That would imply that the market clearing identity in (11.13), with (11.14) inserted, should fail to hold exactly. This is generally the case with commodity market data. The standard way out is to replace that market clearing identity with an explicit price formation mechanism

$$\Delta P_t = k(Z_t, X_t) \tag{11.15}$$

where Z_t is the market's excess supply:

$$Z_t = Q_t - C_t - \Delta S_t \tag{11.16}$$

Equation (11.15) might be viewed as a sort of Walrasian adjustment scheme implicit in the market 'invisible hand' mechanism, or just an inverted version of (11.14). In either case it is made necessary by unobserved stocks. This formulation is essentially the price relationship which was estimated by Fisher, Cootner and Bailey (1972) for their Copper Market model. The other possibility is of course that the mechanistic type of expectations process used to derive (11.14) is the wrong one. The alternative is to specify P_t^e as a rationally formed expectations process. This has been attempted in Gilbert, Hughes Hallett and Ghosh (1984). However, the estimation theory of rational expectations models in not well established, nor has any consensus emerged on a suitable specification of that expectations process. In view of its controversial nature, that issue requires separate investigation.

A more detailed specification of the model used in this chapter will be found in the appendix.

3.2 The stabilisation criteria

We controlled the copper model over a period of 40 quarters, from 1971.1 to 1980.4. The model was estimated on data up to 1978.4, so the stabilisation period extends two years beyond the sample period. Moreover, 1971 is a sensible starting point since it was a year in which the market exhibited excess supply. The instrument available to the stabilisation agency was purchases or sales of a buffer stock maintained by the agency (copper being easily stored and of high unit value). The target variables are deviations of the market (LME) price from an initial pre-determined trend, and deviations of the buffer stock level from a constant level set at 1½ million tonnes. The predetermined price trend was set by the historical price trend.

Specifying the exact objectives of stabilisation has proved controversial in the past. The orthodox objective is to maximise a discounted sum of producers' and consumers' surplus (e.g. Just et al. (1978), Newberry and Stiglitz (1982)). However, Cochrane (1980), among others, has attacked that formulation, arguing that consumers and producers are more concerned with price levels because they identify prices, rather than an abstract economic surplus measure, with welfare. In practice this argument must contain an element of truth, and many authors (e.g. Arzac and Wilkinson (1979), Dixon and Chen (1982)) have concentrated on price levels in empirical work. Moreover, economic surplus also has its limitations as a measure of social welfare in stochastic or nonlinear econtexts (Turnovsky (1978)).

We use a very simple objective function here (involving just market prices and the buffer stock levels) as a means of generating conditionally optimal market interventions. The resulting stabilisation programme can then be judged in terms of whatever measures of financial cost, stability, or general welfare are considered appropriate. Alterations to this specification of the objective function could be used to trace the trade-offs available between the chosen cost and benefit measures.

The relative priorities were specified by setting $\underset{\sim}{Q}$ to be diagonal with constant elements. There are therefore neither joint target nor intertemporal penalties except in so far as the buffer stock level reflects cummulated purchases. The relative penalties were 100 on squared deviations of (log) prices, 1 on squared buffer stock deviations, and 0.1 on squared buffer stock purchases or sales. However, since there are over 25 different rules to be evaluated, the results are more easily discussed in terms of the costs and stabilisation benefits of the various decision rules, rather than by inspecting prices and buffer stock holdings. We used three measures of cost:

(i) the expected Net Present Value of the programme in (1975\$b) allowing for transaction, warehousing and overhead costs at the rates assumed in Bhaskar, Gilbert and Perlman (1978);

(ii) the expected maximum finance (1975\$b) required by the programme, defined as the maximum (outward) cash flow implied by the transactions in (i);

(iii) the expected maximum buffer stock (m. tonnes).

We also used three measures of net benefits:

(iv) the expected root mean square error of prices about the trend;

(v) the mean deviation of prices about that trend;

(vi) a measure of the transfer benefit to the Third world (the 'South') from the developed countries (the 'North') constructed from three elements: (a) the discounted deflated changed in producers' profits. If pre-stabilisation production is q_0 and stabilised production is q_1, then the change in profits is approximately $\frac{1}{2}(q_0 + q_1)\Delta p$ where Δp is the change in the price resulting from stabilisation; (b) the discounted deflated change in consumers' surplus $-\frac{1}{2}(c_0 + c_1)\Delta p$; (c) the discounted deflated revenues of the buffer stock. Summing these by countries within a group gives the North-South transfer. These transfer figures are all evaluated under risk neutrality (Newberry and Stiglitz (1981) p. 93).

3.3 The information sets

The control exercises assume historical values for the noncontrollable exogenous variables, with the exception that net sales by the United States (GSA) strategic stockpile of copper were set at zero and the total amount sold (225,000 tonnes) over the period was transferred to the stabilisation authority at the start of the exercise. Sales by the GSA (or at least the timing of these sales) have in practice been motivated by considerations of price stabilisation, even if this has not always been the result. We therefore assume that had the United States been a signatory of a stabilisation agreement of the type envisaged, then its stockpiling sales would have been coordinated with the activities of the buffer stock.

If the stabilisation rules are not fully stochastic in taking historical values for the noncontrollable variables it is because we have, at present, no satisfactory model for forecasting the important variables –industrial production in the OECD countries, and monetary and trade variables. Unlike the copper market model, such an auxiliary forecasting model would at best be an impressionistic attempt to capture the relationships between the exogenous variables. To do that requires a model of the entire world economy, and it is naive to suppose an auxiliary model of a few simple equations would give an adequate impression of the dynamic relationships which hold between these variables. Moreover, although market agents may not have access to a fully specified world model, they are subjected to a battery of forecasts and comments generated within the financial and governmental communities and are therefore much better informed than an agent abliged to rely on some simple auxiliary model. Not only is the construction of a world model beyond the scope of this exercise, but it would also oblige us to take a simplified view of a number of the major controversies in macroeconomics which might unnecessarily prejudice the conclusions we reach on the more limited questions we wish to answer. So, for comparison purposes, we have used historical values.

3.4 The optimal intervention rules

The results of the optimal interventions quoted below were all computed using the model, preferences, and information sets, given above in the closed loop stochastic control rule (11.8) and they include the optimal revisions described immediately after equation (11.8). Since it is possible to intervene on a daily (or even hourly) basis in the copper market, we assume that the buffer stock manager knows the current and past prediction errors in V_t of (11.2). Future disturbances, however, are all forecasted at their current expected values.

3.5 The bandwidth rules

The bandwidth intervention rules were modelled by stochastic simulations of the copper market model with buffer stocks held constant except for the changes necessary to hold prices within a specified range. By specifying different bandwidths, and different purchasing/sales reactions when intervention is signalled, we can simulate different priorities for smooth prices and different attitudes to which fluctuations should be treated as sufficiently serious to warrant action.

Having set the bandwidth and a central 'trend', the interventions are computed by means of a sequence of one step simulations, each incorporating the information on the realisations of random variables up to and including the current period. Buffer stock purchases or sales are set at zero while the simulated price series remain within the band. But in periods when the simulated price exceeds the band, the price equation is inverted and the model solved for the buffer stock change required to force the price back to the nearer boundary subject to the buffer stock remaining non-negative, and in some cases subject to the financial commitment implied by the cumulated *net* purchases remaining below some limit.

In order to deal with the stochastic nature of the market, each simulation result given below represents the mean of 100 stochastic simulations where the random variables are drawn from normal distributions having the same mean and variance as those estimated from the sample period (the random sampling technique is due to McCarthy (1972)). The schemes studied were:

A: Single bandwidths of ±1%, ±5%, ±10%, ±15% about a predetermined nominal price trend estimated by regression using the historical price series over the simulation period.

B: Two-tier bandwidths of ±2.5/5% and ±7.5/15% about the same nominal price trend. Prices within the inner band again cause no buffer stock interventions, while prices beyond the outer band lead to the full interventions necessary to force prices back to the nearest boundary (subject to the non-negativity constraint). However, when simulated prices lie between inner and outer bands, then interventions are computed at half the rate necessary to return prices to the nearer inner boundary. The inner band was intended to trigger interventions in anticipation of large price fluctuations, and thus to capture the limited discretion which is actually found in existing stabilisation agreements (e.g those for tin and rubber, and those for managing exchange rates).

C: Each one step simulation is Schemes A or B is replaced with a k step simulation based on all the information and expectations available at period t. If intervention is found to be required in period t+k, then the buffer stock change $\frac{1}{k}(\Delta S_{t+k})$ is applied in period t (for any integer $k \geqslant 2$). This rule contains an explicit anticipations mechanism, and attempts to smooth target and instrument trajectories and to cut the cost of intervening.

D: The ±5% single bandwidth exercise was rerun with a borrowing limit imposed on the authority's operations. Once the limit is reached, the authority is unable to make further purchases. The limit was set successively at $2.5b, $5b and $10b.

Finally, each exercise in group A and B was replaced with the stabilisation authority being forced, in each of the last 8 quarters, to sell $1/n^{th}$ of its remaining stock (where n is the number of quarters till termination). These self-liquidating schemes, denoted AS and BS respectively, are included as a 'control group' to show up the corresponding optimal rule's ability to anticipate.

3.6 The simple feedback rules

Stochastic simulations were also used to determine the coefficients of the simple feedback rules described in section 2.4. These rules were fitted using closed loop optimal intervention sequences, each one derived from a simulation of the stochastic elements of the information sets described above, together with the same model and objective function in each case. Thus the first information set, Ω_1, yields an initial open loop control sequence (1971.1 to 1980.4) by (11.8) as a starting point. Then, for each of the 40 intervention periods, 100 drawings from the sample estimates of the density functions of the random variables in the problem were taken. This generated 100 sets of closed loop optimal interventions; $\tilde{x}_t^{(i)*}$ for t = 1 ... 40 and each i = 1 ... 100 in turn. The various simple rules were specified as proposed in section 2; equations (11.9), (11.10), (11.11) and (11.12). The parameters of these 4 types of rule were fitted by ordinary least squares regression on the pseudo-data just generated. For the time varying rules, there were 40 rules each based on a sample size of 100. For the fixed (time invariant) rules, (11.9), the data was pooled to give one rule estimated on a sample of 4000 'observations'. Note that these rules were all estimated with the explanatory and dependent variables measured in deviations from their ideal values.

4. RESULTS: OPTIMAL INTERVENTION RULES

The results of the benchmark optimal stabilisation exercise (OC) about the 1971-80 historical trend are shown in figure 11.1 and table 11.1 (row 1). Intervention certainly does lead to a substantial reduction in the variations of market prices, and it is particularly effective in the periods of greater instability (1972-75 and 1978-80). The variability of prices (as measured by their RMSE) has been halved compared to recent history, and it is 25% less than the fluctuations inherent in the unstabilised market (table 11.1, part (c)).[5] However, these interventions require substantially greater finance than was previously thought. A stockpile of 2½million tonnes and finance of $5.2 billion are required, which contrasts with earlier suggestions of 0.8 million tonnes and $1.1 billion (UNCTAD (1976)) or 2 million tonnes and $3 billion (Bhaskar et al. (1978)). Hence stabilisation is possible but it is expensive.

On the other hand the optimised objective function values w*, which represent the function actually optimised inclusive of constraints on acceptable levels for the buffer stock, clearly show the advantage of stabilisation. Compared to that implied by the natural variability of prices, this stabilisation index falls to one third of its no intervention value; and, compared to the historical prices of 1971-80, it is one quarter of its no intervention level.

We have removed the implication that a market authority would know the most appropriate trend about which to stabilise prices, by repeating exercise OC with the preassigned price trend computed as the projection of the historical price trend before the interventions commence (estimated from data for 1956-70). The results

Table 11.1.* The results of optimal stabilisation rules about unadjusted historical trends

Exercise	Buffer Stock Weight	NPV (1975$b)	Maximum Finance (1975$b)	Maximum Stock (m.tonnes)	Mean Price Deviation (c/lb)	Price RMSE (c/lb)	Gains to 'South' (1975$m)	w*
(a) about the 1971-1980 historical trend								
OC	1.0	–0.2	5.2	2.5	–1.3	9.9	–173.2	22.8
OCS	1.0	–0.1	5.2	2.5	–2.3	10.8	–221.0	33.0
(b) about the 1956-1970 historical trend (informationally feasible)								
FS	1.0	0.5	8.7	3.2	0.8	11.2	–80.4	79.1
(c) with no intervention								
stochastic simulation	0	0	0	0	0	14.2	0	67.6
deterministic simulation	0	0	0	0	0	7.9	0	42.2
historical prices	0	0	0	0	0	18.5	0	82.7

Note: the mean deviation and RMSE figures in tables 11.1–11.5 are all computed about the historical (1971.1 to 1980.4) trend.

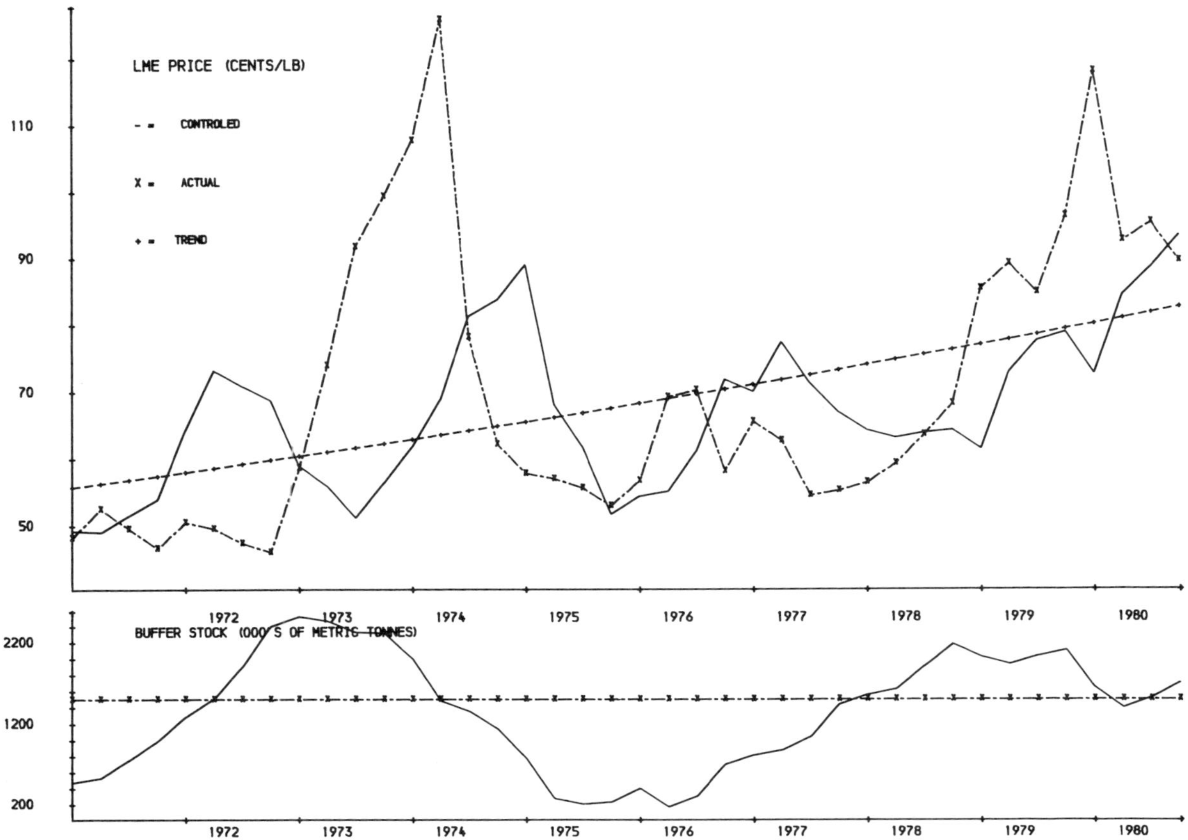

Figure 11.1 The optimal stabilisation rule

are in table 11.1 (row 3); exercise FC. They underline the extreme importance of incorporating suitable information describing the appropriate level about which prices should best be stabilised. Although the net present values are less negative, the finance required rises 67% while the RMSE rises by only 14%. Evidently forcing information feasibility makes the market more difficult and expensive to control, but there is no need to suffer any serious loss in the level of stabilisation provided that extra finance can be found. However, these RMSE figures reflect price variations only. The corresponding increases of 200% or more in w*, which reflect the movements of both prices *and* buffer stocks, are much larger. That demonstrates the extent of the extra work now required of the buffer stock in order to achieve a comparable degree of price stability.

5. RESULTS: BANDWIDTH INTERVENTION RULES

Statistics summarising the results of the various bandwidth schemes are given in table 11.2 (bandwidth schemes about the regression trend of the stabilisation period) and in table 11.3 (bandwidth schemes with a borrowing limit imposed).

5.1 Stabilisation about current trends

From table 11.2 it is clear that no major benefit is obtained from adopting a very narrow price range. For example, in exercise A the root mean square error of the price is not effectively reduced by narrowing the range from ± 5% to ± 1%, and broadly similar results were found to hold for the other schemes. This result is expected since the narrower the range adopted, the lower the probability that the authority will be able to hold the price beneath the ceiling in any boom period. The extent to which the price then rises above the ceiling is thus more or less independent of the range specified. The financial requirements of these schemes are also largely invariant to the bandwidth. In contrast financing falles with increasing bandwidths in the 'discretionary' two-tier schemes.

A second conclusion is that substantially greater finance is required by these schemes than by the corresponding optimal stabilisation rules of table 11.1, and the stockpile of around 6 million tonnes is more than seven times the facility envisaged by UNCTAD (1976). In fact 220% more finance only reduces the RMSE to 60% of its level in table 11.1. The suboptimality of bandwidth rules thus appears in higher costs rather than in lower stabilising power. The fact that extra stability can be gained by 'throwing money at the problem', even with a decision rule which treats each period separately, shows that this suboptimality has to do with being unable to anti-

Table 11.2. Standard bandwidth simulations using the regression trend

Exercise	Bandwidth %	NPV (1975$b)	Maximum Finance (1975$b)	Maximum Stock (m.tonnes)	Mean Deviation (c/lb)	RMSE (c/lb)	Gains to 'South' (1975$m)
(a) permanent schemes:							
A	1	–1.7	16.6	6.4	1.5	5.7	56.5
A	5	–1.6	16.0	6.3	1.5	6.7	53.7
A	10	–1.5	15.7	6.2	1.6	8.6	57.8
A	15	–1.5	16.4	6.4	2.1	11.7	82.1
B	2.5/ 5	–3.2	35.7	13.9	1.7	9.0	63.0
B	7.5/15	–1.2	24.6	10.5	0.9	12.7	26.0
(b) self-liquidating schemes:							
AS	1	–3.1	12.9	5.3	–2.2	16.7	–127.4
AS	5	–2.9	12.6	5.2	–2.2	16.7	–127.0
AS	10	–2.8	12.4	5.2	–2.1	17.2	–121.6
AS	15	–3.1	13.4	5.5	–1.7	19.1	–100.9
BS	2.5/ 5	–5.8	25.9	10.8	0.6	26.9	–23.7
BS	7.5/15	–2.6	19.0	8.7	–0.3	22.6	–53.9

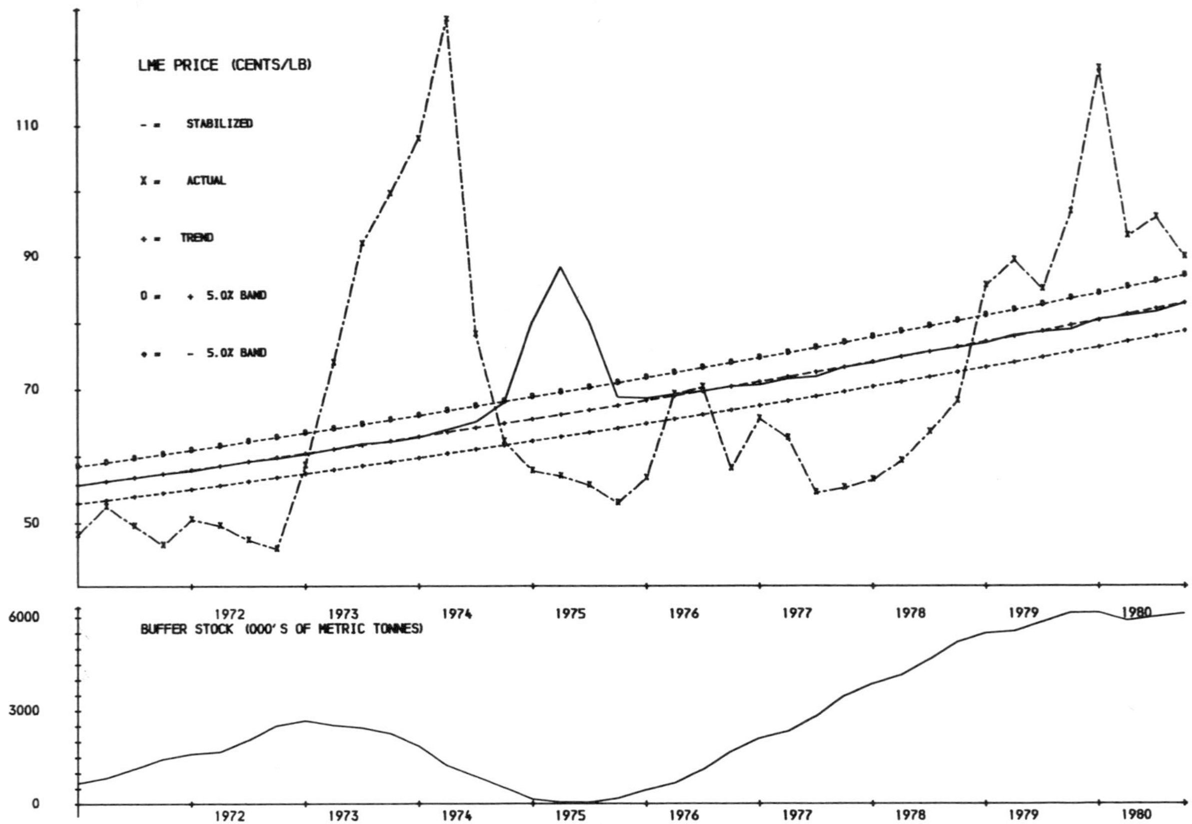

Figure 11.2 The ±5% standard bandwidth intervention rule

cipate subsequent developments. On the other hand, these schemes were up to 2½ times better than 'no intervention' in terms of RMSE. A band of ±5% or less does more than just counteract random fluctuations; the RMSE figures, being lower than that of the deterministic simulation, indicate that the market's natural cycle has been smoothed (see figure 11.2).

5.2 Stabilisation with an anticipations mechanism

The two-tier bandwidth schemes (B in table 11.2) were supposed to provide extra stabilising power through the 'discretionary' interventions between inner and outer bands in anticipation of large price fluctuations. However the market's dynamics were strong enough to render the inner band irrelevant in nearly every period, so that the results actually turned out to be significantly inferior to the standard schemes. The ±2.5/5% scheme gives slightly less stability than a ±10% standard scheme but at more than twice the cost. The ±7.5/15% scheme provides slightly less stability than the ±15% standard rule at 50% increased cost. This happens because, although it correctly anticipates the need to intervene when prices are rising but lie between the inner and outer bands, the half power part of the rule does too little to prevent a full intervention in the following period; but it does diminish the manager's ability to carry out that full intervention. In addition, where prices then exceed the outer band, interventions return prices to that outer boundary. So, in those intervals, the stabilisation is equivalent to that of a standard rule with the extra anticipatory interventions which would not have been undertaken in the corresponding standard rule.

The explicitly anticipating bandwidth schemes, based on the k step simulations (C), were no more successful than the two-tier schemes. This might be expected since they are little more than a multi-tier extension of the two-tier rule. Moreover these rules are only distinct from schemes A or B when the latter do not involve intervention in every period. In practice every single bandwidth rule studied has required intervention in 35, or more, of the 40 decision intervals; and 80% of them needed 39 interventions. So separate results for scheme C are not available in most cases.

The failure of the bandwidth rules B and C stress that anticipatory interventions, deduced from past information only, are unlikely to be successful in a market with strong dynamics. But anticipations would not be important in a market with weaker dynamics. In other words, anticipations which take into account expectations of the future (and the implications of the market's dynamics in particular) tend to be more important for markets where stabilisation is a serious issue.

Further support for the proposition that anticipations of future activity are a key feature of successful intervention comes from the increased dominance of optimal rules over simple bandwidth rules in the self-liquidating schemes. Obliging the buffer stock authority to sell out by the terminal period raises the RMSE by 10% (for no extra finance) in table 11.1, row 2. In contrast the self-liquidating schemes of table 11.2 require 20% less finance but yield threefold increases in RMSE. The optimal interventions are conditioned on the required terminal sales and are therefore less inclined to accumulate in early periods.

5.3 Stabilisation with borrowing restrictions

The scheme in which the buffer stock authority is subject to a borrowing constraint (table 11.3) show substantially inferior performances to that of the unconstrained

Table 11.3 Single bandwidth intervention schemes with borrowing limits

Exercise	Band-width %	Borrowing Limit $b	NPV (1975$b)	Maximum Stock (m.tonnes)	Mean Deviations (c/lb)	RMSE (c/lb)	Gains to 'South' (1975$m)
D	5	2.5	–3.6	9.9	1.1	20.6	51.8
D	5	5	–3.9	10.0	0.8	19.6	13.3
D	5	10	–4.4	9.7	–0.9	10.3	–64.9

schemes; Indeed, the schemes in which the constraint is imposed at $2.5 billion and $5 billion have root mean square errors that are significantly larger than those obtained in the absence of intervention. This suggests that if bandwidth schemes have any merit it is that they can at least contain substantial departures of the price on the down-side. Any attempt to make the financial requirements of the scheme more reasonable by imposing borrowing limits at a level that is likely to bite may well result in the scheme actually destabilising the market price (see, for example, figure 11.3), confirming that having limited resources makes it more important to predict when they will be needed most.

6. RESULTS: SIMPLE FEEDBACK RULES

6.1 Time invariant feedbacks

Of the simple geedback rules considered, (11.9) –represented here by rules 1 and 4 in table 11.4– has the simplest structure. We experimented with values of p=1,... ,9

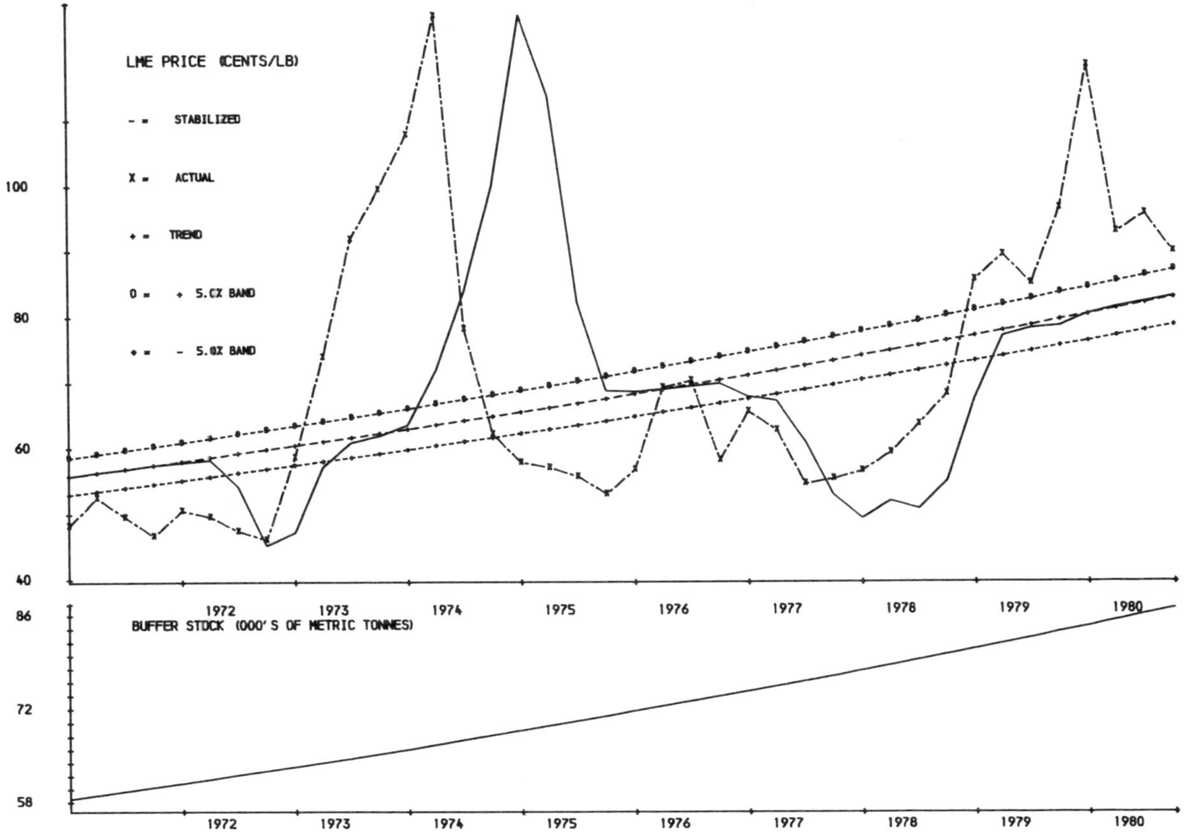

Figure 11.3 The ±5% standard bandwidth intervention rule with finance limited to $5 billion

but report only the main results in table 11.4. A general finding was that the first three lags supplied most (over 50%) of the explanatory power for movements in the buffer stock interventions. The fourth lag, plus trend, constant and seasonal dummies, also increased the explanatory power significantly in terms of the F statistic for those extra variables. But the fifth and subsequent lags failed to improve their tracking performance to any significant extent.

In rule 1, the coefficients on deviations of prices and buffer stocks from their ideal paths both have the correct negative sign for a control rule which aims at stabilisation. But, of the two targets, deviations of prices from their desired path appears to be the more important determinant of the necessary interventions. In fact, the price deviation term has 25 times more impact and is three times more significant than the buffer stock term. This is partly because unit price deviations attract 100 times the penalty on a unit buffer stock deviation in the criterion by which the interventions were selected. However this result becoms obscured as the feedback lags are lengthened in rule 4. Successive lags in the buffer stock form highly colinear variables because they are successive cumulations of the same variable. Not surprisingly it is virtually impossible to distinguish the individual impacts of the various buffer stock feedbacks in rule 4, nor indeed of the first three buffer stock intervention variables (which supply the difference between those buffer stock levels). In fact only ΔBS_{t-4} has a reasonably well determined coefficient, and this suggests that the price feedback terms are still the important factor. Moreover, the price feedback coefficients have on average the correct (negative) sign while the average buffer stock feedback coefficient is very small and has the wrong sign.

The estimated price feedback coefficients in rule 4, on the other hand, showed relatively small covariances, suggesting that each lag independently contributes a genuine extra degree of control. This is not surprising since the feedback mechanism of rule 1, inserted into the model, can only superimpose a first order autoregressive adjustment process on the development of prices. But both the model and the optimal stabilisation rules generate powerful cycles, so one should not expect a one lag feedback mechanism to be effective at smoothing the evolution of a market subject to a more complex dynamic structure. Indeed, to be able to eliminate the discrepancy between the unstabilised price trajectory and its ideal (trend) path theoretically requires a feedback control rule such as (11.9) where $p-1$ is at least as large as the order of difference equation determining that error (Salmon (1982)). The copper model has up to 41 lags (and the ideal values follow a zero order difference equation), so rule 1 describes an error correction mechanism of much too low an order to smooth prices of this market. Rule 4 is evidently better, showing a threefold increase in explanatory power. But it cannot be expected to be a very effective con-

Table 11.4 The fitted coefficients of simple feedback rules (t-ratios in brackets). Dependent variable ΔBS_t.

Explanatory Variable	Rule 1	Rule 2	Rule 3	Rule 4	Rule 5	Rule 6
$LME_{t-1}-LME^d_{t-1}$	−0.414 (11.06)	−0.486 (12.26)	0.121 (8.7)	−0.124 (2.1)	0.318 (4.8)	0.510 (12.8)
$LME_{t-2}-LME^d_{t-2}$				0.348 (4.1)	−0.068 (0.8)	0.431 (9.6)
$LME_{t-3}-LME^d_{t-3}$				−0.632 (7.4)	−0.596 (7.1)	−1.110 (26.5)
$LME_{t-4}-LME^d_{t-4}$				0.251 (4.2)	0.455 (7.6)	0.491 (16.7)
$BS_{t-1} - BS^d_{t-1}$	−0.016 (3.26)	−0.014 (2.84)	−0.495 (157.1)	−74.10 (1.8)	−83.70 (2.1)	−26.70 (1.5)
$BS_{t-2} - BS^d_{t-2}$				29.67 (0.6)	42.52 (0.9)	−3.30 (0.2)
$BS_{t-3} - BS^d_{t-3}$				82.86 (1.7)	76.01 (1.6)	65.59 (3.1)
$BS_{t-4} - BS^d_{t-4}$				−38.60 (0.9)	−34.90 (0.9)	36.20 (2.0)
ΔBS_{t-1}				74.56 (1.8)	84.24 (2.1)	26.03 (1.4)
ΔBS_{t-2}				44.40 (1.0)	41.27 (1.0)	29.30 (1.5)
ΔBS_{t-3}				−38.50 (0.9)	−34.90 (0.9)	−36.10 (1.9)
ΔBS_{t-4}				0.197 (9.9)	0.204 (10.5)	−0.102 (10.2)

Table 11.4 continued

e_t		−0.256 (5.41)			0.455 (13.1)	
LME^e_{t+1}			−0.218 (17.1)			−0.123 (37.6)
LME^e_{t+2}						0.868 (22.9)
LME^e_{t+3}						−0.063 (1.6)
LME^e_{t+4}						−0.219 (7.8)
BS^e_{t+1}			0.531(176.0)			1.011 (54.1)
BS^e_{t+2}						−0.277 (11.4)
BS^e_{t+3}						−0.170 (7.6)
BS^e_{t+4}						0.123 (9.7)
Constant	0.210 (21.9)	0.212 (22.2)	0.203 (4.0)	0.071 (7.2)	0.065 (6.8)	1.608 (14.9)
Trend	−0.001 (2.7)	−0.001 (3.5)	0.001 (7.8)	0.002 (5.1)	0.003 (9.0)	0.006 (23.6)
Q1	−0.225 (23.1)	−0.225 (23.2)	−0.030 (8.7)	−0.252 (23.1)	−0.258 (24.3)	0.165 (19.1)
Q2	−0.340 (35.9)	−0.340 (36.0)	−0.232 (71.6)	−0.254 (16.6)	−0.267 (17.8)	−0.056 (4.8)
Q3	−0.083 (8.8)	−0.083 (8.8)	−0.148 (46.1)	0.060 (4.7)	0.051 (4.1)	−0.174 (20.2)
$\bar{R}^2$	0.300	0.305	0.924	0.780	0.791	0.963
F	279.77	245.72	5813.4	799.71	800.27	3508.5
RSS	173.15	171.86	18.16	51.82	49.37	7.76

Sample size = 4000. RSS = residual sum of squares. Durbin-Watson statistics are not valid as all equations contain lagged dependent variables. Q_1, Q_2, Q_3 are quarterly dummies.

trol mechanism when incorporated into the model; its stabilising power is unlikely to match its explanatory power. This is confirmed in table 11.5 (see section 6.5 below).

In addition most of the price feedback response in rule 4 is delayed, with lags spread between 6 and 12 months compared to the 3 months of rule 1. This sort of 'inertia' implies that interventions should respond to 'permanent' price deviations analogous to an adaptive price expectations process.

In contrast, the buffer stock variable, BS_t, cumulates the value of the intervention instrument since the start of the exercise and therefore represents a tth order error correction mechanism. Hence there is no advantage, in terms of error correction properties, in extending the buffer stock feedback lags.

6.2 Time varying feedbacks

We have attempted to fit feedback rules in the time varying form (11.10). But all the rules of this type were inferior to the corresponding time invariant rules, and they are therefore not reported in table 11.4.

The main problem with time varying rules was instability of the estimated coefficients, both with respect to the specified structure of the feedback mechanism and with respect to the time index. Varying the composition of the feedback mechanism caused changes in the feedback coefficients and some changes of sign. The variability of those coefficients over different intervention periods, and the consequent wide variations in the specification of the feedback mechanism, made this kind of 'simple' rule hard to use effectively. The upshot of these difficulties was low average explanatory power compared to (11.9) with the same number of lags, and insignificant improvements in mean stabilising performance (but with wide variations) when applied to the model. There appear to be advantages to pooling the 'data' across time periods in order to select a stable simple control rule.

6.3 The importance of information innovations

Rules 2 and 5 of table 11.4 repeat rules 1 and 4 except that the impact of the first price feedback term is split between its previous anticipated value and the latest information innovation. This is done by fitting a control rule of the form (11.11) with p = 1 and p = 4 respectively, where the feedback coefficients are all time invariant and the only innovations term is that in current prices.

The innovations term, e_t, is significant but with a coefficient which is unstable with changes in the specification of the feedback mechanism. The remaining coefficients are scarcely affected, with the exception of the coefficient of LME_{t-1} itself (in rule 2) and a shift of weight to the last two lags of the price feedback mechanism (in rule 5). The improvement in the fit of rules 2 and 5 over rules 1 and 4 is statistically insignificant. These results might suggest that bad forecasts of the noncontrollable variables, or large stochastic shocks, are not very damaging for a sensible feedback rule. However, that conclusion must certainly be qualified. Rules 2 and 5 show only that information innovations are not important in simple feedback rules. But, although the optimal rules appear to be explained reasonably well, it may be exactly the remaining unexplained movements which depend on the information innovations. The doubling of both the coefficient of e_t and its significance, when exchanging rule 2 for rule 5, supports that view. It may also be that an error once made calls for relatively small revisions in a strategy which is different, and inferior, to that which would have been chosen in the absence of that error. If optimal policy revisions can add little to the success of intervention [6], then it becomes more important to make those interventions anticipate correctly in the first place.

6.4 The importance of anticipations variables

Rules 3 and 6 of table 11.4 indicate the very important role which an anticipations mechanism can play in generating an effective stabilisation rule. The anticipations variables LME^e_{t+i} and BS^e_{t+i}, for i = 1 . . . 4, are the mathematical expectations of the associated variables predicted by the model plus an optimal open loop sequence of buffer stock purchases/sales, both conditional on the previous information set Ω_{t-1}. They are therefore rational expectations of market prices and buffer stock levels, assuming a rational intervention strategy and knowledge of Ω_{t-1} (Hughes Hallett (1981)). They represent the relevant short term point projections of future developments if it is assumed (for lack of further evidence) that the authority will make optimal interventions, or if the simple rules appear about as effective as optimal rules. But if it is perceived that neither assumption is correct on average, then these expectations should be conditioned on the simple rather than the optimal rule. Moreover, unless one can argue that these anticipations are plausible proxies for some wider information sets, to which agents have access but we do not, then a simple rule incorporating them is no longer 'simple'. If agents actually *computed* such anticipations they would deduce the optimal interventions at the same time.

In view of these qualifications, rules 3 and 6 are offered as a means to study the scope for improving stabilisation rules with anticipations, rather than as serious 'simple' rules for implementation. Adding anticipations terms produces threefold increases in the $\bar{R}^2$ goodness of fit statistic, and up to ninefold falls in the residual sum of squares. The improvements in the F statistics are equally dramatic. They leave no doubt about the significance of the additional explanatory power provided by these anticipations terms.

There is not a great deal to choose between rule 3 and rule 6 in terms of regression diagnostics (the loss of degrees of freedom tends to outweigh the lower residual sum of squares). All the coefficients in rule 3 are significant, but price movements have smaller impacts and are less significant, while buffer stock levels have larger impacts and are more significant, than in the other rules. This suggests that more information about past and expected future events is contained in the cumulative buffer stock levels than in the individual price movements. The buffer stock coefficients also have the correct signs. They indicate that higher stocks than desired would, ceteris paribus, trigger sales. Meanwhile, a predicted rise in stocks implies that purchases would be advanced to the current period in order to exert downward pressure an that rising price trend. Similarly if a price rise is predicted, then current buffer stock sales would be increased to help reduce that upward price trend in advance. But if prices have been above the desired level then, ceteris paribus, extra stock would be bought which is not a stabilising action. Nevertheless the average of the price coefficients is negative, and that provides an appropriate reaction to 'permanent' price deviations indicated by rational expectations (rather than the mechanical process suggested earlier by the structure of rule 4).

The most significant terms by far in rule 3 are the buffer stock levels themselves. Indeed, apart from an adjustment for the desired buffer stock level, the current buffer stock *level* is more or less just a simple average of its past level and future expected level. Consequently anticipations appear to be very important for successful intervention, but they enter the decision rules in a very simple way (similar in spirit, in this case, to the two-tier bandwidth rules of table 11.2). Note that we examine the potential role of anticipations variables here, and not whether sophisticated or simple anticipations will be required to fullfil that role.

Many of the same remarks apply to the four period feedback/feedforward rule 6. The buffer stock variables dominate, although their significance and individual impacts is obscured by the associated multi-collinearity. Delayed reactions of between 9 and 12 months dominate the feedback structure in prices whereas the anticipations mechanism places most weights on the immediate future with a 3 to 6 months lead. The small increase in exemplanatory power over rule 3, and the continued dominance of B^e_{t+1}, confirm that anticipations terms enter a 'good' decision rule in a simple way.

6.5 Stabilisation by simple feedback rules

We examined the stabilising ability of two representative feedback rules from table 11.4 by substituting them into the copper model and then simulating the augmented model over the same control interval, using the same information sets as before. Table 11.5 sets out the summary statistics of the market's performance under rules 3 and 5; that is under the best of the rules with and without anticipations. The results

Table 11.5 The performance of simple feedback rules

	NPV (1975\$b)	Max Finance (1975\$b)	Max Stock (m.tonnes)	Mean Price Deviations (c/lb)	RMSE Price Deviations (c/lb)	Transfer to South (1975\$m)
Rule 3	–1.2	5.74	2.64	–0.21	11.04	–146.1
Rule 5	–5.9	15.23	4.85	4.85	17.36	–4.6

show once again the value of including anticipations in a stabilisation rule. Although the power of these two rules to explain movements in the optimal interventions over the control period was not very different, their ability to stabilise the market over the same period is quite different. The root mean square error of prices under rule 5 is 60% higher than that under rule 3. Moreover it costs nearly three times as much financing to achieve even that poor result. Rule 3, unlike rule 5, produces better results than no intervention at all. In fact the sole desirable feature of rule 5 is that, unlike rule 3, it does not generate any noticeable transfer away from countries of the 'South'. Rule 3, on the other hand, produces results not very much worse than those of the optimal rule (compare figure 11.4).

7. CONCLUSIONS

Comparison of the bandwidth schemes with the optimal stabilisation rule confirms the suboptimality of the bandwidth schemes.[7] Optimal rules achieve the same order of stabilisation as a 12.5% simple bandwidth rule (interpolation from table 11.2) but at less than *one third* of the cost. This is largely because the optimal solution avoids the problem of the price breaking out of range by relaxing the extent to which it wishes to contain the price as its stock becomes undesirably low or high. The point is that comparisons between table 11.2 or 11.3 and table 11.1 are to the disadvantage of the optimal stabilisation rules since the latter incorporates explicit

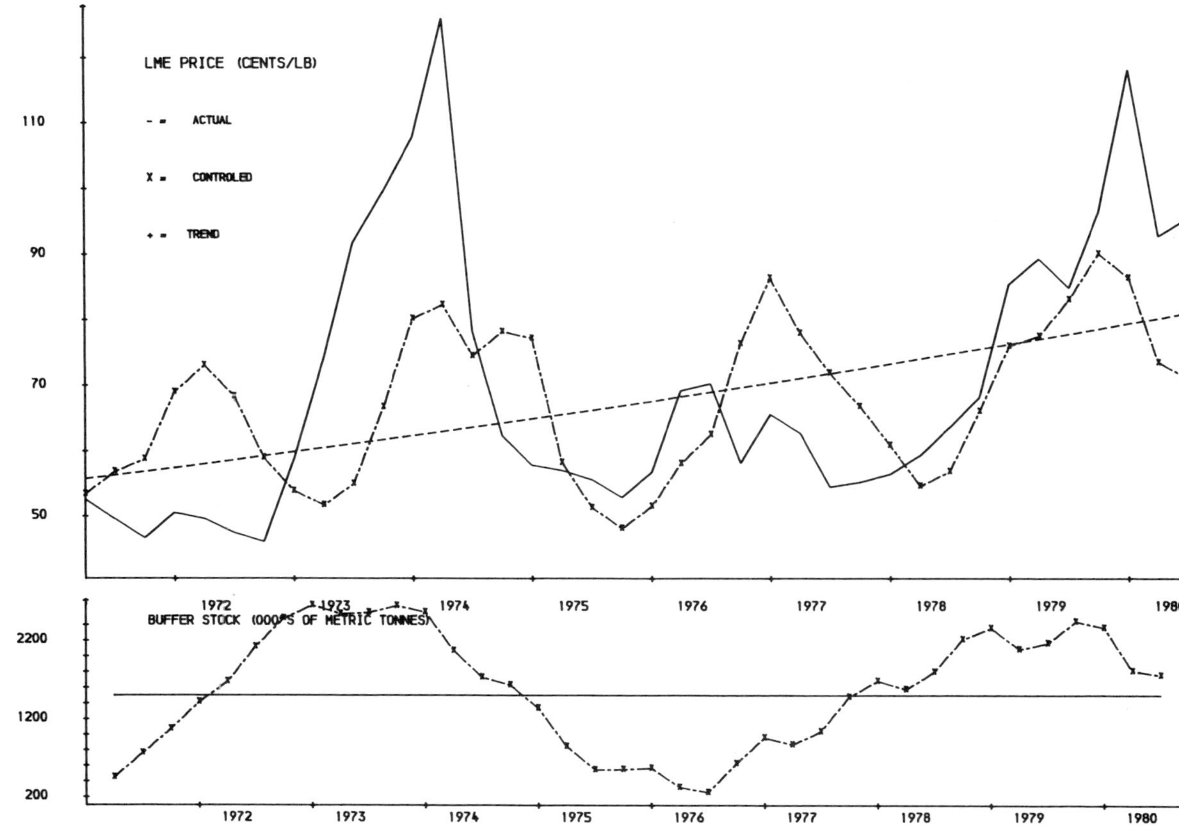

Figure 11.4 The simplest feedback control rule with anticipations (rule 3)

penalties to holding and to changing the buffer stock. No bandwidth scheme allows for such penalties, but attempts to approximate them by imposing a borrowing limit ruins the stabilisation performance. For example, a ± 5% bandwidth with a borrowing limit of $5b, which is almost exactly the financial requirement of the optimal intervention rule, has a RMSE for prices twice as large as that achieved by the optimal rule and nearly three times that of the same bandwidth rule with unlimited finance. This poor performance makes it clear that of one is anxious to limit the financial commitment to the stabilisation exercise, this is better done by penalising the buffer stockholding within a control context than by imposing a rigid borrowing limit on a bandwidth scheme in which the authority's commitment is otherwise unlimited. A policy of trading one objective (price stabilisation) against the other (financial commitment) is more effective than a policy of switching from one to the other.

Compared to the optimal control run OC, the simple feedback rule 3 produces an RMSE which is 10% higher at a 10% greater finance requirement. Rule 5 is correspondingly 70% worse on the RMSE criterion and costs three times as much. The comparison with the bandwidth schemes is more interesting. Rule 3 gives a marginally better stabilisation result (in terms of the RMSE) than a ±15% standard bandwidth rule, and at one third of the cost. It does not involve losses which are as large as the standard bandwidth schemes since their stock requirements are nearly three times larger. Excepting rules 3 and 6 which contain anticipations terms, these simple rules are automatic in that discretion cannot be exercised once it has been decided to follow them. In contrast optimal rules and rules 3 and 6 depend on anticipations of future events and therefore permit discretion.

Our experiments with the simple feedback rules confirm that anticipations play an extremely important role in successful stabilisation rules. It appears that rather simple rules incorporating a sophisticated expectations mechanism are the most successful, but the question of whether these superior feedback/feedforward rules can still be regarded as 'simple' remains unresolved. Tables 11.4 and 11.5 establish that it is anticipations which *can* make stabilisation rules effective; but they do not show whether it is good anticipations, or just some forward looking mechanism, which is crucial. Nor is it clear how crude an anticipations mechanism one should accept as a reasonable characterisation of the typical decision maker's information set.

In summary, some specific conclusions are:

(a) Significant stabilisation of the copper market would have been possible; but it would have been substantially more expensive than previously suggested.

(b) Stabilisation does not generally benefit the third world producers of copper.
(c) Simple and bandwidth rules are no mauch for optimal rules. But it is questionable whether simple rules which are sophisticated enough to anticipate successfully would in fact by 'simple' enough to warrant abandoning optimal rules.
(d) It is not sensible to limit the financial requirements by imposing a borrowing limit as this is likely to end up by destabilising prices.
(e) The importance of anticipations terms indicates the high value which should be placed on discretionary information introduced by the stabilisation authorities. This in turn underlines the importance of full stochastic or closed loop control, as distinct from pure feedback decision rules (optimal or otherwise).

APPENDIX: A MODEL OF THE WORLD COPPER MARKET

Our model is of the basic form of (11.13) with (11.14) replacing the stock equation for observed (producers' and consumers') stocks. Production is disaggregated by geographical area and as ore or scrap. Consumption is disaggregated by area, and stocks are disaggregated by ownership and area. This disaggregation obliges us to consider trade flows. Until 1979, most copper sold in the United States was sold at the U.S. Producers' Price which differed from the free market (London Metal Exchange, henceforth LME) price which formed the basis for pricing in the remainder of the non-Socialist world. Our model takes the LME price to be determined in the manner discussed in section 3, and is designed for use in the post-1979 one price regime. However, at the estimation stage, the two prices must be treated separately. The price of aluminium, the main substitute for copper, is also endogenous to this model.

The model was estimated on a sample of seasonally unadjusted quarterly data, over 1956.1 to 1978.4, using single equation techniques. It has been conventional to specify econometric models as either linear in levels or linear in logarithms, although there is no theoretical justification for either specification. We have specified our model as linear in all quantities and log-linear in all prices. This unconventional choice maintains the identities across quantities but allows linear decomposition of relative price variables. In Ghosh, Gilbert and Hughes Hallett (1983) we report the outcome of tests which show that our specification is more acceptable than either the log or the linear specifications. The complete estimated model is set out in Gilbert, Hughes Hallett and Ghosh (1984).

(i) *Production*

Production of refined copper is disaggregated between the United States (US) and the rest of the world (RW), and as primary copper produced from ore or secondary copper produced from scrap. The general form of the primary production equations is

$$xPR_t = \beta_0 + \beta_1 t + \beta_2 xPR_{t-1} - \beta_3 xPRS_{t-1} - \beta_4 xCXS_{t-1} \tag{A.1}$$

$$+ \sum_{i=1}^{n} \beta_{5i}(\ln xP_{t-i} - \ln USWHP_{t-i})$$

$$+ \text{seasonals} + \text{dummies} \qquad (x = US, RW)$$

The inclusion of a lagged dependent variable may be justified on a standard partial adjustment argument. xPRS is the level of producers' stocks. Hendry and Ungern-Sternberg (1981) have emphasised the importance of including integral error correction mechanisms in dynamic specifications. This is accomplished here by the variable xCXS, which is excess supply cumulated over four quarters. In the United States the price variable xP is the US Producers' Price (USPP), whilst in the non-US area it is the LME price. In both cases the price is deflated by the US Wholesale Price Index (USWHP). In the non-US area the distributed lag β_{5i} was estimated as a 41 quarter unrestricted fourth order Almon polynomial; but in the US, where the price response is less well defined, a block-triangular shape was imposed on this distribution.

The form of the secondary equation is

$$xSR_t = \beta_0 + \beta_1 t + \beta_2 xSR_{t-1} - \beta_3 xPRS_{t-1} - \beta_4 xCXS_{t-1} \tag{A.2}$$

$$+ \beta_5 xCR_{t-1} + \beta_6(\ln LME_{t-1} - \ln USWHP_{t-1}) + \text{seasonals} + \text{dummies.}$$

The inclusion of refined consumption, xCR, reflects the fact that a large proportion of scrap is new scrap generated in the manufacture of semi-fabricated products. In secondary production the LME price is appropriate in the US area since the bulk of US secondary production is due to independent producers selling at the US Merchants' Price which closely follows the LME price.

(ii) *Consumption*

Consumption of refined copper is disaggregated by five areas: the United States (US), Canada (CN), Europe (EU), Japan (JP) and the Residual World (RW). For each area consumption is related to short distributed lags in industrial production (IP_t) and in the price of copper (LME_t) relative to that of aluminium ($ALPP_t$). The general form of the relationship is:

$$xCR_t = \beta_0 + \beta_1 t + \beta_2 xCR_{t-1} + \sum_{i=0}^{5} \beta_{3i} xIP_{t-i} \qquad \text{(A.3)}$$

$$- \sum_{i=1}^{20} \beta_{4i}(\ln LME_{t-i} - \ln ALPP_{t-i}) + \text{seasonals} + \text{dummies}$$

For x = RW, xIP is the OECD total industrial production index. The β_{3i} distributed lag is unrestricted, but for x = CN and x = RW the restriction $\beta_{3i} = 0$ for $i > 1$ was statistically acceptable. The hypothesis that $\beta_2 = 0$ was acceptable for all but the US and RW areas. The price substitution distributed lag, β_{4i}, was poorly defined except for Europe, and the best results were obtained by inclusion of a block triangular weighted variable, together with its first difference. Except for the RW area, the estimated long run price elasticities are very low and it appears unlikely that we have identified any significant long term substitution against copper except through the time trend. Long term substitution between materials involves an investment in technology, equipment and research. It therefore requires very large price movements.

(iii) *Stocks*

Consumer stocks data are available for three areas: The US, Europe and Japan. We model consumer stock holdings by partial adjustments to a desired stock level, supplemented by terms reflecting the fact that consumers can be flexible as to the time at which they place orders. For $0 < \lambda < 1$,

$$\Delta xCRS_t = \lambda(xCRS_t^* - xCRS_{t-1}) - xPP_{t-1} \qquad (x = US, EU, JP) \qquad \text{(A.4)}$$

where xPP_t is purchases postponed from period t to period t+1 (which may happen because of strikes, and because of anticipations or speculative activity) and $xCRS_t^*$ is the desired level of stocks. Let

$$xCRS_t^* = \alpha_0 + \alpha_1 t + \alpha_2 xCR_{t-1} - \alpha_3 USINT_t \qquad (x = US, EU, JP) \qquad \text{(A.5)}$$

where USINT is the US commercial bank annual prime rate. But if consumers' expectations are regressive, purchases will be postponed or advanced depending on whether the LME price is currently high or low. If deliveries take time, as in Japan, local market prices reflect LME prices with a lag and lagged values of the LME price will be important. Additionally, in the United States, where miners' strikes are fully anticipated, consumers will typically advance their purchases prior to a strike. Thus

$$xCRS_t = \beta_0 + \beta_1 t + \beta_2 xCRS_{t-1} + \beta_3 xCR_{t-1} - \beta_4 USINT_t \tag{A.6}$$

$$- \sum_{i=0}^{n} \beta_{5i}\, \Delta lnLME_{t-i} + \beta_6 \Delta xST_t^e + \text{seasonals} \qquad (x = US, EU, JP)$$

where xST_t^e is (for x = US only) a dummy variable taking the value 1 in the quarter prior to the start of a miners' strike. In order to obtain a reasonable fit in the European and Japanese equations, additional lagged stock variables were included and in the European equation the interest rate was lagged.

Stocks are also held for non-speculative reasons by governments and producers. The United States and Japanese governments have held significant stocks of copper during this period, but we take the movements in their stockholdings to be exogenous. If US producer stocks are passive

$$\Delta USPRS_t = USPR_t + USSR_t - USCR_t - \Delta USCRS_t + USNMR_t - \Delta USGRS_t \tag{A.7}$$

where $USNMT_t$ is US net imports of refined copper and $USGRS_t$ is the United States (GSA) stockpile of copper. US producers adjust their stockholdings by changing their production levels. We have not attempted to model the stock behaviour of non-US producers since there are no satisfactory data on these stockholdings.

The separate treatment of production and pricing in the United States requires an explanation of net imports into the United States. We also need to model the small net flow of the refined copper between the socialist block and the non-socialist world. US net imports are modelled as a second order autoregressive relationship with dependence on the state of supply and demand in that market. Also imports are naturally higher during US miners' strkes. Thus,

$$USNMR_t = \beta_0 + \beta_1 t + \beta_2 USNMR_{t-1} + \beta_3 USNMR_{t-2} - \beta_4 USXS_t \tag{A.8}$$

$$- \beta_5 USST_t + \text{seasonals}$$

where $USXS_t = USPR_t + USSR_t - USCR_t - USCRS_t - USGRS_t$, and $USST_t$ is a dummy variable with value 1 during strikes. Socialist countries' net imports ($SONMR_t$) appear to be uncorrelated with other variables, and were modelled as:

$$\mathrm{SONMR}_t = \beta_0 + \beta_1 t + \beta_2 \mathrm{SONMR}_{t-1} + \beta_3 \mathrm{SONMR}_{t-2} + \text{seasonals} \tag{A.9}$$

(iv) *Prices*

There is no need to provide an explanation of the US producers' price since the two price system has been abandoned and the US producers' price now moves directly in relation to the LME price. The LME price equation is of the form (11.13) augmented by terms taking into account the direct effects of inflation on the price (primary commodities are frequently regarded as inflation hedges, so that inflation will react directly onto the copper price), plus level error correction terms relating the copper price to the general level of prices in equilibrium. This gives an equation of the form

$$\begin{aligned}\Delta \ln \mathrm{LME}_t - 0.25\ \mathrm{USINT}_{t-1} &= \beta_0 + \beta_1 t - \beta_2 \mathrm{AGXS}_t + \beta_3 \mathrm{AGXS}_{t-1} \\ &- \beta_4(\ln \mathrm{LME}_{t-1} - \ln \mathrm{USWHP}_{t-1}) - \beta_5(\ln \mathrm{LME}_{t-4} - \\ &- \ln \mathrm{USWHP}_{t-4}) + \beta_6 \Delta_4 \ln \mathrm{USWHP}_{t-1} + \text{seasonals}\end{aligned} \tag{A.10}$$

The restriction on the interest rate coefficient is appropriate since prices are quarterly data. AGXS_t is aggregate excess supply, and is defined as

$$\begin{aligned}\mathrm{AGXS}_t &= \tfrac{1}{2}(\mathrm{AGTR}_t + \mathrm{AGTR}_{t-1}) - \mathrm{AGCR}_t - \mathrm{SONMR}_t \\ &- \Delta \mathrm{AGCRS}_t - \Delta \mathrm{AGGRS}\end{aligned} \tag{A.11}$$

where AGTR is aggregate refined production, AGCR is aggregate refined consumption, and AGCRS is aggregate consumers' stocks of refined copper and AGGRS is aggregate government stock. The inclusion of AGXS_{t-1} in (A.10) reflects the fact that information dated at period t may not in fact be known to the market until t+1. However, in the stabilisation exercises, the impact of buffer stock sales and purchases is confined to the period of intervention with coefficient $\beta_2 + \beta_3$.

Accurate modelling of the aluminium price would entail building a full model of the aluminium market, which is beyond the scope of this chapter. Instead, we specify the change in the aluminium price as a distributed lag of the change in the US copper producers' price, estimated by an unrestricted second Almon polynomial, plus an error correction mechanism with respect to the US energy price (USENP).

This formulation implies that, in the long run, the aluminium price rises proportionally with the energy price, but in the short run it is responsive to the copper price:

$$\ln ALPP_t = \beta_0 + \beta_1 t - \beta_2(\ln ALPP_{t-1} - \ln USENP_{t-1}) \qquad \text{(A.12)}$$

$$+ \sum_{i=1}^{5} \beta_{3i} \ln USPP_{t-i} + \text{seasonals}$$

NOTES

* Financial support from the UK Social Science Research Council is gratefully acknowledged.

1) An approach to solving this information problem is given in Gilbert, Hughes Hallett and Ghosh (1984).
2) For simplicity we take R –or equivalently π_1, π_2, π_3– to be known. More complicated algorithms which treat these quantities as stochastic are reviewed by Kendrick (1981).
3) The details are set out in Hughes Hallett and Rees (1983), ch. 7.
4) Salmon and Young (1979) suggest that these rules may also have certain robustness properties.
5) The 1970's was a difficult stabilisation period, as indicated by a historical RMSE some 30% higher than the corresponding mean stochastic simulation. The recessions in 1973/74 and 1979/80 led to substantial stockpiling –see figure 11.1.
6) There is some independent evidence that this is not the case for the copper market (Hughes Hallett (1981)).
7) The optimal control exercises are pseudo-stochastic, being run using the historical disturbances, and are thus not strictly comparable with the genuinely stochastic bandwidth simulations. To check the comparisons we ran a set of pseudo-stochastic bandwidth simulations using the same set of disturbances. The statistics from these simulations were sufficiently close to those from the stochastic simulations to justify those comparisons.

REFERENCES

Arzac, E.R. and M. Wilkinson (1979), 'Stabilisation policies for United States feedgrain and livestock markets', *Journal of Economic Dynaimcs and Control,* 1, pp. 39-58.

Bhaskar, K.N., C.L. Gilbert and R.A. Perlman (1978), 'Stabilisation of the international copper market: A simulation study', *Resources Policy,* 4, pp. 13-24.

Brandsma, A.S., A.J. Hughes Hallett and N. van der Windt (1983), 'Optimal control of large nonlinear models: An efficient method of policy search applied to the Dutch economy', *Journal of Policy Modelling,* 5, pp.253-270.

Brandt, W. (1980), *North-South: A Programme for Survival,* Pan Books, London.

Chow, G.C. (1975), *Analysis and Control of Dynamic Economic Systems,* J. Wiley and Sons, New York.

Cochrane, W.W. (1980), 'Some nonconformist thoughts on welfare economics and commodity stabilisation policy', *American Journal of Agricultural Economics,* 62, pp. 508-511.

Dixon, B.L. and W.H. Chen (1982), 'A stochastic control approach to buffer stock management in the Taiwan rice market', *Journal of Development Economics,* 10, pp. 187-207.

Fisher, F.M., P.H. Cootner and M.N. Bailey (1972), 'An econometric model of the world copper industry', *Bell Journal of Economics and Management Science,* 3, pp. 568-601.

Friedman, M. (1953), 'The effects of a full-employment policy on economic stability: A formal analysis' in *Essays in Positive Economics,* University of Chicago Press, Chicago.

Ghosh, S., C.L. Gilbert and A.J. Hughes Hallett (1982), 'Optimal stabilisation of the copper market: The problem of information', *Resources Policy,* 8, pp. 201-214.

Ghosh, S., C.L. Gilbert and A.J. Hughes Hallett (1983), 'Tests of functional form in dynamic econometric models: Some empirical experience', *Empirical Economics,* 8, pp. 63-69.

Gilbert, C.L., A.J. Hughes Hallett and S. Ghosh (1984), *Stabilising Speculative Commodity Markets,* Oxford University Press, Oxford (forthcoming).

Goldstein, W. (1982), 'Redistributing the world's wealth: Cancun summit discord', *Resources Policy,* 8, pp. 25-40.

Granger, C.W.J. and P. Newbold (1977), *Forecasting Economic Time Series,* Academic Press, New York.

Gustafson, R.L. (1958), *Carryover Levels for Grains,* U.S. Dept. of Agriculture, Technical Bulletin no. 1178.

Hendry, D.F. and T. von Ungern-Sternberg (1981), 'Liquidity and inflation effects on consumers' expenditure' in A.S. Deaton (ed), *Essays in the Theory and Measurement of Consumers' Expenditure,* Cambridge University Press, Cambridge and New York.

Hughes Hallett, A.J. (1981), 'Measuring the importance of stochastic control in the design of economic policies', *Economics Letters,* 8, pp. 341-347.

Hughes Hallett, A.J. and H.J.B. Rees (1983), *Quantitative Economic Policies and Interactive Planning,* Cambridge University Press, Cambridge and New York.

Just, R., E. Lutz, A. Schmitz and S.J. Turnovsky (1978), 'The distribution of welfare gains from pure stabilisation: An international perspective', *Journal of International Economics,* 8, pp. 551-563.

Kendrick, D.A. (1981), *Stochastic Control for Economic Models,* McGraw-Hill, New York.

Kydland, F.E. and E.C. Prescott (1977), 'Rules rather than discretion: The inconsistency of optimal plans', *Journal of Political Economy,* 85, pp. 473-591.

Lucas, R.E. (1976), 'Econometric policy evaluation: A critique' in K. Brunner and A.H. Meltzer (eds.), *The Phillips Curve and Labour Markets,* North-Holland, Amsterdam.

McCarthy, M.D. (1972), 'Some notes on the generation of pseudo-structural errors for use in stochastic simulation studies' in B.G. Hichman (ed.), *Econometric Models of Cyclical Behaviour: Vol. I,* Columbia University Press, New York.

Mirrlees, J.A. and N.Stern (1972), 'Fairly good plans', *Journal of Economic Theory,* 4, pp. 268-288.

Newbery, D.M.G. and J.E. Stiglitz (1981), *The Theory of Commodity Market Stabilisation,* Oxford University Press, Oxford.

Newbery, D.M.G. and J.E. Stiglitz (1982), 'Optimal commodity stockpiling rules', *Oxford Economic Papers,* 34, pp. 403-427.

Norman, A.L. (1974), 'On the relationship between linear feedback control and first period certainty equivalence', *International Economic Review,* 15, pp. 209-215.

Philips, A.W. (1954), 'Stabilisation policy in a closed economy', *Economic Journal,* 64, pp.290-323.

Philips, A.W. (1957), 'Stabilisation policy in the time-form of lagged responses', *Economic Journal,* 67, pp. 265-277.

Salmon, M. (1982), 'Error correction mechanisms', *Economic Journal,* 92, pp. 615-629.

Salmon, M. and P.C. Young (1979), 'Control methods and quantitative economic policy' in S. Holly, B. Rustem and ' Zarrop (eds.), *Optimal Control for Econometric Models: An approach to Economic Policy Formulation,* McMillan and Co., London.

Theil, H. (1964), *Optimal Decision Rules for Government and Industry,* North-Holland, Amsterdam.

Turnovsky, S.J. (1978), 'The distribution of welfare gains from price stabilisation: A survey of some theoretical issues' in F.G. Adams and S.A. Klein (eds.), *Stabilising World Commodity Markets,* Lexington Books, Lexington, Mass.

UNCTAD (1976), *Integrated Programme for Commodities,* ID/RES/93 (IV), Geneva.

PART V

DECENTRALISATION AND MULTI-SECTOR PLANNING

CHAPTER 12

BEHAVIOURAL ASSUMPTIONS IN DECENTRALISED STABILISATION POLICIES

J.W. Neese and R.S. Pindyck
Massachusetts Institute of Technology, USA

1. INTRODUCTION

Macroeconomic policy in the United States is very much the product of a decentralised control process, as is best exemplifed by the separation of monetary and fiscal policy. [1] In the past two or three decades monetary and fiscal policy have not always been coordinated or based on the same objectives. There have been periods in which the objectives differed, and also periods in which the objectives were the same but the world views on which policies are based differed. It has been argued that decentralisation has limited our ability to control the economy effectively.

Kydland (1975) and Pindyck (1976, 1977) have analysed optimal decentralised monetary and fiscal policies in the context of Nash non-cooperative strategies, and that work suggests that the separation of monetary and fiscal policy may indeed be important in limiting our ability to stabilise the economy. Monetary policy operates with longer lags than fiscal policy, so that the proper phasing of the two is critical. The literature on optimal stabilisation policies based on centralised control has shown that the relative *timing* of monetary and fiscal expansion is as important as amounts of expansion. Thus, monetary and fiscal policies that are not well coordinated may turn out to be sub-optimal, and policies designed with different objectives in mind may result in economic performance that is far from either objective.

This chapter shows that decentralisation of macroeconomic control can not only lead to 'sub-optimal' macroeconomic performance, but can also severely limit our ability to make accurate macroeconomic forecasts. Usually the reason given for our inability to predict (or control) the economy is that our models are not good enough –i.e. we simply do not know enough about the structure of the economy.

Hughes Hallett, A.J. (ed.) Applied Decision Analysis and Economic Behaviour

ISBN 90-247-2968-8. Printed in The Netherlands

Here we show that even with the 'correct' model, the multitude of behavioural possibilities for various policy making bodies may seriously limit our ability to predict. Even if the Federal Reserve (henceforth called the 'Fed') announces its macro-targets and trade-offs, and even if the Executive Branch and Congress do likewise, to the extent that those targets differ (as they often have in the past) a wide spectrum of very different 'optimal' policies may be possible. Macroeconomic prediction may thus face the same problem that makes the prediction of prices and output in oligopolistic markets so difficult –there are simply too many unpredictable behavioural possibilities.

Fair (1978) recently began to illustrate this problem by showing that the design of an optimal fiscal policy, and the effect of that policy, are highly dependent on the assumptions made (and their validity) about the behaviour of the Fed. Fair used his econometric model (1976) to calculate optimal fiscal policies under two alternative assumptions about Fed behaviour: first, that the Fed behaved 'passively' by keeping short term interest rates fixed; and second, that the Fed behaved 'actively' by varying the short term interest rate in response to an (empirically estimated) feedback rule relating it to changes in the price level, employment, and growth in GNP. As expected, Fair found that the fiscal authority was better able to meet its objectives when the Fed held interest rates fixed.

While Fair demonstrated that the optimal fiscal policy depends on the Fed, he restricted the Fed to a narrow range of plausible but naive behavioural options. In addition, his model of decentralised control was asymmetric, and ignored the dependency of optimal monetary policy on fiscal behaviour. In this chapter we show how a wider range of plausible bahvioural assumptions for each authority can lead to a wide range of monetary and fiscal policies, and a wide range of trajectories for economic targets.

The behavioural assumptions that we explore here include fixed levels or rates of growth for policy instruments, fixed feedback rules such as that used by Fair to describe an 'active' Fed policy, open loop and closed loop Nash non-cooperative policies, and the 'coordinated' policy implied by a Nash cooperative equilibrium. In order to make the calculation of optimal policies for this range of behavioural assumptions computationally feasible, we use a linear econometric model together with quadratic cost criteria. The model, the behavioural assumptions, and the optimisation experiments are described in the next section. Our computational results are presented in section 3, and section 4 discusses their implications for macroeconomic policy and prediction.

2. POLICY FORMULATION UNDER ALTERNATIVE BEHAVIOURAL ASSUMPTIONS

We examine the implications of alternative behavioural assumptions in the context of a small linear economic model of the U.S., with quadratic criteria functions for the fiscal and monetary authorities. The model is a modified and updated verion of one constructed earlier by Pindyck (1973), and contains eight behavioural equations together with a tax relation and two accounting identities. Fiscal policy works through government expenditures G, and monetary policy through the short term interest rate (Treasury bill rate) RS. [2] The model is summarised in the Appendix, and described in detail in Neese (1979) and Pindyck and Rubinfeld (1981).

We use the model to calculate policies for the period 1969-1 through 1973-4. A five year horizon should be at least as long as any likely to be used for actual policy planning, and this particular period precedes the oil price increases and rapid inflation of 1974 and recession of 1975.

Decentralised policies are interesting when authorities have different and conflicting objectives. For those cases in which one or both authorities optimise, we assume that the fiscal authority pursues an unemployment rate (UR) target, and the monetary authority an inflation rate (INF) target. Optimisation for the fiscal authority means minimising the cost functional

$$J_1 = \tfrac{1}{2}(0.5)(UR_{20} - UR^*_{20})^2 + \tfrac{1}{2}\sum_{t=0}^{19}\left\{(0.5)(UR_t - UR^*_t)^2 + (.01)(G_t - G^*_t)^2\right\}, \tag{12.1}$$

and for the monetary authority the cost functional

$$J_2 = \tfrac{1}{2}(0.5)(INF_{20} - INF^*_{20})^2 + \tfrac{1}{2}\sum_{t=0}^{19}\left\{(0.5)(INF_t - INF^*_t)^2 + (.6)(RS_t - RS^*_t)^2\right\} \tag{12.2}$$

Target rates for unemployment (UR^*_t) and inflation (INF^*_t) are both set at 2%. Policy variable targets follow historical averages over the control period: the real government spending target G^*_t grows at a 0.12% quarterly rate from \$139.5 billion (1958 dollars) in 1968-4; the short term interest rate target RS^*_t is constant at 5.7%. [3]

We consider behavioural assumptions corresponding to varying degrees of sophistication on the part of each authority, as well as varying degrees of cooperation between the authorities. All of these behavioural assumptions have been cited at one time or another as being either representative or ideal bases for the design of macroeconomic policy, and all have a degree of plausibility and realism. The alternatives we examine are as follows:

(i) *One-sided fixed policy paths.* Here, one authority sets its policy variable on a fixed path (following what Fair (1978) calls a 'passive' policy), and the other authority designs an optimal policy. We apply this first to the calculation of an optimal fiscal policy, and then an optimal monetary policy. As 'passive' policies we use the policy targets: G_t^* and RS_t^*. We label these runs M.EXOG for the case of a fixed monetary policy and an optimal fiscal policy, and F.EXOG for the opposite case.

(ii) *Use of reaction functions.* Here, one authority varies its policy from period to period according to a reaction function (what Fair (1978) calls an 'active' policy), while the other authority pursues an optimal strategy, calculated by taking the first authority's reaction function into account. We estimate fiscal and monetary reaction functions via two-stage least squares, employing time series data over the period 1956-1 to 1976-1 to capture historically 'averaged' policy formation.

Because of autocorrelation, the fiscal reaction function is estimated with government spending first differenced:

$$\Delta G = \underset{(-1.59)}{-1.148} - \underset{(-2.56)}{0.0669}\,\Delta GNP - \underset{(-2.24)}{0.1318}\,INF + \underset{(3.24)}{0.442}\,UR_{-1} + \underset{(6.01)}{2.415}\,WARDUM \tag{12.3}$$

$$R^2 = 0.315,\ \ F(4/76) = 8.74,\ \ SER = 1.171,\ \ DW(0) = 1.97$$

where WARDUM is a dummy variable with value 1.0 from 1965-1 to 1968-3 and 0 otherwise and accounts for increased government expenditures during the Vietnam War.[4]

The monetary reaction function is estimated in level form and is more sensitive than the fiscal one to policy target changes. It is very much in line with Fair's, and has the monetary authority 'leaning against the wind':

$$RS = \underset{(2.28)}{0.988} + \underset{(12.65)}{0.872}\,RS_{-1} + \underset{(1.62)}{.07383}\,INF_{-1} - \underset{(-2.43)}{0.161}\,UR + \underset{(1.95)}{0.0235}\,\Delta GNP + \underset{(1.23)}{0.0112}\,\Delta GNP_{-1} \tag{12.4}$$

$$R^2 = 0.867,\ \ F(5/75) = 98.03,\ \ SER = 0.513,\ \ DW(0) = 1.84,\ \ \hat{\rho} = 0.2246.$$

We label these runs M.REACT and F.REACT for the cases where the monetary and fiscal authorities respectively follow reaction functions, and the other authority optimises.[5]

(iii) *Open and closed loop Nash non-cooperative strategies.* Here, the fiscal authority minimises J_1 and the monetary authority minimises J_2, with each authority taking the other's optimal behaviour into account. In the open loop case, each authority designs its optimal policy at the beginning of the planning period, and then sticks to that policy throughout the entire period. In the closed loop case, each authority designs a control rule at the beginning of the planning period, and then uses that rule, together with observations of the state of the economy, to continually revise policy. This should not be confused with the notion of closed loop optimal control in the centralised case; we are viewing the economy as decentralised but *deterministic,* so that the closed loop strategy allows adaptation to the *evolving strategy of the other authority.* [6] The optimal policy calculations are based on the solutions derived in Pindyck (1977). We label the open loop and closed loop runs COMPET.0 and COMPET.C respectively.

(iv) *Nash cooperative strategy.* This provides a basis for determining the relative 'bargaining power' of the two authorities, and exploring how they might cooperate in designing *coordinated* monetary and fiscal policies. In this framework, monetary and fiscal instruments are manipulated to minimise a weighted sum of J_1 and J_2:

$$\underset{\substack{\{G_t\} \\ \{RS_t\}}}{\text{Min}}\ J = \alpha J_1 + (1-\alpha) J_2 \tag{12.5}$$

By varying α between 0 and 1 and solving the resulting set of parametric optimisation problems, we can obtain the pareto-optimal frontier in the space of realised outcomes (J_1, J_2). Determining the value of α most likely to prevail through a cooperative agreement requires a theory of bargaining. We use the Nash (1953) cooperative equilibrium because of its generality and robustness. [7]

Any Nash cooperative equilibrium is, of course, relative to a particular threat point, and the threat point should represent a *non-cooperative* equilibrium. We choose as a threat point the closed loop Nash non-cooperative equilibrium described above. We label this run BARGAIN.

3. COMPUTATIONAL RESULTS

Some preliminary observations aid in understanding the results. First, a model simulation generated by letting G and RS follow their target paths produces 'nominal' trajectories for UR and INF that differ significantly from the historical data (see Tables 12.1 and 12.2) While the actual rate of inflation fluctuated around 5% over most of the control period, climbing to nearly 9% in the final quarter, nominal infla-

Table 12.1 Control Variables

Government spending (billions of 1958 dollars)

Year/ Experiment	Nominal	Historical	M.EXOG	F.EXOG	M.REACT	F.REACT	COMPET.0	COMPET.C	BARGAIN
1968 4	139.3	146.0	139.3	139.3	139.3	139.3	139.3	139.3	139.3
1969 1	139.5	144.6	150.4	139.5	141.0	138.8	152.5	152.4	139.8
1969 2	139.7	145.0	150.8	139.7	141.7	138.6	153.4	153.0	140.5
1969 3	139.8	143.5	151.9	139.8	142.6	138.5	155.3	154.5	142.0
1969 4	140.0	143.1	152.7	140.0	143.7	138.7	156.8	155.6	143.0
1970 1	140.2	141.5	153.3	140.2	144.9	139.1	158.1	156.6	144.3
1970 2	140.3	139.8	154.0	140.3	146.2	139.6	159.2	157.5	145.1
1970 3	140.5	139.9	154.6	140.5	147.2	140.2	160.1	158.2	146.0
1970 4	140.7	140.4	154.9	140.7	148.2	141.0	160.7	158.7	146.7
1971 1	140.8	139.9	155.0	140.8	148.8	141.8	160.9	158.9	146.9
1971 2	141.0	138.6	154.8	141.0	149.2	142.5	160.7	158.7	146.6
1971 3	141.2	140.6	154.4	141.2	149.4	143.1	160.3	158.3	145.9
1971 4	141.4	140.8	154.0	141.4	149.7	143.8	159.8	157.9	145.5
1972 1	141.5	142.6	153.6	141.5	150.3	144.5	159.3	157.5	145.3
1972 2	141.7	142.1	153.5	141.7	151.2	145.2	158.9	157.3	145.1
1972 3	141.9	141.4	153.0	141.9	151.9	145.8	158.2	156.7	144.8
1972 4	142.0	142.1	152.3	142.0	152.3	146.5	157.0	155.7	144.7
1973 1	142.2	143.2	151.4	142.2	152.4	147.0	155.7	154.6	144.0
1973 2	142.4	141.0	152.4	142.4	154.1	147.5	156.7	155.6	144.5
1973 3	142.5	141.3	150.4	142.5	152.0	148.1	153.6	152.8	142.6
1973 4	142.7	141.4	142.7	142.7	142.7	148.5	142.7	142.7	137.9

Table 12.1 (cont.)

Short term bond rate (annual percentage)

Year/ Experiment	Nominal	Historical	M.EXOG	F.EXOG	M.REACT	F.REACT	COMPET.0	COMPET.C	BARGAIN
1968 4	5.70	5.59	5.70	5.70	5.70	5.70	5.70	5.70	5.70
1969 1	5.70	6.09	5.70	6.61	6.08	6.06	7.96	7.03	5.16
1969 2	5.70	6.20	5.70	6.39	6.25	5.94	7.71	6.92	5.07
1969 3	5.70	7.02	5.70	6.21	6.31	5.85	7.52	6.83	5.01
1969 4	5.70	7.35	5.70	6.09	6.23	5.81	7.38	6.77	4.98
1970 1	5.70	7.21	5.70	6.03	6.08	5.81	7.30	6.74	4.98
1970 2	5.70	6.68	5.70	6.02	5.89	5.86	7.25	6.73	5.01
1970 3	5.70	6.33	5.70	6.06	5.68	5.93	7.24	6.75	5.07
1970 4	5.70	5.35	5.70	6.11	5.49	6.03	7.24	6.77	5.14
1971 1	5.70	3.84	5.70	6.16	5.37	6.13	7.23	6.78	5.21
1971 2	5.70	4.25	5.70	6.20	5.33	6.21	7.21	6.79	5.29
1971 3	5.70	5.01	5.70	6.23	5.40	6.29	7.16	6.79	5.36
1971 4	5.70	4.23	5.70	6.25	5.53	6.35	7.09	6.76	5.43
1972 1	5.70	3.44	5.70	6.26	5.67	6.38	7.00	6.71	5.51
1972 2	5.70	3.77	5.70	6.25	5.84	6.40	6.87	6.64	5.59
1972 3	5.70	4.22	5.70	6.21	6.02	6.37	6.70	6.52	5.68
1972 4	5.70	4.86	5.70	6.13	6.16	6.28	6.46	6.34	5.76
1973 1	5.70	5.70	5.70	6.00	6.27	6.11	6.17	6.12	5.79
1973 2	5.70	6.60	5.70	5.86	6.43	5.93	5.91	5.91	5.79
1973 3	5.70	8.32	5.70	5.75	6.45	5.77	5.75	5.76	5.74
1973 4	5.70	7.50	5.70	5.71	5.94	5.71	5.71	5.71	5.71

Table 12.2 Target Variables

Year/ Experiment	Rate of unemployment (percent)								
	Nominal	Historical	M.EXOG	F.EXOG	M.REACT	F.REACT	COMPET.0	COMPET.C	BARGAIN
1968 4	3.30	3.40	3.30	3.30	3.30	3.30	3.30	3.30	3.30
1969 1	3.53	3.40	3.53	3.53	3.53	3.53	3.53	3.53	3.53
1969 2	3.57	3.43	2.82	3.57	3.47	3.62	2.68	2.69	3.54
1969 3	3.82	3.57	2.79	3.85	3.66	3.92	2.66	2.66	3.73
1969 4	4.03	3.57	3.01	4.15	3.87	4.19	3.03	2.97	3.79
1970 1	4.34	4.17	3.15	4.53	4.14	4.53	3.32	3.21	3.93
1970 2	4.63	4.73	3.28	4.90	4.40	4.84	3.61	3.43	4.04
1970 3	4.94	5.17	3.44	5.25	4.65	5.15	3.90	3.68	4.17
1970 4	5.22	5.87	3.62	5.56	4.86	5.41	4.17	3.92	4.29
1971 1	5.49	5.90	3.77	5.85	5.02	5.65	4.41	4.14	4.40
1971 2	5.67	5.90	3.86	6.06	5.09	5.80	4.57	4.28	4.49
1971 3	5.78	6.03	3.90	6.19	5.08	5.90	4.67	4.38	4.55
1971 4	5.81	5.97	3.90	6.25	4.99	5.93	4.72	4.42	4.58
1972 1	5.86	5.77	3.91	6.32	4.90	5.97	4.79	4.48	4.63
1972 2	5.92	5.63	3.96	6.42	4.82	6.03	4.87	4.57	4.70
1972 3	5.99	5.60	4.00	6.52	4.75	6.10	4.95	4.65	4.79
1972 4	6.02	5.33	4.04	6.59	4.68	6.13	5.02	4.72	4.87
1973 1	6.07	4.93	4.13	6.67	4.67	6.17	5.13	4.84	4.97
1973 2	6.05	4.90	4.18	6.67	4.65	6.14	5.18	4.90	5.06
1973 3	6.06	4.80	4.13	6.68	4.56	6.11	5.17	4.82	5.11
1973 4	6.09	4.77	4.28	6.70	4.74	6.08	5.20	4.97	5.33

Table 12.2 (cont.)

Rate of inflation (annual percentage)

Year/ Experiment	Nominal	Historical	M.EXOG	F.EXOG	M.REACT	F.REACT	COMPET.0	COMPET.C	BARGAIN
1968 4	5.00	5.50	5.00	5.00	5.00	5.00	5.00	5.00	5.00
1969 1	4.48	4.30	5.43	4.47	4.61	4.42	5.61	5.60	4.51
1969 2	4.64	5.20	6.32	4.59	4.89	4.48	6.56	6.56	4.77
1969 3	4.10	6.20	5.49	3.93	4.32	3.87	5.45	5.53	4.44
1969 4	3.85	5.00	5.27	3.57	4.09	3.59	4.97	5.14	4.44
1970 1	3.44	5.90	5.06	3.07	3.73	3.17	4.55	4.80	4.25
1970 2	3.15	4.90	4.87	2.73	3.50	2.90	4.20	4.50	4.17
1970 3	2.86	3.60	4.63	2.44	3.29	2.67	3.88	4.19	4.05
1970 4	2.64	5.40	4.47	2.23	3.20	2.51	3.65	3.97	3.98
1971 1	2.54	6.00	4.41	2.12	3.24	2.46	3.55	3.87	3.94
1971 2	2.59	5.50	4.44	2.16	3.42	2.53	3.56	3.87	3.96
1971 3	2.75	3.40	4.55	2.30	3.71	2.69	3.65	3.95	4.01
1971 4	2.89	3.50	4.64	2.42	4.00	2.83	3.71	4.00	4.06
1972 1	2.95	5.60	4.65	2.45	4.18	2.89	3.71	3.99	4.05
1972 2	3.01	2.70	4.67	2.49	4.38	2.95	3.74	4.00	4.04
1972 3	3.12	3.40	4.71	2.57	4.57	3.06	3.79	4.03	4.03
1972 4	3.20	4.50	4.67	2.63	4.64	3.15	3.76	3.98	3.99
1973 1	3.32	5.60	4.64	2.75	4.67	3.29	3.78	3.97	3.95
1973 2	3.44	6.80	4.78	2.90	4.83	3.46	4.04	4.19	3.97
1973 3	3.48	7.20	4.69	2.98	4.67	3.57	4.04	4.15	3.79
1973 4	3.46	9.00	3.77	3.03	3.51	3.67	2.97	3.11	3.11

tion drops from 5% to 2.5% and climbs back to only 3.5%. Likewise, while actual unemployment increased from 3.5% to nearly 6% and then decreased to below 5%, nominal unemployment increases steadily from 3.5% to 6%. This means that as far as our policy experiments are concerned, 1969 to 1973 was an uncomplicated period characterised by moderate inflation but rising unemployment. Consequently, relative to the fiscal incentive, there is less monetary 'gain' from further reductions in the already low rate of inflation. If fiscal policies are nearly as effective as monetary policies, then the balancing of incentives in non-cooperative policies will trade off increased inflation for decreased unemployment.

A policy effectiveness comparison can be made by comparing the simulation responses of inflation or unemployment to equally costly steps in the two policy instruments. Since short term interest rate deviations are weighted $\sqrt{10}$ times less heavily than government spending deviations, moving RS by 100 basis points from its target is as costly to the Fed as a $7.767 billion change in G from its target is to the fiscal authority. If we compare the changes in UR and INF that result first from a 100 basis point drop in RS, and second from a $7.767 billion increase in G, we find that the fiscal authority enjoys far greater short term effectiveness, while monetary and fiscal policies are almost equally effective after about 10 to 12 quarters.

Our policy results are summarised in the form of the cost frontier in figure 12.1. Referring to that figure, note first that each authority improves its position relative to the nominal by following an optimal strategy when the other holds to its target policy (M.EXOG, F.EXOG). Also,the non-optimising authority does better by following a reaction function than by sticking to its target policy (M.REACT, F.REACT). Open loop and closed loop Nash competition, on the other hand, prove expensive for both authorities; the fiscal authority reduces its cost only slightly from the nominal while inflicting a substantial cost increase on the monetary authority (COMPET.0, COMPET.C). Since both authorities do better under closed loop non-cooperative behaviour, its choice as the bargaining 'threat point' is appealing. The Nash bargain weights the two cost functions nearly equally, offering both authorities substantial cost reduction (BARGAIN).

The various trajectories are shown graphically in figures 12.2 through 12.5. (To avoid cluttering these graphs, the historical and open loop Nash competitive paths are omitted.) All of the trajectories are also recorded in Tables 12.1 and 12.2. Note that the convergence of policy variables to their target values in the last 1 or 2 quarters in all cases of optimising behaviour is due to end point effects (target variables are affected only after the end of the planning horizon).

Let us examine the simplest asymmetric case, M.EXOG and F.EXOG first. Note that when the Fed is held to its 5.7% target short term rate, fiscal policy can

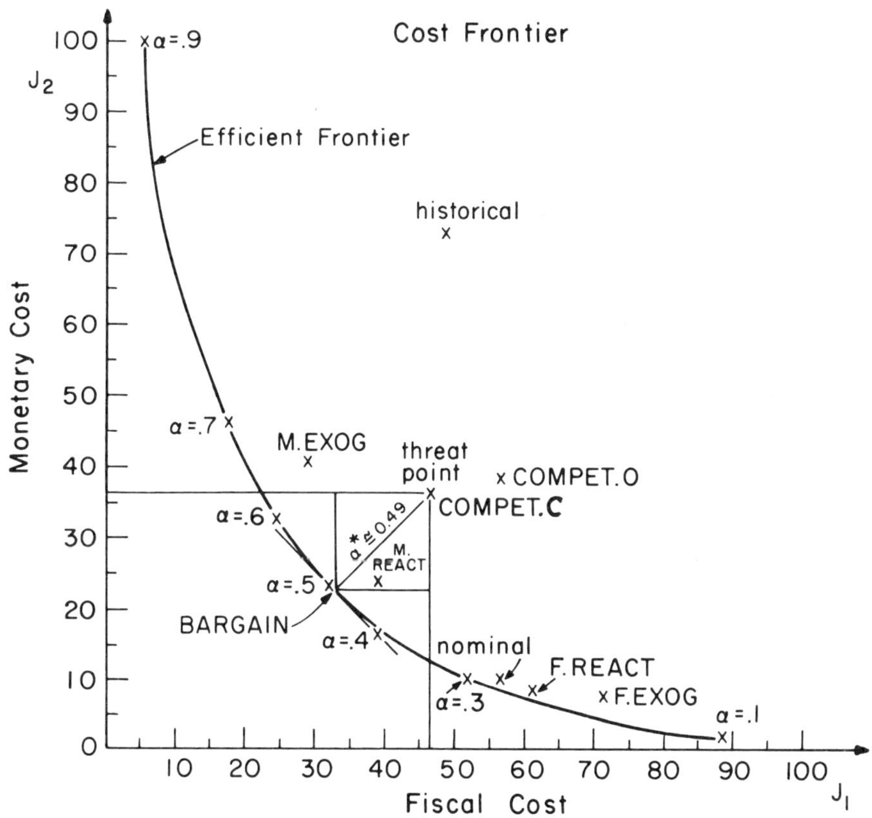

Figure 12.1 Cost frontier

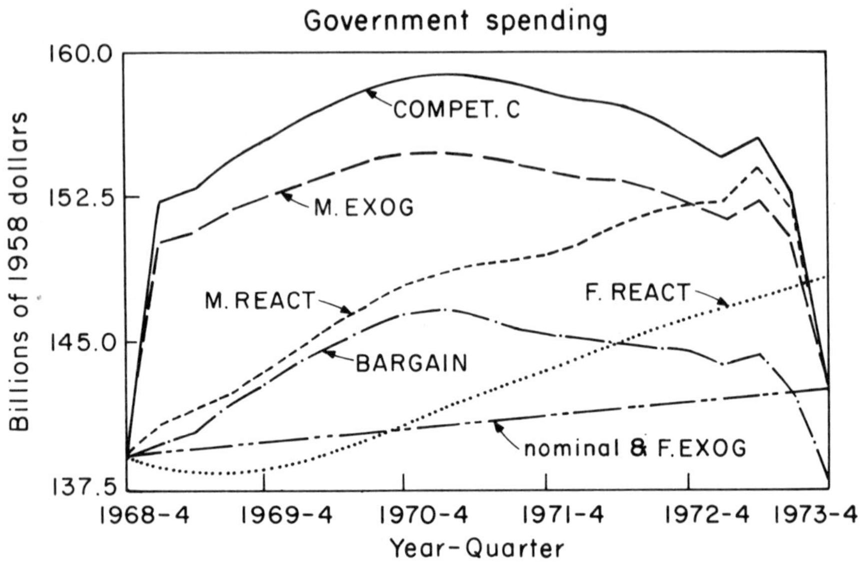

Figure 12.2 Government spending

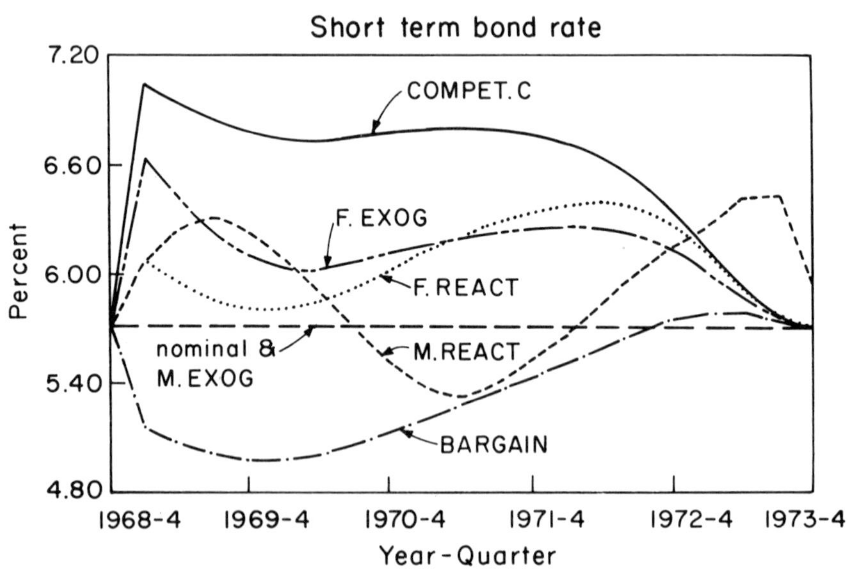

Figure 12.3 Short term bond rate

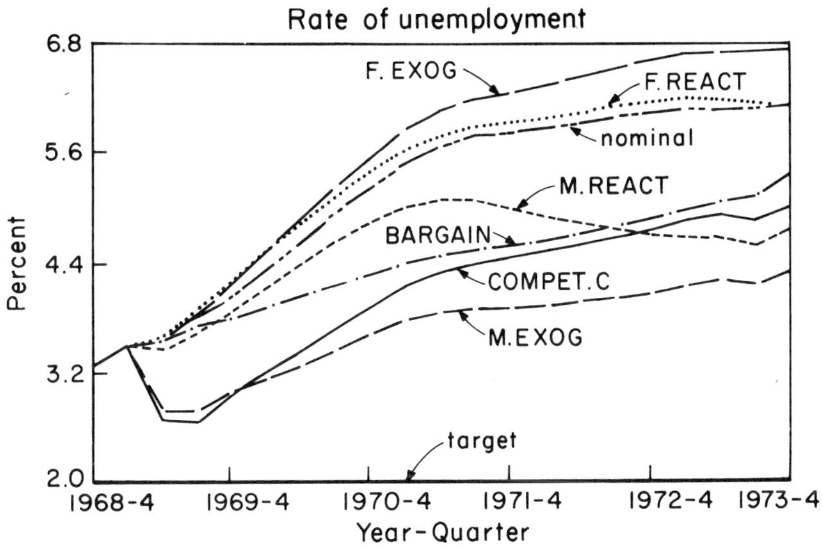

Figure 12.4 Rate of unemployment

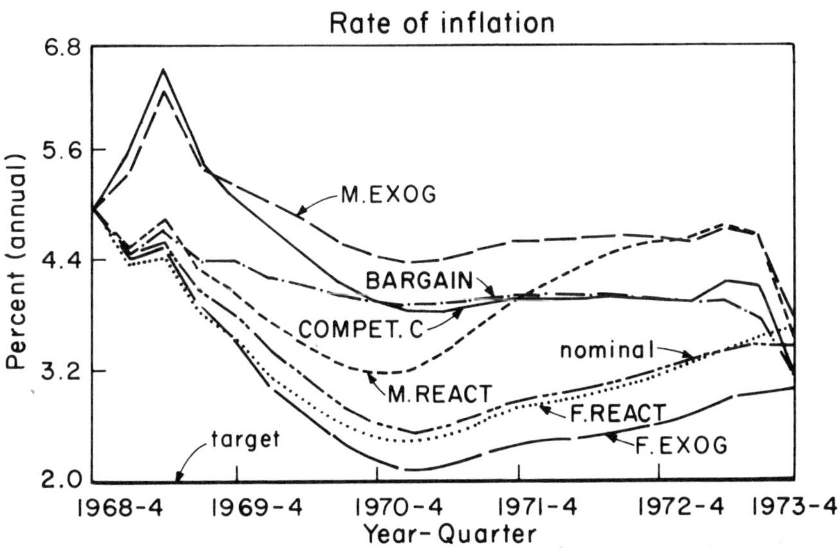

Figure 12.5 Rate of inflation

achieve marked success by immediately increasing government spending to about \$150 billion (a \$12 billion or 8.5% policy excursion), and maintaining it at about that level until the final quarter. There would seem to be less incentive for the Fed to pursue such an aggressive policy when the fiscal authority follows its target spending paths, since, except in the first year, the nominal rate of inflation is already low. However, the lower penalty on monetary policy excursions (by a factor of $\sqrt{10}$) makes it optimal to sharply increase RS by 91 basis points (a 16% policy excursion), and then reduce it again. The result is that inflation is reduced almost to the 2% target by 1970.

We see from the reaction function experiments that a suboptimal feedback strategy based on averaged, historical policy formation can be much superior to following a fixed path. The effectiveness of the monetary reaction function is limited by an inability to anticipate the future effects of changes in G (note the drop in RS during 1970), but nonetheless restrains fiscal policy from the degree of success achieved in the M.EXOG experiment; the average reduction in unemployment is held to 1 percent with an equal increase in inflation. Similarly, the use of a reaction function by the fiscal authority greatly limits the gain to the Fed from an optimal policy. The limited success of monetary policy (F.REACT) is more attributable to the fact that G is below its target path during the first two years than to interest rate changes themselves.[8]

Let us now turn to the open and closed loop Nash non-cooperative policies (COMPET.0 and COMPET.C). These policies are more aggressive than in any of the other experiments, but are also relatively counterproductive. The fiscal short term advantage brings substantial reduction in unemployment early on, while producing a sharp inflationary spike. Soon thereafter the sharp increase in RS checks the fiscal momentum and leads to a stand-off which holds until the end of the control period. Thus, the fiscal authority succeeds in lowering the unemployment rate about 1.2 percent (with an equal increase in inflation), but only by incurring a heavy policy cost. Consequently, the fiscal cost is reduced only marginally and while the Fed's cost nearly quadruples, it remains the smaller of the two.

Strategy adjustment makes possible a closed loop equilibrium which is less costly to both authorities than the open loop. Because monetary policy operates with longer lags, the Fed is forced into a strategy which improves its position relative to the open loop case while conceding greater gain to the fiscal authority. The Fed's closed loop initial interest rate increase is much smaller than its open loop increase, since this induces a fiscal spending reduction. Most of the gain is fiscal as spending is reduced only marginally, so that unemployment is lower and inflation higher than in the open loop case.

Both authorities could clearly do better by choosing less counterproductive strategies (for instance, by duplicating the M.REACT policies), and this is indeed what we observe in the Nash bargaining solution. In this case (BARGAIN), the Fed pursues an *expansionary* short term interest rate policy in return for a substantial reduction in fiscal aggressiveness. As a result, both authorities achieve nearly identical cost reductions (relative to the threat point) by allowing symmetrical policy relaxation while leaving the overall unemployment-inflation trade-off unchanged. While this might at first be construed as a fiscal 'victory', note that the resulting value of α is close to 0.5, so that the two cost criteria are weighted about equally. In addition, government spending increases only gradually, indicating indirect monetary control over early period inflation rates by preventing the fiscal authority from capitalising on its short term policy advantage.

4. IMPLICATIONS FOR MACROECONOMIC POLICY AND PREDICTION

These results corroborate Fair's finding that the design and effect of optimal fiscal policy are highly dependent on behavioural assumptions concerning the Fed, and extends that finding to optimal monetary policy. Fiscal policy is more effective when the Fed holds short term interest rates fixed than when it follows an (empirically estimated) reaction function. Similarly, monetary policy is more effective when the fiscal authority holds spending to a fixed path than when it 'actively' responds via a reaction function. Due to the lag in monetary policy effecttiveness, inability to accurately anticipate policy results hampers the monetary authority more than the fiscal authority, and leaves the monetary reaciton more open to manipulation.

We also find that the decentralisation of macroeconomic control can indeed lead to 'sub-optimal' macroeconomic performance, particularly when both authorities use 'sophisticated' but non-cooperative policies. Open loop Nash non-cooperative behaviour produces counterproductive policies which favour the fiscal authority in the short run, but which lead to a stand-off in the medium term. Because it operates with shorter lags, the fiscal authority can adapt its strategy to changing events better than the monetary authority in the closed loop Nash case, but strategies remain directly counterproductive. The Nash cooperative solution shows tha the resolution of conflicting objectives can leave both authorities much better off, not so much because either is better able to attain its target variable objectives, but more because each can limit the use of its policy instrument.

As is often the case in models of oligopoly, more sophisticated *non-cooperative* behaviour makes everyone worse off than less sophisticated behaviour. To the extent that actual macroeconomic objectives are in conflict and policies are uncoordinated, simple modes of policy formation by each authority (e.g. the use of 'reaction function' rules or even adherence to fixed policy variable target paths) may be more desirable from the point of view of overall economic performance. 'Optimal' policy design may be of little value unless decentralised policies are reasonably well ccordinated.

The diversity of the policy results obtained here also shows that the decentralisation of macroeconomic control can limit our ability to make accurate forecasts. Even with the 'correct' model, the range of behavioural possibilities for various policy making bodies can lead to a wide range of outcomes. Just as knowing the objectives of oligopolistic firms is not sufficient to forecast industry output, knowing fiscal and monetary objectives may also not be sufficient to forecast the macroeconomy —there remain too many unpredictable behavioural possibilities.

APPENDIX: THE ECONOMETRIC MODEL

This model is similar to one used by Pindyck (1973) in earlier studies of optimal stabilisation policies. GNP and its components are in real terms (1958 dollars), and total investment is disaggregated, so that separate equations explain consumption C, fixed non-residential investment INR, residential investment IR, and change in inventories IIN. The remaining behavioural equations explain the long term interest rate RL, the rate of growth of the price level RGP[9], the rate of growth of the money wage rate RGW, and the unemployment rate UR. Disposable income is computed by applying an average tax rate to GNP, and an identity keeps track of the stock of inventories INV.

The equations are listed below. All of the behavioural equations were estimated over the period 1956-1 to 1976-1, using two-stage least squares in combination with a Cochrane-Orcutt autoregressive correction. (t-statistics are shown in parentheses beneath each estimated coefficient).

GNP: $$GNP = C + INR + IR + IIN + G \qquad (A.1)$$

Disposable Income, YD: $$YD = 0.11925\ GNP \qquad (A.2)$$

Inventories, INV: $$INV = INV_{-1} + IIN/4.0 \qquad (A.3)$$

Consumption, C[10]:

$$C = \underset{(0.58)}{1.77276} + \underset{(2.98)}{0.14020}\,(YD - TR)$$

$$+ \underset{(2.62)}{0.47305}\,TR + \underset{(9.50)}{0.78927}\,C_{-1} + \underset{(4.00)}{44.1008}\,\Delta WLTH - \underset{(-1.74)}{0.18347}\,(RS + RS_{-1} + RS_{-2} + RS_{-3}) \qquad (A.4)$$

$R^2 = 0.9993$, $SER = 2.386$, $F(5/75) = 2.17\ E{+}04$, $DW(0) = 2.13$.

Non-residential Investment, INR:

$$\Delta INR = \underset{(-3.61)}{-0.00531}\,(INR_{-1} + INR_{-2})$$

$$+ \underset{(3.92)}{0.08036}\,\Delta YD + \underset{(6.06)}{0.06307}\,\Delta YD_{-1} + \underset{(4.16)}{0.05266}\,\Delta YD_{-2} + \underset{(4.82)}{0.04912}\,\Delta YD_{-3}$$

$$+ \underset{(2.88)}{0.05246}\,\Delta YD_{-4} - \underset{(-2.17)}{1.35601}\,\Delta RL_{-4} \qquad (A.5)$$

$R^2 = 0.6170$, $SER = 0.960$, $F(4/76) = 30.60$, $DW(0) = 1.94$, $\hat{\rho} = 0.2238$.

Residential Investment, IR:

$$IR = \underset{(-0.53)}{-0.33033} + \underset{(4.50)}{0.01149}\,YD$$

$$+ \underset{(1.98)}{0.47200}\,(RL_{-2} - RS_{-2}) - \underset{(-2.19)}{0.38887}\,RS_{-1} + \underset{(12.97)}{1.29240}\,IR_{-1} - \underset{(-4.88)}{0.451751}\,IR_{-2} \qquad (A.6)$$

$R^2 = 0.977$, $SER = 0.944$, $F(5/75) = 637.2$, $DW(0) = 1.93$.

Inventory Investment, IIN:

$$IIN = \underset{(-3.31)}{-4.10794} + \underset{(4.18)}{0.13038}\,YD_{-1}$$

$$+ \underset{(4.51)}{0.37372}\,\Delta_2 YD - \underset{(-4.44)}{0.56866}\,\Delta_2 C - \underset{(-3.90)}{0.40114}\,INV_{-1} + \underset{(4.00)}{0.36996}\,IIN_{-2} \qquad (A.7)$$

$R^2 = 0.8178$, $SER = 2.15$, $F(5/75) = 67.3$, $DW(0) = 1.85$.

Long Term Interest Rate, RL:

$$RL = \underset{(1.52)}{0.12535} + \underset{(1.91)}{0.04534}\,RS + \underset{(3.04)}{0.13063}\,\Delta RS$$

$$+ \underset{(28.86)}{0.94306}\,RL_{-1} \qquad (A.8)$$

$R^2 = 0.9846$, $SER = 0.156$, $F(3/77) = 1946$, $DW(0) = 2.10$.

Rate of Inflation, RGP[11]:

$$RGP = -0.00156 + 0.21818\, RGW + 0.00011934\, \Delta_2 YD + 0.00763\, DUM + 0.32983\, (RGP_{-1} + RGP_{-2}) \quad (A.9)$$
$$\qquad (-0.86) \qquad (1.76) \qquad (2.66) \qquad (3.45) \qquad (7.23)$$

$R^2 = 0.745$, SER = 0.0033, F(4/76) = 55.6, DW(0) = 1.98 .

Rate of Growth of Wage Rate, RGW:

$$RGW = 0.01677 + 0.48601\, RGP - 0.00116\, UR_{-3} \quad (A.10)$$
$$\qquad (5.32) \qquad (4.65) \qquad (-2.12)$$

$R^2 = 0.2891$, SER = 0.0056, F(2/78) = 15.86, DW(0) = 2.19 .

Unemployment Rate, UR[12]:

$$UR = 0.50222 - 0.04062\, \Delta YD_{-1} - 0.00128\, (GNP_{-1} - GNPP_{-1}) + 0.93255\, UR_{-1} \quad (A.11)$$
$$\qquad (3.00) \qquad (-7.36) \qquad (-1.90) \qquad (27.22)$$

$R^2 = 0.9399$, SER = 0.318, F(3/77) = 401.1, DW(0) = 1.73 .

NOTES

* An earlier version of this paper was presented at the Economic Dynamics and Control Conference, Cambridge University, Cambridge, England, June 20, 1979. The work leading to this paper was supported by the National Science Foundation under Grant No. SOC76-05837, and that support is gratefully acknowledged. We also appreciate the helpful comments and suggestions made by David Castanon, Michael Athans, and Edwin Kuh.

1) Fiscal policy is itself decentralised to some extent. Tax schedules, transfer schedules, and trade policy may, for example, be controlled, or at least influenced, to a greater or lesser extent by different Congressional committees and by the President.
2) The model was actually constructed with a ninth behavioural equation descibing money demand, which provided the linkage between the supply of money and the short term interest rate. Following Fair (1978), however, we manipulate the short term interest rate directly as a policy variable, and thus drop this additional behavioural equation.
3) Relative weights for J_1 and J_2 correspond to a 'reasonable' policy/target mix in a centralised experiment in which the joint authority pursues both unemployment and inflation rate objectives. Percent deviations in G are weighted 10 times, and in RS $\sqrt{10}$ times more heavily than those in INF and UR. Equal weights lead to greater fiscal than monetary policy cost-effectiveness and pronounced end effects in G.
4) Note that feedbacks through policy targets are weak; each 2% of unemployment, for example, creates quarterly increases in G of $1 billion. This feedback is strengthened indirectly through the dependence on GNP. This result might be expected to the extent that fiscal policy changes are more the products of political than purely economic events.
5) We also calculated policies for the 'symmetric' case in which *both* authorities follow reaction function. For brevity this result is omitted here, but can be found in Neese (1979).
6) It is important to stress that the open loop and closed loop modes of behaviour yield different solutions, since they imply different assumptions on the part of each authority regarding its own allowed behaviour as well as the allowed response of the other authority. In the open loop mode the first authority assumes that the second will not adjust his strategy in response to changes in each period in the first's policy –and thus in response to changes in the state of the economy. In the closed loop mode, each authority operates under the assumption that the other will adjust his strategy, and thus each authority recognises that changes in his own choice of strategy will change the state of the economy and hence change the strategy of the other authority. It is this *difference in operating assumptions that leads* to the difference in the solutions. For further discussion, see Ho (1970) and Pindyck (1977).

7) Nash's solution is based on the premise that the relevant measure of 'relative power' which determines the outcome of the bargaining process is given by the relative utilities at the 'threat point' or point of no agreement. This is plausible, since each authority is willing to bargain only in so far as it expects to acrue a pay-off over and above that attained at the threat point. It seems reasonable that both authorities should be willing to accept a division of the net incremental gains in a proportion directly related to th losses incurred by *not* making an agreement. Nash demonstrated that his solution to the bargaining problem is he *only* solution (J_1^*, J_2^*) that satisfies axioms of rationality, feasibility, pareto-optimality, independence of irrelevant alternatives, symmetry, and independence with respect to linear transformations of the set of pay-offs. Furthermore, the solution is such that the product $(J_1^* - J_1^0)(J_2^* - J_2^0)$, where (J_1^0, J_2^0) corresponds to the threat point, is maximised. For a proof and further discussion of Nash cooperative behaviour, see Owen (1968). For an application to an oligopoly problem, see Hnyilicza and Pindyck (1976).
8) Remember that unlike our experimental fiscal policy objective, historical fiscal policy emphasised reducing an inflation rate of nearly 5% when unemployment was around 3.5%. Also, the fiscal reaction is felt almost as soon as a monetary strategy can affect the economy, and therefore cannot be manipulated by monetary policy.
9) Our inflation rate target is just INF = 400 RGP.
10) TR is transfer payments, and WLTH is an index of real household net worth.
11) DUM = Dummy variable for OPEC oil price hikes: 1.0 over 1973-4 to 1974-1, 0 elsewhere.
12) GNPP is real potential GNP, and is essentially a 4% trend line.

REFERENCES

Fair, R.C. (1976), *A Model of Macroeconomic Activeity, Volume II: The Empirical Model,* Ballinger Publishing Company, Cambridge.

Fair, R.C. (1978), 'The sensitivity of fiscal policy effects to assumptions about the behaviour of the Federal Reserve', *Econometrica,* 46, pp. 1165-1180.

Hnyilicza, E. and R.S. Pindyck (1976), 'Pricing policies for a two-part exhaustible resource cartel: The case of OPEC', *European Economic Review,* 8, pp. 139-154.

Ho, Y.C. (1970), 'Differential games, dynamic optimisation and generalised control theory', *Journal of Optimisation Theory and Applications,* 16, pp. 179-209.

Kydland, F.E. (1975), 'Non-cooperative and dominant player solutions in discrete dynamic games', *International Economic Review,* 16, pp. 321-335.

Nash, J.F. (1953), 'Two-person cooperative games', *Econometrica,* 21, pp. 128-140.

Neese, J.W. (1979), 'Optimal control studies of interactions between monetary and fiscal authorities in the U.S. economy', Master's theses, MIT, Department of Ocean Engineering.

Owen, G. (1968), *Game Theory,* W.B. Saunders, Philadelphia.

Pindyck, R.S. (1973), *Optimal Planning for Economic Stabilisation,* North-Holland, Amsterdam.

Pindyck, R.S. (1976), 'The cost of conflicting objectives in policy formulation', *Annals of Economic and Social Measurement,* 5, pp. 239-248.

Pindyck, R.S. (1977), 'Optimal economic stabilisation policies under decentralised control and conflicting objectives', *IEEE Transactions on Automatic Control,* AC-22, pp. 517-530.

Pindyck, R.S., and D.L. Rubinfeld (1981), *Econometric Models and Economic Forecasts,* 2nd edition, McGraw-Hill, New York.

CHAPTER 13

STABILITY ANALYSIS OF LARGE SCALE ECONOMIC SYSTEMS WHICH HAVE A MULTI–TIME SCALE PROPERTY

Djordjija B. Petkovski
University of Novi Sad, Yugoslavia

1. INTRODUCTION

The problem of controlling large scale economic systems has led to the introduction of the state space forms as an alternative representation of traditional model forms in various theoretical and empirical studies of dynamic economic systems, especially in the application of optimal decision rules for macroeconomic planning and policy models. The application of optimal control techniques to macroeconomics has demonstrated the potential of optimal control theory for macroeconomic growth theory, development and stabilisation (Shell (1967), Kendrick and Taylor (1970), Dobell and Ho (1967)). To open up the field of econometric modelling to the techniques of optimal control econometric models, in either structural, reduced or final form, have usually been translated into state space form; see for example Preston and Wall (1973).

Many recent studies have been concerned with control and policy analysis in large scale systems. A combination of structural considerations for large scale systems, plus policy and decision analysis, in a hierarchical framework can do much to enhance our ability to cope with the complexity inherent in large scale economic systems. In this paper, we apply the multi-level system theory to large scale economic systems for two main purposes. First, the econometric models essentially include a very large number of interdependent variables; hence, the computation time involved in policy experiments is often excessive. Second, there is usually a natural way to decompose the model into fundamental subsystems which agree with the

Hughes Hallett, A.J. (ed.) Applied Decision Analysis and Economic Behaviour

ISBN 90-247-2968-8. Printed in The Netherlands

economic structural aspects. The focus of our attention in this chapter is on interconnected economic systems which have a multi-time scale propoerty. We consider a large scale composite system with one high level subsystem and N–1 lower level subsystems. Two basic assumptions are made:

(i) The lower level subsystems S_2, S_3, ..., S_N have inherently faster dynamics than the higher level subsystem S_1;

(ii) Insight and sufficient knowledge about the system are available to identify the multi-time scale behaviour.

In dealing with optimisation in large scale systems there appear to be two main problems:

(i) The actual 'size' of the problems which leads to computational difficulties;

(ii) Centralised control of large interconnected systems is generally unrealistic because the cost of communication between numerous information gathering networks is prohibitive. To overcome these difficulties a design methodology is presented for obtaining decentralised strategies for decision makers, such that the information processing and control policy decisions are delegated to a set of agents. The simplification of the computation is based on a time scale separation of the subsystems. One of the most basic issues that arise in this class of problems is the stability of the composite system.

The outline of this chapter is the following. Section 2 contains a rough description of the preliminary concepts: economic models in state space form, and decentralised control strategy. The mathematical model of multi-time scale systems is given in section 3, where the main characteristics of such systems are discussed. A centralised control strategy for multi-time scale systems is prposed in section 4. In section 5 the conditions for the stability of interconnected systems under time scale separation of the subsystems are established. The stability results are illustrated via an example of a second order system. Section 6 contains the conclusions. The proofs of the theorems are given in an Appendix.

2. PRELIMINARY CONCEPTS

2.1 The basic model

Economic systems have recently received a great deal of attention from control engineers as one of the broader and more fruitful areas of control theory applications. This arises naturally in describing both the macroeconomic and microeconomic behaviour of economic systems. More recently, the state space form as an alternative representation of traditional forms has emerged in various theoretical and empirical studies of dynamic economic systems. The realisation problem and the problem of how the state space approach can be integrated into the traditional econometric models will not be considered in this chapter. Various methods and results are available for the problem of realisation (Ho and Kalman (1976), Silverman (1971), Chow (1975)). Some numerical results of an operational algorithm for constructing a minimal realisation are given by Myoken and Uchida (1983), in which the canonical minimal realisations of some well-known economic models are illustrated numerically.

Despite the high efficiency of modern computing machinery, the formidable complexity of systems with large numbers of economic variables makes a direct analysis unattractive. However, by grouping variables of a large evonomy into a relatively small number of subsystems, that economy can be decomposed into various interconnected subsystems. The focus of attention in this chapter is on large scale system S, composed of N–1 interacting subsystems $S_1, S_2, \ldots, S_N$ where each individual subsystem is only a 'small' part of the whole system. Many economic phenomena may be modelled in this manner. The mathematical model of the whole system S can be represented as

$$\dot{x}_i(t) = A_{ii}x_i(t) + \sum_{j=1}^{N} A_{ij}x_j(t) + B_{ii}u_i(t) \quad , \quad i = 1,2, \ldots, N \tag{13.1}$$

$$y_i(t) = C_i x_i(t) \quad , \quad i = 1,2, \ldots, N \tag{13.2}$$

where $x_i(t)$, $x_i \in R^{n_i}$, is the state of economy; $u_i(t)$, $u_i \in R^{m_i}$ is the vector of exogenous variables (inputs); $y_i(t)$, $y_i \in R^{r_i}$ is the vector of endogenous variables (outputs). (Mehra (1974) contains a useful comparison of econometric and control jargon). Finally, A_{ii}, A_{ij}, B_{ii} and C_i are known matrices of appropriate dimensions; and A_{ij}, $A_{ij} \in R^{n_i x n_j}$, denotes the interconnection from S_i to S_j.

Equations (13.1) and (13.2) provide a basis for representing many econometric models in a control framework. From an economic standpoint, the state variables $x_i(t)$ include, for example, incomes, residential construction, durable consumption, investment, inventories, etc. The control vectors $u_i(t)$ have entries such as tax rates, government expenditures, money supply and other policy variables. The output vector variables are usually a linear transformation of the state variables. Finally, the elements of the matrices A_{ii}, A_{ij}, B_{ii}, and C_i involve the parameters that specify alternative channels of influences and economic effects among the system variables.

2.2 A decentralised control strategy

In classical control and decision making problems, the system is handled in a centralised fashion. The decisions of control policies and their implementation are all made according to the preference of a single, central supervisor. However, centralised control of large interconnected systems is generally unrealistic because of the excessive computational costs and because of the heavy costs of communication between a large number of information gathering networks. Hence, an important problem of decentralisation arises where the information processing and control decisions can be delegated to a set of agents. For an excellent survey of decentralised control methods for large scale systems see Sandell et al. (1978).

Therefore, in this chapter, we consider a dynamic system which has a set of control inputs and a set of measurement equations. It is to be controlled to achieve certain objectives. The objectives may be to optimise or stabilise the overall system. In a number of cases in economics both objectives can be achieved through the optimisation of a cost function (the term welfare function is also used), such as

$$J = \int_0^\infty (x'Qx + \sum_{i=1}^N u_i'R_iu_i)dt \tag{13.3}$$

The weighting matrices Q and R_i in the decentralised quadratic performance criterion (13.3) are symmetric positive definite matrices and have special significance. While Q accounts for the relative cost of deviating the state variables from the desired level, the matrices R_i stand for the cost of operating the controls away from their desired levels. The matrices Q and R_i are normally diagonal and have relative magnitudes that reflect the costs of the control effort compared to output deviations (or 'failures').

The problem now is to determine the control law $u_i(t)$, $i=1,2,\ldots,N$, for the system described by equation (13.1), subject to the known information (measurement) constraints (13.2), which minimises the cost function (13.3).

The information available to the decision makers consists of two parts:

(i) Prior information – this includes information on the system structure, values of the parameters, cost function, and so on.

(ii) A posteriori information – this includes measurements obtained during the control period itself.

The decision makers have to generate the control law based on their prior information and as much posteriori information as is available at each decision point. In this chapter, we consider a case of decentralised control and centralised off-line computations (see figure 13.1). This occurs when the information pattern is decentralised but the control laws are computed in a centralised manner (Petkovski and Athans (1981)). Thus, there is more than one control law, each of which transforms a set of measurements into a set of controls. This reduces the complexity of the communication system required and simplifies the on-line computations. The control law which minimises (13.3) has the general form

$$u_i(t) = E_i C_i x(t) \qquad i = 1, 2, \ldots, N \tag{13.4}$$

where E_i is a time-invariant matrix and the matrix C_i defines the a posteriori information available to the agent i at time t (Petkovski and Athans (1981)).

3. TWO–TIME SCALE SYSTEMS

It is common procedure in practice to work with mathematical models that are simple, but less accurate, than the best available model of a given system. In going from the most complex to the most simplified model, the trade-off is between computational convenience and modelling adequacy. Not only should a model be faithful in terms of the physical reality which it represents, but it should also provide the planner or the analyst with enough information to enable him to act on the system in an informed manner. In other words, a satisfactory model is a good aid to decision making which at the same time achieves the right level of trade-off between accuracy and computational convenience.

Methods for the approximate control of dynamic systems have received a great deal of attention on recent years. A great variety of reduced-order modelling techniques exist for general systems (see for example the bibliography of Genesia and Milanese (1976)). The reduction of computation and the simplification of structure are of particular concern in the control of large scale systems (Sandell et al. (1978), Koktović et al. (1976), Petkovski and Rakić (1979), Petkovski (1977, 1978)).

A characteristic that one can observe in many economic systems is the existence of sectors with different speeds of adjustment. These can be recognised when viewing the time variations of the dynamic system states. In this section, we shall consider what is called the two-time scale behaviour of systems.

Defintion 1: The system

$$\dot{x}(t) = Ax(t) \tag{13.4}$$

will be called a two-time scale system if the absolute values of the eigenvalues of A, represented as $\lambda(A)$, can be separated into two disjoint non-empty sets V and W such that

$$|v_i| \ll |w_i| \qquad \text{for all } v_i \in V \text{ and } w_i \in W \tag{13.5}$$

where '≪' denotes 'significantly smaller' (i.e. the left hand side of (13.5) is several orders of magnitude less than the right hand side).

For any two-time scale systems the ratio

$$\mu = \frac{|v_1|}{|w_1|} \ll 1 \tag{13.6}$$

where v_1 is the largest eigenvalue in V and w_1 is the smallest eigenvalue in W, will define the parameter needed to measure the system's time scale separation.

In this section, we consider the large scale hierarchical system with one higher level subsystem and N–1 lower level subsystems. Thus

$$\dot{x}_1(t) = A_{11}x_1(t) + \sum_{j=2}^{N} A_{1j}x_j(t) + \sum_{j=2}^{N} B_{1j}u_j(t) \tag{13.7}$$

$$\mu\dot{x}_j(t) = A_{j1}x_1(t) + A_{jj}x_j(t) + B_{jj}u_j(t) \qquad j = 2, 3, \ldots, N \tag{13.8}$$

where $x_1 \in R^n$, $x_j \in R^{m_j}$, and $\sum_{j=2}^{N} m_j = m$. Here x_1 is the state of the slow subsystem, and x_j, j=2,3, . . . ,N are the state vectors of the fast subsystems. The low level subsystems $S_2, S_3, \ldots, S_N$ have inherently faster dynamics than the high level subsystem S_1. The parameter μ, which is a small positive number, is assumed to be the same for the N–1 subsystems, and indicates how much faster they are with respect to the higher level subsystem. In other words, three basic assumptions are made: (i) The lower level subsystems have inherently faster dynamics than the higher level subsystems; (ii) Prior insight and knowledge about the system to identify the two-time scale behaviour are available; and (iii) The subsystems are recursively connected, from (13.8) to (13.7) but not vice versa.

An important question which arises in modelling of two-time scale linear systems is, how should the state variables x(t) be reordered so that states which contain predominantly slow modes are placed in $x_1(t)$? For example, one approach to the identification of slow dynamic variables is to rely upon designer insight into the dynamic structure of the system. For many widely studied dynamic systems the choice between slow and fast variables may be obvious. Detailed discussion how should state variables x(t) be reordered so that the states which contain predominantly slow modes are placed in $x_1(t)$ is given by Phillips (1980).

As an example, an economic system which has a multi-time scale consider the hierarchical decision structure in a company. Local decision makers (workers at lower levels in the hierarchy) make day to day decisions. At the same time they feed the central decision making agent (manager at a higher level in the hierarchy) with information on their activities. Based partly on this information and partly on other information, the central decision maker makes decisions at a slower rate (for example, weekly or monthly).

In a similar way, we can consider the hierarchical decision structure in national planning. Companies are able to adjust their decisions monthly or seasonally, but the government policy and interventions are typically changed either annually or every few years.

4. DECENTRALISED CONTROL SYSTEM DESIGN

In this section we shall investigate whether a priori knowledge about the dynamics of the subsystems would help in determining control strategies for the large scale interconnected systems. We shall use the knowledge that the subsystems can be grouped according to whether their dynamics are slow or fast with respect to each other. The objective is a control law that satisfies two criteria: (i) Computational simplicity; and (ii) Information structure constraints. There are at least two strong practical reasons to neglect the parameter μ during the design of the decentralised control law. One reason is that the presence of the 'parasitic' parameter μ can make the dimensionality of a dynamic system prohibitively high. Another, less apparent, reason is that the interaction of fast and slow phenomena in high order systems results in 'stiff' numerical problems which require expensive numerical integration routines. Furthermore, the presence of the parameter μ is likely to complicate the design of decentralised control law.

However, it is shown in this chapter that the design of stabilising decentralised feedback control for (n+m)th-order systems, governed by equations of the form (13.7) and (13.8) can be reduced to the design of stabilising feedback control for nth-order systems whose state equations are derived by setting $\mu=0$ in equations (13.7) and (13.8). In other words, the main objective is to solve smaller order problems and develop decentralised control strategy with reduced information in different time scale.

Notice that if A_{jj}, $j=2,3,\ldots,N-1$ are stable matrices (in the sense that the eigenvalues of the matrices A_{jj} all have negative real parts), and if $\mu=0$, then equations (13.7) and (13.8) reduce to the system

$$\dot{x}_1(t) = A_o x_1(t) + \sum_{j=2}^{N} B_{oj} u_j(t) \tag{13.9}$$

where the new system matrices are

$$A_o = A_{11} - \sum_{j=1}^{N} A_{1j} A_{jj}^{-1} A_{j1} \tag{13.10}$$

$$B_{oj} = B_{1j} - A_{1j} A_{jj}^{-1} B_{jj} \qquad j = 2, 3, \ldots, N \tag{13.11}$$

We shall call the system S_o, given by equation (13.9), a degenerate system. Using the decentralised control strategy proposed in Section 2.2, we can define a decentralised control law in the form

$$u_j(t) = E_j C_j x_1(t) \tag{13.12}$$

Inserting (13.12) into (13.9) we obtain the closed loop degenerate system

$$\dot{x}_1(t) = (A_o + \sum_{j=2}^{N} B_{oj} E_j C_j) x_1(t) \tag{13.13}$$

which will be assumed to be stable.

Now the state equations of the (n+m)th order closed loop system governed by equations (13.8) and (13.9) are evidently,

$$\dot{x}_1(t) = D_1 x_1(t) + D_2 x^{(2)}(t) \tag{13.14}$$

$$\mu \dot{x}^{(2)}(t) = D_3 x_1(t) + D_4 x^{(2)}(t) \tag{13.15}$$

where

$$D_1 = A_{11} + \sum_{j=2}^{N} B_{1j} E_j C_j \tag{13.16}$$

$$D_2 = [A_{12}, A_{13}, \ldots, A_{1N}] \tag{13.17}$$

$$D_3 = \begin{bmatrix} A_{21} - B_{22} E_2 C_2 \\ A_{31} - B_{33} E_3 C_3 \\ \vdots \\ A_{N1} - B_{NN} E_N C_N \end{bmatrix} \tag{13.18}$$

$$D_4 = \text{diag}(A_{jj}) \qquad j = 2, 3, \ldots, N \tag{13.19}$$

and $$(x^{(2)})' = [x_2', x_3', \ldots, x_N'] \tag{13.20}$$

One of the most basic issues that arises in this class of problems is the stability of the composite system, equations (13.14) and (13.15). In the next section we consider the conditions under which the stability analysis of the reduced system (13.13) is valid for the full system, (13.14) plus (13.15).

5. STABILITY ANALYSIS

Stabilisation of a decentralised dynamic system is more difficult than for a centralised dynamic system since all the information which is needed to make a 'correct' decision is not available in any one place. A decentralised information pattern thus implies certain structural restrictions on stabilisation policies. A degree of cooperation among decision makers is necessary so that their actions are coordinated rather than contradictory to the stabilisation of a dynamic system. The problem becomes more complicated if a simplified model of the system is also used for decision making.

In this section we give the stability analysis of large scale economic systems which have a multi-time scale property.

Theorem 1: If A_{jj}, j=2,3,...,N are stable matrices, then there exists a $\mu_o > 0$ such that for every $\mu \in (0, \mu_o]$ the closed loop composite system (13.14) and (13.15) is asymptotically stable.

Proof: See Appendix 13.1.

The significance of this theorem lies in the fact that it reduces the design of a stabilising feedback control law of an (n+m)th order system governed by state equations of the form (13.7) and (13.8) – where μ is small and A_{jj}, j=2,3,...,N satisfy the Routh-Hurwitz theorem (Gantmacher (1959)) – to the design of a stabilising feedback control law for nth order system governed by a state equation of the form (13.9). In other words, the stability of the full system (13.7) and (13.8) (in the sense that eigenvalues of the closed loop system matrix have negative real parts) is insensitive to the effects of variations in the parameter μ. If $\mu_o > 0$ exists such that (13.7) and (13.8) is a stable system for all $0 \leqslant \mu \leqslant \mu_o$ then the degenerate system S_o in (13.9) is also stable.

However, a more basic problem is how variations in the value of the parameter

μ, which indicates how much 'faster' the subsystems on the lower level are with respect to the higher level, influences the stability of the composite system. In other words, if the closed loop system (13.7) and (13.8) is observed to be stable, so that $\mu \leqslant \mu_o$ by theorem 1, the stability of the system remains in question if the parameter μ can change value while the system is operating. Thus, a problem of particular significance is the determination of a numerical upper bound μ^* such that the asymptotic stability of (13.7) and (13.8) is guaranteed for all $\mu < \mu^*$. Stability properties of singularly perturbed systems have been investigated by several authors over the last two decades (see Kakotović et al. (1976) for a survey). However, like theorem 1, these papers contain no expression for calculating an upper bound for the parameter μ. One exception is the paper by Zien (1973) where μ^* was obtained in terms of the transition matrices of the reduced and boundary layer systems.

In this section we give a new approach to computing stability of large scale composite systems with a multi-time scale property. First, define a new parameter γ such that

$$\gamma = \frac{1}{\mu} \tag{13.21}$$

Hence $\mu \to 0$ implies $\gamma \to \infty$. The following relationship can be established between the parameter μ and its nominal value μ_1,

$$\mu = \mu_1 + \Delta\mu \tag{13.22}$$

Then

$$\Delta\mu = -\frac{\Delta\gamma}{(\Delta\mu + \gamma_1)\gamma_1} \tag{13.23}$$

where

$$\Delta\gamma = \gamma - \gamma_1 \tag{13.24}$$

In this case $\Delta\mu$ and $\Delta\gamma$ are some nonlinear functions of t. Therefore, if we define the range on $\Delta\gamma$ so that the closed loop sytem (13.7) and (13.8) remains stable, then $\Delta\mu$ is uniquely defined by (13.23).

Hence *Theorem 2:* If the closed loop system (13.7) and (13.8) is stable for some $\mu = \mu_1$ it will remain stable for all $\mu = \mu_1 + \Delta\mu$ where $\Delta\mu$ is given with (13.23) and $\Delta\gamma$ satisfies the inequalities

$$\lambda_{min}^{-1}(Y) = \lambda_{min} \leqslant \Delta\gamma \leqslant \gamma_{max} = \lambda_{max}^{-1}(Y) \tag{13.25}$$

for all $t \in [0, \infty)$, where

$$Y = Q^{-1}(\bar{D}'P + P\bar{D}); \tag{13.26}$$

Q is an arbitrary symmetric, positive definite matrix;

$$\bar{D} = \begin{bmatrix} 0 & 0 \\ D_3 & D_4 \end{bmatrix}; \tag{13.27}$$

and P is a positive definite solution of the linear Lyapunov matrix equation,

$$\bar{D}'P + P\bar{D} = Q \tag{13.28}$$

Finally, $\lambda_i(Y)$ denotes an eigenvalue of the matrix Y.

Proof: See Appendix 13.2.

Remark 1. Notice that we are only interested in the upper bound of the parameter μ as we know that the system is stable for all $\mu \in (0, \mu_0]$.

We observe that the computation of the upper bound μ^* by Theorem 2 is much easier than the computation of μ^* suggested by Zien (1973) because it requires merely solving algebraic linear Lyapunov matrix equation, there is no need for finding transition matrices. Therefore, the basic strategy in the proposed approach for stability analysis of large scale economic systems with multi-time scale property is:
(1) Decompose the economic system by classifying the economic variables into a number of groups that describe subeconomies of the system, according to whether their dynamics are relatively slow or fast;
(2) Formulate constraints on the information among the subeconomies, expressed through the parameter μ, which indicates how much 'faster' the subsystems on the lower level are with respect to the higher level; and
(3) Conclude stability of the entire economy from the stability indices of the reduced system and the interactions among subeconomies on the higher and lower level.

We conclude this section with an example. Consider the second order system,

$$\begin{bmatrix} \dot{x}_1 \\ \mu \dot{x}_2 \end{bmatrix} = \begin{bmatrix} 1 & 1 \\ 0 & -1 \end{bmatrix} \begin{bmatrix} x_1 \\ x_2 \end{bmatrix} + \begin{bmatrix} 0 \\ 0.5 \end{bmatrix} u(t) \tag{13.29}$$

We want to reduce the decision making problem from the system model of second order to the model of first order. Notice that $a_{22} = -1$, is stable, for $\mu = 0$, the system (13.29) reduces to the degenerate system

$$x_1(t) = x_1(t) + 0.5u(t) \tag{13.30}$$

The control

$$u(t) = -4.2361 x_1(t) \tag{13.31}$$

minimises the quadratic performance index (13.3) with the weighting matrices Q=1 and R=1. This control stabilises the high order system (13.29), which has the closed loop matrix

$$A_c = A + BEC \tag{13.32}$$

where

$$E = -4.2361 \quad \text{and} \quad C = [1\ 0]. \tag{13.33}$$

Suppose $\mu_1 = 0.01$. We then get

$$A_c = \begin{bmatrix} 1 & 1 \\ -211.8 & -100 \end{bmatrix} \tag{13.34}$$

Define the Lyapunov matrix equation (13.29) with

$$Q = \begin{bmatrix} 20 & 0 \\ 0 & 20 \end{bmatrix} \tag{13.35}$$

Now, from the conditions (13.25) it follows that,

$$\Delta\gamma \in (-25.2525, \ \infty) \tag{13.36}$$

and the corresponding value for $\Delta\mu$ can be calculated from (13.23),

$$\Delta\mu \in (0, \ 0.01338) \tag{13.37}$$

Therefore, the allowable variations in the perturbation parameter μ which identifies the two-time scale behaviour of the system (13.29) are nearly 34% of its nominal value μ_1.

6. CONCLUSIONS

This paper has been concerned with the state space approach to decentralised control problems of large scale dynamic economic systems, composed of many similar interacting subsystems. The subsystems classification was based on a time scale separation.

A new criterion for asymptotic stability of interconnected systems that have a multi-time scale characteristic has been derived. It has been shown how the Lyapunov function can be used to estimate the permissable range of parameter μ which indicates how much 'faster' are the subsystems on the lower level with respect to the higher level.

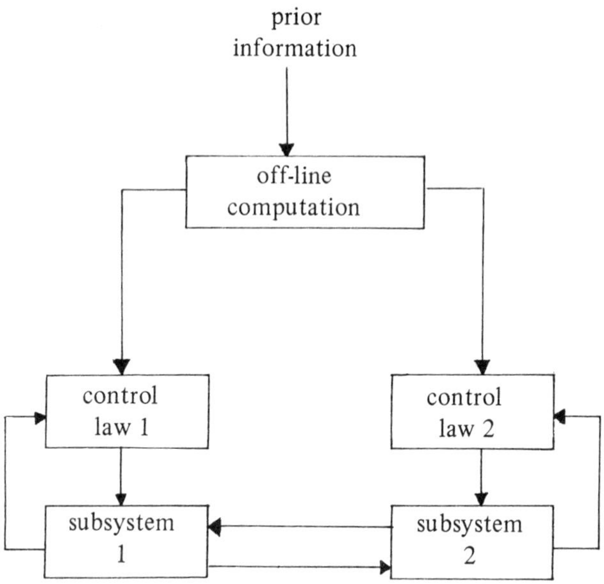

Figure 13.1. Two coupled systems controlled via decentralised control strategy

APPENDIX 1 Proof of Theorem 1.

The proof of Theorem 1 requires the following lemma.

Lemma 1: In the case of a system governed by the state equations,

$$\dot{x}_1(t) = I_1 x_1(t) + I_2 x_2(t) \tag{A.1}$$

$$\mu \dot{x}_2(t) = I_3 x_1(t) + I_4 x_2(t) \tag{A.2}$$

Let I_4 be a stable matrix. Then, if

$$\underline{E} = I_1 - I_2 I_4^{-1} I_3 \tag{A.3}$$

is a stable matrix, there exists a $\mu_o > 0$ such that for every $\mu \in (0, \mu_o]$ the equilibrium state $x_1 = 0$ and $x_2 = 0$ of the system is asymptotically stable.

Proof: See Zien (1973).

Therefore to prove Theorem 1 we must prove that,

(a) D_4 is stable (A.4)

(b) $\underline{E} = D_1 - D_2 D_4^{-1} D_3$ is stable (A.5)

The condition (a) is satisfied since $D_4 = \mathrm{diag}(A_{jj}), j = 2, 3, \ldots, N$ and $A_{jj}, j = 2,3,\ldots,N$ are stable.

To prove that the matrix $\underline{E}$ in (A.5) is stable, notice that (A.5) implies that,

$$\underline{E} = A_{11} + \sum_{j=3}^{N} B_{1j} E_j C_j - \begin{bmatrix} A_{12}A_{22}^{-1} & 0 & \cdots & 0 \\ 0 & A_{13}A_{33}^{-1} & \cdots & 0 \\ \vdots & \vdots & & \vdots \\ 0 & 0 & \cdots & A_{1N}A_{NN}^{-1} \end{bmatrix} \begin{bmatrix} A_{21}-B_{22}E_2C_2 \\ A_{31}-B_{33}E_3C_3 \\ \vdots \\ A_{N1}-B_{NN}E_NC_N \end{bmatrix} \tag{A.6}$$

making use of equations (13.16) – (13.19).

Now, it can easily be shown that the matrix $\underline{E}$ can be represented as

$$\underline{E} = A_{11} - \sum_{j=2}^{N} A_{1j} A_{jj}^{-1} A_{j1} + \sum_{j=2}^{N} (B_{1j} - A_{1j} A_{jj}^{-1} B_{jj}) E_j C_j \tag{A.7}$$

i.e., the matrix $\underline{E}$ is identical to the closed loop matrix of the degenerate system (13.9). Therefore $\underline{E}$ is a stable matrix.

APPENDIX 2 Proof of Theorem 2.

The proof is based on Lyapunov's theory. Choose the positive definite Lyapunov function as $V(x) = x'(t)Px(t)$. Taking the time derivative along the solution of the system (13.10) and (13.11) and using equation (13.27), $\dot{V}(x)$ may be represented as

$$\dot{V}(x) = -x'(t)\,(Q + \gamma(t)\bar{D}'P + \gamma(t)P\bar{D})x(t) \tag{A.8}$$

To prove the condition (13.25) we use the following lemma.

Lemma 2 (Thrall and Thornheim (1975)): If A and B are symmetric matrices and A is positive definite, there exists a nonsingular matrix S such that

$$S'(A + B)S = I + G \tag{A.9}$$

where the matrix G is a diagonal matrix whose elements are eigenvalues of $A^{-1}B$.

Therefore, using the results of Lemma 2, it can easily be concluded that the composite system (13.10) and (13.11) will remain stable if the following inequality is satisfied,

$$1 - \gamma(t)\lambda_j(Q^{-1}(\bar{D}'P + P\bar{D}) > 0 \qquad j = 1, 2, \ldots, n+m \tag{A.10}$$

i.e.

$$1 - \gamma(t)\lambda_j(Y) > 0 \qquad j = 1, 2, \ldots, n+m \tag{A.11}$$

where the matrix Y is defined by (13.26) for all $t \in [0, \infty)$. Now, under the usual assumption that $\lambda_{max}(Y) > 0$, it follows that

$$\gamma_{max} = \lambda_{max}^{-1}(Y) \tag{A. 12}$$

In a similar way if $\lambda_{min}(Y) < 0$ then

$$\gamma_{min} = \lambda_{min}^{-1}(Y) \tag{A.13}$$

i.e. the composite system remains stable if

$$\gamma(t) \in (\gamma_{min}, \gamma_{max}) \tag{A.14}$$

NOTES

* Research supported in part by the U.S.–Yugoslav Scientific and Technological Cooperation, under Grant ENERGY–401.

REFERENCES

Chow, G.C. (1975), *Analysis and Control of Dynamic Economic Systems,* John Wiley and Sons, New York.

Dobell, A.R. and Y.C. Ho (1967), 'Optimal investment policy: an example of a control problem in economic theory', *IEEE Transactions on Automatic Control,* AC-12, pp. 4-14.

Gantmacher, F.R. (1959), *The Theory of Matrices,* Chelsea Publishing Co., New York.

Genesio, R. and M. Milanese (1976), 'A note on the derivation and use of reduced-order models', *IEEE Transactions on Automatic Control,* AC-21, pp. 118-122.

Ho, B.L. and R.E. Kalman (1966), 'Effective construction of linear state-variable methods for input-output functions', *Regelungstechnik,* 14, pp. 545-548.

Kendrick, D. and L. Taylor (1970), 'Numerical solution of nonlinear planning methods', *Econometrica,* 38, pp. 453-467.

Kotović, P.V., R. O'Malley and P. Sannuti (1976), 'Singular perturbations and order reduction in control theory – an overview', *Automatica,* 12, pp. 123-132.

Mehra, R.K. (1974), 'Identification in control and econometrics; similarities and differences', *Annals of Economic and Social Measurement,* 3, pp. 21-48.

Myoken, H. and Y. Uchida (1983), 'Minimal canonical form realisation for multivariable econometric systems', *International Journal of Systems Science,* (in press).

Petkovski, D.B. (1977), 'Application of ϵ-method to linear dynamic systems decoupled into N subsystems', *Automatic Control Theory and Applications,* 5, pp. 66-71.

Petkovski, D.B. (1978), 'Calculation of optimum feedback gains for output constrained regulators', *Journal of Numerical Methods in Engineering,* 12, pp. 1873-1878.

Petkovski, D.B. and M. Athans (1981), 'Robustness of decentralised output control designs with application to an electric power system', Third IMA Conference on Control Theory, University of Sheffield, Academic Press, New York, pp. 859-880.

Petkovski, D.B. and M.Rakić (1979), 'Series solution of feedback gain for output-constrained regulators', *International Journal of Control,* 30, pp. 661-668.

Preston, A.J. and K.D. Wall (1973), 'Some aspects of the use of state space models in econometrics', PREM Discussion Paper No. 6, Imperial College, University of London.

Phillips, R.G. (1980), 'Reduced order modelling and control of two-time-scale discrete systems', *International Journal of Control,* 31, pp. 765-781.

Sandell, N.R., P. Varaiya, M. Athans and M. Safanov (1978), 'Survey of decentralised control methods for large-scale systems', *IEEE Transactions on Automatic Control,* AC-23, pp. 108-128.

Shell, K. (ed.) (1967), *Essays on the Theory of Optimal Control Growth,* MIT Press, Cambridge, Massachusetts.

Shensa, M.J. (1971), 'Parasitics and stability of equilibrium points on nonlinear networks', *IEEE Transactions on Circuit Theory,* CT-18, pp. 481-484.

Silverman, L.M. (1971), 'Realisation of linear dynamic systems', *IEEE Transactions on Automatic Control,* AC-16, pp. 554-567.

Thrall, R.M. and L. Thronheim (1975), *Vector Spaces and Matrices,* John Wiley and Sons, New York.

Zien, L. (1973), 'An upper bound for the singular parameter in a stable singularly perturbed system', *Journal of the Franklin Insitute,* 295, pp. 373-381.

CHAPTER 14

THE LOCATION OF A FIRM ON A NETWORK

Pierre Hanjoul and Jacques-François Thisse
University of Louvain, Belgium

'On ne fait point de l'industrie entre le ciel et terre; il faut se poser quelque part sur le sol'.

L. Walras, *Eléments d'économie politique pure.*

1. INTRODUCTION

Since the pioneering work of Launhardt and Weber (1909), the location theory of the firm has developed from a particular model of the firm in which the location decision criterion is the minimisation of transportation costs.[1] Actually it is not surprising that this model, called hereafter *Weberian*, still is the basic reference in the field in spite of its difference with the neo-classical model of the firm. One has only to remember the minor position held by spatial economics in the mainstream economics over several decades.[2] Despite appearances, this theoreticl hiatus is of no serious consequences for the study of location problems. Indeed, the Weberian model now appears to be a short-cut leading to the neo-classical model. The argument is simple and it will be used in several propositions of this chapter: a place which maximises the profit of the firm at the same time minimises the transportation cost included in the profit.[3] Consequently, the characteristics of the Weberian model solution remain valid for the neo-classical model solution. This explains why, in some parts of the chapter, we follow the lines of proofs given elsewhere. Unfortunately, there are exceptions to that equivalence rule which, not surprisingly, correspond to location problems which are not easy to deal with from both the theoretical and numerical points of view. Such a problem is discussed in section 3.

The objection has sometimes been raised against the neo-classical approach that the decision of locating a firm is not guided by profit maximisation. The firm would

Hughes Hallett, A.J. (ed.) Applied Decision Analysis and Economic Behaviour

ISBN 90-247-2968-8. Printed in The Netherlands

rather attempt to capture as many amenities as possible linked to certain places. The chosen location would then represent a compromise between these different location factors. To such a criticism we may answer that it is not clear why the locational decision should escape the principles of microeconomic theory, when they should continue to be applied to other decisions of the firm. Furthermore, it is possible to partially reconcile the different approaches –Weberian, neo-classical and behaviourist– by showing that, under rather general conditions, they obey the same spatial logic whereas, of course, the locations actually chosen in each case are not the same.[4]

The approach followed in firm location theory is original. Indeed, rather than characterising the equilibrium location by means of first-order conditions, it aims at the characterisation of a part of space containing one (or the) equilibrium location(s). As expected, the set of candidate locations diminishes progressively with the introduction of additional hypotheses. This gives rise to a *reduction process,* the stages of which are defined in terms of what we call *localisation theorems.* In most of the problems considered here, the following results are obtained: (i) the set of candidate locations is, under very mild assumptions, given by a finite subset of the network; (ii) the places in this subset are either markets or nodes endowed with a high degree of centrality; (iii) in some cases, only the markets are to be considered.

An interesting characteristic of the location model lies in the fact that the theoretical analysis can be applied to an operational analysis. The above-mentioned 'finiteness' property leads to a discrete formalisation and, therefore, to the use of 0-1 programming techniques. A large number of operational models have thus been built by engineers. Most of them, however, focus on the minimisation of production and/or transportation costs. But, as in theoretical work, the integration of price variables and the extension to more general objective functions have only recently been made. Unfortunately, the 'trick' given above proves to be useless in the present case: as the quantities of outputs and inputs are not known a priori, one can no longer use the Weberian model to find the solution to the general problem. Nevertheless, we shall see that the neo-classical model often admits, as a particular case, another famous location model, namely the *simple plant location problem.* Given an efficient solution to the latter problem, it is possible to apply it to models dealing with profit maximisation and to exploit its numerical properties.

This chapter presents some propositions and solution methods of the equilibrium location of a neo-classical firm on a transportation network. Two market structures are considered: quasi-perfect competition (Section 2) and spatial monopoly (Section 3). Our conclusions are displayed in section 4.

2. THE SPATIAL EQUILIBRIUM OF A FIRM IN QUASI-PERFECT COMPETITION

In this section, we study the location and production policy of a firm within a spatial competitive economy. The model is defined in 2.1. In 2.2 we set forth the localisation theorems and formalise the reduction process. Finally, in 2.3, we discuss some economic and geographical implications of the results obtained and propose various extensions of the basic model.

2.1 The location and production problem

2.1.1 The geographical structure

We suppose, following a well-established tradition in location theory, that there exists only one transportation mode. (The case of several modes will be discussed later on). Literature in spatial analysis abounds with mathematical representations of the corresponding transportation space. They have metric spaces in common and are divided in two classes, namely the continuous and the network representations. The first ones suppose that a distance, generally derived from a norm, is defined a priori on a convex subset of the plane with a non-empty interior. The analytical and geometrical properties of the distance express the main characteristics of the network that we intend to describe.[5] By contrast, the second ones aim at integrating the characteristics of configureation, position and site of the real network in the definition of the basic subset. The distance is constructed from this subset. In other words, instead of being imposed a priori, the properties of the distance arise from the structure of the basic subset. In what follows, network representations alone are considered.[6]

Definition 1: We call *network* any subset X of $\mathbb{R}^2$ which satisfies the following properties:

(i) $X = \bigcup_{i=1}^{n} h_i([0,1])$, where n is a positive integer and h_i a continuous injection from [0,1] in $\mathbb{R}^2$, $i = 1 \ldots n$;

(ii) $h_i(\theta) \neq h_{i'}(\theta')$ for any $i \neq i'$, with $i, i' \in \{1 \ldots n\}$ and any $\theta \neq \theta'$, with $\theta, \theta' \in\,]0,1[$;

(iii) X is connected.

The set of *vertices* associated with X is given by $V = \{v \in X;\ \exists i \in \{1 \ldots n\}\ v = h_i(0) \text{ or } v = h_i(1)\}$.

With the network X we may associate a graph G whose constituent elements are the following: (i) the set of vertices is V; (ii) the family of edges is $(\{h_i(0), h_i(1)\};$

$i \in \{1 \ldots n\}$). A pair of vertices is then repeated as many times as there are mappings h_i satisfying the property $\{v, v'\} = \{h_i(0), h_i(1)\}$. A straightforward implication of the definition of X is that G is connected in the sense of graph theory. The graph G is therefore the graph-theoretic counterpart of the network X, which itself is not a graph in the strict sense.[7] The reason for introducing G is that it allows us to save a number of definitions. To endow X with some properties, it is sufficient to pose the corresponding hypotheses on G using the language of graph theory.

A *route between* $x \in X$ and $x' \in X$ is a subset R of X for which there exists an homeomorphism h from [0,1] on R such that $\{x, x'\} = \{h(0), h(1)\}$.[8] In particular, $h_i([0,1])$ with $i \in \{1 \ldots n\}$, is a route linking the vertices $h_i(0)$ and $h_i(1)$; it is called a *basic route.* Obviously, there is a bijection between the set of basic routes of X and the family of edges of G.

Every basic route $h_i([0,1])$ is endowed with a positive length L_i. If $0 \leqslant \theta' \leqslant \theta'' \leqslant 1$, the length of the subroute $h_i([\theta', \theta''])$ is by definition equal to $(\theta'' - \theta')L_i$. The length of a route R is then given by the sum of the lengths of the routes and subroutes which constitute it.[9]

Definition 2: The *distance between* $x \in X$ *and* $x' \in X$ is equal to the length of the shortest route between $x \in X$ and $x' \in X$; it is denoted by $d(x,x')$.

Clearly, the mapping d is a metric on X and the function $d(v,h_i(\theta))$ is concave with respect to θ for any $v \in V$ and any basic route $h_i([0,1])$.

Definition 3: The *set of locations,* denoted by S, is a subset of the network; $s \in S$ stands for a possible location.[10]

2.2 The technology of the firm

Because of space, it is possible for the firm to divide its production activities into several geographically separated plants. Roughly speaking, we may consider two polar cases of the spatial division of production. The first one, called *horizontal* division, supposes that each plant carries ot the whole production process. In this case, the spatial division is associated with a geographical segmentation of output and input markets, each plant being linked to a particular segment. The second one, called *vertical* division, admits the possibility of ranking the plants according to an order based on technological links, plant i supplying plant i+1 and being itself supplied by plant i–1. Here, the spatial division corresponds to a breaking up of the production process made with the aim to internalise the comparative advantages of certain places. The transportation costs of the intermediate goods is then more than compensated by the gains realised on production costs.

Clearly, between those two cases of spatial division of production, we can imagine a whole range of intermediate situations: The description of a technological structure covering all situations is possible but proves to be very cumbersome notationally. To simplify matters, we only consider the case of a single-plant firm in the remainder of this section. (Note, however, that the multi-plant case is briefly discussed in 2.3.7).

The set of outputs (inputs) of the firm is represented by $G_0(G_i)$ and any output (input) by $g \in G_0(G_i)$.

Definition 4: The firm has a single plant; the production function of this plant is strictly convex and independent of the chosen location.[11]

2.1.3 The economic environment of the firm

The spatial factor creates difficulties in the perfect competition model to the extent that the basic assumption about firms' behaviour, i.e. firms perceive their supply and demand functions as perfectly elastic, seems to lose all meaning in a spatial economy. Indeed, it is hard to imagine why firms would not enjoy the monopoly power resulting from the geographical spreading of production and consumption. Consequently, for the firms to take the prices as given, we have to assume that they operate within a particular spatial market structure.[12] In this case: for every good, there exists a finite number of market places where the firms can buy or sell the good considered. Each good therefore passes through a market place and the corresponding transportation cost from or to that place is paid by the firms.[13] We then admit that the number of such market places is low compared to the number of firms involved, so that each of them should perceive its supply and demand functions as perfectly elastic. In each market place the law of supply and demand determines the market price which is taken as given by the firms. As a result, each good is characterised by a price system, one price per market place, and not by a unique price as in perfect competition. The so-obtained market structure is called *quasi-perfect competition.*[14] There is no need here to go into further details. At this stage, it is worth noticing that the location theory of the firm has mainly developed within the framework of quasi-perfect competition, even when this has not always been made clear.

For our problem, the economic information needed by the firms is contained in the prices at the different market places and in the transportation cost functions.

Definition 5: The set of market places of the output (input) $g \in G_0(G_i)$ is a subset

M_g of the set of vertices V. the market price of output (input) $g \in G_o(G_i)$ in $m \in M_g$ is given and denoted by π_{gm}.[15]

Let M be defined by $\cup \left\{ M_g ; g \in G_o \cup G_i \right\}$; a point in M is denoted by m.

Definition 6: The unit transportation cost of good $g \in G_o \cup G_i$ between market place $m \in M_g$ and location $s \in S$ is given by a non-negative, increasing and concave function $t_g[d(m,s)]$ of the distance such that $t_g(o) = 0$.

The above specification admits as particular cases the linear function $t_g = r_g . d(m,s)$, the affine function $t_g = f_g + r_g . d(m,s)$ if $m \neq s$ and $t_g = 0$ otherwise, and the power function $t_g = r_g . [d(m,s)]^{\alpha}$ with $\alpha \in]0,1[$, which can all be found in textbooks on transportation economics.

It is well known that the transportation activity exhibits numerous indivisibilities in fixed as well as in variable factors and, consequently, that the average transportation cost decreases with distance.[15] In our model, this would amount to requiring either a discontinuity at the origin, i.e. a positive fixed transportation cost f_g, or the strict concavity of t_g. In either case the linear function, so popular in spatial economics, should be prohibited. Yet it still has an interest so far as it simplifies the study of the impact of site characteristics in some location problems. Indeed, a constant transportation rate r_g can be viewed as a simple measure of the transportability of good g from or to $m \in M_g$.

Note also that $t_g[d(m, h_i(\theta))]$ is concave with respect to θ for every basic route $h_i([0,1])$ since $d(m, h_i(\theta))$ is concave with respect to θ and t_g increasing and concave in distance.

The firm chooses its production policy from prices net of transportation costs, and not from market prices. The former, unlike the latter, depends on the firm locational decision.

Definition 7: For output $g \in G_o$, the firm-price associated with market place $m \in M_g$ is given by

$$p_{gm}[d(m,s)] = \pi_{gm} - t_g[d(m,s)] \tag{14.1}$$

while the firm-price of input $g \in G_i$ at $m \in M_g$ is expressed by

$$p_{gm}[d(m,s)] = \pi_{gm} + t_g[d(m,s)] . \tag{14.2}$$

If q_{gm} stands for the non-negative quantity of output $g \in G_o$ (the non-positive quantity of input $g \in G_i$) sold (bought) at market place $m \in M_g$, the profit function of the firm can be written as

$$P(\underline{Q},s) = \sum_{g \in G_o \cup G_i} \; \sum_{m \in M_g} p_{gm}[d(m,s)] \cdot q_{gm} \tag{14.3}$$

where $\underline{Q}$ denotes the vector of quantities q_{gm}.

2.1.4 The location and production problem of the firm

Let $f(\underline{Q})$ be the production function of the firm defined on the set of vectors of quantities $q_g = \sum_{m \in M_g} q_{gm}$. For the sake of simplicity, it is supposed that each good $g \in G_o(G_i)$ is produced (consumed) by the firm.

Definition 8: The *location and production problem (LPP) of the firm is given by* the non-linear program

$$\underset{\underline{Q},s}{\text{maximise}}\; P(\underline{Q},s) \tag{14.4}$$

s.t.

$$q_{gm} \geqslant 0, \;\forall g \in G_o \text{ and } m \in M_g,$$

$$q_{gm} \leqslant 0, \;\forall g \in G_i \text{ and } m \in M_g$$

$$f(\underline{Q}) = 0, \; s \in S.$$ [17]

A solution of the LPP, denoted $(\underline{Q}^*, s^*)$, is called a *spatial equilibrium of the firm* in quasi-perfect competition.

The following comments are in order.

(i) The LPP is basically a constrained optimisation problem in that the non-negativity (non-positivity) constraints on the quantities of output (input) cannot be disregarded. There is no reason, indeed, to suppose that they will be all satisfied at the equilibrium. Better, we shall see that there exists an equilibrium in which only one quantity q_{gm} is different from zero per output and per input. The proposition that the market places with which the firm is connected are given a priori therefore implies that the associated solution is often suboptimal from the firm's point of view.

(ii) Owing to the non-negativity and non-positivity constraints on quantities, a change in firm location is likely to bring about substitution effects between markets. In other words, apart from the traditional substitution effects between quantities, we observe that the variations in firm-prices associated with a relocation of the firm can imply a restructuring of the producer's commercial policy to the advantage of some markets and to the detriment of others. From the analytical point of view, this means that the properties of comparative statics can be valid for a given variation of a price and yet cease to be valid for the opposite variation.

(iii) There is another substitution effect to indicate, namely the one relative to transportation inputs. In view of Definition 6, it is clear that transportation inputs vary with the quantities of goods. Accordingly, the substitution effects between transportation inputs are of the same nature as the substitution effects between goods.

2.2 The reduction process

2.2.1 The production policy

To a certain extent, the following result allows us to characterise the production policy of the firm in quasi-perfect competition; the proof is obvious and is omitted.

Proposition 1: If $(\underline{Q}_e, s_e)$ is a spatial equilibrium of the firm, then there exists an equilibrium $(\underline{Q}^*, s^*)$ such that $s^* = s_e$ and that for each output (input) $g \in G_o(G_i)$, q^*_{gm} is positive (negative) for only one market place $m \in M_g$.

In other words, each output (input) is sold (bought) on a single market place at the equilibrium $(\underline{Q}^*, s^*)$. Clearly, this market place is the one –or one of those– for which the firm-price corresponding to location s^* is the highest (lowest) possible. In what follows, we shall limit ourselves to the equilibria of this type. Interestingly, the above property permits a substantial simplification in the writing of the LPP at the equilibrium. The non-zero quantity of good $g \in G_oUG_i$ in $\underline{Q}^*$ and the corresponding market place, market price and firm-price are respectively denoted by q^*_g, m^*_g, π^*_g and p^*_g, so that the maximum profit can be written as

$$P^* = \sum_{g \in G_oUG_i} p^*_g[d(m^*_g, s^*)] \cdot q^*_g . \tag{14.5}$$

Let M^* be the subset $\{m^*_g ; g \in G_oUG_i\}$ of M. A point x of the network is said to be *efficient* with respect to the set M^* of market places if and only if there exists no location $s \in S$ such that $d(s,m) \leqslant d(x,m)$ for all $m \in M^*$, the inequality being strict for at least one market place of M^*. We denote by V^*_e the set of efficient vertices associated with the equilibrium $(\underline{Q}^*, s^*)$; of course $M^* \subseteq V_e^*$.

Given (14.1) and (14.2), the maximum profit can be rewritten as

$$P^* = \sum_{g \in G_o \cup G_i} \pi_g^* q_g^* - \sum_{g \in G_o \cup G_i} t_g[(m_g^*, s^*)] \ |q_g^*| . \tag{14.6}$$

For every $m \in M^*$, we set:

$$T_m^*(s) = \sum_{\{g \in G_o \cup G_i ; m_g^* = m\}} t_g[d(m_g^*, s)] \ |q_g^*| \tag{14.7}$$

and

$$T^*(s) = \sum_{m \in M^*} T_m^*(s) . \tag{14.8}$$

Hence (14.6) amounts to

$$P^* = \sum_{g \in G_o \cup G_i} \pi_g^* q_g^* - T^*(s^*) . \tag{14.9}$$

We can easily deduce from (14.9) that s^* is a minimiser of $T^*(s)$ and that every minimiser $\bar{s}$ of $T^*(s)$ is such that $P(\underline{Q}^*, \bar{s}) = P^*$. Consequently, as pointed out in the introduction, the properties of the Weberian model solution extends to the solution of the LPP.

2.2.2 The Hakimi theorem

The next property, called Hakimi theorem, yields a very neat characterisation of the location policy of the firm.

Proposition 2: There exists a spatial equilibrium $(\underline{Q}^*, s^*)$ of the firm such that s^* belongs to the set V_e^* of efficient vertices. Furthermore, $s^* \in V_e^*$ for any equilibrium $(\underline{Q}^*, s^*)$ if one of the following conditions holds:
(a) the unit transportation cost of at least one good $g \in G_o \cup G_i$ is strictly concave in distance; (b) the unit transportation costs are linear or affine in distance and the production function is continuously differentiable.[18]

Proof: (i) Let $(\underline{Q}^*, s^*)$ be an equilibrium. If $s^* \in V_e^*$, the first part of the statement is verified. Then, assume that s^* is an intermediate point of a basic route $h_i([0,1])$ whose vertices are v_1 and v_2. Substituting $h_i(\theta)$ for s in (14.7) and (14.8), we see that $T_m^*[h_i(\theta)]$ and, consequently, $T^*[h_i(\theta)]$ are concave with respect to θ. It then follows from the theorem of minimisation of a concave function that $T^*[h_i(\theta)]$ is constant on [0,1] (see, e.g. Berge (1966), p. 204). Accordingly, v_1 is a minimiser of $T^*(s)$ and $P(\underline{Q}^*, v_1) = P^*$.

Let us now suppose that v_1 is not efficient with respect to M^*. Then $\hat{s} \in S$ would exist such that $T^*_m(\hat{s}) \leqslant T^*_m(v_1)$, the inequality being strict for at least one $m \in M^*$.

Consequently, we would have $T^*(\hat{s}) < T^*(v_1)$ and $P(\underline{Q}^*, \hat{s}) > P^*$, which contradicts the assumption that $(\underline{Q}^*, s^*)$ is an equilibrium. The solution $(\underline{Q}^*, v_1)$ therefore satisfies the first part of the statement.

(ii) From the strict concavity of one transportation cost function, it follows that, for any equilibrium $(\underline{Q}^*, g^*)$, $T^*[h_i(\theta)]$ is strictly concave with respect to θ, so that any minimiser of $T^*[h_i(\theta)]$ must belong to $\{0,1\}$. As this holds for any basic route, V contains any minimiser of $T^*(s)$. Since the argument is independent of the particular equilibrium considered, statement (a) of the second part of the proposition is proved.

Let us now consider statement (b) and assume that an equilibrium $(\underline{Q}^*, s^*)$ exists such that s^* is an intermediate point of a basic route with vertices v_1 and v_2. Then we know that $P(\underline{Q}^*, v_1) = P^*$. The firm-prices of goods $g \in G_o \cup G_i$ in v_1 are different from the corresponding firm-prices in s^*: some increase while others decrease. Moreover, the iso-production surfaces are smooth since the production function is of type C_1. Hence $\underline{Q}^*$ is not a maximiser of $P(\underline{Q}, v_1)$ so that $\underline{Q}_1$ may be found such that $P(\underline{Q}_1, v_1) > P^*$, a contradiction. That completes the proof.

The above proposition has several interesting implications from both the economic and geographical points of view. For clarity, their discussion is postponed to subsection 2.3. In what follows, we shall try to pursue the reduction process and to characterise *nested* subsets of the network that necessarily contain an equilibrium location. For that, of course, we must introduce some additional restrictions of the LPP.

2.2.3 *The market place property*

To begin with, let us consider the transportation cost functions. Roughly speaking, it can be said that the real costs consist of a *fixed component* which is independent of the transport length and which has its origin in the indivisibilities of the transportation activity, and of a *variable component* which is a function of that length and the result of the movement itself. This difference is reflected in either positive fixed and marginal costs –see the affine function– or in a marginal cost arbitrarily high at zero and decreasing beyond zero –see the power function. In both cases, when compared with points situated in the vicinity of $m \in M_g$, the choice of the market place m as location allows the firm to reduce the transportation cost of good g more than the costs associated with the other goods increase. Market places therefore appear as *local equilibria.* [19] Clearly, as the proportion of the fixed component in t_g increases, the domain of optimality of m enlarges. From a certain threshold, we can then expect the domains corresponding to the different market places to cover the whole network. To deal with this formally, we suppose that functions t_g also depend on a parameter γ which expresses the relative importance of fixed and variable components in the formation of transportation costs. By convention, γ is considered as an inverse measure of the degree of scale economies in transportation: the smaller γ, the larger the fixed component. For example in the case of the affine function, γ is the ratio of the marginal cost to the fixed one; in the case of the power function, γ is the exponent of distance.

Definition 9: The unit transportation cost $t_g[d(m,s)\gamma]$ of good $g \in G_o \cup G_i$ is said to belong to *class* LT iff the following conditions hold:

(i) $t_g[d(m,s),\gamma]$ is a non-negative, increasing and concave function of the distance and a continuous function of γ on $[0,\gamma_0]$;

(ii) $t_g[d(m,s),0] = k_g > 0, \quad \forall m \in M_g, \quad \forall s \neq m;$ (14.10)

(iii) if $P(\underline{Q}, s; \gamma)$ denotes the profit of the firm corresponding to a given value of γ, then $\underline{Q}$ with $f(\underline{Q}) = 0$ and $s \in S$ exist such that

$$P(\underline{Q}, s; 0) > 0. \text{ [20]} \tag{14.11}$$

The next result gives us a characterisation of the equilibrium location more precise than Proposition 2.

Proposition 3: Assume that the unit transportation costs of goods $g \in G_o \cup G_i$ belong to class LT. Then there exists $\bar{\gamma} > 0$ such that, for any $\gamma \in [0, \bar{\gamma}]$ and any spatial equilibrium $(\underline{Q}^*, s^*)$ of the firm, the following properties hold:

(a.) there is an equilibrium $(\underline{Q}^*, m^*)$ with $m^* \in M^*$;

(b.) if M^* does not contain a pair of adjacent matket places, or if at least one of the conditions (a) and (b) is satisfied, then $s^* \in M^*$. [21]

Proof: (a') Set $\tilde{P}(s;\gamma) = \max\{P(\underline{Q}, s; \gamma); f(\underline{Q}) = 0\}$. To calculate $\tilde{P}(s;\gamma)$, as in Proposition 1, we may limit ourselves to the vectors $\underline{Q}$ with a non-zero component per good $g \in G_o \cup G_i$ and such that $f(\underline{Q}) = 0$. Let $\underline{Q}$ be any such vector and let π_g and m_g be the market prices and the market places associated with. For $m \in M$, we have:

$$P(\underline{Q},m;0) = \sum_{g \in G_o \cup G_i} \pi_g q_g - \sum_{\{g;m_g \neq m\}} k_g |q_g|.$$

On the other hand, for any $s \in S - M$

$$P(\underline{Q},s;0) = \sum_{g \in G_o \cup G_i} \pi_g q_g - \sum_{g \in G_o \cup G_i} k_g |q_g|.$$

It is then clear that $P(\underline{Q},m;0) \geqslant P(\underline{Q},s;0)$, the inequality being strict when $q_g \neq 0$ and $m = m_g$ for at least one good $g \subset G_o \cup G_i$.

Hence, if $\underline{Q} \neq 0$, we obtain:

$$\max_{m \in M} P(\underline{Q},m;0) > \max_{s \in S-M} P(\underline{Q},s;0). \tag{14.12}$$

Maximising both members of (14.12) with respect to $\underline{Q}$ as defined aboven, then yields:

$$\max_{m \in M} \tilde{P}(m;0) > \max_{s \in S-M} \tilde{P}(s;0) \tag{14.13}$$

where the inequality is strict by (14.11); and (14.13) guarantees that the optimal solution of $\gamma = 0$ is different from $\underline{Q} = 0$.

Now, for any s, the function $\tilde{P}(s;\gamma)$ is continuous in γ by the theorem of maximisation (Berge (1966), p. 122). Consequently, $\max_{m \in M} \tilde{P}(s;\gamma)$ and $\max_{v \in V-M} \tilde{P}(v;\gamma)$ are also continuous. In view of (14.13) and given that $\max_{s \in S-M} \tilde{P}(s;0) = \max_{v \in V-M} \tilde{P}(v;0)$, $\bar{\gamma} > 0$ may be found such that

$$\max_{m \in M} \tilde{P}(m;\gamma) > \max_{v \in V-M} \tilde{P}(v;\gamma) \tag{14.14}$$

for any $\gamma \in [0,\bar{\gamma}]$. The LHS of (14.14) is therefore positive. Proposition 2 ensures that $\max_{v \in V} \tilde{P}(v;\gamma) = \max_{s \in S} \tilde{P}(s;\gamma)$ for all values of γ. It therefore follows from (14.14) that

$$\max_{m \in M} \tilde{P}(m;\gamma) = \max_{s \in S} \tilde{P}(s;\gamma) = P^*(\gamma) > 0 \text{ for all } \gamma \in [0,\bar{\gamma}].$$

(b.) If $s^* \in V$, (a.) shows that $s^* \in M^*$. Otherwise s^* is an intermediate point of a basic route with vertices v_1 and v_2. An argument similar to that of Proposition 2 can be used to establish that $(\underline{Q}^*, v_1)$ and $(\underline{Q}^*, v_2)$ are equilibria too. It then follows from (a.) that $\{v_1, v_2\} \subseteq M^*$, a contradiction.

The second part of (b.) results immediately from (a.) and Proposition 2. That completes the proof.

2.2.4 *The median principle*

It would be interesting to have localisation theorems yielding sufficient conditions for a given site of V_e^*, or of M^*, to be an equilibrium location. Not surprisingly, one cannot derive general results. Nonetheless, in two particular but meaningful cases, it is possible to characterise very precisely the equilibrium location. To do this it is assumed that the unit transportation costs are linear in distance. This seems to contradict the argument developed in 2.3.3. For the sake of simplicity, however, we find it convenient to use linear functions each time that the shape of the transportation cost is not essential for the problem considered. The analysis of the attractiveness of particular network sites belongs to this category. In such cases, indeed, we try to describe simply but exhaustively the main characteristics intervening in the comparative analysis implied by the Hakimi theorem For a market place $m \in M^*$, it is reasonable to think that those characteristics are expressed by the quantity $|q_g^*|$ and the transportability, inversely measured by r_g, of the goods g transported from or to m. Hence, the magnitude

$$w_m^* = \sum_{\{g \in G_o \cup G_i;\, m_g^* = m\}} r_g \cdot |q_g^*| \tag{14.15}$$

can be viewed as a measure of the attractiveness of m. It is called the weight of the market place.

For any $s \in S$, the profit $P(\underline{Q}^*, s)$ then becomes:

$$P(\underline{Q}^*, s) = \sum_{g \in G_o \cup G_i} \pi_g^* q_g^* - \sum_{m \in M} w_m^* d(m,s)\,. \tag{14.16}$$

Let us assume that a vertex of the network exists around which the purchases and the sales of the firm are distributed. Formally, this property can be stated as follows:

Definition 10: Let $(\underline{Q}^*, s^*)$ be a spatial equilibrium of the firm. The vertex $\bar{v} \in V$ is said to be central for $\underline{Q}^*$ iff the following two conditions hold:

(i) $\bar{v}$ is a cutting-vertex of graph G;

$$\text{(ii)} \quad \sum_{m \in M^* \cap V_k} w_m^* \leqslant \sum_{m \in M^* - V_k} w_m^*, \quad \forall k = 1 \dots K \tag{14.17}$$

where $V_1 \dots V_k$ denote the sets of vertices belonging to the connected components of $X - \{\overline{v}\}$.

Proposition 4: Let $(\underline{Q}^*, s^*)$ be a spatial equilibrium of the firm. If $\overline{v} \in S$ is a central vertex for $\underline{Q}^*$, then $(\underline{Q}^*, \overline{v})$ is an equilibrium. Furthermore, if for $k = 1 \dots K$ the inequality is strict in (14.17), we have $s^* = \overline{v}$.

Proof: Assume that $s^* \in V_k U \{\overline{v}\}$. Since $\overline{v}$ is a cutting vertex of G, we have $d(m,s^*) = d(m,\overline{v}) + (d(\overline{v},s^*)$ for any $m \in M^* - V_k$. Hence we obtain:

$$T^*(\overline{v}) \leqslant \sum_{m \in M^* \cap V_k} w_m^* [d(m,s^*) + d(s^*,\overline{v})] + \sum_{m \in M^* - V_k} w_m^* [d(m,\overline{v}) + d(\overline{v},s^*)]$$

$$- \sum_{m \in M^* - V_k} w_m^* d(\overline{v},s^*)$$

$$\leqslant T(s^*) + [\sum_{m \in M^* \cap V_k} w_m^* - \sum_{m \in M^* - V_k} w_m^* \} d(\overline{v},s^*)$$

$$\leqslant T^*(s^*). \tag{14.18}$$

It then follows from (14.16) and (14.18) that

$$P(\underline{Q}^*,\overline{v}) = \sum_{g \in G_o U G_i} \pi_g^* q_g^* - T^*(\overline{v}) \geqslant \sum_{g \in G_o U G_i} \pi_g^* q_g^* - T^*(s^*) = P^*,$$

in which the equality holds when $\sum_{m \in M^* \cap V_k} w_m^* = \sum_{m \in M^* - V_k} w_m^*$ or when $s^* = \overline{v}$.

That completes the proof.

In the case when G is a tree –which amounts to saying that there is a single route between any pair of network sites– every vertex which is not a tip is a cutting-vertex. Moreover, condition (14.17) means that $\overline{v}$ is the median of the w_m^*-distribution. Reinterpreting Proposition 4, we then obtain the median principle:

Proposition 5: Let $(\underline{Q}^*, s^*)$ be a spatial equilibrium of the firm. If the graph G is a tree, then s^* is a median of the w_m^*-distribution.[22]

2.2.5 The majority theorem

Intuitively, we expect a market place to be an equilibrium location when its weight is higher than the weight of the other market places.

Definition 11: Let $(\underline{Q}^*, s^*)$ be a spation equilibrium of the fim. We say that $\bar{m} \in M^*$ is a dominant market place for $\underline{Q}^*$ if and only if

$$w^*_{\bar{m}} \geqslant \sum_{\substack{m \in M^* \\ m \neq \bar{m}}} w^*_m . \tag{14.19}$$

Proposition 6: Let $(\underline{Q}^*, s^*)$ be a spatial equilibrium of the firm. If $\bar{m} \in M^*$ is a dominant market place for $\underline{Q}^*$ then $(\underline{Q}^*, \bar{m})$ is an equilibrium. Furthermore, if the inequality in (14.19) is strict we have $s^* = \bar{m}$.[23]

Proof: We have:

$$\begin{aligned} T^*(\bar{m}) &\leqslant \sum_{\substack{m \in \underline{M}^* \\ m \neq \bar{m}}} w^*_m [d(m,s^*) + d(s^*,\bar{m})] \\ &\leqslant T^*(s^*) + [\sum_{m \in M^*} w^*_m - 2 w^*_{\bar{m}}]\, d(s^*,\bar{m}) \\ &\leqslant T^*(s^*) . \end{aligned} \tag{14.20}$$

Consequently, given (14.16) and (14.20), we get:

$$P(\underline{Q}^*, \bar{m}) = \sum_{g \in G_o U G_i} \pi^*_g q^*_g - T^*(\bar{m}) \geqslant \sum_{g \in G_o U G_i} \pi^*_g q^*_g - T^*(s^*) = P^*,$$

where the equality holds provided that $w^*_{\bar{m}} = \sum_{\substack{m \in M^* \\ m \neq \bar{m}}} w^*_m$ or $s^* = \bar{m}$. That completes the proof.

2.2.6 The reduction process

The following flow-chart diagram expresses the reduction process in a nutshell; the set of candidate sites associated with each stage of the process is indicated inside the corresponding box.

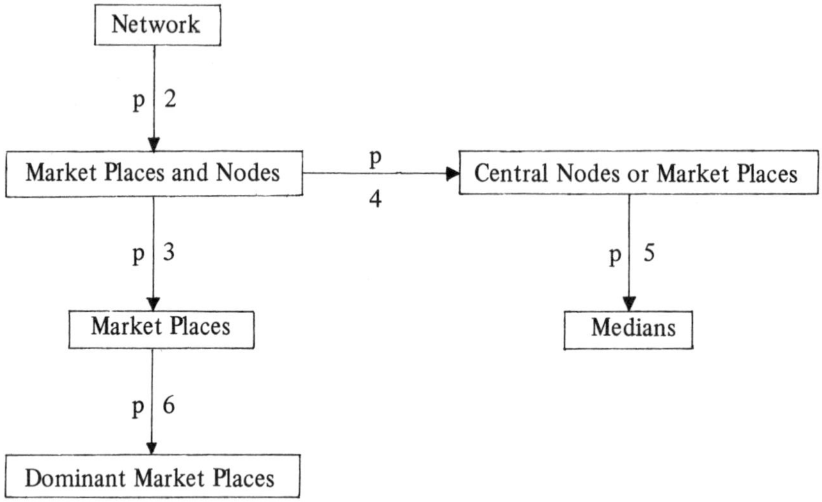

2.3 Implications and extensions

The reduction process has several interesting implications for both spatial economics and regional industrial development planning. In the following, we briefly discuss some of them.

2.3.1 The 'discontinuity' of the locational decision

We have seen that the set of candidate sites, initially given by a continuous set, ends up in a finite subset of the network. In other words, the LPP has been shown to be a continuous problem with corner solutions. This is relatively rare in economics where interior solutions are very often encountered. Not surprisingly, the corner solutions result from the concavity of the transportation cost function.

The corner solution property, which looks more formal than intuitive, expresses in theoretical language the frequent empirical observation that location decisions are in fact discontinuous in nature. In reality, as in theory, we do not observe marginal adjustments in locations but rather a long run spatial inertia possibly followed by relocations in distant places. Stated differently, relocations do not occur in the small but in the large.

In the same manner, we notice that changes in the economic environment of the firm may not affect the optimality of the site previously chosen. The inertia observed in existing locations results from the combination of the low mobility of the installations with the finiteness of the location problem.

2.3.2 *The spatial hierarchy*

A hierarchical process of space is associated with the reduction process. From network sites, we are led first to the (efficient) vertices, that is the nodes and the market places; and afterwards to the market places alone, the nodes in turn being eliminated. Among nodes and market places, a site endowed with a high degree of centrality in the network has some chance to be chosen by the firm. This is particularly true when that site is also an outlet or an input source of the firm. Such a hierarchy corresponds, roughly speaking, to that suggested by armchair observations.

The reduction process also sheds some light on the problem of spatial agglomeration. Most probably, indeed, other production activities are already set up at several candidate sites of V_e^*. This, together with the inertia of existing locations, suggests that firms cluster in a few places as they enter into business. Of course, this is no more than an indication and sound analysis is still required. Again, however, this location theory appears to correspond to experience.

2.3.3 *The multi-factor approach*

The model considered here integrates most of the location factors discussed in old treatises of economic geography. The main factors are: existence of transport infrastructures, of heavy raw materials, of qualified or cheap manpower; geographical concentration of customers in a small area; proximity of a region offering a vast range of services. Unlike the traditional approach in economic geography, we do not resort here to a single factor analysis to explain actual locations. Of course, single factor analyses remain relevant in the present model as far as they correspond to cases –probably rarer than one would imagine– where one location factor dominates the others. For the rest, we have to turn to a multi-factor approach which explains the locational decisions through the combination of several factors. In principle the combination changes with the firm and spatial econometrics allows us to estimate it. To illustrate, the reader could easily construct some of the possible combinations corresponding to the different stages of the reduction process.

2.3.4 *The comparative advantage method*

The finiteness property has interesting implications as to the choice of a location by the firm. There is no need to use sophisticated methods for determining the equilibrium location. (Note that this is no longer true in the case of the multiplant firm; see section 3). It suffices to make a *pairwise comparison* of the candidate sites and to choose the most advantageous one.[24] For that, we have to define precisely the set of locations to be investigated. The set V_e^* is not known a priori because M^* is not known. Consequently, the search for the equilibrium location must be carried out inside a larger set, namely the set V^* formed by the vertices efficient with respect to the set M of market places. As $V^* \subseteq V$, V^* is obviously finite.

2.3.5 *On the spatial strategy of industrial development planning*

The majority theorem brings to light, at least from the point of view of theory, the difficulty of creating a growth pole at a given site by establishing an attractor firm there. According to this proposition, a sufficient condition for a newly established firm to attract independent upstream and downstream production units, is that this firm should constitute a dominant market for some of its suppliers and buyers. Obviously, such a condition is very restrictive. Thus it is not surprising that, in the real world, the linkage effects generated even by a large firm often reveal themselves insufficient to promote the local development, and that several experiences of planned development have led to the setting up of 'cathédrales dans le désert'. Needless to say, this interpretation is only indicative and must be completed by more general analyses.

We conclude this section by the discussion of some extensions of the LPP.

2.3.6 *The impact of a multi-modal system*

When there are several transport modes, the unit transportation cost of good $g \in G_0 U G_i$ between two places is no longer a function of the distance between them. It can be worthwhile for the firm to lengthen some hauls in order to benefit from the lower tariffs attached to certain modes. Obviously, the route followed depends on the relative position of the destimations with respect to the different networks. As a result the unit transportation cost of good $g \in G_0 U G_i$ is a piecewise function, one piece per mode effectively used. In addition, it turns out necessary to introduce a new set of points, the *junction points,* corresponding to connections between networks. If the unit transportation costs are concave in distance within each network, it is possible to show, using Theorem 3 of Louveaux et al. (1982), that an equilibrium location belongs to the set of junction points, market places and nodes of the different networks. This result generalises Proposition 2. Furthermore, if the unit transportation costs belong to class LT for every mode, nodes which are not market places or junction points may be disregarded for small values of γ. Such a property therefore extends Proposition 3. Unfortunately, we cannot take the reduction process further and eliminate the junction points because they are the points where the structure of transportation costs changes.

Finally, notice that the above results also hold in the case of a transportation network divided into different tariff zones. Indeed, the breaking points play a role similar to that of the junction points.

2.3.7 *The vertical division of production*

Assume that the firm has several plants organised on the pattern of vertical division.[25] In this case, the equilibrium location of plant i depends directly on the location of the downstream and upstream plants $i-1$ and $i+1$ appearing in the production process. Here the locational interdependence among plants takes the shape of a *chain-effect.* If unit transportation costs of intermediate goods are concave in distance, it can be shown, using an inductive argument about locations (see also Theorem 2 of Wendell and Hurter (1973)) and Proposition 2, that an equilibrium configuration exists such that all plants located at efficient network vertices. Clearly, this is another generalisation of Proposition 2. Interestingly, the a priori possible separation of some production stages is not necessarily observed at the equilibrium. Two or several potential plants can be grouped togethe at the same place. Such will be the case, for example, if links between some plants dominate other links. Furthermore, if unit transportation costs of intermediate goods are of class LT then, for small values of parameter γ, at least one equilibrium configureation of plants is included in the set of market places.

2.3.8 The impact of locational constraints

Until now it has been assumed that V_e^* is included in S. One may wonder whether introducing locational constraints would lead to a refutation of the finiteness property. This answer is as follows. In order for S to be closed –which is very convenient when constraints are binding– we suppose that no point of some open subset of X containing points of V_e^* is a possible location. For each vertex $\hat{v} \in V_e^* - S$, we consider the points of S visible from $\hat{v}$; that is the possible locations $\hat{s} \in S$ for which there exists a route between $\hat{v}$ ($\neq \hat{s}$) and $\hat{s}$ included in X–S. Intuitively, the locations visible from $\hat{v}$ are the first ones encountered from $\hat{v}$. It is then easy to see that the proof of Proposition 2 can be repeated provided that the efficient vertices not belonging to S should be replaced by the efficient locations visible from them. Thus locational constraints do not affect the finite nature of the LPP, even when they lead to an increase in the number of candidate sites. They do not affect either the interpretation given to the candidate sites. Indeed, the nodes or the market places which are not possible locations are to be replaced by 'neighbouring' locations. The same holds for Proposition 3 when transportation cost functions are of class LT. Finally, Propositions 4 and 6 can be extended in the following way: the equilibrium location is visible from the central vertex (the dominant market place) when all its adjacent vertices belong to S.

2.3.9 A remark about general equilibrium in space

Let us finally discuss the validity of the reduction process for the whole set of firms in the economy, which are not transportation firms. For reasons obvious to the reader familiar with general equilibrium analysis, it is supposed that the technologies of transportation firms have constant returns. This implies that unit transportation cost functions are linear in distance and quantities. We also assume, at least for the moment, that an equilibrium price system exists at the market places. Applying Proposition 2 to each firm separately shows that firms which are not transportation firms are all established at network vertices. Consequently, the location index à la Arrow-Debreu can only vary through V, so that the dimension of the commodity space is finite. For a given configuration of consumers, the equilibrium existence theorem can then be used to obtain the equilibrium price system.[26] Given the foregoing, the resulting equilibrium locations belong to the set of vertices.

3. THE EQUILIBRIUM OF THE FIRM IN SPATIAL MONOPOLY

We deal here with the location and price monopoly of a firm which is a monopolist inside a given territory. The model is discussed in 3.1; several hypotheses made in 2.1 are maintained. In 3.2 and 3.3 respectively, we study the equilibrium location of a single-plant and multi-plant firm. Finally, some extensions of the model are considered in 3.4.

3.1 The problem of the spatial monopolist

3.1.1 The production cost of the firm

The network and distance are described by Definitions 1 and 2. Concerning the possible locations (Definition 3), we keep the assumption $V \subseteq S \subseteq X$. Purely for notational convenience, we suppose that the firm produces a *single* output denoted by g_o; i.e. $G_o = \{g_o\}$. The quantity of output, the set of its market places and its unit transportation cost are denoted respectively by q_o, M_o and $t_o[d(m,s)]$.

It is also assumed, at least for subsection 3.2, that the firm has a single plant. The corresponding production function (Definition 3) is as follows:

Definition 12: The quantity of input $g \in G_i$ required to produce the quantity q_o of the output is given by[27]

$$q_g = a_g\, q_o + b_g \tag{14.21}$$

where a_g and b_g are non-negative constants such that $(a_g, b_g) \neq (0,0)$.

At first glance, the assumption of a unique production technique seems to be very restrictive. Yet it entails no substantial loss of generality. Indeed, when the firm faces a set of different techniques of that type, the properties obtained below hold for the equilibrium technique chosen by the firm. The only restriction needed for Proposition 9 is that the coefficients a_g and b_g should be constant.[28]

Definition 5 is kept as regards the inputs, while Definition 6 is maintained.

From the foregoing, it then follows that the production cost of quantity q_o, the firm being established at $s \in S$, is given by:

$$C(q_o,s) = \sum_{g \in G_i} \left\{(a_g q_o + b_g) \,.\, \min_{m \in M_g} [\pi_{gm} + t_g[d(m,s)]\,]\right\} \tag{14.22}$$

where it has been supposed that the firm buys every input at the lowest firm-price (in the sense of Definition 7). This expression can be simplified into:

$$C(q_o,s) = \alpha(s) \,.\, q_o + \beta(s) \tag{14.23}$$

where

$$\alpha(s) = \sum_{g \in G_i} \left\{a_g \,.\, \min_{m \in M_g} [\pi_{gm} + t_g[d(m,s)]\,]\right\} \tag{14.24}$$

and

$$\beta(s) = \sum_{g \in G_i} \left\{b_g \,.\, \min_{m \in M_g} [\pi_{gm} + t_g[d(m,s)]\,]\right\} \tag{14.25}$$

In (14.23) the marginal cost of production, represented by $\alpha(s)$, depends only upon the location chosen by the firm. The same holds for the fixed cost of production $\beta(s)$. From the concavity of $t_g[d(m,h_i(\theta))]$, we deduce that $\alpha[h_i(\theta)]$ and $\beta[h_i(\theta)]$ are concave with respect to θ for any basic route.

3.1.2 The price policy of the firm

Within a given territory the firm is confronted with a system of demand functions, one function per market place. As a result, the firm is able to choose a price policy maximising its profit. Because of space, different types of policy can be implemented. In the following, we will limit ourselves to the most common industrial practice.[29] For that, we have to distinguish between two kinds of price. The delivered price is the price actually paid by the customer at the market place. It includes the unit transportation cost. The mill price is the price charged at the firm's door. It does not include the unit transportation cost.[30] The price policies studied in this section are the following: (i) discriminatory pricing, (ii) uniform delivered pricing, and (iii) uniform mill pricing. As usual, the first policy supposes that the firm charges a price π_m maximising the profit obtained at each market place $m \in M_o$, independently of the prices set elsewhere.[31] The mill price associated with m, defined by $p_m(s) = \pi_m - t_o[d(m,s)]$, changes with the market place. In the second policy, the firm charges the same delivered price π at all market places. As the costs of transporting the output are paid by the firm, the mill price corresponding to $m \in M_o$, defined by $p_m(s) = \pi - t_o[d(m,s)]$, decrease with distance: there is freight absorption. Finally, in the last policy, the firm sets a mill price p which is the same for everybody. The transportation cost is passed on to the customers, and the delivered price at $m \in M_o$, defined by $\pi_m(s) = p + t_o[d(m,s)]$, increases with distance.

The system of demand functions is described next:

Definition 13: The demand of good g_o at market place $m \in M_o$ is given by a non-negative, non-increasing and continuous function $D_m[\pi_m(s)]$ of the delivered price at m; moreover $\lim_{\pi_m(s) \to +\infty} D_m[\pi_m(s)] = 0$.

3.1.3 The problem of the spatial monopolist

Let q_m denote the quantity of output sold on market place $m \in M_o$.

Definition 14: The problem of the spatial monopolist (PSM) is given by the non-linear program

$$\underset{\underline{\pi},\underline{p},\underline{q},s}{\text{maximise}}\ P(\underline{\pi},\underline{p},\underline{q},s) = \sum_{m \in M_o} p_m q_m - C\Big(\sum_{m \in M_o} q_m, s\Big) \tag{14.26}$$

s.t.

$$\pi_m = p_m + t_o[d(m,s)], \quad \forall\, m \in M_o$$

$$0 \leqslant q_m \leqslant D_m(\pi_m), \quad \forall\, m \in M_o, \quad \text{and } s \in S.$$

There are extra constraints $\pi_m = \pi_{m'}$ $(p_m = p_{m'})$ for any pair $\{m,m'\}$ of market places in the case of uniform delivered (mill) pricing.

A solution to the PSM is called a spatial equilibrium of the monopolist. The following comments are in order:

(i) Introducing the variables q_m into the PSM is justified by the fact that it may not be profitable to the firm to supply a market place with a positive demand. Indeed, given (14.23), P can be rewritten as follows:

$$P = \sum_{m \in M_o} [p_m - \alpha(s)]\, q_m - \beta(s). \qquad (14.27)$$

Accordingly, as soon as $p_m < \alpha(s)$, i.e. the mill price corresponding to $m \in M_o$ is less than the marginal cost of production, $q_m = 0$ and market place m is not supplied. On the other hand, if $p_m \geqslant \alpha(s)$, i.e. the mill price is larger than or equal to the marginal cost of production, then $q_m = D_m(\pi_m)$ and the demand at m is met. Setting

$$B_m(\pi_m, p_m, s) = \max\left\{0, p_m - \alpha(s)\right\} D_m(\pi_m),$$

we see that the PSM can be reformulated as follows:

$$\underset{\underline{\pi}, \underline{p}, s}{\text{maximise}} \; P(\underline{\pi}, \underline{p}, s) = \sum_{m \in M_o} B_m(\pi_m, p_m, s) - \beta(s) \qquad (14.28)$$

s.t.

$$\pi_m = p_m + t_o[d(m,s)], \quad \forall\, m \in M_o, \quad \text{and } s \in S.$$

(ii) Both uniform delivered and mill price policies imply a decrease in the equilibrium profit of the firm when compared with the discriminatory price policy. This results immediately from the addition of further constraints to the PSM. Nevertheless, they have the advantage to be applicable to a larger range of situations since they do not require the market places to be clustered.

(iii) In the PSM, unlike the LPP, it is often profitable to the firm to sell its output on several market places. In the discriminatory pricing case, those places, as well as the corresponding delivered prices, are selected by equating marginal revenue to the marginal cost of production plus transport. When the firm follows a uniform delivered price policy, it supplies those market places whose equilibrium price (net of the corresponding marginal cost of transportation) is not smaller than the marginal cost of production. Finally, in the uniform mill pricing case, the firm supplies those market places with a positive demand at the equilibrium price plus transportation costs.

3.2 The location of the single-plant firm

In the following, we give localisation theorems correponding to the three price policies considered in 3.1.2.

3.2.1 *The delivered price case*

We first examine the case of discriminatory pricing. This means that $B_m(\pi_m, p_m, s)$ is to be replaced by $B_m(\pi_m, s) = \max\{0, \pi_m - t_o[d(m,s)] - \alpha(s)\} D_m(\pi_m)$. Hence the profit of the spatial monopolist can be written as

$$P(\underline{\pi}, s) = \sum_{m \in M_o} B_m(\pi_m, s) - \beta(s). \tag{14.29}$$

For every basic route $h_i([0,1])$, it is clear that $B_m[\pi_m, h_i(\theta)]$ and consequently $P[\underline{\pi}, h_i(\theta)]$ are convex functions of θ. Using an argument similar to that of Proposition 2 we obtain:

Proposition 7: Assume that the monopolist chooses a discriminatory price policy. Then there exists a spatial equilibrium $(\underline{\pi}^*, s^*)$ of the monopolist which satisfies $s^* \in V_e^*$. Furthermore, if condition (a) of Proposition 2 holds any equilibrium is such that $s^* \in V_e^*$.

We know that uniform delivered pricing is a particular case of discriminatory pricing in which π_m is replaced by π. From the above proposition, it then follows:

Proposition 8: Assume that the monopolist chooses a uniform delivered price policy. Then there exists a spatial equilibrium (π^*, s^*) of the monopolist for which $s^* \in V_e^*$. Furthermore, if condition (a) of Proposition 2 holds, $s^* \in V_e^*$ for any equilibrium.

In the case of a (discriminatory or uniform) delivered price policy, the quantities demanded on the different market places are independent of the location chosen by the firm; they depend only upon the price set there. Accordingly, as in the LPP, we can separate profits into two functions representing, on the one hand, the gross profit and, on the other, the transportation costs. The reduction process appraoch of section 2 therefore applies to the spatial monopolist implementing delivered prices. For that reason, Proposition 7 and 8 can be viewed as the counterpart of Proposition 2. In a similar manner, it would be possible to state results equivalent to Propositions 3, 4, 5 and 6.[32]

Finally, notice that the finiteness property contained in Propositions 7 and 8 holds for *any* given system of delivered prices. Furthermore, it can be shown that Proposition 7 remains valid when the assumption of clustered markets is relaxed, to include the possibility of resale among customers.

3.2.3 *The mill price case*

We now assume that the spatial monopolist follows a uniform price policy. In this case, $B_m(\pi_m, p_m, s)$ is expressed as $B_m(p, s) = \max\{0, p - \alpha(s)\} . D_m\ [p + t_o[d(m,s)]]$

while the profit becomes

$$P(p,s) = \sum_{m \in M_o} B_m(p,s) - \beta(s)\,. \tag{14.30}$$

Unlike the above case, functions $B_m(p,s)$ and $P(p,s)$ are generally not convex with respect to θ along basic routes. At a fixed mill price the quantities demanded change with the firm location, so that it is no longer possible to isolate variable s within one transportation cost function. As a consequence, we cannot expect to establish as general localisation theorems for the uniform mill pricing case as those for the other cases. To make a Hakimi-like claim, we need additional assumptions on the demand functions.

For the next property, we suppose that the equilibrium profit of the monopolist is positive.

Proposition 9: Assume that the monopolist chooses a uniform mill price policy and that the demand functions are convex. Then there exists a spatial equilibrium (p^*,s^*) for the monopolist, such that $s^* \in V_e^*$. Furthermore, if condition (a) of Proposition 2 is satisfied, $s^* \in V_e^*$ for any equilibrium.

Proof: Let (p^*,s^*) be an equilibrium. For the proof, the following intermediate results are established: (i) s^* is efficient with respect to M^*; (ii) there exists an equilibrium (p^{**},s^{**}) such that $s^{**} \in V$; (iii) if condition (a) of Proposition 2 holds, then $s^* \in V$.

(i) Assume that s^* is not efficient with respect to M^*. Then $\bar{s} \in S$ would exist such that, where M_o^* denotes the set of market places supplied from the firm located at s^*,

$$\alpha(\bar{s}) \leqslant \alpha(s^*)$$

$$\beta(\bar{s}) \leqslant \beta(s^*)$$

$$D_m[p^* + t_o[d(m,\bar{s})]] \geqslant D_m[p^* + t_o[d(m,s^*)]], \quad \forall\, m \in M_o^*$$

where at least one of the inequalities is strict. (Notice that the convexity of functions D_m together with Definition 13 implies that those functions are decreasing on their support). Given that $P^* > 0$ we have $p^* - \alpha(s^*) > 0$. Hence we obtain:

$$\begin{aligned} P^* &= [p^* - \alpha(s^*)] \sum_{m \in M_o^*} D_m[p^* + t[d(m,s^*)]] - \beta(s^*) \\ &< [p^* - \alpha(\bar{s})] \sum_{m \in M_o^*} D_m[p^* + t[d(m,\bar{s})]] - \beta(\bar{s}) < P(p^*, \bar{s}), \end{aligned}$$

which is a contradiction.

(ii) Given Definition 13 and the convexity of function D_m, there exists for every $\pi'_m \geqslant 0$ a supporting line with a slope $-a_m(\pi'_m) \leqslant 0$ and a non-negative intercept $b_m(\pi'_m)$ such that

$$D_m(\pi_m) \geqslant a_m(\pi'_m)[b_m(\pi'_m) - \pi_m] \quad \text{for} \quad \forall \pi_m \geqslant 0$$

and

$$D_m(\pi'_m) = a_m(\pi'_m) \cdot [b_m(\pi'_m) - \pi'_m].$$

Therefore

$$D_m(\pi_m) = \left\{\max\ a_m(\pi'_m) \cdot [b_m(\pi'_m) - \pi_m]\,;\quad \pi'_m \geqslant 0\right\}. \tag{14.31}$$

It then follows from (14.30) and (14.31) and the positiveness of the equilibrium delivered prices that

$$P^* = \max\left\{\overline{P}(\underline{\pi}', p, s);\ \underline{\pi}' \geqslant 0,\quad p > 0 \ \text{ and } \ s \in S\right\}$$

where

$$\overline{P}(\underline{\pi}', p, s) = \max\left\{0, p - \alpha(s)\right\} \cdot \sum_{m \in M_o} \left\{a_m(\pi'_m) \cdot [b_m(\pi'_m) - p - t_o[d(m,s)]]\right\} - \beta(s).$$

Set $a(\underline{\pi}') = \sum_{m \in M_o} a_m(\pi'_m)$.

If, for at least one $m \in M_o$ we have $a_m(\pi'_m) > 0$, then $a(\underline{\pi}') > 0$ and we set

$$b(\underline{\pi}', s) = \sum_{m \in M_o} \left\{a_m(\pi'_m) \cdot [b_m(\pi'_m) - t_o[d(m,s)]]\right\} / a(\underline{\pi}').$$

If not, $a_m(\pi'_m) = 0$ for all $m \in M_o$ and $b(\underline{\pi}', s)$ is given any arbitrary value. In both cases, $\overline{P}(\underline{\pi}' p, s)$ becomes

$$\overline{P}(\underline{\pi}', p, s) = a(\underline{\pi}') \max\left\{0, p - \alpha(s)\right\} \cdot [b(\underline{\pi}', s) - p] - \beta(s).$$

This expression being quadratic in p for $p \geqslant \alpha(s)$, it is easy to see that:

$$\overline{P}(\underline{\pi}', s) = \max\left\{\overline{P}(\underline{\pi}', p, s)\,;\ p \geqslant 0\right\}$$

$$= \tfrac{1}{4}\, a(\underline{\pi}') \cdot [\max\left\{0, b(\underline{\pi}', a) - \alpha(s)\right\}]^2 - \beta(s). \tag{14.32}$$

Given $\underline{\pi}'$, $\overline{P}[\underline{\pi}', h_i(\theta)]$ is convex with respect to θ on any basic route $h_i([0,1])$ so that $\overline{P}(\underline{\pi}',s)$ has a maximiser in V. Hence, $\overline{P}(\underline{\pi}',s)$ is maximised at some $(\underline{\pi}'^*,s^*)$ with $s^* \in V$; of course $\overline{P}(\underline{\pi}'^*,s^*) = P^*$. Considering now the value p^* for which $\overline{P}(\underline{\pi}'^*,s^*) = \overline{P}(\underline{\pi}'^*,p^*,s^*)$, it is straightforward that $P(p^*,s^*) = P^*$ with $s^* \in V$.

(iii) Assume that $s^* \notin V$. Then some basic route $h_i([0,1)]$ and $\theta^* \in]0,1[$ may be found such that $s^* = h_i(\theta^*)$. Since $P^* > 0$, (14.32) implies that $a(\underline{\pi}'^*) > 0$ and

$$b(\underline{\pi}'^*,s) - \alpha(s) > 0 \tag{14.33}$$

for $s = s^*$.

As (14.33) is continuous with respect to s, the strict inequality holds in a neighbourhood of s^*. In other words, $\epsilon > 0$ exists for which $0 \leqslant \theta^* - \epsilon < \theta^* + \epsilon \leqslant 1$ and (14.31) is satisfied for $s \in h_i([\theta^* - \epsilon, \theta^* + \epsilon])$. Now condition (a) of Proposition 2 implies that at least one of the functions $-\alpha[h_i(\theta)]$, $-\beta[h_i(\theta)]$, and $b[\underline{\pi}^*, h_i(\theta)]$ is strictly convex on $[\theta^* - \epsilon, \theta^* + \epsilon]$. Therefore $\overline{P}[\underline{\pi}'^*, h_i(\theta)]$ must be strictly convex. Consequently,

$$P^* = \overline{P}(\underline{\pi}'^*, s^*) < \max\left\{\overline{P}[\underline{\pi}'^*, h_i(\theta^* - \epsilon)],\ \overline{P}[\underline{\pi}'^*, h_i(\theta^* + \epsilon)]\right\},$$

which contradicts the fact that $P^* = \max\left\{\overline{P}(\underline{\pi}',s);\ \underline{\pi}' \geqslant \underline{0} \text{ and } s \in S\right\}$. That completes the proof.

The convexity of the demand functions seems to be essential for the finiteness property to hold in the proof above. This is confirmed by the following example in which demand functions are not convex and in which the unique equilibrium location is an intermediate point of the network.

Example 1: The network is described by the segment $[0,1]$; the output can be sold on two market places located respectively at $\theta = 0$ and $\theta = 1$; the demand function is the same and given by $\max\{0, c-\pi^2\}$ where c is a positive constant sufficiently large for the two market places to be supplied at the equilibrium; the unit transportation cost of the output is equal to d(m,s); and, finally, there is no production cost. Given that the demands are positive at the equilibrium, the location must belong to the interval $[\max\{0,p+1-\sqrt{c}\}, \min\{1,\sqrt{c}-p\}]$ and the profit function can be written as $P(p,\theta) = p.[2c-(p+\theta)^2 - (p+1-\theta)^2]$. It is then easy to see that $\theta = ½$ is the only solution to $\partial P/\partial\theta = 0$.

In addition, even when the assumptions of Proposition 9 hold, we can construct examples to show that the profit-maximising location may not belong to V when the mill price is not set at the equilibrium level.

It should now be clear to the reader that the choice of a price policy by the firm has substantial implications for the spatial organisation of production.[33] Compared with delivered pricing, mill pricing would therefore favour a larger geographical decentralisation of locational decisions since it may lead the firm to establish at an intermediate point of the network.[34]

Let us now consider the solution methods. The solution to the PSM with discriminatory pricing can be obtained as follows. For each location $s \in V_e$ and market place $m \in M_o$, we compute the price $\pi^*_m(s)$ maximising $\{\pi_m - \alpha(s) - t_o[d(m,s)]\} \cdot D_m(\pi_m)$. We then evaluate functions $B_m[\pi^*_m(s),s]$ and add them to get $P(\underline{\pi}^*, s)$. The equilibrium location is found by comparing the values of this function at the locations in V_e. We can similarly proceed in the case of uniform delivered pricing given the caveat that $\pi^*(s)$ maximises $\sum_{m \in M_o} \{\pi - \alpha(s) - t_o[d(m,s)]\} \cdot D_m(\pi)$. Finally, a general solution method of the PSM with uniform mill pricing does not exist yet. Using a branch-and-bound method seems to be reasonable. Nevertheless, the above method can be implemented in the case of convex demands.

3.3 The location of the multiplant firm

3.3.1 The multiplant policy of the spatial monopolist

It is advantageous to the spatial monopolist, *ceteris paribus,* to be established near the output markets whatever the price policy. Transportation costs are reduced in the case of delivered prices, and sales are increased in the case of mill prices. Customers being dispersed over space, it becomes profitable to the firm to open several plants on the pattern of the horizontal division of production. Such a tendency is offset by the existence of indivisibilities in production; the more plants we have, the higher the overhead costs. The number of plants to set up is therefore the outcome of a trade-off between transportation costs and overhead costs.[35] Not surprisingly, this trade-off will be solved differently depending upon the price policy implemented by the spatial monopolist.[36]

Because of the (possible) existence of several plants a new set of variables, the allocation variables, is needed. The role of these variables is to answer the question 'who supplies who?' and, therefore, to permit the determination of the market areas. We have to specify the agent who chooses, out of a configuration $I \subseteq S$, the plant which provides a given market place. In the case of delivered pricing, it seems natural to admit that this choice is made by the monopolist. The allocation rule is then the following: the plant with the lowest marginal production and transportation cost is chosen, that is $\min_{s\in I} \{\alpha(s) + t_o[d(m,s)]\}$. But in the case of mill pricing, it is reasonable to suppose that the customers select the plant they want to buy from. Clearly, they will choose the plant with the lowest possible delivered price, i.e. $\min_{s\in I}\{p + t_o[d(m,s)]\}$, which amounts to the nearest plant.

The multiplant spatial monopolist problem (MSMP) can be formulated as follows:

$$\underset{\underline{\pi},\, I}{\text{maximise}}\ P(\underline{\pi}, I) = \sum_{m\in M_o} \max_{s\in I} B_m(\pi_m, s) - \sum_{s\in I} \beta(s) \tag{14.34}$$

s.t.

$$I \subseteq S,$$

when the firm adopts a discriminatory price policy (we replace $\underline{\pi}$ and π_m by π if the delivered price is uniform).

The customers located at m can be equally distant from several plants in configuration I. To deal with this possibility, we set $S_m(I) = \{s\in I;\ d(m,s) = \min_{s'\in I} d(m,s')\}$.

When the firm adopts a uniform mill price policy, the MSMP becomes

$$\underset{p,\, I}{\text{maximise}}\ P(p, I) = \sum_{m\in M_o} \max_{s\in S_m(I)} B_m(p,s) - \sum_{s\in I} \beta(s) \tag{14.35}$$

s.t.

$$I \subseteq S.$$ [37]

3.3.2 The delivered price case

Let us consider the MSMP given by program (14.34). It is easy to see that the variables specific to each plant depend upon each other only through the allocation variables. When these are specified, each plant can determine its price and location policy independently from others. (Note that, when the delivered price is uniform, the price variable must be specified at the same time as the allocation variables. In that case, the locations only can be decentralised to the plants). This implies that, within any equilibrium of the spatial monopolist, each plant maximises its own profit conditionally upon the market area devoted to it in the equilibrium considered. Accordingly, Propositions 7 and 3 can be used to obtain an equilibrium configuration I^* such that $I^* \subseteq \bigcup_{s\in I^*} V_e^*(s)$; $V_e^*(s)$ denoting the set of efficient vertices for the plant at $s \in I$. For analogous reasons the other localisation theorems established in section 2 are applicable to each plant considered separately. In consequence, the whole reduction process described in 2.2.5 remains true for a multiplant firm following a (discriminatory or uniform) delivered price policy.

The above leads to a substantial simplification in the search for a solution to (14.34). Indeed, it allows us to replace S by V_e in (14.34) so that a profit-maximising configuration may be obtained by solving a finite problem. But the enumerative method becomes intractable as soon as the problem becomes large, so we have to resort to 0–1 programming techniques. In the present case, there is no need to design a completely new algorithm. It is possible to use a property of (14.34), and to fall back on an already solved problem. More specifically, when the delivered prices are fixed, the program reduces to the well known simple plant location problem (SPLP), for which there exists a particularly efficient solution method.[38] The approach then consists in linking the search for the equilibrium prices to one or several resolutions of the corresponding SPLP. The method is described in detail in Hansen and Thisse (1977) for the discriminatory pricing case. For a treatment of the uniform delivered pricing case, the reader is referred to Hansen, Thisse and Hanjoul (1981). In both cases, it appears therefore that the solution of the MSMP with delivered prices is known.

3.3.3 The mill price case

In the program (14.35), the separability mentioned above ceases to hold. Indeed, as customers patronise the nearest plant, the relocation of a plant closer to a customer served previously by another plant affects the market area of both of them. In other words, the market area of a given plant is determined at the same time as the whole configuration of locations. Accordingly, it is not possible to deal with the location of each plant separately and to use Proposition 9. Unfortunately, that proposition cannot be generalised to the multiplant firm, as the following counter-example shows.

Example 2: The network is given by the segment $[0,1]$; the output can be sold in two market places located respectively at $\theta = 0$ and $\theta = 0.5$; their demand functions are identical and given by max $\{0.3-\pi\}$; the unit transportation costs, while the marginal production cost reduces to the transportation cost of the output is equal to 2.2 d(m,s); finally, there are no fixed costs, while the marginal production cost reduces to the transportation cost of a single input from $\theta = 1$ and is given by $2d(1,\theta)$. Clearly, the firm will never open more than two plants. Consequently, we can limit ourselves to consider the case of two plants given that the case of a single plant obtains as a particular case with two identical locations. Denote the locations of the two plants by θ_1 and θ_2. If Proposition 9 holds in the present model, then a profit-maximising configuration must be included in $V = \{0, 0.5, 1\}$. Some simple calculations show that the best solution in $\underline{V}$ is given by $\{0, \underline{0.5}\}$ with a profit equal to 1.125. Considering now the locations $\overline{\theta}_1 = 0.216$ and $\overline{\theta}_2 = 0.5$, we can see that the profit at $(\overline{\theta}_1, \overline{\theta}_2)$ is 1.127. Accordingly, the profit at $(\overline{\theta}_1, \overline{\theta}_2)$ is higher than the profit yielded by any configuration in V.

In conclusion, it appears that the reduction process fails to hold in the case of the MSMP with uniform mill pricing.

3.4 Extensions

3.4.1 The problem of the public spatial monopolist

We briefly discuss here some properties of the PSM in the case of a public enterprise. The production costs are as in Definition 12. The inverse demand functions are continuous and non-increasing, and they are denoted by $\pi_m(q_m)$ where q_m is the quantity of output sold on $m \in M_o$. The objective of the firm is to maximise the net social benefit by

$$A(\underline{q}, s) = \sum_{m \in M_o} \left\{ \int_o^{q_m} \pi_m(y)\,dy - [\alpha(s) + t_o[d(m,s)]]\, q_m \right\} - \beta(s) \quad (14.36)$$

For any given $s \in S$, it is easy to see that the optimal delivered price at $m \in M_o$ is equal to the marginal cost of production plus the marginal cost of transportation. As a result the firm budget shows a deficit equal to $\beta(s)$. Not se well known is the fact that V_e^* contains a socially optimal location. Stated differently, the public monopolist will locate at some efficient network vertex. Interestingly this property can be extended to the case of the multiplant firm and to the public monopolist with a budget constraint. All of that, therefore, suggests that the nature of the locational decisions of the public monopolist is similar to that of the private monopolist. The reader is referred to Erlenkotter (1977) for a description of the corresponding solution methods.

3.4.2 The spatial Cournot oligopoly

The properties of the PSM are now extended to a different market structure called spatial Cournot oligopoly. Consider an industry made of n firms selling an homogenous product. Firm i is located at $s_i \in V$, and its production costs are as described in Definition 12. The strategies of firm i are the quantities q_{im} sold on the market places $m \in M_o$. The inverse demand functions $\pi_m(\sum_{j=1}^{n} q_{jm})$ are strictly decreasing, continuous, and such that $q_{im}\,\pi_m(\sum_{j=1}^{n} q_{jm})$ is concave with respect to q_{im} for $m \in M_o$ and $i = 1 \ldots n$. Finally the profit function of firm is given by

$$\sum_{m \in M_o}^{n} \left\{\pi_m(\sum_{j=1}^{n} q_{jm}) - \alpha(s_i) - t_o[d(m,s)]\right\} q_{im} - \beta(s_i) \tag{14.37}$$

Let us assume that the industry is initially at a Cournot equilibrium.[39] Hence, each firm may supply several market places and each market place may be supplied by several firms.[40] Firm n+1 considers the possibility of entering the industry, choosing a location and a sales policy. The incumbent firms will most probably react to the entry of firm n+1 by changing their production, even if they should decide not to modify their location because of the low mobility of their installation. For each possible location of the entrant, we will therefore observe a different Cournot equilibrium. Here also, it can be shown that the new firm may limit itself to the vertices of V_e as possible locations. Hence, the entrant will compare the profit obtained at each of the corresponding Cournot equilibria and will select the vertex yielding the highest profit. We thus arrive at a characterisation of the equilibrium location of the entrant similar to the one derived in the PSM.[41]

4. CONCLUSIONS

The properties developed in this chapter have some interesting inplications for both transportation and regional development policies. Plassard (1977) has shown how a mythical sounding thesis has been exploited in several countries to justify the building up of large transportation infrastructures, such as interstate highway systems, by the induced development of the regions involved. In turn, this thesis has given rise to a theory, called 'theory of linear development', which states that new production should appear along the main lines of communication, thus promoting the economic growth of the associated regions through the usual multiplier effects. The overview of the literature provided by Plassard indicates that this theory is not supported by empirical evidence. The reduction process presented in this chapter confirms Plassard's criticims and suggests a 'theory of point developments'. We cannot expect the new firms to establish alongside the main lines of transportation. Rather they would choose a site among a limited number of candidates corresponding to place already developed –the markets– or to places with a high degree of centrality in the transportation network –the nodes. Thus one of the main effects of improved transport technology would be a tendency to increase the relative advantage of larger versus smaller centres, but it would probably not lead to a spatial diffusion of growth along the network. Of course, this does not imply that the setting up of new turnpikes or waterways will have no significant impact upon the future locational patterns. A new line can disturb the hierarchy of the candidate sites by strengthening the attractiveness of some of them at the expense of others. It can also generate new candidate sites by the creation of nodes. In both cases, however, the effect should be different from that predicted by the theory of linear development because of the finiteness of most locational decisions. Empirical studies devoted to land use should be undertaken to test the relevance of the above argument. Interestingly, the few existing results in this field (reported by Plassard (1977)) seem to support our conclusions.

Most of our results have been obtained in the context of quasi-perfect competition and spatial monopoly. Clearly, these market structures correspond to polar cases, and properties concerning spatial oligopolies would be desirable. The study of locational decisions within such a market structure is at the heart of spatial competition theory.[42] Nevertheless, the existing models are still very simplified in terms of transportation. Space is modelled by a line or a circle, while transport rates are constant. Recently some attempts have been made to fit those problems into network location theory. Unfortunately, certain difficulties concerning the existence and the characterisation of a stable locational configuration arise even in the simplest cases.[43] The reason for this is to be found in the quasi-absence of properties of the network structure. In our opinion, there is no doubt that the development of such a theory should constitute one of the main lines of research in the future. We hope that the approach proposed and the results obtained here will help to the construction of a sound theory of the spatial organisation of economic activities.

NOTES

1. A good historical survey of firm location theory is found in Ponsard (1983).
2. Also it is not surprising that the first serious attempts to reconcile the two approaches are contemporary with the work of Isard in regional science which mark the revival of spatial studies in economics; see, e.g. Isard (1956), Moses (1957), and Alonso (1967).
3. See Thisse and Perreur (1977) for a detailed discussion of that property.
4. To this effect, the reader is referred to Thisse and Papageorgiou (1981).
5. An illustration is given by the block and the round norms studied by Thisse, Ward and Wendell (1984).
6. For a survey of 'continuous' location theory, see Hansen and Thisse (1983).
7. Sometimes X is called a topological graph.

8. It is of some interest to notice that the set of routes endowed with the operation of concatenation is a groupoïd.
9. In the jargon of geometry, a route is a rectifiable Jordan arc.
10. When the concept of branching is considered, the model easily extends to the case of locations which do not belong to the network.
11. As usual, the assumption of convexity is made to guarantee the existence of an equilibrium. Without changing the results, it could be replaced by the compactness of the production possibility set. Concerning the second assumption, we must notice that the production technique actually used by the firm may change with its location.
12. Although ignored by many economists, this observation is by no means novel. See, for example Enke (1942).
13. The market places are therefore the spatial counterpart of the 'Walrasian auction'.
14. The localisation theorems of this section remain valid in the case of ubiquitous inputs sold at constant and uniform prices.
15. There are plenty of references; see, e.g. Isard (1956) and Locklin (1972).
16. See, e.g. Ponsard (1971).
17. It is of some interest to notice that land does not appear as an input in the LPP. This corresponds to a well-established tradition in location theory where the firms are assumed to be 'spaceless'; The reason for this assumption is the following. The location models à la Weber stand for locational decisions within a regional space. In this context, the relative position of sites proves to be the fundamental spatial variable. Hence the idea of simplifying the analysis by neglectint land consumption. By contrast, land consumption may become essential if the firm has to choose within an urban space. Furthermore, the assumption of spaceless firms permits us to bring out the sites generating a relative surplus because of their advantageous situation. It is this surplus which is the foundation for land competition. Note, in passing, that the whole surplus does not necessarily go to the landlord in a regional space.
18. The hypothesis of a production function of class C_1 is not very restrictive compared to that of convexity. Moreover, since Weber, it is often assumed in firm location models that quantities of output are given a priori. In that case, the LPP reduces to the choice of a location and of a production technique so that the hypothesis of convexity of the production function becomes unnecessary. In this sense, Proposition 2 generalises Proposition 2 and 2A of Eswaran et al. (1981) to the case of a general network. Similarly, it extends to profit maximisation the theorem obtained in operations research for transportation cost minimisation. See, for instance Theorem 1 of Wendell and Hurter (1973); but the

basic result is due to Hakimi (1964). Many other references could be given about particular aspects of that proposition; e.g. the results of Sakashita (1968) and Mathur (1979).

19. See Theorem 4 of Louveaux et al. (1982).
20. Obviously, the affine and power functions belong to class LT.
21. Clearly, functions P and T as they appear in the proof are defined for any given value of γ.
22. The median principle has a long history in location theory going back to Edgeworth; see Rosenhead (1973) for a brief outline of the development of the principle.
23. The majority principle was established by Witzgall (1964) in the case of the Weberian model. As such, it generalises the property of the dominant material index stated by Weber (1909).
24. That procedure is similar to that of cost-benefit analysis.
25. The horizontal division of production is meaningless in quasi-perfect competition. Indeed, if $(\underline{Q}^*,s^*)$ is a spatial equilibrium of the single-plant firm, it is profitable for the firm to replicate that solution as many times as there are possible plants. Such is no longer the case when the market price becomes quantity-sensitive. The horizontal division of production is at the heart of the problem of the spatial monopolist; see section 3.
26. See, for example, Debreu (1982).
27. Unlike section 2, we take the quantities of inputs as non-negative here.
28. In particular, the results of this section remain valid for a linear homogeneous production function.
29. See Phlips (1983), Essay 1, for a survey of spatial price policies.
30. In short, the delivered (mill) price in the spatial monopoly corresponds to the market (firm) price of the quasi-perfect competition model.
31. Actually, the price charged on a market place can still influence the price policy at another market place when the marginal cost of production is not constant. However, this kind of interdependence does not contradict the assumption of clustered markets since it does not operate through resales among customers.
32. Among other things, this implies that Propositions 7 and 8 remain true for much broader a class of production functions than that described in Definition 12. This will not be true for Proposition 9.
33. Greenhut, Mai and Norman (1982) reach a similar conclusion but in a different model.
34. This is in accord with other results obtained by Phlips (1983).
35. See, for example Beckenstein (1975).

36. We do not consider here the possibility for the spatial monopolist to deter entry by establishing several plants; to this end, see Eaton and Lipsey (1979).
37. For simplicity's sake, we have assumed that customers equidistant from different plants choose the one most profitable to the firm.
38. See the DUALOC algorithm of Erlenkotter (1978). The properties of the simple plant location problem are discussed in Krarup and Pruzan (1983) and Wolsey (1983).
39. The existence and uniqueness of a Cournot equilibrium is guaranteed by the assumptions made on the demand and cost functions; see, e.g. Szidarovsky and Yakowitz (1982).
40. Interestingly, cross-hauling can emerge at the Cournot equilibrium. Firm im located at $s_i = m_i \in M_o$, can sell on market place $m_j \in M_o$ while firm j, established at $s_j = m_j$, can supply market place m_i. Spatial Cournot oligopoly therefore accounts for intra-industry trade; for more details, see Brander (1981).
41. The Nti and Shubik (1981) approach to entry in a Cournot industry can be adapted to deal with spatial Cournot oligopoly.
42. See, e.g. Dorward (1982), Graitson (1982) and Phlips and Thisse (1982).
43. See Wendell and McKelvey (1981) and Hakimi (1983).

REFERENCES

Alonso, W. (1967), 'A reformulation of classical location theory and its relation to rent theory', *Papers of the Regional Science Association,* 19, pp. 23-44.

Beckenstein, A.R. (1975), 'Scale economies in the multiplant firm: Theory and empirical evidence', *Bell Journal of Economics,* 6, pp. 644-657.

Berge, C. (1966), *Espaces topologiques. Fonctions multivoques,* Dunod, Paris.

Brander, J.A. (1981), 'Intra-industry trade in identical commodities', *Journal of International Economics,* 11, pp. 1-14.

Debreu, G. (1982), 'Existence of competitive equilibrium', in: K.J. Arrow and M.D. Intriligator (eds.), *Handbook of Mathematical Economics, Volume 2,* North-Holland, Amsterdam.

Dorward, N. (1982), 'Recent developments in the analysis of spatial competiton and their implications for industrial economics', *Journal of Industrial Economics,* 31, pp. 133-151.

Eaton, B.C. and R.G. Lipsey (1979), 'The theory of market pre-emption: The persistence of excess capacity and monopoly in growing spatial markets', *Economica,* 46, pp. 149-158.

Enke, S. (1942), 'Space and value', *Quarterly Journal of Economics,* 57, pp. 627-637.

Erlenkotter, D. (1977), 'Facility location with price-sensitive demands: Private, public and quasi-public', *Management Science,* 24, pp. 378-386.

Erlenkotter, D. (1978), 'A dual-based procedure for uncapacitated facility location', *Operations Research,* 16, pp. 992-1009.

Eswaran, M., Y. Kanemoto and D. Ryan (1981), 'A dual approach to the locational decision of the firm', *Journal of Regional Science,* 21, pp. 469-490.

Graitson, D. (1982), 'Spatial competition à la Hotelling: A selective survey', *Journal of Industrial Economics, 31, pp. 13-25.*

Greenhut, M.L., Mai Chao-Cheng and G. Norman (1982), 'Impact on optimum location of different pricing strategies, market structures and customer distributions over space', University of Reading (mimeo).

Hakimi, S.L. (1964), 'Optimum location of switching centres and the absolute centres and medians of a graph', *Operations Research,* 12, pp. 450-459.

Hakimi, S.L. (1983), 'On locating new facilities in a competitive environment', *European Journal of Operational Research,* 12, pp. 29-35.

Hansen, P. and J.-F. Thisse (1977), 'Multiplant location for profit maximisation', *Environment and Planning,* 9, pp. 63-73.

Hansen, P. and J.-F. Thisse (1983), 'Recent advances in continuous location theory', *Sistemi Urbani* (forthcoming).

Hansen, P., J.-F. Thisse and P. Hanjoul (1981), 'Simple plant location under uniform delivered pricing', *European Journal of Operational Research,* 6, pp. 94-103.

Isard, W. (1956), *Location and Space-Economy,* MIT Press and Wiley and Sons, New York.

Krarup, J. and P.M. Pruzan (1983), 'The simple plant location problem: Survey and synthesis', *European Journal of Operational Research,* 12, pp. 36-81.

Launhardt, W. (1882), 'Die Bestimmung des zweckmässigsten Standortes einer gewerblichen Anlage', *Zeitschrift des Vereins Deutscher Ingenieure,* 26, pp. 106-116.

Locklin, P. (1972), *Economics of Transportation,* Irwin, Homewood, IL.

Louveaux, F., J.-F. Thisse and H. Beguin (1982), 'Location theory and transportation costs', *Regional Science and Urban Economics,* 12, pp. 529-546.

Mathur, V.K. (1979), 'Some unresolved issues in the location theory of the firm', *Journal of Urban Economics,* 6, pp. 299-318.

Moses, L. (1957), 'Location and the theory of production', *Quarterly Journal of Economics,* 72, pp. 259-272.

Nti, K.O. and M. Shubik (1981), 'Non-cooperative oligopoly with entry', *Journal of Economic Theory,* 24, pp. 187-204.

Phlips, L. (1983), *The Economics of Price Discrimination,* Cambridge University Press, Cambridge.

Phlips, L. and J.-F. Thisse (1982), 'Spatial competition and the theory of differentiated markets: An introduction', *Journal of Industrial Economics,* 31, pp. 1-9.

Plassard, F. (1977), *Les autoroutes et le développement régional,* Economica, Paris.

Ponsard, C. (1971), 'Note sur la localisation de la branche d'activité dans une structure de concurrence quasi-parfaite', *Revue d'Economie Politique,* 81, pp. 1028-1031.

Ponsard, C. (1983), *A History of Spatial Economic Theory,* Springer Verlag, Berlin and New York.

Rosenhead, J. (1973), 'Some comments on 'A note on the location depots' by Ralph D. Snyder', *Management Science,* 19, pp. 831-832.

Sakashita, N. (1968), 'Production function, demand function and location theory of the firm', *Papers of the Regional Science Association,* 20, pp. 109-122.

Szidarovsky, F. and S. Yakowitz (1982), 'Contributions to Cournot oligopoly theory', *Journal of Economic Theory,* 28, pp. 51-70.

Thisse, J.-F. and Y.Y. Papageorgiou (1981), 'Reconciliation of transportation costs and amenities as location factors in the theory of the firm', *Geographical Analysis,* 13, pp. 189-195.

Thisse, J.-F. and J. Perreur (1977), 'Relations betweent he point of maximum profit and the point of minimal total transportation costs: A restatement', *Journal of Regional Science,* 17, pp. 227-234.

Thisse, J.-F., J.E. Ward and R.E. Wendell (1984), 'Some properties of location problems with block and round norms', *Operations Research* (forthcoming).

Weber, A. (1909), Über den Standort der Industrien (Tübingen). English translation: 'The theory of the location of industry', The University of Chicago Press, Chicago, IL.

Wendell, R.E. and A.P. Hurter (1973), 'Optimal locations on a network', *Transportation Science,* 7, pp. 18-33.

Wendell, R.E. and R.D. McKelvey (1981), 'New perspectives in competitive location theory', *European Journal of Operational Research,* 6, pp. 174-182.

Witzgall, C. (1964), 'Optimal location of a central facility. Mathematical models and concepts', U.S. Department of Commerce. National Bureau of Standards.

Wolsey, L. (1983), 'Some fundamental properties of discrete location models', in: Thisse, J.-F. and H.G. Zoller (eds.), *Location Analysis of Public Facilities,* North-Holland, Amsterdam.

EPILOGUE

CHAPTER 15

STYLE IN MULTISECTORAL MODELLING

David Kendrick
University of Texas, USA

1. INTRODUCTION

The need for multisectoral models of the U.S. economy has increased in the last few years as the economy has been buffeted by large changes in relative prices and by rapid growth in some sectors and decay in others. Thus Leontieff models of the type developed by Almon, Buckler, and Reimbold (1974) are required. However, the models should not only have quantity equations but also price equations; see Henaff (1980). Moreover, since relative price changes have been large it would be useful to have models that permit substitution between factors of production as do the general equilibrium models created (i) for the developing countries by Adelman and Robinson (1978), Dervis, de Melo, and Robinson (1982), and Kelley and Williamson (1981); and (ii) for the United States by Jorgenson (1982) and his associates, and by Fullerton, Shoven and Whalley (1980). The models also should employ efficient computational methods so that they can be disaggregated to include many sectors and can also be extended to include many time periods and many regions.*

One approach that meets all these requirements is the one developed by Johansen (1974). These models are multisectoral and permit substitution between factors. In their original form they are nonlinear in the levels of the variables but they are converted to the equivalent linear model in percentage rates of change of the variables. This type of model has been applied to Norway by Longva, Lorentsen, and Olsen (1980), to Brazil by Taylor, Bacha, Cardoso, and Lysy (1980), and to Australia by Dixon and Powell (1979). The present paper is a step toward the application of this kind of methodology to the United States economy.

The development of this type of model is a complex process. Therefore the process has been divided into a number of parts. The first part was to install a simple version of the model on the CDC computer of the University of Texas. The 39 equa-

Hughes Hallett, A.J. (ed.) Applied Decision Analysis and Economic Behaviour

ISBN 90-247-2968-8. Printed in The Netherlands

tion Miniature ORANI model contained in Dixon (1979) and in Dixon, Parmenter, Sutton, and Vincent (1982) was selected as a starting point. This model was first restated using a slightly more intuitive notation and then coded in the GAMS language. The GAMS language, which was developed by Meeraus (1983), makes the computable version of the model much easier to understand than the usual Fortran statement. Finally, the model was solved and the solution sent to Australia where Peter Dixon confirmed that the original model yielded the same solution.

This paper was then drafted to serve two purposes. The first purpose was to make it easier for others to enter this field of work by providing a slightly more intuitive mathematical statement of the Dixon (1979) model and by providing an accompanying GAMS statement of the model so those with access to that language could easily begin to do numerical experiments with a small but rich general equilibrium model. The second purpose was to put some ideas on the elements of style in economic modelling into writing. There are three sources for the idea of writing a paper on the elements of style in economic modelling. One of the sources is the famous little book by Strunk and White (1959) which is entitled simply *The Elements of Style.* This book contains a set of pithy rules for effective writing such as 'use definite, specific, concrete language' and 'omit needless words'. The second source is long conversations with Alexander Meeraus of the World Bank about effective modelling practices –many of which are basically matters of style. The third source is the experience of teaching the art and science of economic modelling to many graduate students over the last fifteen years.

This chapter contains a discussion of the proposed rules for economic modelling with style, and an application of these rules to the Miniature ORANI model. The first section provides a list of the rules. The second section contains a statement of the nonlinear model in the level variables. The third section repeats the model statement, but in the linearised form with percentage-rates-of-change variables. The fourth section includes a description of the data and the fifth section presents the results of the solution of the model. Finally Appendix A contains a GAMS statement of the model.

2. THE ELEMENTS OF STYLE

In the tradition of Strunk and White a list of the elements of style will be given. Then later in this section each of the rules will be elaborated. However, unlike the Strunk and White rules, these elements are not the product of long years of utilisation; rather they are a new list that is being put forward for discussion and debate.

The overall spirit of the rules is that in developing, solving, and explaining large economic models it is essential that every effort be made to be precise and clear.

The elements are as follows:

1. Make a complete mathematical statement of the model
2. Use sets to define the domains
3. Provide a list of variables, parameters, and equations
4. Use mathematical –not FORTRAN– variable names
5. Use subscripts for indices and superscripts for variable names
6. Use single letters for indices
7. Do not use sector numbers as subscripts
8. Use words under complex equations
9. Input raw data and show the transformations

Next, each of these rules are considered in turn.

2.1 Make a complete mathematical statement of the model

This rule seems obvious – and yet it is frequently broken. Some model builders begin their work with a mathematical statement of the model, and provide this to their local Fortran programmer and request that the model be solved. Then as modifications are developed they are not made in the mathematical statement but rather in the Fortran code. Soon the only reliable version of the model is the Fortran code. Resolutions are made by the analyst to work out a new mathematical statement at the time the project is completed. Meanwhile the model becomes so complex that only the programmer really knows what is in it. Finally the programmer quits to take a more lucrative position and the analyst realises that it will take many months to train a new programmer. So the results of the model are written up, defended to the hilt in all seminars (since it is no longer possible to make changes), and the model is quietly laid to rest.

Later, others attempt to resurrect the model either to check the results or to use it as a starting point for another project. However, they soon discover that the only reliable documentation of the model in in pages and pages of Fortran code and that it is therefore impossible to check the results or to use the model as a beginning point for a new project.

Builders of such computer models sometimes claim that their models are too complex to be represented mathematically. If this is the case then they are also to complex to be understood and are therefore of little value for economic analysis. Also, it is claimed that mathematical models usually employ only one method such as simulation or optimisation, whereas large computer models employ a variety of models. However, the mathematics of these models with multiple methods can be written in a clear fashion. Finally, it is claimed that mathematical variable names consist of only a single letter while Fortran variable names include seven or more letters; thus the computer model can be more complex than the mathematicl model. However, the judicious use of indices and the of subscripts and superscripts permit the development of very large numbers of mathematical variables.

In summary, it is extremely useful to have a concise mathematical statement of economic models. Analysts shoud not allow their models to be represented only as pages of Fortran code.

2.2 Use sets to define the domains

Models of any size usually include multiple commodities, sectors, and factors. The ability to understand and use such models is greatly enhanced if the sets over which the model is defined are established at the outset and identified with indices and with set names. For example, a model might include two commodities (food and clothing) and two sectors (agriculture and manufacturing). The domain for the problem would be the sets

$$c \epsilon C = \{\text{food, clothing}\}$$

$$i \epsilon I = \{\text{agriculture, manufacturing}\}$$

Then all variables, parameters and equations can be defined over these domains.

The advantage of this kind of problem specification is not only the clarity and precision of expression, but it also facilitates the solution of the models on computers. Computer languages have been developed to read set specifications of the type used above and thus it becomes relatively easy to alter the domain of definition of the problem by simply redefining the elements in the sets.

2.3 Provide a list of variables, parameters, and equations

This rule is widely observed with the exception that investigators occasionally forget to include a list of parameters. Also, there is sometimes a failure to keep the list up to date as the model develops, with the result that some subsections of the model are difficult to understand.

From the point of view of the computer implementation of models, these lists are valuable in that they permit cross checking and therefore aid in the debugging process.

2.4 Use mathematical –not Fortran– variable names

The mathematical statement of the model should use single letter variable names rather than multi-letter names as in Fortran. Thus the single letter q should be used instead of the Fortran PRODUCTION. While it is indeed easier to remember what PRODUCTION means than to remember what q stands for, the use of singlė letters permits a much more parsimonius statement of the model. Thus the model can be written on one or two pages instead of many, and it is easier to comprehend.

Furthermore, if the model is coded into Fortran the production variable should be coded as q rather than as PRODUCTION. It is important to use the same variable names in the computer program as in the mathematical statement since this makes careful checking of the model much easier. Greek letters such as α should be coded in Fortran as ALPHA. Of course if α stands for crop yield an argument can be made that the Fortran variable name of YIELD would be easier to understand. While it is indeed true that this makes the computer code easier to read, it makes the translation and checking from the mathematical to the computer statement much more difficult. It is my conviction that quality in model building is enhanced if the computer program is the handmaid of the mathematical statement of the model rather than vice versa. Therefore the variable names in the computer program should correspond to the mathematical names rather than the other way round.

If the rule above is violated then, at the very least, a table giving the equivalence between mathematical and Fortran variable names should be provided.

2.5 Use subscripts for indices and superscrips for variable names

This is an unusual rule, but one which will facilitate the development of computable general equilibrium models. Computer codes will soon be developed to translate the input to text processors into other computer languages which can be used to solve economic models. An example, which is described in Kendrick (1982), translates models written in the Unix word processing language nroff-neqn into the modelling language GAMS. The nroff-neqn version provides a verbal and mathematical description of the model and the GAMS version is used to solve the model. In this case the translator must distinguish between subscripts and superscripts which are used as a part of the variable names and those which are used as indices. For example consider the variables p_i^d, the domestic price of good i, and the variable p_i^f, the foreign price of good i. In this case i is an index for the set of commodities but d and f are really parts of the variable name. If the indices are listed as subscripts, and the variable names as the variable itself and the accompanying superscripts, the translator can distinguish between them and therefore produce a correct model in the modelling language.[1]

2.6 Use single letters for indices

The reason for this rule is simple aesthetics. For example the variable for the production of the ith commodity in the rth region in time period t is easier to read if it is written without commas between the subscripts, i.e. as x_{irt} instead of $x_{i,r,t}$ and that the commas are not necessary so long as each index consists of a single letter.

2.7 Do not use sector numbers as subscripts

Understandability is enhanced if sectors are not numbered but rather named. Thus instead of using numbers such as sector one and sector two, it is better to use names such as agriculture and manufacturing. For example, the text describing such a model would not read q_1 and q_2 to represent production in agriculture and manufacturing but rather would read q_i for $i \epsilon I$ with $I = \{\text{agriculture, manufacturing}\}$.

One reason for this rule is that it is much easier to read

$$x_{ijrt} \quad \begin{array}{l} i \epsilon \{\text{agriculture}\} \\ j \epsilon \{\text{manufacturing}\} \\ r \epsilon \ \text{Northeast} \\ t \epsilon \ 1983 \end{array}$$

to mean the input of agricultural products to manufacturing in the Northeastern region in 1983 than it is to read

$$x_{1221}$$

and to remember that it refers to the first commodity (agriculture) input to the production of the second commodity (manufacturing) in the second region (Northeast) in the first period (1983).

2.8 Use words under complex equations

When equations become very complex it is useful to display words in brackets under the equation in order to facilitate the readers' understanding. That style is not used in this chapter, but it is used extensively in a series of books on industrial planning which have been edited by Stoutjesdijk and Meeraus. For example see the notation in Kendrick and Stoutjesdijk (1978), viz

$$\sum_{p \epsilon P} a_{cpi} \; z_{pit} > \sum_{j \epsilon J} x_{cijt} + \sum_{\ell \epsilon L} e_{ci\ell t} \qquad \begin{matrix} c \epsilon C \\ i \epsilon I \\ t \epsilon T \end{matrix}$$

Output of final products	>	Domestic shipments of final products	+	Exports of final products

2.9 Input raw data and show the transformations

The model input should show the data in its least processed form and all operations performed on that data should be explicitly shown. Modelling languages such as TROLL, TSP and GAMS greatly facilitate this procedure. When using them it is natural to follow this rule. However, there remain many cases in which the transformations are not explicitly shown and therefore cases in which it is difficult or impossible to replicate the work of other investigators.

In summary, these rules are put forth as a suggested list for debate among modellers. The reader will doubtless even observe that one or more of these rules are broken in the accompanying application to the Miniature ORANI model. For example, words are not used under the equations. However, it is hoped that this list will stir a debate which will enable all of us to improve the efficiency of communication of economic model specifications and results.

3. THE MODEL IN LEVELS

The model consists of five sets and two subsets of indices, twenty-four groups of variables and five types of equations. Each of these will be described in turn.

3.1 Sets

$c \epsilon C$ = Commodities

$s \epsilon S$ = Sources of commodities

SD = Domestic source
SF = Foreign source

$i \in I$ = Industries
$f \in F$ = Factors of production
$h \in H$ = Households

Commodities have only two sources: domestic and foreign. Thus the set S has only these two elements and one element is in each of the two subsets SD and SF.

3.2 Variables

Two conventions are adopted in the notation for the variables. First a tilde over a variable indicates the percentage rate of change of that variable. Thus c represents the level of consumption and $\tilde{c}$ represents the percentage rate of change of consumption. The second convention is for superscripts and subscripts. Superscripts are used as a part of the variable name. Thus c^n is nominal consumption and c^r is real consumption. In contrast subscripts are used only for indices. For example c^n_{cs} is nominal consumption of commodity c from source s, viz the nominal consumption of food that is imported. The variables used in the model appear in table 15.1:

Table 15.1. The variables of the Miniature ORANI model

b	balance of trade	p^c	consumer price index
c^n	nominal consumption	p^k_i	prices of capital stocks
c^r	real consumption	ϕ	exchange rate
d^f	shift factor for foreign demand	q_{ci}	output
e_c	exports	t_c	import duty
e^T	total exports	v_c	export subsidy
k_i	sectoral capital demand	w	wage rate
κ_i	sectoral capital stock	w^s	wage shift factor
ℓ^f	labour force	x_{csi}	intermediate commodity demands
ℓ_i	labour demand in each industry	y^e	household expenditures
m^T	total imports	z_i	industry activity level
p_{cs}	prices for commodities in domestic currency		
p^*_{cs}	prices for commodities in foreign currency		

3.3 Relationships

The model contains five groups of equations as follows:

* demand equations
* production functions
* price equations
* market clearing equations
* miscellaneous identities

Each type of equation is replicated for the appropriate number of commodities, industries, factors of production, and types of households. For example a simple model might have production functions for two types of commodities (food and clothing) and two industries (agriculture and manufacturing) with two factors of production (labour and capital).

One unusual aspect of this model is that there is not a one-to-one relationship between commodities and industries. Rather each industry can produce several commodities. Also, each commodity is labelled as to its source, namely domestic or imported. Thus the simple model mentioned above would have four commodities instead of two, i.e. domestic and imported food and domestic and imported clothing.

The model will be represented here in a sparse form by simply stating the sets, variables, and equations with relatively few comments. The reader who would like a more generous explanation is referred to Dixon (1979) or Dixon, Parmenter, Sutton and Vincent (1982).

Demand

(i) demand for domestic and imported goods

total utility

$$U = \min_{c \in C} \left\{ u_c / \upsilon_c \right\} \tag{15.1}$$

utility for each commodity from all sources

$$u_c = \prod_{s \in S} c_{cs}^{\alpha_{cs}} \qquad c \in C \tag{15.2}$$

where

u_c = utility from consumption of commodity c

c_{cs} = consumption of commodity c from source s

υ_c = a positive parameter

The specification of equations (15.1) and (15.2) embodies the assumption that there is no substitution between different commodities such as food and clothing, but that there is substitution between the same commodity from different sources, i.e. between imported and domestic clothing.

(ii) household budget constraint

$$\sum_{c\epsilon C} \sum_{s\epsilon S} p_{cs}\, c_{cs} = y^e \qquad (15.3)$$

where

y^e = expenditure by households

p_{cs} = prices

From equations (15.1) – (15.3) one can derive household demand functions of the form

$$c_{cs} = f(p_{cs}, y^e) \qquad c\epsilon C,\ s\epsilon S \qquad (15.4)$$

(iii) demand for domestic goods by foreigners

$$p^*_{cs} = e_c^{-\tau}\, d^f_c \qquad c\epsilon C,\ s\epsilon SD \qquad (15.5)$$

where

p^*_c = foreign currency price of good c

e = exports

d^f = shift factor in demand for exports

Production functions

This model is more general than most in that it permits multiple commodities to be produced by a single industry. Thus in addition to the usual output variables q and commodity inputs x and factor inputs k and ℓ, there is also an activity variable for each industry z. This activity variable is used on the one hand to determine the output of each commodity by each industry, q_{ci} and on the other hand to determine the inputs of commodities x_{ci} and of factors k_i and ℓ_i.

The production possibility frontier is used to determine the mix of outputs from the activity level, and the production function is used to determine the demand for commodity inputs and factor inputs.

(i) production possibility frontier

These relations are obtained by solving the following maximisation problem for each industry.

$$\max \xi_i = \sum_{c \epsilon C} \sum_{s \epsilon SD} p_{cs} q_{ci} \qquad i \epsilon I \qquad (15.6)$$

subject to

$$\left(\sum_{c \epsilon C} \beta_{ci} q_{ci}^2 \right)^{1/2} = z_i \qquad i \epsilon I \qquad (15.7)$$

where

β_{ci} = positive parameters
q_{ci} = output of commodity c by industry i
z_i = activity level for industry i

(ii) production functions

The production functions are two level functions. The top level is a Leontief production function which permits no substitution between an aggregate of primary factor inputs and the aggregates of the various commodity inputs. The second level is a Cobb-Douglas production function which represents the production of (i) the aggregate of factor inputs from capital and labour inputs, and (ii) the aggregate commodity inputs from domestic and imported commodity inputs. The result of this specification is that there is substitution between capital and labour, but not between these factors and the commodity inputs. Also, there is substitution between the imported and domestic variant of each commodity, but not between domestic commodities nor between imported commodities.

These production functions are therefore:

$$z_i = \min \left[\frac{f_i}{a_i^f}, \frac{x_{1i}^{\dagger}}{a_{1i}}, \frac{x_{2i}^{\dagger}}{a_{2i}}, \ldots \right] \qquad i \epsilon I \qquad (15.8)$$

where

f_i = Cobb-Douglas combination of primary factor inputs to industry i

$x_{ci}^{\dagger}$ = inputs to industry i of a Cobb-Douglas combination of commodity c from from domestic and foreign sources and where the Cobb-Douglas combination for factors is given by:

$$f_i = k_i^{\alpha_i^k} \ell_i^{\alpha_i^\ell} \qquad i \epsilon I \qquad (15.9)$$

and the Cobb-Douglas combination for inputs is defined by:

$$x_{ci}^{\dagger} = \prod_{s \epsilon S} x_{csi}^{\alpha_{csi}} \qquad c \epsilon C,\ i \epsilon I \qquad (15.10)$$

Price equations

There are three sets of price equations in the model. The first set is a group of functions which require that prices of outputs and inputs be set in such a way as to equate the cost of inputs and the value of outputs. The other two sets of price equations are for exports and imports. They relate prices in domestic and foreign currencies by using the exchange rate, tariffs, and export subsidies.

(i) cost function

$$\sum_{c \epsilon C} p_{cs} q_{ci} = \sum_{c \epsilon C} \sum_{s' \epsilon S} p_{cs'} x_{cs'i} + p^{k_i} . k_i + w \ell_i \qquad i \epsilon I,\ s \epsilon SD \qquad (15.11)$$

(ii) exports

$$p_{cs}^{*} v_c \phi = p_{cs} \qquad s \epsilon SC,\ c \epsilon C \qquad (15.12)$$

where

ϕ = exchange rate

v_c = one plus the ad valorem rate of export subsidy

(iii) imports

$$p_{cs} = p_{cs}^{*} t_c \phi \qquad s \epsilon SF,\ c \epsilon C \qquad (15.13)$$

where

t_c = one plus the ad valorem tariff rate

Market clearing equations

The market clearing equations require that no more of any commodity or factor be used than is available. There is one of these equations for each commodity. Also, there is one for each type of capital. However, there is only a single equation for labour. This specification thus embodies the assumption that capital cannot be shifted between industries while labour is perfectly mobile between industries.

(i) commodities

$$\sum_{i \epsilon I} q_{ci} = \sum_{i \epsilon I} x_{csi} + c_{cs} + e_c \qquad s\epsilon SD,\ c\epsilon C \qquad (15.14)$$

(ii) labour

$$\sum_{i \epsilon I} \ell_i = \ell^f \qquad (15.15)$$

where

ℓ^f = labour force

(iii) capital

$$k_i = \kappa_i \qquad i\epsilon I \qquad (15.16)$$

Miscellaneous identities

These identities are for foreign trade, price and wage measures, and for real consumption.

(i) foreign trade

total imports

$$m^T = \sum_{c \epsilon C} \left(\sum_{i \epsilon I} (p^*_{cs}\, x_{csi}) + c_{cs} \right) \qquad s\epsilon SF \qquad (15.17)$$

total exports

$$e^T = \sum_{c \epsilon C} p^*_{cs}\, e_c \qquad s\epsilon SD \qquad (15.18)$$

balance of trade

$$b = e^T - m^T \qquad (15.19)$$

(ii) consumer price index

$$p^c = \sum_{c\epsilon C} \sum_{s\epsilon S} p_{cs}^{\mu_{cs}} \qquad (15.20)$$

(iii) wage rate

$$w = (p^c)^\theta \, w^s \qquad (15.21)$$

(iv) real consumption

$$c^r = y^e/p^c \qquad (15.22)$$

4. THE MODEL IN PERCENTAGE RATES OF CHANGE

The model is restated here in percentage rates of change. The sets are not restated since they are identical to those used in the previous subsections. Also, the variables are not restated since the same variables will be used here as in the previous section except that they will have a ∿ over them to indicate that they are defined as percentage rates of change. The derivations are not included here since they are available in part in Dixon (1979) and in Dixon, Parmenter, Sutton, and Vincent (1982).

4.1 Demand equations

The demand equations relate nominal consumption of each good c from each source s to total expenditure and to prices. For example one equation would be for domestic food and another for imported food.

Demand for domestic and imported goods

$$\tilde{c}^n_{cs} = \epsilon_{cs}\, \tilde{y}^e + \sum_{c'\epsilon C} \sum_{s'\epsilon S} \eta_{csc's'}\, \tilde{p}_{c's'} \qquad c\epsilon C,\ s\epsilon S \qquad (15.23)$$

where

ϵ = expenditure elasticity
η = cross price elasticities

In the case at hand, $\epsilon_{cs} = 1$ because of the form of the utility function (15.1). Also, changes in the prices of the cth domestic or imported good will not affect the demand for the c'^{th} domestic or imported good. That is, there is substitution between domestic and imported goods of the same commodity type but not among goods of different commodity types, i.e.

$$\eta_{csc's'} = 0 \qquad \text{if } c \neq c' \qquad (15.24)$$

Demand by foreigners for domestic goods

$$\tilde{p}^*_{cs} = -\gamma_c \tilde{e}_c + \tilde{d}^f_c \qquad c\epsilon C,\ s\epsilon SD \qquad (15.25)$$

Note that this demand function is stated in the form p = f(q), rather than in the more familiar form q = f(p) where p is price and q is quantity demanded.

4.2 Production functions

Supply response equations

$$\tilde{q}_{ci} = \tilde{z}_i + (\tilde{p}_{cs} - \sum_{c'\epsilon C} r_{c'i} \tilde{p}_{c's}) \qquad c\epsilon C,\ s\epsilon SD,\ i\epsilon I \qquad (15.26)$$

where

r_{ci} = share of revenue from commodity c in industry i

Production functions

(i) input demand function for commodities

$$\tilde{x}_{csi} = \tilde{z}_i - (\tilde{p}_{cs} - \sum_{s'\epsilon S} \alpha_{cs'i} \tilde{p}_{cs'}) \qquad c\epsilon C,\ s\epsilon S,\ i\epsilon I \qquad (15.27)$$

where

α_{csi} = share of expenditure by industry

(ii) input demand function for capital

$$\tilde{k}_i = \tilde{z}_i - (\tilde{p}^k_i - \alpha^\ell_i \tilde{w} - \alpha^k_i \tilde{p}^k_i) \qquad i\epsilon I \qquad (15.28)$$

where

α^ℓ_i = share of expenditure on labour

α^k_i = share of expenditure on capital

(iii) input demand function for labour

$$\tilde{\ell}_i = \tilde{z}_i - (\tilde{w} - \alpha_i^{\ell}\tilde{w} - \alpha_i^{k}\tilde{p}_i^{k}) \qquad i\epsilon I \qquad (15.29)$$

4.3 Price equations

Commodities

$$\sum_{c\epsilon C} r_{ci}\tilde{p}_{cs} = \sum_{c\epsilon C}\sum_{s'\epsilon S} s^{c}_{cs'i}\tilde{p}_{cs'} + s_i^k\tilde{p}_i^k + s_i^{\ell}\tilde{w} \qquad s\epsilon S^* \qquad (15.30)$$

where

s^c_{csi} = cost share for commodity cs

s_i^k = cost share for capital

s_i^{ℓ} = cost share for labour

Exports

$$\tilde{p}_{cs} = \tilde{p}^*_{cs} + \tilde{v}_c + \tilde{\phi} \qquad s\epsilon SD,\ c\epsilon C \qquad (15.31)$$

Imports

$$\tilde{p}_{cs} = \tilde{p}^*_{cs} + t_c + \tilde{\phi} \qquad s\epsilon SF,\ c\epsilon C \qquad (15.32)$$

4.4 Market clearing equations

Commodities

$$\sum_{i\epsilon I} m_{ci}\tilde{q}_{ci} = \sum_{i\epsilon I} w^i_{csi}\tilde{x}_{csi} + w^c_{cs}\tilde{c}^n_{cs} + w^e_c\tilde{e}_c \qquad c\epsilon C,\ s\epsilon SD \qquad (15.33)$$

where

m = industry
w^i = shares of intermediates in aggregate demand
w^c = shares of consumption in aggregate demand
w^e = share of exports in aggregate demand

Labour

$$\sum_{i \in I} w_i^{\ell} \tilde{\ell} = \tilde{\ell}^f \qquad (15.34)$$

where

w_i^{ℓ} = share of total employment in industry i

Capital

$$\tilde{k}_i = \tilde{\kappa}_i \qquad i \in I \qquad (15.35)$$

4.5 Miscellaneous identities

Total imports

$$\tilde{m}^T = \sum_{c \in C} n_c^m (\tilde{p}_{cs}^* + \sum_{i \in I} (w_{csi}^i \tilde{x}_{csi}) + w_{cs}^c \tilde{c}_{cs}^n) \qquad s \in SF \qquad (15.36)$$

where

n_c^m = share of commodity c in total imports

Total exports

$$\tilde{e}^T = \sum_{c \in C} n_c^x (\tilde{p}_{cs}^* + \tilde{e}_c) \qquad s \in SD \qquad (15.37)$$

where

n_c^x = share of commodity c in total exports

Balance of trade

$$\tilde{b} = (1/100)(e^T \tilde{e}^T - m^T \tilde{m}^T) \qquad (15.38)$$

Consumer price index

$$\tilde{p}^c = \sum_{c \in C} \sum_{s \in S} \mu_{cs} \tilde{p}_{cs} \qquad (15.39)$$

where

μ_{cs} = share of good cs in total household consumption

Wage rate

$$\tilde{w} = \theta\, \tilde{p}^c + \tilde{w}^s \tag{15.40}$$

where

θ = wage indexation parameter

Real consumption

$$\tilde{c}^r = \tilde{y}^e - \tilde{p}^c \tag{15.41}$$

5. THE DATA

The data for this model is presented in compact form in a single table just as it is done in Dixon (1979). This data is shown in table 15.2 which is an input output table for an imaginary economy with two commodities (food and clothing), two in-industries (agriculture and manufacturing), and two factors (capital and labour). Furthermore each commodity can be produced domestically or imported. Also, each industry can produce something of both goods. The data in this table are not used directly in the model. Rather a variety of transformations of the data are used to compute the parameters which are used in the model. These transformations are outlined in Dixon (1979) and are given in detail in the GAMS statement in the Appendix. They are not repeated here.

Table 15.2. Input-output data base

		Industries		House-			Row
		Agric	Manuf	holds	Exports	–Duty	Totals
Domestic	Food	10	8	17	19		54
	Clothing	15	1	34	1		51
Imported	Food	1	8	1		–1	9
	Clothing	5	2	10		–5	12
Factors	Labour	20	20				40
	Capital	10	5				15
Totals		61	44	62	20		
Outputs	Food	45	9				54
	Clothing	16	35				51

In addition to the data in table 15.2 only one other small data table is required to complete the listing of all the data which is used in the model. This data is the export demand parameters and is given in table 15.3.

Table 15.3. Export demand parameters

Food	0.5
Clothing	0.05

6. RESULTS

The results given here were intended to be used only to confirm that this model yields the same results as the model described in Dixon (1979). An earlier draft of this paper was sent to Australia and Peter Dixon solved the miniature ORANI model with the exogenous variable settings shown here and obtained the same results as those shown here.

6.1 Exogenous variables

The exogenous variable settings which were used for the trial solution are given in tables 15.4 to 15.7.

Table 15.4. Scalar variables

$\tilde{\phi}$	0.0
$\tilde{w}^s$	0.0
$\tilde{y}^e$	2.0

Table 15.5. Commodity variables

	t	$\tilde{v}$	d^1	$\tilde{e}$
Food	0.0	0.0	1.0	–
Clothing	0.0	–	1.0	1.0

Table 15.6. Industry variables

	κ
Agric	3.0
Manuf	3.0

Table 15.7. Commodity-source variables

		$\tilde{p}^*$
Food	Imported	–2.0
Clothing	Imported	–2.0

6.2 Endogenous variables

The solution of the model is given in tables 15.8 to 15.12.

Table 15.8. Scalar variables

$\tilde{b}$	0.2
$\tilde{c}^r$	3.6
$\tilde{e}^T$	3.2
$\tilde{\ell}^f$	4.0
$\tilde{m}^T$	2.0
$\tilde{p}^c$	−1.6
$\tilde{w}$	−1.6

Table 15.9. Commodity variables

	$\tilde{v}$	$\tilde{e}$
Food	–	4.5
Clothing	−2.6	–

Table 15.10. Industry variables

	k	ℓ	$\tilde{p}^k$	$\tilde{z}$
Agric	3.0	4.3	−.3	3.8
Manuf	3.0	3.7	−.9	3.5

Table 15.11. Commodity-source variables

		$\tilde{c}^n$	$\tilde{p}$	p^*
Food	Domestic	3.5	−1.2	−1.2
Clothing	Domestic	3.5	−1.6	0.9
Food	Imported	4.2	−2.0	–
Clothing	Imported	3.9	−2.0	–

Table 15.12. Commodity-industry variables, $\tilde{q}$

	Agric	Manuf
Food	3.9	3.8
Clothing	3.6	3.5

7. SUMMARY

This chapter has provided a set of rules for 'style' in multisectoral modelling which will hopefully stir a debate. Style is extremely important in improving the efficiency of communication about the specification of and the results from multisectoral modelling exercises.

The application to the ORANI model is designed to decrease the 'cost of entry' into the multisectoral modelling field by providing easy access to a small but intricate numerical multisectoral model stated in the GAMS language. Also this application serves to illustrate the application for the rules set out in the first part of the chapter.

APPENDIX: A GAMS statement of the model

```
$ TITLE   A MINIATURE VERSION OF ORANI 78

SETS
        C           COMMODITIES
                    / FOOD
                      CLOTHING /
                      CA            AGRICULTURAL COMMODITIES
                                    / FOOD /
                      CM            MANUFACTURED COMMODITIES
                                    / CLOTHING /

        F           FACTORS
                    / LABOUR
                      CAPITAL /
        H           HOUSEHOLDS
                    / FAMILIES /
        I           INDUSTRIES
                    / AGRIC         AGRICULTURE
                      MANUF         MANUFACTURING /
        S           SOURCES
                    / DOMESTIC
                      IMPORTED /
                      SD            SOURCES : DOMESTIC
                                    / DOMESTIC /
                      SF            SOURCES : IMPORTED
                                    / IMPORTED /
*       CP          CPRIME – COPY OF COMMODITIES SET
                    ALIAS(C,CP);
*       SP          SPRIME – COPY OF SOURCES SET
                    ALIAS(S,SP);

SETS    CCP         (C,CP) PAIRS WHERE C IS NOT EQUAL TO CP;
        CCP(C,CP) $ (ORD(C) NE ORD(CP)) = 1.;
        DISPLAY CCP;
```

```
*       BASIC DATA AND PARAMETERS

*       TABLE AMC  ACCOUNTING MATRIX FOR COMMODITIES
                        INDUSTRIES   HOUSEHOLDS  EXPORTS  IMPORT
                       AGRIC  MANUF   FAMILIES     EXP     DUTY

FOOD . DOMESTIC          10     8        17         19
CLOTHING.DOMESTIC        15     1        34          1
*
FOOD.IMPORTED             1     8         1                  -1
CLOTHING.IMPORTED         5     2        10                  -5


        TABLE AMF  ACCOUNTING MATRIX FOR FACTORS
                       AGRIC   MANUF

 LABOUR                  20      20
 CAPITAL                 10       5


        TABLE AMQ  ACCOUNTING MATRIX FOR OUTPUTS
                       AGRIC   MANUF

 FOOD                    45       9
 CLOTHING                16      35
 ;

*       TOTALS FOR ACCOUNTING MATRIX DATA

 AMC(C,S,'TOTAL') = SUM(I, AMC(C,S,I)) + AMC(C,S,'FAMILIES')
                    + AMC(C,S,'EXP') + AMC(C,S, 'DUTY') ;

 AMF(F,'TOTAL') = SUM(I, AMF(F,I)) ;

 AMQ(C,'TOTAL') = SUM(I, AMQ(C,I)) ;

 PARAMETER AMT   ACCOUNTING MATRIX FOR COLUMN TOTALS ;
 AMT(I) = SUM((C,S), AMC(C,S,I)) + SUM(F, AMF(F,I)) ;
 AMT('FAMILIES') = SUM((C,S), AMC(C,S,'FAMILIES'));
 AMT('EXP') = SUM((C,S), AMC(C,S,'EXP')) ;
 DISPLAY AMC,  AMF,AMT,  AMQ ;
```

```
PARAMETER GAMMA (C)  EXPORT DEMAND PARAMETERS
/ FOOD          .5
  CLOTHING      .05 /


TABLE EPSILON (C,S)  INCOME ELASTICITIES
               DOMESTIC    IMPORTED
FOOD              1.          1.
CLOTHING          1.          1.


SCALAR THETA  ADJUSTMENT PARAMETER FOR WAGE RATE /1.0/


PARAMETER WL(I)  SHARE OF TOTAL EMPLOYMENT
/ AGRIC         .5
  MANUF         .5 /


*           DERIVED DATA AND PARAMETERS

PARAMETERS
   ALPHA(C,S,I)            SHARE OF EXPENDITURE BY INDUSTRY
   ALPHAK(I)               SHARE OF EXPENDITURE ON CAPITAL
   ALPHAL(I)               SHARE OF EXPENDITURE ON LABOUR
     ALPHAE(C,S)           SHARE OF GOOD CS IN EXPEND ON C
     ETABAR(C,S,CP,SP)     COMPENSATED PRICE ELASTICITIES
     SB(C,S)               SHARE OF GOOD CS IN HOUSEHOLD BUDGET
   ETA(C,S,CP,SP)          UNCOMPENSATED PRICE ELASTICITIES
   ELEVEL                  BASE PERIOD EXPORT LEVEL – NOT A RATE
   M(C,I)                  INDUSTRY MARKET SHARE
   MLEVEL                  BASE PERIOD IMPORT LEVEL – NOT A RATE ;


   ALPHA(C,S,I) = AMC(C,S,I) / (SUM(SP, AMC(C,SP,I)) ) ;
   ALPHAK(I) = AMF ('CAPITAL',I) / (SUM(F, AMF(F,I)) ) ;
   ALPHAL(I) = AMF ('LABOUR',I) / (SUM(F, AMF(F,I)) ) ;
     ALPHAE(C,S) = AMC(C,S,'FAMILIES') /
                   (SUM(SP, AMC(C,SP, 'FAMILIES')) ) ;
     ETABAR(C,S,CP,SP) = ALPHAE(CP,SP) ;
```

```
   ETABAR(C,S,C,S) = -1.0 + ALPHAE(C,S) ;
   ETABAR(C,S,CP,SP) $ CCP(C,CP) = 0.0 ;
   SB(C,S) = AMC(C,S,'FAMILIES') / AMT('FAMILIES') ;
ETA(C,S,CP,SP) = - EPSILON(C,S) * SB(CP,SP)
                 + ETABAR(C,S,CP,SP) ;
ELEVEL = AMT('EXP') ;
M(C,I)    = AMQ(C,I) / AMQ(C,'TOTAL') ;
MLEVEL = SUM(C, AMC(C,'IMPORTED','TOTAL')) ;


PARAMETERS
   MU(C,S)          WEIGHTS FOR THE CPI
   NM(C)            SHARE IN TOTAL IMPORTS
   NX(C)            SHARE IN TOTAL EXPORTS
   R(C,I)           REVENUE SHARE
   SC(C,S,I)        COST SHARE
   SK(I)            COST SHARE FOR CAPITAL
   SL(I)            COST SHARE FOR LABOUR
   WC(C,S)          SHARE OF CONSUMPTION IN DEMAND
   WE(C)            SHARE OF EXPORTS IN DEMAND
   WI(C,S,I)        SHARE OF INTERMEDIATES IN DEMAND ;

   MU(C,S) =  SB(C,S) ;
   NM(C) = AMC(C,'IMPORTED','TOTAL') /
           SUM(CP, AMC(CP,'IMPORTED','TOTAL')) ;
   NX(C) = AMC(C,'DOMESTIC','EXP') / AMT('EXP') ;
   R(C,I) = AMQ(C,I) / SUM(CP, AMQ(CP,I)) ;
   SC(C,S,I) = AMC(C,S,I) / AMT(I) ;
   SK(I) = AMF('CAPITAL',I) / AMT(I) ;
   SL(I) = AMF('LABOUR',I) / AMT(I) ;
   WC(C,SD) = AMC(C,SD,'FAMILIES') / AMC(C,SD,'TOTAL') ;
   WC(C,SF) = AMC(C,SF,'FAMILIES') /
              (AMC(C,SF,'TOTAL') - AMC(C,SF,'DUTY')) ;
   WE(C) = AMC(C,'DOMESTIC','EXP') /
           AMC(C,'DOMESTIC','TOTAL') ;
   WI(C,SD,I) = AMC(C,SD,I) / AMC(C,SD,'TOTAL') ,
   WI(C,SF,I) = AMC(C,SF,I) /
                (AMC(C,SF,'TOTAL') - AMC(C,SF,'DUTY')) ;
```

```
DISPLAY  ALPHA,  ALPHAK,  ALPHAL,  ALPHAE,  ETABAR,  SB ;
DISPLAY  ETA,    ELEVEL,  M,       MLEVEL,  MU,      NM ;
DISPLAY  NX,     R,       SC,      SK,      SL,      WC ;
DISPLAY  WE,     WI ;
```

VARIABLES

* ALL VARAIBLES ARE RATES OF CHANGE UNLESS OTHERWISE NOTED
* ENDOGENOUS VARIABLES

B	BALANCE OF TRADE
CN(C,S)	CONSUMPTION–NOMINAL
CR	CONSUMPTION–REAL
E(CA)	EXPORTS OF AGRICULTURAL COMMODITIES
ET	TOTAL EXPORTS
K(I)	CAPITAL DEMAND
L	TOTAL EMPLOYMENT
LI(I)	LABOUR DEMAND BY INDUSTRY
MT	TOTAL IMPORTS
P(C,S)	PRICES FOR COMMODITIES IN DOMESTIC CURRENCY
PC	PRICES : CONSUMER PRICE INDEX
PK(I)	PRICE OF CAPITAL
PSTAR(C,SD)	PRICE OF COMMODITIES IN FOREIGN CURRENCY
Q(C,I)	OUTPUT
V(CM)	EXPORT SUBSIDY FOR THE MANUF COMMODITY
W	WAGE RATE
X(C,S,I)	INTERMEDIATE COMMODITY DEMANDS
Z(I)	INDUSTRY ACTIVITY LEVEL

* EXOGENOUS VARIABLES

DF(C)	DEMAND : FOREIGN (SHIFT)
E(CM)	EXPORTS OF MANUFACTURED GOODS
KAPPA(I)	SECTORAL CAPITAL STOCKS
PHI	EXCHANGE RATE
PSTAR(C,SF)	PRICES FOR COMMODITIES IN FOREIGN CURRENCY
T(C)	IMPORT DUTY
V(CA)	EXPORT SUBSIDY FOR THE AGRI COMMODITY
WS	WAGE SHIFT FACTOR
YE	HOUSEHOLD EXPENDITURES

```
*  PARAMETERS USED IN EQUATIONS
*
*      ALPHA(C,S,I)       SHARE OF EXPENDITURE BY INDUSTRY
*      ALPHAK(I)          SHARE OF EXPENDITURE ON CAPITAL
*      ALPHAL(I)          SHARE OF EXPENDITURE OF LABOUR
*      EPSILON(C,S)       INCOME ELASTICITIES
*      ETA(C,S,CP,SP)     CROSS PRICE ELASTICITIES
*      ELEVEL             BASE PERIOD EXPORT LEVEL
*      GAMMA(C)           EXPORT DEMAND PARAMETERS
*      M(C,I)             INDUSTRY MARKET SHARE
*      MLEVEL             BASE PERIOD IMPORT LEVEL
*      MU(C,S)            WEIGHTS FOR CPI
*      NM(C)              SHARE IN TOTAL IMPORTS
*      NX(C)              SHARE IN TOTAL EXPORTS
*      R(C,I)             REVENUE SHARE
*      SC(C,S,I)          COST SHARE
*      SK(I)              COST SHARE FOR CAPITAL
*      SL(I)              COST SHARE FOR LABOUR
*      THETA              ADJUSTMENT PARAMETER FOR WAGE RATE
*      WC(C,S)            SHARE OF CONSUMPTION IN DEMAND
*      WE(C)              SHARE OF EXPORTS IN DEMAND
*      WI(C,S,I)          SHARE OF INTERMEDIATES IN DEMAND
*      WL(I)              SHARE OF TOTAL EMPLOYMENT


EQUATIONS

       CON            CONSUMPTION
       EXPD           EXPORT DEMANDS
       SUPPLY         SUPPLY RELATIONS
       INDCOMM        INPUT DEMAND FOR COMMODITIES
       INDCAP         INPUT DEMAND FOR CAPITAL
       INDLAB         INPUT DEMAND FOR LABOUR
       PRICOMM        PRICE EQUATIONS FOR COMMODITIES
       PRIEXP         PRICE EQUATIONS FOR EXPORTS
       PRIIMP         PRICE EQUATIONS FOR IMPORTS
       BALDCOMM       BALANCE EQUATION FOR DOMESTIC COMMODITY
       BALLAB         BALANCE EQUATION FOR LABOUR
       BALCAP         BALANCE EQUATIONS FOR CAPITAL
       IMPORTS        IMPORTS
       EXPORTS        EXPORTS
       BALTRADE       BALANCE OF TRADE
       CPI            CONSUMER PRICE INDEX
       WAGE           WAGE RATE
```

```
        REALC           REAL CONSUMPTION
        SHIFTFD         SHIFT FACTOR FOR FOREIGN DEMAND
        EXM             EXPORTS OF MANUFACTURED GOODS
        CAPSTOCKS       SECTORAL CAPITAL STOCKS
        EXCHANGE        EXCHANGE RATE
        PFC             FOREIGN CURR PRICES OF IMPORTED GOODS
        DUTY            IMPORT DUTY
        EXPSUB          EXPORT SUBSIDY FOR THE AGRIC COMMODITY
        WAGESHIFT       WAGESHIFT FACTOR
        HOUSEEXP        HOUSEHOLD EXPENDITURES  ;


*     CONSUMPTION
 CON(C,S) ..     CN(C,S)  =E=  EPSILON(C,S) * YE +
                               SUM((CP,SP), ETA(C,S,CP,SP) * P(CP,SP)) ;

*     EXPORT DEMAND
 EXPD(C,SD). .    PSTAR(C,SD)  =E=  – GAMMA(C) * E(C) + DF(C) ;

*     SUPPLY RELATIONS
 SUPPLY(C,SD,I). .    Q(C,I)  =E=  Z(I) + ( P(C,SD)
           – SUM(CP, R(CP,I) * P(CP,SD) ) ) ;

*     INPUT DEMAND FOR COMMODITIES
 INDCOMM(C,S,I). .     X(C,S,I)  =E=  Z(I) – ( P(C,S) –
                               SUM( SP, ALPHA(C,SP,I) * P(C,SP) ) ) ;

*     INPUT DEMAND FOR CAPITAL
 INDCAP(I). .    K(I)  =E=  Z(I) – (PK(I) – ALPHAL(I) * W
                             – ALPHAK(I) * PK(I) ) ;

*     INPUT DEMAND FOR LABOUR
 INDLAB(I). .    LI(I)  =E=  Z(I) – (W – ALPHAL(I) * W
                                  – ALPHAK(I) * PK(I) ) ;

*     PRICE EQUATIONS FOR COMMODITIES
 PRICOMM(SD,I). .    SUM(C, R(C,I) * P(C,SD) )  =E=
                     SUM( (C,SP), SC(C,SP,I) * P(C,SP) )
                     + SK(I) * PK(I) + SL(I) * W ;

*     PRICE EQUATIONS FOR EXPORTS
 PRIEXP(C,SD). .    P(C,SD)  =E=  PSTAR(C,SD) + V(C) + PHI ;
```

```
*      PRICE EQUATIONS FOR IMPORTS
 PRIIMP(C,SF)..    P(C,SF)  =E=  PSTAR(C,SF) + T(C) + PHI ;

*      BALANCE EQUATIONS FOR DOMESTIC COMMODITIES
 BALDCOMM(C,SD)    SUM(I, M(C,I) * Q(C,I) )  =E=
                   SUM(I, WI(C,SD,I) * X(C,SD,I) )
                   + WC(C,SD) * CN(C,SD) + WE(C) * E(C) ;

*      BALANCE EQUATION FOR LABOUR
 BALLAB..    SUM(I, WL(I) * LI(I) )  =E=  L ;

*      BALANCE EQUATION FOR CAPITAL
 BALCAP(I)..    K(I)  =E=  KAPPA(I) ;

*      IMPORTS
 IMPORTS..    MT  =E=  SUM( (C,SF), NM(C) * ( PSTAR(C,SF) +
                       SUM(I, WI(C,SF,I) * X(C,SF,I) ) +
                       WC(C,SF) * CN(C,SF) ) ) ;

*      EXPORTS
 EXPORTS..    ET  =E=  SUM((C,SD), NX(C) * PSTAR(C,SD) + NX(C) * E(C)) ;

*      BALANCE OF TRADE
 BALTRADE..    B  =E=  (1/100) * ( (ELEVEL * ET) – (MLEVEL * MT) ) ;

*      CONSUMER PRICE INDEX
 CPI..    PC  =E=  SUM( (C,S), MU(C,S) * P(C,S) ) ;

*      WAGE RATE
 WAGE..    W  =E=  (THETA * PC) + WS ;

*      REAL CONSUMPTION
 REALC..    CR  =E=  YE – PC ;


*   EXOGENOUS VARIABLES
*      SHIFT FACTOR FOR FOREIGN DEMAND
 SHIFTFD(C)..    DF(C)  =E=  1. ;

*      EXPORTS OF MANUFACTURED GOODS
 EXM(CM)..    E(CM)  =E=  1. ;
```

```
*     SECTORAL CAPITAL STOCKS
 CAPSTOCKS(I)..   KAPPA(I) =E= 3. ;

*     EXCHANGE RATE
 EXCHANGE..   PHI =E= 0. ;

*     FOREIGN CURR PRICES OF IMPORTED GOODS
 PFC(C,SF)..   PSTAR(C,SF) =E= -2. ;

*     IMPORT DUTY
 DUTY(C)..   T(C) =E= 0. ;

*     EXPORT SUBSIDY FOR THE AGRICULTURAL COMMODITY
 EXPSUB(CA)..   V(CA) =E= 0. ;

*     WAGE SHIFT FACTOR
 WAGESHIFT..   WS =E= 0. ;

*     HOUSEHOLD EXPENDITURES
 HOUSEEXP..   YE =E= 2. ;


OPTION LIMROW = 25, LIMCOL = 25 ;

MODEL ORANI /ALL/ ;

SOLVE ORANI USING LP MINIMISING PC ;



* DISPLAY OF EXOGENOUS VARIABLES

 PARAMETERS
     EXSCALAR    EXOGENOUS SCALAR VARIABLES
     EXCOMM      EXOGENOUS COMMODITY VARIABLES
     EXINDUS     EXOGENOUS INDUSTRY VARIABLES
     EXCS        EXOGENOUS COMMODITY AND SOURCE VARIABLES ;

     EXSCALAR('PHI') = PHI.L ;
     EXSCALAR('WS') = WS.L ;
     EXSCALAR('YE') = YE.L ;
```

```
    EXCOMM(C,'T')    = T.L(C) ;
    EXCOMM(CA,'V')   = V.L(CA) ;
    EXCOMM(C,'DF')   = DF.L(C) ;
    EXCOMM(CM,'E')   = E.L(CM) ;

    EXINDUS(I,'KAPPA') = KAPPA.L(I) ;

    EXCS(C,SF) = PSTAR.L(C,SF) ;

    DISPLAY EXSCALAR, EXCOMM, EXINDUS, EXCS ;


*  DISPLAY OF ENDOGENOUS VARIABLES

 PARAMETERS

   ENSCALAR ENDOGENOUS SCALAR VARIABLES
   ENCOMM   ENDOGENOUS COMMODITY VARIABLES
   ENINDUS  ENDOGENOUS INDUSTRY VARIABLES
   ENCS     ENDOGENOUS COMMODITY AND SOURCE VARIABLES
   ENCI     ENDOGENOUS COMMODITY AND INDUSTRY VARIABLES
   ENCSI    ENDOGENOUS COMMODITY SOURCE AND INDUSTRY
                 VARIABLES ;

   ENSCALAR('B')    = B.L ;
   ENSCALAR('CR')   = CR.L ;
   ENSCALAR('ET')   = ET.L ;
   ENSCALAR('L')    = L.L ;
   ENSCALAR('MT')   = MT.L ;
   ENSCALAR('PC')   = PC.L ;
   ENSCALAR('W')    = W.L ;

   ENCOMM(CM,'V')   = V.L(CM) ;
   ENCOMM(CA,'E')   = E.L(CA) ;

   ENINDUS(I,'K')   = K.L(I) ;
   ENDINUS(I,'LI')  = LI.L(I) ;
   ENIDNUS(I,'PK')  = PK.L(I) ;
   ENINDUS(I,'Z')   = Z.L(I) ;

   ENCS('FOOD-DOM','CN')   = CN.L('FOOD','DOMESTIC') ;
   ENCS('CLOTH-DOM','CN')  = CN.L('CLOTHING','DOMESTIC') ;
   ENCS('FOOD-IMP','CN')   = CN.L('FOOD','IMPORTED') ;
   ENCS('CLOTH-IMP','CN')  = CN.L('CLOTHING','IMPORTED') ;
```

```
ENCS('FOOD–DOM', 'P')     = P.L('FOOD', 'DOMESTIC') ;
ENCS('CLOTH–DOM', 'P')    = P.L('CLOTHING', 'DOMESTIC') ;
ENCS('FOOD–IMP', 'P')     = P.L('FOOD', 'IMPORTED') ;
ENCS('CLOTH–IMP', 'P')    = P.L('CLOTHING', 'IMPORTED') ;

ENCS('FOOD–DOM','PSTAR') = PSTAR.L('FOOD','DOMESTIC') ;
ENCS('CLOTH–DOM','PSTAR') = PSTAR.L('CLOTHING','DOMESTIC') ;

ENCI(C,I) = Q.L(C,I) ;

ENCSI(C,I,S) = X.L(C,S,I) ;

DISPLAY ENSCALAR, ENCOMM, ENINDUS, ENCS, ENCI, ENCSI ;
```

NOTES

* I am indebted to Peter Dixon for his comments on an earlier draft of this chapter and to the Institute for Constructive Capitalism of the University of Texas for research support.

1. This subscript-superscript convention is not a part of GAMS but rather of the modelling language described in Kendrick (1982).

REFERENCES

Adelman, I. and S. Robinson (1978), *Income Distribution Policies in Developing Countries*, Stanford University Press, Stanford, California.

Almon, C., Jr., M.B. Buckler, L.M. Horwitz, and T.C. Reimbold (1974), *1985: Interindustry Forecasts of the American Economy*, Lexington Books, Lexington, Massachusetts.

Dervis, K., J. De Melo, and S. Robinson (1982), *General Equilibrium Models for Development Policy*, Cambridge University Press, Cambridge, England.

Dixon, P.B. (1979), 'A skeletal version of Orani 78: Theory, data, computations, and results', Preliminary Working Paper No. OP-24, Impact Research Center, Industrial Assistance Commission, 608 St. Kilda Road, Melbourne, Victoria, 3004, Australia.

Dixon, P.B., B.R. Parmenter, J. Sutton, and D.P. Vincent (1982), *ORANI: A Multisectoral Model of the Australian Economy*, North Holland Publishing Company, Amsterdam.

Dixon, P.B. and A.A. Powell (1979), *Structural Adaptation in an Ailing Economy*, Melbourne University Press, Carlton, Victoria, 3053, Australia.

Fullerton, D., J.B. Shoven and J. Whalley (1980), 'Dynamic general equilibrium impact of replacing the U.S. income tax with a progressive consumption tax', National Bureau of Economic Research Conference Paper No. 55, October.

Henaff, P. (1980), 'An input-output model of the French economy', Masters Thesis, University of Maryland, College Park, Maryland.

Johansen, L. (1974), *A Multi-Sectoral Study of Economic Growth,* Second Edition, North Holland Publishing Company, Amsterdam, The Netherlands.

Jorgenson, D.W. (1982), 'An econometric approach to general equilibrium analysis', in: M. Hazewinkel and A.H.G. Rinnooy Kan (eds.), *Current Developments at the Interface Economics, Econometrics, Mathematics,* pp. 217-233, D. Reidel Publishing Company, The Netherlands.

Kelley, A.G. and J.G. Williamson (1981), 'The sources of third world urbanisation and city growth', Working Paper, Development Research Department, The World Bank, Washington, D.C.

Kendrick, D.A. (1982), 'A mathematical-computer language for linear programming problems', Paper No. 82-8, Center for Economic Research, The University of Texas, Austin, Texas 78712.

Kendrick, D.A. and A.J. Stoutjesdijk (1978), *The Planning of Industrial Investment Programs: A Methodology,* John Hopkins University Press, Baltimore, Maryland.

Longva, S., L. Lorentsen and O.Olsen (1980), 'Energy in the multi-sectoral growth model MSG', Central Bureau of Statistics, Oslo, Norway.

Meeraus, A. (1983), 'An algebraic approach to modelling., *The Journal of Economic Dynamics and Control,* 5, pp. 81-108.

Strunk, W., Jr. and E.B. White (1959), *The Elements of Style,* The Macmillian Company, New York.

Taylor, L., E.L. Bacha, E.A. Cardoso, and F.J. Lysy (1980), *Models of Growth and Distribution for Brazil,* Oxford University Press, Oxford, England.

ADVANCED STUDIES IN THEORETICAL AND APPLIED ECONOMETRICS
VOLUME 3

---

1. J.H.P. Paelinck (ed.) Qualitative and Quantitative Mathematical Economics, 1982. ISBN 90 247 2623 9.
2. J.P. Ancot (ed.) Analysing the Structure of Economic Models, 1984. ISBN 90 247 2894 0.
3. Dr. A.J. Hughes Hallett (ed.) Applied Decision Analysis and Economic Behaviour ISBN 90 247 2968 8.